The Beatles and Fandom

The Beatles and Fandom

Sex, Death and Progressive Nostalgia

Richard Mills

BLOOMSBURY ACADEMIC
LONDON • NEW YORK • OXFORD • NEW DELHI • SYDNEY

BLOOMSBURY ACADEMIC
Bloomsbury Publishing Inc
1385 Broadway, New York, NY 10018, USA
50 Bedford Square, London, WC1B 3DP, UK
29 Earlsfort Terrace, Dublin 2, Ireland

BLOOMSBURY, BLOOMSBURY ACADEMIC and the Diana logo
are trademarks of Bloomsbury Publishing Plc

First published in the United States of America 2020
Paperback edition first published 2021

Copyright © Richard Mills, 2020

For legal purposes the Acknowledgments on p. viii constitute
an extension of this copyright page.

Cover design by Louise Dugdale
Cover image © William Lovelace/Stringer/Getty images

All rights reserved. No part of this publication may be reproduced or
transmitted in any form or by any means, electronic or mechanical,
including photocopying, recording, or any information storage or retrieval
system, without prior permission in writing from the publishers.

Bloomsbury Publishing Inc does not have any control over, or responsibility for,
any third-party websites referred to or in this book. All internet addresses given
in this book were correct at the time of going to press. The author and publisher
regret any inconvenience caused if addresses have changed or sites have
ceased to exist, but can accept no responsibility for any such changes.

Library of Congress Cataloging-in-Publication Data
Names: Mills, Richard, 1964– author.
Title: The Beatles and fandom: sex, death and progressive nostalgia / Richard Mills.
Description: [1st.] | New York: Bloomsbury Academic, 2019. |
Includes bibliographical references and index. |
Summary: "The first book to address Beatles' fan culture, focusing on
the subcultures of sex, death, and nostalgia."–Provided by publisher.
Identifiers: LCCN 2019025884 (print) | LCCN 2019025885 (ebook) |
ISBN 9781501346620 (hardback) | ISBN 9781501346637 (epub) |
ISBN 9781501346644 (pdf)
Subjects: LCSH: Beatles–Influence. | Popular music fans. |
Heritage tourism–England. | Tribute bands (Musical groups)
Classification: LCC ML421.B4 M57 2019 (print) | LCC ML421.B4 (ebook) |
DDC 782.42166092/2–dc23
LC record available at https://lccn.loc.gov/2019025884
LC ebook record available at https://lccn.loc.gov/2019025885

ISBN: HB: 978-1-5013-4662-0
PB: 978-1-5013-8319-9
ePDF: 978-1-5013-4664-4
eBook: 978-1-5013-4663-7

Typeset by Newgen KnowledgeWorks Pvt. Ltd., Chennai, India

To find out more about our authors and books visit
www.bloomsbury.com and sign up for our newsletters.

Ars longa, vita brevis

Contents

Acknowledgements	viii
Introduction: *The Beatles and Fandom: Sex, Death and Progressive Nostalgia*	1
1 'She Loves You': *Beatles Monthly*	27
2 (Un)conventional: Beatles fan conventions	53
3 'Paperback Writer', journalists as superfans: Hunter Davis, Ian MacDonald and Philip Norman	75
4 'Fanaticism' and the Beatles	99
5 'Images of broken light': The Beatles on YouTube	113
6 *Paul Is Undead*: Fan fiction, slash fiction and literary fiction	137
7 'I play the part so well': Beatles tribute bands	169
8 'Ticket to Ride': English cultural tourism and Beatles fans	179
Conclusion: Paul is dead: A fan's story	201
Notes	215
References	217
Discography	229
Personal interviews	231
Appendices	235
Index	241

Acknowledgements

I am very grateful to the School of Arts and Humanities at St Mary's University, Twickenham, for supporting the production of this book. Current colleagues Michael and Pauline Foster, Maria Mellins, Carole Murphy, Kim Salmons and Russell Schechter along with Bloomsbury's editorial team, Leah Babb-Rosenfeld, Katherine De Chant and Amy Martin, have supported my work along the way. I would also like to thank the four anonymous readers of my initial proposal.

I owe a particular debt of gratitude to Anne-Marie Barry, Dr Jon Hackett and Dr Michelle Paull for their unstinting support and for sharing ideas and books with me; without them, this book would not have happened. Finally, I would like to thank all my family and friends who helped me to complete this book.

Introduction

The Beatles and Fandom: Sex, Death and Progressive Nostalgia

Since the beginning of Beatlemania in 1963 numerous subcultures have built up around the Beatles. The most significant of these fan cultures surrounding the band have been the *Beatles Monthly* fanzine, which started in 1963; fan conventions, which began after the Beatles' split in 1974; the cult of journalists/'superfans', who have built careers writing partial and biased accounts of the band; media discourses on Beatles 'fanatics' such as Mark Chapman; fans who use YouTube to reinvent the Beatles' canon of work in innovative and exciting ways; fan fiction, literary fiction and slash fiction, which give fans control over their fictional reimaginings of the Beatles, often placing their idols in the most unusual, surreal and erotic dream scenarios; Beatles cultural tourism where fans have a psychological and creative engagement with famous Beatles spaces such as Abbey Road Studios in London and the Cavern club in Liverpool; and, lastly, Beatles tribute acts: fans who want to be the Beatles and form tribute bands as the ultimate act of devotion. In eight chapters I will delineate the eccentric, creative and often aesthetically dazzling new directions Beatles fans have taken the Beatles art; to paraphrase the epigraph for this book: Beatles art is long because of its stunning quality; it is folk music for the ages, and this longevity, and its reinvention into new forms, is because of the Beatles fans.

Sex and death

Sex and death are two other themes that recur in this text. Death is closely linked to nostalgia and both of these themes are the *sine qua non* of the Beatles story. For instance, the metaphorical death of the Beatles after their break-up in 1970 has fuelled the progressive nostalgia of fan conventions for forty-seven years. The death of John Lennon and George Harrison has also added pathos, drama and 'progressive nostalgia' (another workable definition is creative regretfulness) to the Beatles story. The Beatles' work is imbued with pathos and melancholy because of these tragic events. Songs, videos and album covers have an added emotional realism in the present because the past is colliding with the present, creating new complex psychological imaginings where past/present/future coexists in an imaginative melange. For example, the video for 'You've Got to Hide Your Love Away' on the *Beatles Anthology* shows a series of nostalgic images that feed into the present: the sadness of gazing on the youthful boyish Beatles creates a mournful nostalgia but concurrently these 'joyful' images fill the viewer with optimism.

Sexuality is an integral part of this book. *Beatles Monthly* is predicated on the Beatles' good looks and these appealing images are sold to fans, and the letters page in *Beatles Monthly* is a forum for euphemistic sexuality. Conventions too are affirmed on the Beatles' image, as are tribute bands and YouTube, and, of course, slash fiction is explicitly sexual.

Sex and nostalgia are in many ways twin themes. The free love of the permissive 1960s is synonymous with the Beatles, and famously enshrined in Larkin's poem 'Annus Mirabilis': 'Sexual intercourse began / In nineteen sixty-three / (which was rather late for me) / Between the end of the Chatterley ban / And the Beatles' first LP' (Larkin 2012: 90). The Beatles' music and appearance is concerned with love and sex, and when a first-generation fan gazes at or listens to the Beatles, they are nostalgic for their youthful sexual freedom. Death is closely linked to sex and nostalgia as ghostly spectres of the Beatles resonate through the corridors of our memory. The Beatles' songs and their image are a *momento mori* for baby boomers' younger selves. This nostalgic feeling is Janus-faced; we gaze at our own mortality and simultaneously mourn our own past every time we look at the youthful Beatles. As my questionnaire for Beatleweek in August 2017 puts it, 'Sex and Death are at the core of Beatles fandom'. Death is obviously central to Chapter 4 on Mark Chapman and Michael Abram, but *Beatles Monthly* and slash are masturbation fantasies.

Amorous fixation

The Beatles and Fandom: Sex, Death and Progressive Fandom is a cultural chronology of fandom becoming more explicit. In Chapter 1, I examine the suppressed sexuality of the letters in *Beatles Monthly* from 1963 to 1969 to the more explicit porn of slash fiction in 2017. Fred Vermorel calls these moments of fandom 'benchmarks' of extreme behaviour reaching a tipping point with David Bowie's famous last Ziggy Stardust concert at the Hammersmith Odeon in 1973:

> Beatlemania, or from the advent of screaming as an accepted mode of behavior in concerts: a kind of acceleration or intensification. There are also plateaus, benchmarks. A line from the Johnnie Ray concerts in the mid-1950s to the David Bowie final Ziggy concert where people couldn't believe what the fans were doing. Which was hushed up at the time. I spoke to one music critic who was there and really shocked. To quote *Starlust*, a fan we called Julie told us:
> 'I was at the Hammersmith Odeon when Bowie killed off Ziggy in '73. I got trampled to death! A lot of men were throwing off their underwear and showing their

c**ks all over the place. A lot of fluid was flying about. One girl was actually sucking someone off at the same time as trying to listen to what was going on. I thought it was so extraordinary because nobody had any inhibitions. I remember that around me nobody gave a shit really about doing these things because it was rumoured that maybe this was the last time Bowie would perform. Maybe this was the last time Ziggy would be here. And everyone's got to get in on this because otherwise you're just a square. So everyone just took their clothes off. And w**king was nothing. There was a guy next to me who was w**king in time to one track and I thought: My God! What does he do when he's alone? Then I suddenly realized that all the things I'd been doing were perfectly OK. Because here were people doing it with each other and sharing it. How wonderful, you know. So get off on that. And I thought I'd never seen so many c**ks in my life.' (Duffett 2017)

Sex is a major theme in many chapters but it becomes intense and explicit with slash fiction, especially as our convergence culture of the internet allows such instant dissemination of the most Gothic sexuality. My chapter on fan, literary and slash fiction also stresses that fandom is often predicated on quite wholesome desire; again in an interview with Mark Duffett, Vermorel elucidates,

I've often felt that as well. Also, some of the most lurid, pornographic fan fantasies are actually about wanting to be someone's friend. They don't really want to screw these people, but they would like to get a phone call from them in the middle of the night – asking for advice or solace as a friend would. Reciprocity. Just a kind of easy friendship – a yearning for recognition or innocent love – in the way that the psychologist Alfred Binet called fetishism a form of love: 'amorous fixation', he called it. (Duffett 2017)

In a very real sense, *The Beatles and Fandom: Sex, Death and Progressive Nostalgia* is a history of 'amorous fixation': whether that is a capriciously inconsistent journalist such as Philip Norman or the Bootleg Beatles' Neil Harrison, who has spent his professional career pretending to be a hero (John Lennon) he doesn't know personally but 'loves'.

The Beatles story is a history of sex in the twentieth century, feminism, misogyny, bacchanalian orgies, fans' orgasms at concerts and gay liberation (Brian Epstein's sex life was illegal until the Sexual Offences Act in 1967). One of the most eccentric books in the Beatles canon is *Sex and the Beatles: 400 Entries* by Jeff Walker. In his book, Walker demonstrates that *Beatles Monthly* and the Beatles PR machine were eager to clean up the Beatles' image. He writes, 'Brian Epstein re-made the Beatles' image basically for American consumption. Deft PR lowered the sexual profile of these typically-oversexed rock 'n' rollers: These were squeaky-clean albeit wisecracking lads; not wild horn-dogs devilishly exploiting the groupie scene' (Walker 2014: 115). The fans screaming too was an act of obfuscation; they orgasmed and urinated their way through concerts. Freud identified this sexual peccadillo in 'Obsession and Phobias' in 1895: 'Once, at the theatre seeing a man who attracted her, she had felt an erotic desire, accompanied (as spontaneous pollutions in women always are) by a desire to urinate'

(Freud 2013: 8); fascinatingly Freud's phrase 'spontaneous pollutions' demonstrates how important the work of Barbara Ehrenreich et al. in the essay 'Beatlemania: Girls Just Want to Have Fun' is in highlighting institutional misogyny of the male canon and the sexism built into the machinery of the music business. So the Beatles' image was a 'Trojan horse' (Gross 1966); Walker cites Australian journalist Glenn A. Baker on the Beatles' sex lives at the height of Beatlemania:

> Lennon in particular, must have been consumed with perverse delight by the grand confidence trick which he and his colleagues were perpetuating upon the whole western world. By day they won the hearts of mum, dad, and the garden gnome with cheeky, innocent charm and by night, according to more than a few observers, they hurled themselves into bacchanalian orgies beyond the comprehension of the humble folk who paid them. (Walker 2014: 115)

The Beatles phenomenon can be understood in terms of sex and death; the Eros and Thanatos drive positions the Beatles at the head of a multimillion-dollar creative industry where they and fans are engaged in a strange *quid pro quo* of sexist music industry, sexual exploitation and fans' transgression of this odious machinery through sex, *Beatles Monthly* and screamingly orgiastic concerts; this misalliance is an exchange of power structures from above and below. *The Guardian* journalist Peter Conrad illustrates the power structures of Beatlemania's hidden sexuality; and his writing review of Foucault conflates the death-drive with sexuality: two powerful forces in the history of Beatles fans and each is understood in terms of power relations of music industry machinery versus appropriation by fans (see my Chapter 4 on the violent transgression by Mark Chapman and Michael Abram). Writing about Pompidou's execution of two prisoners in 1971, Conrad evokes the perverse gratifications of Beatles and fans alike:

> One of the best pieces here is a short, impassioned assault on Georges Pompidou's guillotining of two prisoners in 1971. Their abrupt end demonstrates that the whole penal system is impelled by 'the desire for death, the fascination with death'; and that lust – symbolized by the rearing, phallic, blood-stained shape of the guillotine – was grounded, for Foucault, in a fatal sexual curiosity. This complicity between sex and death revealed to him 'the fascism in us all', just as it provoked Genet's sexual rhapsodies about the Nazis. The revelation was meant to be shocking: Foucault would not have enjoyed the spectacle of academics convening fascist rallies to enforce the credo of political correctness. And, in the years before his death from an Aids-related illness in 1984, he made a kind of self-destructive atonement for what he had discovered about his unholy, illiberal, inhumane nature. (Conrad, *Guardian* 2001)

Progressive nostalgia

The theoretical methodological approach to this book is outlined here: the fans' story, the mini-narrative which informs the wider grand narrative of Beatles history, is predicated on sex, death, *mal d'archive*, Freud's repetition compulsion, transformative nostalgia and progressive nostalgia, all themes which are introduced here and which recur throughout the book. The key idea here is 'transformative or progressive nostalgia', which is fans making the old new: fans ensuring that the Beatles are a progressive and living culture because fans appropriate the Beatles phenomenon into new hybrid forms which mix the past and present together to create a Beatles future: new bricolage Beatles art that is a mix of the fans' ingenuity in fan vids (mashed Beatles' music), slash fiction, tribute bands and the creative psychogeography of Richard Porter's and Jackie Spencer's walking tours. All these cultural activities are progressive nostalgia: that is, reimagining the old. The antithesis of this is *mal d'archive* and repetition compulsion in the Chapman/Abram chapters, where I apply the theories of Derrida and Freud to demonstrate that Chapman/Abram were traumatized subjects who could not move forward; they were mired in the stasis and paralysis of violent fantasy. Throughout the book, I contrast their Thanatos or death drive with the sensual Eros of other Beatles fans; Eros is progressive and Thanatos is regressive and dangerously reactionary. Sex for progressive Beatles fans in *Beatles Monthly* and slash fiction is a moving forward in a life-affirming and experimental way; Chapman's and Abram's Thanatos is an inability to change and look forward, and progressive fandom expresses a frustration with those who cannot adapt and change. There is a clear demarcation between the progressive, sensual and whimsical id of slash fiction and the conservative egotism and reactionary violence of Chapman.

The African American journalist George Nelson, born in New York in 1957, provides a cogent definition of 'progressive nostalgia' and the extent to which this concept applies to the diverse manifestations of Beatles fandom in this book. Writing a review of Anita Baker's *Rapture*, Nelson praises her work for 'its mix of contemporary and historical feel, launching the term *Retro-Nuevo* to name the phenomenon' (Lindberg 2005: 291). In his review of her album, 'Anita Baker: Quiet Storm' in *The Village Voice*, Nelson claims to have invented the term *retro-nuevo* in order to describe the 'embrace of the past to create passionate, fresh expressions and institutions'. He adds, 'It doesn't just refer to music' (Lindberg 2005: 291). Nelson sees this aesthetic in the work of Prince in an album such as *Around the World in a Day* (1985) where he combines retro 1960s psychedelia with the rich textures of black soul music and the funk of Sly and the Family Stone, to make it new. As Nelson contends, this term *retro-nuevo* is applicable not only to music but also to different types of fandom; in Nelson's case as a writer/fan this is especially germane to the term 'journalist-fan', or 'superfan', which I theorize in Chapter 3 in relation to Hunter Davies, Philip Norman and Ian MacDonald, who I argue are passionately subjective Beatles fans. Lindberg et al. in *Rock Criticism from the Beginning* (2005) define these journalist fans in the context of the history of rock criticism. Lindberg makes the point that the rock writing has produced superfans such as Paul Williams, Nik Cohn, Jon Landau, Greil Marcus and Lester Bangs; these writers are opinionated fans, 'rock critics are definitely fans. They start out as "fans" – as record buyers, listeners and collectors – and continue as "fans", even after they become writers' (Lindberg 2005: 75). These writers, especially 'scholar-fan' Grail Marcus, demonstrate that American music has a rich heritage firmly rooted in the past. Marcus aligns this heritage with his highly subjective opinions and exemplifies how journalists are engaged in a profound negation with the past but at the same time making their writing new, what Nelson calls *retro-nuevo*. *Retro-nuevo* is synonymous with progressive nostalgia and this concept provides a deep, thought-provoking riposte to Derrida's *mal d'archive*, which Simon Reynolds analyses in his book *Retromania* (2011) as a hidebound retrospective sickness.

One significant problem with a chronological approach to this subject is that there is the danger of creating a canon of Beatles fandom, and new orthodoxies in the process, but because there is such an endless stream of fan activity concerning the Beatles, it is the only organizational method which makes sense when dealing with such a huge subject matter. There is, however, an important caveat: Chapter 2 on fan conventions discusses the conventions in the post-context break-up of the 1970s, but I break chronology in this chapter to discuss the causality between conventions of the 1970s and Beatleweek in Liverpool in 2017 and The Fest for Beatles Fans in Chicago in 2018.

My thesis that Beatles fandom is progressive and not regressive nostalgia is a seam that runs through the book; Candy Leonard, the author of *Beatleness* (2014), concurs:

> To dismiss the feelings of first-generation Beatle fans as mere 'nostalgia' is to trivialize an extraordinary relationship that has endured for a half century. Fans hand images of the Beatles in their homes and work-places not to evoke bittersweet feelings of nostalgia or to relive their youth, but for the same reasons they display family photos: the images represent relationships that have been and continue to be important, meaningful, and most of all, joyful. One fan (b. '53) talked about her Beatle décor as her 'personal Feng Shui' and arranges her house so that she can see Beatles in any direction she looks. (Leonard 2014: 265)

This idea that fandom is forward looking and progressive is key to the book. Beatles is constantly merging with new technology and making profound links with physical space (tribute performances, museums and walks). Leonard's example demonstrates that the Beatles phenomenon is progressive nostalgia, a serviceable definition of the term is that Beatles fandom furnishes our lives in the here and now, and in the future!

Nostalgia and transformative nostalgia

Progressive nostalgia is central to this book, which is the idea that Beatles history is remade anew, the past is reinvigorated by alloying to new musical forms, new imagining and fantasies of the Beatles phenomenon: fans produce bespoke hybrid texts. Concrete memorabilia is collected by fans who don't remember the 1960s, and who are therefore imagining a period they didn't live through. Objects such as the Beatles *Yellow Submarine*, produced by Corgi in 1969, have a very different connotation to a young fan and to a fan who can remember the 1960s. Geraghty's work is primarily concerned with the increasingly complex links between fandom, memory, and nostalgia, and his work here draws on an admirable amount of other authors' investigations into these specialized fields. He successfully fuses discussions of past, present, and possible futures of media and memory to demonstrate just how meaningful and malleable collecting remains for us. 'Nostalgia and memory are bound up in the creation of a contemporary fan identity', Geraghty notes (3), and quoting Jean Baudrillard from *The System of Objects*, he maintains that all collecting is personal: 'what you really collect is always yourself' (4). Especially in our contemporary socially connected culture, collecting can also signify being 'part of a larger community that shares in the same affective relationship' (35) while articulating our own particular fandoms – and thus identities – individually. Our culture of fandom now celebrates the public history of franchises and storytelling while revealing personal histories that are inherently tied to these cultures, and Geraghty's book helps deconstruct the images we as a culture have of fans and fan culture. (Duffy 2014: http://journal.transformativeworks.org/index.php/twc/article/view/584/444)

Saudade is a Portuguese word meaning a deep melancholy for a lost person or object. In fact fandom is based on this feeling of loss, but this loss is a complex and transformative psychological state that gives fans agency. The feeling of nostalgia transforms the present and helps shape an alternative future where the past is relevant. Transformative nostalgia is an enunciation of the moment predicted on the causality and accumulation of past Beatles culture. All the material in this book is transformative nostalgia as fans' psychology is a mess of paradoxical and contradictory interconnecting strains rather like a kaleidoscope where memories of the past and present concepts flow into each other, creating an ineffable psychological state that can only be expressed through profound theoretical and linguistic expressions. Material objects are wedded to technology which keeps the past alive in a material and simulated form: technology gives access to the corporeal object which in turns fuels imaginative fan whimsy.

> Geraghty argues that the prevalence of and access to digital technologies in our daily lives has not only reminded us of how digital culture is in certain ways replacing older forms of entertainment but also has encouraged fans/collectors to further privilege material objects, as they remain 'solid signifiers of the historical significance of previous media texts' (2). He notes that previous work on toys and collecting 'suggest[s] that the histories of popular culture are being constantly rewritten, re-evaluated, and there is an audience out there that wants to engage with and relive that history in some form or another' (3). (Duffy 2014: http://journal.transformativeworks.org/index.php/twc/article/view/584/444)

The ubiquity of, and fans' access to, cyberspace means that 'new' fans create an imaginative 1960s through memorabilia, while baby boomer fans have a more lucid and more nuanced memory of a culture they lived through and they now experience 1960s as a memory based on reminiscences of an earlier moment in their lives, and also the access to 'memorialized objects' means that old and new perceptions collide and coexist in a psychological mélange of the past, present and future invention. This complex negotiation with the Beatles phenomenon is true of the fan activities discussed in this book: fandom's stalk is rooted in the past, but the plant flowers and blossoms in the present in the form of mashed Beatles tunes, fan vids which galvanize collages from different Beatles historical periods, fan fiction which transforms the past into a weird surrealistic present, tribute acts whose performances are behaviourally and psychologically different for performer and fans at every gig and the material objects of vinyl records, Corgi toys, *Beatles Monthly* magazine and Beatles cuddly toys, all of which are deep moments of enunciation in progressive and transformative fandom.

> *Cult Collectors* arrives at just the right time to explore how the roles of fans and the nature of memorialized objects are shifting thanks to the expansion of the Internet; the World Wide Web has allowed collectors of previously obscure material to become more sophisticated both in their knowledge of media and object histories and in their ability to discuss and reobtain precious items of – or representing – their youth. For Geraghty, the Web, and our access to it, has made 'history more accessible, our memories more tangible, thus bringing the past into the present' (2). Now, with the Internet, 'collecting enables fans to connect with the histories of their favorite media texts in ways they just could not achieve twenty or thirty years ago' (Duffy 2014: http://journal.transformativeworks.org/index.php/twc/article/view/584/444)

I have written about progressive nostalgia in 'Rule Britannia Is Out of bounds': David Bowie and English heritage in *Mad Dogs and Englishness: Popular Music and English Identities* (Brooks, Donnelly and Mills 2017). My work will also incorporate memory and nostalgia as outlined by Mark Duffett, in *Understanding Fandom*, where he argues that 'the imagined memory … becomes a generative resource for other narratives and commodities' (Duffett 2013: 230). I develop this theme in my work of fan 'culture which is reaching far back and far forward' (Brooks, Donnelly and Mills 2017: 53).

Lincoln Geraghty's work on fandom focuses on the extent to which concrete objects such as Lego and Beatles memorabilia from fan conventions have caused a shift in nostalgia and memory. *Beatles Monthly* and Beatles Corgi toys, for instance, become a 'personalised memory' (Geraghty 2014: 8) as opposed to a mass-produced standardized object. Beatles fandom becomes a new form of nostalgia where 'The Internet becomes an archive, a virtual space that fans can enter whenever they like to access memories and images that contribute to metanarratives of their favourite franchise' (Geraghty 2014: 8). In other words, when a physical Beatles product is digitized, 'the lines between past and present … are increasingly porous' (Geraghty 2014: 9). The physical objects *Beatles Monthly*, vinyl, Beatles fan fiction, the music of tribute bands and Beatles walks are all remediated through 'digital collaborative spaces shared with other fans' (2014: 9). Beatles conventions are also unmoored in a similar manner, fans post their fan conventions experience and in so doing, 'combine and simultaneously represent, contest and invert, the physical real space of there were bought and acquired virtual spaces of the web where fans share their experience of the convention, the city and the pictures taken' (2014: 9). Bought memorabilia becomes a highly personal object as well as an object to be traded. So memory and nostalgia are transformed into contemporary and living commodities.

One of the most cogent definitions of 'progressive nostalgia' was raised in an interview I had with Candy Leonard, author of *Beatleness: The Fans' Eye View*. She used the song 'For No One' from the *Revolver* album as an example of 'progressive nostalgia'; she said that she was a 9-year-old child when she saw the Beatles on *The Ed Sullivan Show* in 1964, and that a huge impact of this was a nostalgic moment that has resonated for most of her adult life, but this nostalgia also has progressiveness grafted onto it as a fan experiences the songs in the here and now. Leonard says that she listens to 'the song 'For No One' with adult ears' (Leonard 2018), imbuing the song with a completely new psychological context: Beatles art is a kaleidoscopic weave of childhood nostalgia (Leonard's experience of *The Ed Sullivan Show*) and whatever the listener's mindset is in the here and now, this is classic reception and fandom theory, art that resonates is art that wends its way into the future with its shadow close behind. Such a contemporary listening experience also challenges any negative stigma surrounding fandom, for as Leonard points out, having memorabilia and picture of the Beatles in not a kitsch retrogressive *mal d'archive*, it is progressive as the pictures are creating a sophisticated psychological process of non-linear memory: progressive memory if you like. Memories are fused with forward-looking, optimistic thoughts in this complicated psychological process; and it should be stigma free, as 'nobody ridicules pictures of your family and loved one around the house, workplace and your phone. ... There's a reference to them (pictures of the Beatles) because of the gifts they gave to us as kids' (Leonard 2018). Leonard's meditation on progressive fandom provides a convincing and serviceable definition for my book: 'The meaning is created in that meeting space between the text and the fan', and she goes on to rescue the word fan from the pathological tradition (discussed in Chapter 4) by saying that the 'obsessive fan is more discriminating than the casual fan because there is such a rich seam of art there' (Leonard 2018); in other words, Beatles fans are contemporary aesthetes. In our conversation, Leonard peppers our interview with remarks that illustrate that the Beatles and their fans interfuse to create common meaning: 'They created a generation of people who were with them, who were on the train with them' (Leonard 2018); and the reason that this *quid pro quo* between fans and Beatles was such a massive phenomenon is that there was almost a monolithic cultural communication source in the 1960s unlike a pop sensation in 2018: 'Nobody can be famous on that scale again because communication has fragmented so much since then; it's a different environment now' (Leonard 2018). The 1960s context created a two-way cultural conversation between the pop phenomenon and the mass audience: a democratic exchange predicated on technology.

The pathological tradition and trauma

Beatles fans' cultural trauma at the death of the band in 1969, and the vicarious trauma after the death of John Lennon, is analysed in Chapter 2 on fan conventions in the context of a disturbing event that is overcome through the communal spirit and the social networking of conventions. The cultural trauma of losing the Beatles is diluted by communal activity which brings fandom into the present by letting the past go and looking forwards. Chapman and Abram's illnesses are exacerbated by not being able to belong. Chapman and Abram's psychological scars have primary effects not only on the psychological sense of self but also on affiliation that links individual and community. Both have undergone a traumatized subjectivity which alienates them from community, and their drift towards violence is indicative of a cultural shift away from collective political involvement and towards individualized experience. Chapman and Abram are drawn to murder as the result of alleged childhood abuse (in Chapman's case) and trauma (drug addiction and marriage breakdown in Abram's case): their trauma disrupts their personal histories and makes harmonious integration into society impossible. Their wounded psyches are conceptualized and registered through violence. It is important to note that their mental illnesses were caused by verbal and physical abuse, which is not commensurate with a band breaking up and in no way am I homogenizing the trauma of the death of a band and the childhood/ marriage break-up and drugs traumas of Chapman/Abram, but it is important to point out that communal fan social networks put the isolation of damaged individuals into sharp relief and fan interaction is a healthy riposte to selfish individualism which is a factor in leading loners to be attracted to violence. Freud's theories demonstrate that trauma needs to be mastered and controlled by restaging the trauma through psychoanalysis: by undergoing psychotherapy symptoms of childhood trauma could be alleviated. Trauma is a delayed psychical wound that becomes embedded in one's consciousness only to resurface at a later stage.

In comparing fan conventions to the death drives of Chapman and Abram, it is clear that group activity, or group therapy, can go a long way to preventing violence, and violence happens because of an inability to move forward: conventions are progressive; Chapman and Abram's violence represents an atavistic return of the repressed. In Freud's topography of the mind the conscious mind splits from the unconscious mind so instead of managing a traumatic episode it becomes repressed in the unconscious. This concept of a belated return of repressed memory is the core of trauma theory and results in a reliving of the past: a 'compulsion to repeat' (Freud 1920: 9). He concluded that a 'compulsion to repeat overrides the pleasure principle' (1920: 22). Had Chapman, for instance, received support, not to mention the fact that he should have been denied access to a gun, he would have hopefully been able to assimilate his experience and find a way of controlling and articulating it, and thus be socialized.

Abram's case is very similar to Chapman's; however, it was a marriage breakdown, stress at work and heroin addiction that were the tipping points for Abram; the only significant difference in both cases is that Abram's trauma came later in life.

Nonetheless, Abram, like Chapman, had an inability to move beyond his trauma. The eldest of three children born to Raymond Abram, a labourer, and his wife, Lynda, a factory worker, he grew up with his younger brother and sister in a council house in Stockbridge Village, Liverpool, and attended a local comprehensive. He was a well-adjusted and intelligent student who left with three O-levels and some CSEs. At school he met Jeanette Freeman and within two years their first child was born. They were too young to set up home together, and the teenagers stayed with their own parents. After working in computers, he moved into telesales, selling advertising space. According to his mother it was then that he turned to heroin to ease the pressure of work and marriage. Abram and Ms Freeman had moved into a flat in Page Moss by 1987. Their second child was born two years later. Abram was, his family said, a devoted father but the relationship was marked by violent arguments and eventually collapsed.

Abram was admitted to Whiston Hospital in Merseyside for the first time in March 1990 and was diagnosed as psychotic with paranoid delusions. Over the next nine years he was a frequent visitor to the hospital as his drug addiction worsened and his illness took hold. From the moment that his illness took hold, Abram's narrative is very similar to Chapman's. Abram became haunted by voices in his head and voices from the radio television; and his traumatic marriage breakdown exacerbated his drug use. By the summer of 1999 (six months before he attacked Harrison) Abram had managed to replace heroin with methadone, but his psychosis became increasingly severe. After losing his job and his family in 1996, he moved into a tower block in Woolfall Heights in Huyton. He had threatened to jump from the building, he was convinced that Oasis (the Gallagher brothers) were writing him letters and he became obsessed with Beatles' music. He often slept in the landing of the building because he thought a fat lady and a man in black were living in his flat. The neighbours began to beat him and called him Sheephead and General Custer because of his long blonde hair. He would listen to music constantly and even while walking naked along the balcony. He told his mother that Paul McCartney is a witch but George Harrison is the boss. Mrs Abram was so upset by what she presumed to be her son's schizophrenia that she pleaded with Whiston Hospital to section her son under the Mental Health Act. At this stage Abram's condition had deteriorated so much that George Harrison was an alien from Hell; he thought he was the fifth Beatle and that all the Beatles flew around on broomsticks at night.

In a similar manner to Chapman, Abram had appropriated the Beatles into his psychotic fantasy world; and like Chapman, he was not a Beatles fan per se, but a damaged and traumatized person who happened to like the Beatles among other pop stars such as John Lennon, Bob Marley, Oasis and U2. Both were schizophrenic and delusional: their fractured psyches were similar, and they were both faux fans; however, their social and economic worlds were very different. Abram lived in a ten-floor squalid apartment block and, unlike Chapman, he could not buy a gun and ammunition. Abram was armed with a table lamp, an electrical flex, a pole from a broken statue and a knife; when he attacked Harrison, he felt he was on a mission from God and when George Harrison shouted Hare Krishna at Abram, he was convinced he had been cursed by the devil's tongue. Abram's and Chapman's life stories demonstrate that trauma was the prominent *leitmotif* of their lives and that these problems were accentuated by excessive drug use. There is no process of either Beatles 'fan' having engaged or come to terms with their past, no gradual process of working through the implications of what has happened and both became profoundly perturbed and haunted by a troubled past. Abram and Chapman have buried their toxic pasts; however, their shameful, disturbing and dramatic pasts subsequently and inevitably transmit their existences: Freud's return of the repressed. Here these two men are not Beatles fans but are instead two disturbed subjects 'haunted by a phantom becomes a living tomb or repository in which unspeakable drama ... lies buried yet alive' (Raskin 2008: 94). Abram and Chapman, unlike fans at conventions, writers of fan fiction, tribute act performers, have not been able to come to understand their psychosis, engage with it, confront it or assimilate it as fans at Beatle walks or Beatleweek do: Abram and Chapman appropriate the Beatles phenomenon in a negative, unhealthy, *mal d'archive* and destructive manner which hinders their socialization into a positive and constructive sphere of society or fan grouping. Beatles fans give shape and meaning to the whole Beatles cultural phenomenon, whereas these two subjects are trapped by the trauma of not being able to belong. Abram and Chapman are erroneously stereotyped by the shallow media as Beatles fans, whereas they are violent, haunted and mentally ill people who are pathologized by the press as scary monster fans; in reality they are not fans because they do not belong to any social grouping of fans: they are psychologically scarred and sick people who happen to be Beatles fans.

Jack Jones writes that the source of Chapman's trauma was his father's violence towards him and his mother; Jones describes Chapman's childhood in a Gothic, melodramatic and unsettling language:

> The child awoke in the middle of the night to a sharp slapping sound. Light from the hallway filtered along the edge of a partially opened bedroom door as he waited in a chilled silence for the sound he knew would come again. At last he heard it, a sickening slap of flesh against flesh followed by his father's gruff voice and his mother's muffled sobs. (Jones 1992: 97)

Chapman's childhood trauma exacerbated by his teenage drug use meant it was psychological and unable to relive his trauma, which meant he was living in the past. He appropriated the Beatles' music but it could not channel this act of appropriation into positive creativity, nor could he restage the trauma adequately to a psychotherapist or to a group. So it is perhaps appropriate that he describes John Lennon's murder in the terms of Gothic horror, as he waits to murder Lennon, he identifies with the gargoyles on the Dakota building: 'There were gargoyles ... I leaned against a black rail between them. It's like I was a real gargoyle that had come to life' (Jones 1992: 6). Chapman could not transcend his violent urges, and his Beatles fandom is rejected by writers such as Mark Duffett, who convincingly contends that when this gargoyle came to life, Chapman's violence had nothing to do with his Beatles fandom and everything to do with his fractured psychic which was trapped in the past (Duffett 2013).

Transforming death and trauma

Woody Allen famously posited, 'Sex and death: two things that come once in a lifetime' (*Sleeper*, Dir. Woody Allen 1973), and many fans are now considering being buried in a celebrity-branded coffin: so death that comes once in a lifetime is being adorned with celebrity trappings, a very Allen-esque ending. This phenomenon demonstrates the extent to which all the eight chapters of disparate fan experiences in my book are couched and delivered in the envelope of capitalism, sex, death and nostalgia. Celebrity-styled burials are a reminder that there is a seam of humour running through fandom. Writing in 2013, Jenny Huberman has shown the extent to which celebrity death has been branded. In 'Forever a Fan: Reflections on the Branding of Death and the Production of Value', she gives examples of funeral directors who have fan-themed funerals: *Star Trek*, Kiss, Boston Red Sox urns and *Dr Who* coffins, and as we will see in my chapter on Beatles cultural tourism in Liverpool, when John Lennon's death prompted Liverpool from condemnation to celebration of the Beatles' phenomenon, branding after death ensures that

> the object of fandom often serves as a metonymic representation of the fan's self, the fan brand may come to function very much like a kitomu (this is also known as the kula ring which is the method of exchange in the Trobriand Islands of Papua New Guinea, see Bronislaw Mallinowski's *Argonauts of the Western Pacific* (1922). That is, the intimate association between fan and brand might enable the brand to operate as a vehicle through which individual fans are able to extend their remembered presence across space and time and remain 'in circulation' after death. Additionally, although the brand is not given as a gift its ubiquitous presence in everyday life may facilitate new forms, spaces, and occasions for remembering that do indeed help mourners keep the memory of the deceased alive. (Huberman 2013: 475)

In Beatles fan studies a more accentuated version of the cultural trauma at the Beatles break-up is obviously felt when a member of the band dies, these psychic traumas have a 'productive capacity', that is, 'the brand ... enhances the individual qualities of the deceased rather than rendering them more generic' (2013: 475); this is progressive nostalgia, which combines branding and individual trauma to transform memory of the Beatles into a forward-looking and alive cultural phenomenon, even if you are being buried in a *Yellow Submarine*-shaped coffin or are laid to rest in a full *Sgt. Pepper* regalia. By fans' appropriation of death and through branding, Beatles death (both the break-up of the band and the deaths of Lennon and Harrison) is viewed in the rear-view mirror by fans who are simultaneously keeping their eyes on the road forward.

The main thrust of the book is that Beatles fandom is a living culture; and where there is death, such as the metaphorical death of the Beatles when the band broke up in 1970, there a process of nostalgic transformation takes place: the break-up is turned into a living culture by fan interaction at Beatles conventions. There is violence, tragedy and death in the lives of Mark Chapman and Michael Abram. The narrative of Chapman and Abram highlights two central theme to this study: firstly, Chapman and Abram were culturally trapped in Derrida's *mal d'archive*, and secondly, they were hidebound by Freud's repetition compulsion; both never grew to a progressive understanding of the Beatles and their art, and both never managed to break away from traumatic childhood experiences which left them permanently damaged. Chapman and Abram were rooted in a *mal d'archive* and repetition compulsion which was an unhealthy necrophiliac obsession with the past: they couldn't move forward emotionally, intellectually or creatively so they dragged their heroes (Lennon and Harrison) down into their stasis and psychosis. To Freud, their violence is the return of the repressed (childhood traumas); and to Derrida they are infected with a sickness that made them unable to look forward. This is the distinction between Chapman/Abram and Beatles fans: Chapman/Abram were not fans, but mentally ill subjects who happened to be Beatles fans. Fans, on the other hand, were creative, they took the Beatles phenomenon and pushed it forward by making new art out of Beatles archives. For example, fan vids of John Lennon and George Harrison demonstrate fans taking past images of the dead Beatles and adding music, and their own collages, to create a bricolage art of the singing dead. In a similar manner to fan vids on YouTube, the Beatles themselves brought John Lennon back to life via technology to create a new Beatles song with 'Free as a Bird' and 'Real Love'. New music by Paul, George and Ringo was used to augment old Lennon demos and to make them into new songs. Bringing John back from the dead is a fan activity (Beatles fans and the Beatles themselves) of idiosyncratic art: a mix of found songs that are rewritten to make new work. When fan vids and songs such as 'Free as a Bird' are created, this kind of fan activity eschews the death drive of Chapman by making new Beatles art which pushes the creative envelope, leaving violent killers trapped in a haunting and disturbing psychological stasis of repetitive compulsion and retrospective sickness. Death is appropriated by fans into simulacra texts of the singing dead, which are constantly remixed into new hybrid texts of the old and new, transforming nostalgia into progressive and challenging new artistic directions: death is creatively turned into new art by fans, whether that is a themed Beatles funeral or the progressive sentimentality of a fan vid. To apply Freud's famous distinction in *Melancholia and Mourning* (1920) to Beatles fans: Melancholia is an inability to deal with trauma and grief (the institutionalized Chapman, for example), while Mourning is a verb: an active talking and singing cure which embraces new forms and transcends the past through catharsis. Chapman and Abram's stories illustrate how debilitating it is to be rooted in the past: Beatles fans are not mired in the 1960s because every generation produces new fans and these fans cannibalize the Beatles canon into new exciting expressions. The mash-ups, fan vids, slash, tribute bands, Beatles walks, *Beatles Monthly* (this fanzine was relaunched and repackaged) and conventions of Beatles fandom are a transforming, progressive and living representation of the singing dead. Fan conventions are therapy for those traumatized by loss, whereas Chapman and Abram took revenge and punished society, and dealt with their incipient trauma, by killing and attacking, respectively, two of its icons. Both were psychopaths whose fandom was only a small part of their complex personalities and it can be argued that one of the reasons they targeted celebrities was quite simply for fame.

Writing about Elvis Presley, Greil Marcus demonstrates the importance of death to pop culture; and at the time of writing there are three significant deaths that have impacted on the Beatles story: John Lennon, George Harrison and the death (break-up of the band in 1970). After the demise of the Beatles, we fans are living in the midst of a Beatles explosion:

> Between those Elvises are the Elvises I have followed since Elvis Presley's death. The enormity of his impact on culture, on millions of people, was never really clear when he was alive; it was mostly hidden. When he died, the event was a kind of explosion that went off silently, in minds and hearts; out of that explosion came many fragments, edging slowly into the light, taking shape, changing shape again and again as the years went on. No one, I think could have predicted the ubiquity, the playfulness, the perversity, the terror, and the fun of this: a great, common conversation, sometimes, a conversation between specters and fans, made out of songs, art works, books, movies, dreams; sometimes more than anything cultural noise, the glossolalia of money, advertisements, tabloid headlines, bestsellers, urban legends, nightclub japes. (Marcus 1991: XIII–XIV)

Marcus's writing on Presley demonstrates the extent to which a hugely popular phenomenon is a conversation between the band's spectre and fans: the Beatles phenomenon (or spectre) is transgressed, promoted, performed, written, discussed, transformed, broadcast and walked by Beatles fans.

It is very important to add that my discussion of 'trauma' in Chapter 2 on fan conventions means cultural trauma at the break-up of the Beatles and the death of John Lennon and George Harrison, whereas my use of 'trauma' in Chapter 3 on Mark Chapman, Michael Abram and the pathological tradition is of the word in a psychological sense. It is very important to make this distinction as the cultural trauma experienced by Beatles and Grateful Dead fans is very different to the mental illness and complete psychological breakdowns experienced by sociopaths Chapman and Abram. Fans I interviewed at Liverpool's Beatleweek in 2017 and 2018 and Chicago's The Fest for Beatles Fans in 2018 were keen to speak of the conventions as a 'family', 'a community', 'friends' and 'social networking' that helped to transform the cultural and vicarious trauma of the band's break-up and John Lennon's and George Harrison's deaths into a contemporary and living culture of shared experience and communal support.

Hauntology and progressive nostalgia

The concept of hauntology recurs in this book and it ripples through the chapter on Mark Chapman and Michael Abram as a ghostly reminder of childhood trauma; in this chapter hauntology is the embodied pain of Derrida's concept of concealment which discusses the consequences of concealment in *The Spectres of Marx* (Derrida 1993), the ramifications to Chapman/Abram's 'fandom' are significant. As well as using hauntology in the sense of 'concealment' and repression, I apply Derrida's notion of it as disjunction and non-origin (Derrida 1993) to Mark Fisher and Simon Reynolds's work in my YouTube chapters; here, the YouTube chapter looks at video spectres which are remembered and remixed as nostalgia transformed! 'The old sunlight from other times and other lives' (Fisher 2014: 57), that is, images from the past reworked into bricolage visual texts to unite the past and the present in fans' imaginations. Fisher writes that hauntology 'has been applied to music culture … persistences, repetitions, prefigurations' and that these hauntings can be made into 'escapes from ourselves'. Reynolds too warns about unhealthy retromania but demonstrates that remix culture creates new texts, new escapes and new meanings. Hauntology is used in two important sections of this study, in Chapman/Abram it is a traumatic rupture that prevents growth, and in fans' art hauntology uses rupture, spectres and technological apparitions to create progressive future. In a sense, all the manifestations of fandom discussed – *Beatles Monthly*, fan fiction, Beatles walks, museums and tribute bands are old memories made new. To cite Bob Dylan's 'Visions of Joanna', 'the ghosts of electricity' are remade into progressive nostalgia which is hauntingly new and resonates for future generations of Beatles fans not yet born.

Aspects of fandom

It is important to note that fandom is a very broad church and that the term is so elastic it can be stretched to include almost any act of Beatles worship. Rolling Stone has even, with some justification, described George Harrison as the first Beatles fan:

> George sounded like he really did need you. He was the Beatle who wrote and sang the loneliest songs: 'Don't Bother Me', 'I Want to Tell You', 'Long, Long, Long', 'If I Needed Someone'. He was the one shy boys could relate to, even if we never would have looked that cool in his black turtlenecks or the cowboy gear on the back cover of Rubber Soul. As we know from the biographical details of his life, although anyone can see it in Help!, he sounded lonely because he was lonely. He was the one Beatle who, in a true sense, had originally been a Beatle fan. He was the young kid tagging along behind the older, cooler guys, John and Paul, trying to get in on their bond. George wanted to act cool for them but had to settle for impressing them with his guitar chops instead. He was the original Beatlemaniac, the first fan ever to chase John and Paul down the street. As John remembered shortly before his death, in words that soon turned haunting, 'When George was a kid, he used to follow me and my first girlfriend, Cynthia – who became my wife – around. We'd come out of art school, and he'd be hovering around like those kids at the gate of the Dakota now'. (Rolling Stone 2002)

I hope I haven't stretched the term 'fandom' too widely, but it is important to incorporate the diversity of this subject in the volume, so for the intents and purposes of this book and to keep the thesis concise and coherent, I have to avoid semantic stretches like this description of Harrison as the first Beatles fan. However, I have taken creative licence in describing the journalists Davies, Norman and MacDonald as superfans, but not quite to the extent of this Rolling Stone piece. I include this article as example of the dilemma I faced in streamlining the book to eight chapters and also the perils of defining fandom too widely.

An aspect of fandom which recurs throughout this book is the sense of community that fans shared, for example, a Beatle fan called Deborah McDermott described the communal experience of screaming at the 15 August 1966 Beatles concert in Washington:

> Why did we scream? At the concert, it was absolutely group reaction. It was August, it was hot, it was sticky, as only D. C. can be in August. The place was packed with kids my age. I went with older sister, who is 10 years older than me and now wears it as badge of honour that she saw the Beatles. We were al 14, 15, 16 years old, and that meant screaming and not really listening. I remember being borne away by all the energy around me, there for one purpose. And the energy was what drove all of us to yell and scream. I remember there was a cyclone fence that we were clawing, screaming their names. (Berman 2008: 200)

Another aspect of fandom which is prevalent throughout is the fact that many fans are devoted for life (see my chapter on Beatleweek in Liverpool where fans have attended every convention since it started in 1981) as Iona Gabriel, an American fan, shows: 'They never went out of my mind at all. Even now, if things are overwhelming me, thinking about bills and the house, I'll go and put on my Beatle music. And it just relaxes me; it brings me back to that time when everything was happy. It's excellent therapy. It takes you back' (Berman 2008: 282). In the context of Simon Reynold's discussion of *Retromania*, it is fascinating that Ilona uses the word 'nostalgia'; a discussion of this term is central to an analysis of Beatles fandom: Is the Beatles' music being adapted to something new or is it ossifying? The use of the word 'therapy' also connotes that fans use the Beatles' fantasy in conventions and slash fiction to escape the trauma of the band's break-up or to express sexual desire.

Chapter 1 examines the beginning of Beatles fandom through the history of the fanzine *Beatles Monthly*. The fanzine's full title is the *Beatles Monthly Book*; I have abbreviated it throughout as the punchier *Beatles Monthly*, as it commonly became known to fans and scholars. The publication was produced by the Beatles fan club (mostly female), and it ran from 1963 to 1969. *Beatles Monthly* was first published in August 1963 and continued for seventy-seven editions until it stopped publication after the December 1969 edition. It was revived in 1977 and ceased publication in 2003. *Beatles Monthly* was the first official fanzine on the Beatles; a more accurate title of the fanzine would have been *She Loves You* as the Beatles' image and music were reappropriated by girl fans. The appropriation of the Beatles phenomenon in *Beatles*

Monthly is predicated on girl fans objectifying the Beatles as adored, love fantasies; and although the language used in the fanzine is inoffensive, banal and sanitized for a teen and pre-teen market, there is a heavily sexualized undercurrent throughout. For most of its seven-year history the magazine is divided into distinct sections: Johnny Dean's editorial, a double-spread colour centrefold of a different Beatle every week, 'Letters from Beatles People', 'Beatles News' and 'This Month's Beatle Song'. The Beatles are treated as love objects both visually and linguistically.

Although my discussion of Beatlemania in this chapter is entitled 'She Loves You', I contend that *Beatles Monthly* was not by any means solely for (or comprised of) girl fans. Male fans are discussed here and the chapter is written in the full knowledge that there are performed gender roles in fandom. This chapter is careful not to homogenize female fans or to essentalize fans' identities, as Duffett posits: 'If the cultural world is seen entirely through the prism of gender, there is a danger that we will think in that the ways in which male and female – or for that matter gay and straight – fans pursue their fandom are *inherently* different' (Duffett 2013: 193). My chapter on *Beatles Monthly* is *primarily* concerned with young female fans and the extent to which they appropriate the Beatles into their sexual fantasies; I analyse mostly letters from female fans; I also give examples of male fan letters to show that my work is not solely a textual/empirical study of *Beatles Monthly* focused on female fans. The weight of this chapter is on female fans and the critical methodology here is proto-feminist: *Beatles Monthly* epitomizes the extent to which female fans reverse the male machinery of the music business and the machismo Beatles organization into the web and weft of their romantic and sexual lives.

Although letters in *Beatles Monthly* are overtly gendered in feminine language, there are also letters of male devotion and there is an acknowledgement that a fan letter is a performed identity, not necessarily the innermost truth of fans' minds. Nevertheless, the fact remains that female Beatles fans were empowered by *Beatles Monthly*: a cultural space where the original meanings of the Beatles' image and music are translated into a series of sexual meanings beyond the intentions of original text. Taking the Beatles' image and appropriating it is a feature that has recurred throughout the Beatles' career. The screaming of Beatlemania was the sound of teenage girl fans creating their own identity, and *Beatles Monthly*, especially 'Letters from Beatle People', was the written expression of this fan intensity. Ehrenreich et al. recognized the social and cultural implications of this expression:

> Yet, if it was not the 'movement', or a clear-cut protest of any kind, Beatlemania was the first mass outburst of 1960s to feature women – in this case girls … To abandon control – to scream, faint, dash about in mobs – was, in form if not in conscious intent, to protest the sexual repressiveness, the rigid double standard of female teen culture. It was the first and most dramatic uprising of *women's* sexual revolution. (Ehrenreich, Hess and Jacobs 1992: 85)

The home of Beatles fandom in the 1960s was *Beatles Monthly*. Apart from screaming at concerts, it was one of the few cultural spaces where fans could express their opinions on the Beatles. In 1974 fan conventions replaced the magazine as a space where Beatles fandom continued to flourish. The continuing popularity of the band in this decade was due, in a large part, to forums where endless Beatles-related activities were created and performed: quizzes, art exhibits, competitions and memorabilia swaps.

The founder of the Beatle Fest, Mark Lapidos, in an interview with Susan Lewis from Continental Cable television in 1998, defined the Beatle Fest as an event where fans share a love of the Beatles: 'fans come and celebrate our common love for the Beatles regardless of what age' (Beatle Fest 1998). The main feature of this documentary, even as late as 1998, is the grief resulting from the Beatles' break-up and the death of John Lennon. Lewis interviewed two middle-aged American women called Cherie and Nancy who said that their favourite Beatle was 'John' and Lewis replied that 'You can't say that without getting choked up' (Beatle Fest 1998). In this maudlin and sentimental interview, Cherie states that 'he (John) is never gone as long as he lives in my heart' (Beatle Fest 1998). In a sense this quote is key to understanding the Fest. Fans are motivated by a sense of loss: a deep emotional connection to the band which impels them to come together in a forum where they can openly display their communal affinity.

The Beatles phenomenon has produced a curious hybrid manifested in the journalist/fan. The three main writers in this category are: Hunter Davies (the only authorized Beatles biographer), Ian McDonald (1960s proselytizer, who has written a passionate book which has an essay on every Beatles song ever released) and Philip Norman, a dedicated Lennon fan, who has courted controversy with his dogmatic work on the Beatles. Music journalists are subjective fans: Steven Stark concurs arguing that biographies and journalism are fan literature, 'To a certain extent, almost all books about the Beatles – even the so-called objective histories – are a form of fan literature' (Stark 2006: 1). Davies, Norman and MacDonald are 'writers who look at the Beatles and tend to see themselves' (Stark 2006: 7): the real theme of their most significant Beatles books is themselves and their entirely partial opinions.

Another important discussion in this chapter is gendered fandom and the extent to which an initial 'feminized' Beatles fandom might have given way to a 'masculinized' culture of biographers and journalist-fans. Sheila Whiteley's work on the gender politics of progressive rock and 1960s counterculture is employed here to discuss fandom and gender.

Chapter 4 discusses John Lennon's murderer Mark Chapman and also Michael Abram, who attempted to murder George Harrison in a knife attack in 1999. Both were fascinated by the Beatles and felt that they were on missions from God to kill Lennon and Harrison, respectively. Each explained their respective psychologies in religious terms; Mark Chapman, for example, suggesting that 'a small part of me must be the Devil' (Jones 1992: 98).

Using press coverage (newspapers, television documentaries, films and biographies of the killers) of Chapman and Abram, this chapter will problematize the media's description of them as 'fans'. It is clear that they initially loved the Beatles, but by the time of their attacks, they transformed into eccentric outsiders still erroneously categorized as 'fans', albeit of the obsessive, extreme and dangerous kind by the media: this terminology is typical of media discourses that mistake far outliers as representative of fandom in general. In this chapter I will discuss the extent to which the lives of Chapman and Abram have been used by the media to create a negative stereotype of fan in general. As Duffett contends, Chapman was not a fan when he shot Lennon, 'he was already seriously ill' (Duffett 2013: 108) and a shallow media categorized him as a fan when, in fact, he 'suffered from a personality disorder that did not spring from his fandom' (2013: 108). Chapman's childhood trauma is a theme in this chapter: unlike fans at conventions who create strong social networks to break the melancholy of post-Beatles break-up trauma, Chapman was a lonely and isolated individual who was trapped in a 'repetitive compulsion' of a downward spiralling melancholy and depression: an inability to heal childhood trauma which eventually led to murder.

Chapter 5 discusses the extent to which YouTube has transformed engagement with the Beatles' phenomenon. In a sense, YouTube is the fans' appropriation of the Beatles' image and music away from Apple and into their own bricolage art that is controlled by the fans. In 1995, Apple released a DVD of all the remaining Beatles archives. The difference to other media constructions, such as the press and television, was that the Beatles, their producer George Martin and assorted friends and colleagues reminisced on their own experience of the 1960s. The first and most startling aspect of this attempt to tell their own story was the fact that they contradicted themselves from start to finish: for instance, Anthology Episode 5 (1995) has the three surviving Beatles struggling to remember the details of meeting Elvis Presley in 1965. To the Beatles themselves the chronology of their work was not a seamless series of albums and films but a kaleidoscope of contradictory memories. Added to this mess of opposing impulses was the fact that the DVD, which seemed to point to another exercise in Beatles canon building, included many out-takes and alternative versions of their songs as well as previously unseen footage.

So technology and unreliable memory had inadvertently set off a process of deconstruction. Technology is fundamental for setting these wheels in motion. For the first time the viewer is offered a non-linear and piecemeal version of history. We have access to never before seen clips that are framed in a celluloid shudder, the very ethereality of which eschew fixed historical positions, totality and any sense of grand narrative. We have micro-narratives that have been possible by a technological collage. This is only the first stage in deconstruction as the DVD is not interactive: we are getting an alternative version of the Beatles canon, but is still filtered by Apple Corps.

The YouTube chapter discusses Geraghty's work on 'transformative nostalgia' and discusses the extent to which 'imagined memory' is largely predicated on nostalgia (Duffett 2013: 229). 'Transformative nostalgia' helps fans in their quest to imaginatively inhabit the past (Duffett 2013). For Geraghty, the Web, and our access to it, has made 'history more accessible, our memories more tangible, thus bringing the past into the present' (2). Now, with the internet, 'collecting enables fans to connect with the histories of their favorite media texts in ways they just could not achieve twenty or thirty years ago' (Duffy 2014: http://journal.transformativeworks.org/index.php/twc/article/view/584/444).

Paul Booth's *Digital Fandom 2.0* (2017) will be used to extend my research on social media into areas such as the Digit Gratis Economy, Wikis, MagiQuest (research in this area, for example, will generate ideas concerning immersive environment, comparing MagiQuest to Beatles Rock Band) and Tumblr (a forum for Beatles slash).

Fan fiction grew out of *Spockanalia*, a fanzine started in 1967 by *Star Trek* enthusiasts. The first edition had a letter of encouragement from Leonard Nimoy (Spock from the television series). Here is the birth of fan fiction as genre, by definition, amateur works of fiction. Of course it didn't take Beatles fans long to catch up. Girl fans had been writing romantic stories in notebooks since 1963. Beatles fan fiction evolved from this science fiction genre, and by 2006 Rooftop Sessions (one of the main online forums) had collated thousands of stories. This has become known as 'slash fiction', that is, highly eroticized sexual fantasies by fans, which often star the Beatles in homoerotic stories. This chapter will analyse the cultural capital of slash fiction, with reference to more 'respectable' published fiction: Mark Shipper's *Paperback Writer* (1979); Ian McLeod's *Snodgrass* (2013); and Kevin Barry's *Beatlebone* (2015).

Beatles fan fiction provides a literary arena where the Beatles are re-energized and reborn through imaginative storytelling, creative characterization and carnivalesque language and description. In contrast, the energy in Beatles tribute bands is a physical and performative desire to bring the band back from the dead. Where this desire to reform the Beatles is at its most performative is Beatles tribute acts. Andy Bennett's description of the tribute band phenomenon expresses this Lazarus effect and retrospective urge as 'a postmodern landscape in which the real and the hyperreal blur into one. An often cited explanation for the origin of the tribute band phenomenon is that it began as a response to the perpetual unavailability of original acts' (Bennett 2006: 23).

The final chapter will discuss Beatles-related tourism, museums, city walks and urban renewal with reference to Liverpool and London's tourist industry. Stephanie and Mark Fremaux contend that

> With the increasing ease and affordability of travelling in the mid-twentieth-century, tourism focused on catering to individual needs. Postmodernity ushered in a focus on the individual and through the rise of popular culture, consumerism, and the ease of reproduction, museums were no longer places for high culture where the relics of an imperial past were on display. (Wearing, Stevenson and Young 2010: 29; cited in S. Fremaux and M. Fremaux)

To put it simply, fans now have access to a highly personalized culture remote from 'imperial' museum culture: what Derrida refers to as a ghoulish *mal d'archive*. Simon Reynolds calls this unwholesome process, a blending of 'museum and mausoleum' (Reynolds 2012: 12), but the cultural tourism discussed in this chapter is concerned with a new empirical and immersive experience: new social spheres for fan interaction. For instance, Richard Porter's London Beatles Walks are an opportunity for fan interaction and fresh 'meaning-making' (Fremaux 2013: 10). Chapters 7 and 8 both include a discussion of tribute bands as tribute acts are an indispensable part of cultural tourism of Beatleweek in Liverpool.

Theoretical positions on 'memory' are especially relevant to my work in Chapter 8 of this book, '"Ticket to Ride": English Cultural Tourism and Beatles Fans'. *Social Memory Technology* (2016) by Karen Worcman and Joanne Garde-Hansen is useful for discussing new ways of engaging with heritage cultures through digital memory technologies. Reference will also be made to the analysis of fandom and tourism in Linden and Linden (2017).

Speaking to Mark Duffett I asked him for a definition of 'transformative nostalgia' and his answer provides a cogent overview of my argument: 'fans come from a place of both frustration and fascination with the text and they remake it themselves in ways that suit them and you get a constantly modified end product' (Duffett 2018). Duffett goes on to compare Elvis Presley fandom to the Beatles and he tells me that Elvis was such a huge icon that fans created memes that had very little to do with Elvis. 'Elvis was such a great artist that his meme could travel so far' (Duffett 2018). This description of fandom captures Beatles fans' progressive nostalgia: with the help of technology they transform Beatles art into memes that resonate into the future. The term 'progressive' in the context of my work means to move forward. Duffett is uncomfortable with this term as it denotes politics, and what is progressive about Beatles fandom when it is couched in the historical materialism of capitalism? So a caveat at the beginning of this work, Beatles fans are not necessarily progressive politically as they are caught up in the electronic envelope of the media where agendas are shaped by economic determinism; however, *The Beatles and Fandom: Sex, Death and Progressive Nostalgia* argues that fans do, to some extent, aesthetically move Beatles art forward and utilize technology to transgress their capitalist context: Beatles fandom is aesthetically liberating, but not always politically emancipatory.

My approach to this book is to galvanize research material (one hundred to two hundred interviews with fans, participatory and empirical research at Beatleweek in Liverpool and The Fest for Beatles Fans in Chicago for Chapter 2 on conventions, and writers, books, articles, YouTube, online slash), theoretical arguments and also to contrast Ian MacDonald's poetic prose, which evokes powerful emotion and feeling, with the traditional objective journalese method of Philip Norman and Hunter Davies. In gathering my research material I am aware that there are limitations to this approach: the recycling of mythology, cliché and documentary is cold and most 'facts' concerning the Beatles (with the exception of Mark Lewisohn's) are inaccurate. Also the documentary method epitomized by Hunter Davies is the labour of a 'chronicler'; 'Chroniclers' to Marcus Collins 'produce books without arguments' and writers such as Davies and Norman 'resist the temptation to analyze' (Collins 2017). *The Beatles and Fandom* is not so cautious and plunges into tempestuous seas of theory and this method has two intellectual bonuses: theory produces shifting, unstable insights and meanings and my occasional lapse into poetic subjective language, like MacDonald, produces eccentric changing perspectives.

When one reads chroniclers such as Davies and Norman the reader is taking a different set of perspectives to the book (especially with the benefit of hindsight), but Davies's and Norman's raw material does not offer the dizzying and vertiginous insights of MacDonald's overreaching opinions nor his challenging and opinionated musical analysis. MacDonald offers analysis and theory. His two main ideas are that 1960s is a repository for the best pop music ever produced and the spiritual awakening of 1960s has been replaced by selfish capitalism and materialism. Davies and Norman do not proffer such big ideas; they repeat well-worn Beatles anecdotes because they are professional journalists first and foremost and then Beatles fans second, they lack MacDonald's passion; however, with MacDonald he is a fan first and a journalist second: MacDonald writes subjectively and emotionally about the Beatles employing the prose/poetry of New Journalistic method to convey his very strident opinions.

An important point to be made about Beatles scholarship is that there has simply been far too much of it. When researching this book I was repeatedly reminded, by anyone I happened to mention the project to, that too much ink has already been spilled on the subject. However, I had to remind casual observers that of the approximately 1700 books and articles on the Beatles (according to Mike Brocken and Melissa Davies's *The Beatles Biography* published in 2012) a comprehensive history on Beatles fandom had yet to be written. I am aware that I am writing this book in the wake of Mark Lewisohn's magisterial study of the band, *The Beatles: All These Years, Volume One: Tune In*; John Harris calls for a cessation in Fab scholarship and obsession. Harris writes that 72 per cent of Liverpudlians are in favour of demolishing Ringo Starr's childhood home, presumably out of nostalgia fatigue:

> And consider what state-sponsored Fabs-worship is doing to our appreciation of their own work. Understanding their music's essentials – the liquid excitement of their early period, the creative daring in so much of what they did, the 1,000mph pace at which they developed – is made increasingly difficult by a great blanket of compulsory sentimentality. Put another way, we are reaching a point where a creation as jaw-dropping as, say, A Day in the Life, is in danger of acquiring a leaden kind of tedium, like something from a school hymn book. The Beatles' magic is being crushed: sorry to bring up such grim eventualities, but after the great outpourings that will greet the passing of Paul and Ringo, there will surely be none left. (Harris, 2013)

There is a broad consensus that a glut of books has desiccated all the sap out of the Beatles' work; but the fact remains that a cogent book on the Beatles and fandom has yet to be written. This debate is not new; as early as 1963, Oxford don John Gross wrote that 'surely there is almost nothing an intelligent person really wants to say about them one way or another' (Collins 2017). So two related schools of thought recur in this discussion of the Beatles, firstly, that they are a shallow capitalist manipulation of the masses and therefore not worthy of serious intellectual consideration, and secondly, the verbiage and ink that has been used discussing the band has reached a tipping point. On the first point, psychologist William Sergeant compared Beatlemania to 'the brainwashing of Adolf Hitler' (Collins 2017); Eric Hobsbawm in 1963 said 'nothing of them will survive by 1990' (Collins 2017); educationalist David Holbrook declared the Beatles were nothing more than 'a masturbation fantasy' (Collins 2017). In a very real sense, my book has to overcome two prejudices: that everything about the Beatles cultural phenomenon has been said; and snobbishness about the band as serious area of scholarly pursuit has only been overcome since Wilfrid Mellers's *Twilight of the Gods* (1974); and as I discussed earlier in this introduction, this elitism has morphed into condescension about fan studies: the scorn that was directed at the band is now focused on books written about lowly fans.

The Beatles: The Biography by Mark Spitz claims to have interviewed 600 friends, family and business associates; Albert Goldman claims 'double that number' in *The Lives of John Lennon* and Mark Lewisohn's 'The Beatles: Turn On, Tune In and Drop Out, when it is completed will be 5,000 pages in length' (Collins 2017); all claim to be neutral accounts; I make no such claims in *The Beatles and Fandom*. Another feature of the two most outstanding books on the Beatles is that they don't engage with theory; Mark Lewisohn's *Turn On* only references two academic books, and Ian MacDonald's *Revolution in the Head* cites only five; this is a pitfall that academic writing avoids because academia is predicated on 'interpretation and representation' (Collins 2017). Richard Poirier also wrote in the Paris Review in 1967 that 'The outmoded criteria of literary criticism made it unable to analyse contemporary culture' (Collins 2017). *The Beatles and Fandom* is engaged with fans' interpretation, and it is in the cultural studies tradition that treats the subject seriously.

Any discussion of fandom in an academic context must take account of the aca-fan or aca-fen. The aca-fan (acafen is the plural) is an academic or researcher 'who self-consciously serve and speak for fan communities by using their own identities as fans are, in effect, academic fans or "acafen"' (Duffett 2015: 267). Traditionally fan studies have been at the bottom of the academic pecking order in terms of cultural capital. Bourdieu used the term strictly in a Marxist sense, arguing that cultural capital is a critique of the manner in which the moneyed classes replicated snobbish social attitudes to culture. Although the cultural capital of fandom is low, the Beatles phenomenon has collided and interacted with so much 'high' and 'low' culture that new interstices of meaning have opened up. For instance, when Beatle fandom combines with English heritage culture (on a London Beatles walk, the other two most popular destinations were Shakespeare's Globe and Buckingham Palace), a cultural tourism of high status is created: new Beatles heritage culture, if you like. *The Beatles and Fandom: Sex, Death and Progressive Nostalgia* serves to chronicle the creation of such bricolage and fresh fan spaces; and an ethnographer should ideally be an 'insider' who knows the culture that they are studying well enough to really allow it to speak for itself (Duffett 2015: 263).

My intention for *The Beatles and Fandom* is that it will allow Beatles fans to tell their own story through an academic text that synthesizes academic theory and participant research to create a book that will be passionate, opinionated and lively, and also tempered with mannered, academic objectivity, as aca-fen should avoid 'the affective fallacy says that those emotionally swayed by a text will lose insight and objectivity' (Duffett 2015: 268). So my rationale for this study is to demonstrate the extent to which the aca-fen have 'reduced the distance between fandom and the academy by proclaiming their dual identities' (Duffett 2015: 268).

My characterization of myself as an aca-fan, of inhabiting a 'dual identity', is to try and ensnare the wealth of archival (and living subcultural) material which is shifting constantly and reconfiguring Beatles art at a speed with which it is difficult to keep pace. This intangible or living culture of fan communities is difficult to chronicle because of its scale and because it is adapting and changing in multiple new media forms. One of the problems of a book of this nature is that as soon as it is 'finished', new media flora and fauna are discovered, so with that caveat about the dynamism of fans ringing in my ears, it's time to get to work.

1

'She Loves You': *Beatles Monthly*

Beatles Monthly is significant for fan studies for two main reasons. Firstly, it was a forum for proto-feminist girl fans to express their sexuality – admittedly in a very euphemistic and wholesome manner – and secondly, the publication is an example of transformative or progressive nostalgia. Liam Geraghty, paraphrasing Simon Reynold's thesis in *Retromania* (2011), explains that nostalgia is 'often seen as an inhibiting and emotional phenomenon that reacts against change and modernity, nostalgia not only represents a longing for the past, it is also manifested as dissatisfaction for the present' (Geraghty 2014: 163). In this chapter we will see that *Beatles Monthly* is a forward-looking publication: the girl fans challenge Brian Epstein's cosy boy-next-door image with letters and commentary that are feminist and transgressive. A scrutiny of *Beatles Monthly* demonstrates that new theoretical positions are constantly developing, new perspectives on fans and Beatlemania, more importantly a feminist discussion concerning sexuality and the incipient sexism of the music industry. *Beatles Monthly* is not just relevant as a 1960s cultural artefact, but it is appropriated into new debates by fans. *Beatles Monthly* is an emancipatory feminist space, it is unmoored from its context in later years by technology and there is a sexual subtext: all of these aspects of fandom demonstrating that it is not an 'inhibiting phenomenon' rooted in nostalgia.

Rather than being a mere reactionary colour supplement, the nostalgia represented by this fanzine is 'a more active agent, reflexive and exerting a shaping influence on the past and present; bringing the two periods on an individual's memory together, making a new more fulfilling experience of history and the possibilities it holds for the future' (Geraghty 2014: 164). *Beatles Monthly* is now bought, exchanged and read online, and like all the objects and performances in this book, *Beatles Monthly* has been transformed by the digital remediation. This is what Geraghty calls transformative nostalgia or what I call progressive nostalgia. *Beatles Monthly* is held dear by baby boomer fans, but technology has changed the meaning of *Beatles Monthly* to 'serve as model for future play' (Geraghty 2014: 164). In other words, 'The things we continue to hold dear from childhood, remediated and recycled by new technologies of modern culture, are evocative and thus serve to bring together ideas of thought and feeling' (Geraghty 2014: 164). Through cyberspace these objects are transformed into progressive texts that are no longer anchored to their original print dissemination and reception. *Beatles Monthly* is a digitized ghostly presence which is electronic imprint reminding older fans of the past; it is a ghoul haunting the present with its exchange value; it is a cyber *objet d'art* that creates new meaning in fans' lives because of its remediation by online communities. The meaning of Beatles objects shifts in conjunction with changes in media: the online sale and discussion of *Beatles Monthly* takes it into a new electronic realm which is distinct from its print form, as Geraghty argues: 'Playing with these objects (touching, filming, displaying and collecting) changes how fans relate to memories of the 1960s, or as he puts it, "the reconstruction of personal and public memories of childhood in the digital sphere"' (2014: 165). Technology stimulates a progressive nostalgia where dusty archives are reimagined creatively online and are understood in new fan contexts.

In early 1963 a publisher, Sean O'Mahony, asked Brian Epstein if he could publish a magazine devoted to the Beatles. Epstein and the group agreed and the title launched in August 1963 with a print run of eighty thousand. The fanzine *Beatles Monthly* was produced by the Beatles fan club (mostly female) and it ran from 1963 to 1969. *Beatles Monthly* was founded in 1963. It was first published in August 1963 and continued for seventy-seven editions until it stopped publication after the December 1969 edition. It was revived in 1977 and ceased publication in 2003. *Beatles Monthly* was the first official fanzine on the Beatles.

By the end of the year circulation had grown to 330,000 copies per month. O'Mahony edited the magazine under the name of Johnny Dean. The magazine's photographer, Leslie Bryce, had unrivalled access to the group throughout the 1960s, travelling the world and taking thousands of photographs. In addition, Beatles roadies Neil Aspinall and the late Mal Evans wrote many of the articles, and artist Bob Gibson created numerous cartoons and caricatures of the fab four on a regular basis.

A more accurate title of the fanzine would have been *She Loves You* as the Beatles' image and music were reappropriated by girl fans. The appropriation of the Beatles phenomenon in *Beatles Monthly* is predicated on girl fans objectifying the Beatles as adored, love fantasies. For most of its seven-year history, the magazine was divided into distinct sections: Johnny Dean's editorial, a double-spread colour centrefold of a different Beatle every week, 'Letters from Beatles People', 'Beatles News' and 'This Month's Beatle Song'. The language in the letters page is full of repetitious phrases: love, gorgeous, scream and generally jokey colloquial language that is bubbling under with sexual innuendo.

The first *Beatles Monthly* in August 1963 starts as it means to go on. The first issue has all four Beatles on the cover in their Pierre Cardin collar suits. From the start it is obvious that the fanzine will be devoted to glossy pictures of the fab four. In fact fourteen of the twenty-eight pages in the first issue are glossy photographs of 'the boys' (including a forensic close centre spread). This ratio continued throughout the fanzine's history: 50 per cent pictures and 50 per cent text. In issue No. 2, September 1963, this format continues. The Beatles are described by Margaret Newham, South Shields, Durham, 'a devoted Beatles fan', as 'gorgeous' (*Beatles Monthly*, No. 1, 1963) in a letter section dominated by female fans: Kay McGregor, Margo Higginson, Lesley Banks, Gula Lindross, Valerie Payne, Margaret Newham, Laura Bellany, Maxine Williamson, Virginia Harrop and Samantha Chatnam. This was only occasionally impinged on by a male letter. It is only when the book is rebooted in 1976, with a new introduction by Dean and a contemporary letter pages from 1976, that this demographic changes dramatically: in the 'new' fanzine, the letter writers are mostly male, enquiring about the minutiae of Beatles history, chronology of releases and nerdy facts about the band.

The Beatles organization cannily sells the fanzine to girl fans: the band is often pictured with girl fans (this is especially prevalent in issue No. 5). The fanzine prints letters that obsess over the Beatles appearance. Alison from Stubbington, Hants, writes in issue No. 3, 'if you take Paul's hair and eyebrows, Ringo's eye and neck and George's chin and ears; put them together and you will have most handsome face to grace that has, or ever will, grace the pages of pop star mag' (*Beatles Monthly*, No. 3, 1963). Theresa Wareham, Dagenham, Essex, asks 'if we can have one (a picture) of all of them in swimming trunks' (*Beatles Monthly*, No. 3, 1963). By this stage of the publication the fans are calling the shots and demanding pictures of 'Paul's handsome suntanned face' (*Beatles Monthly*, No. 5, 1963); the Beatles 'improperly clad' (*Beatles Monthly*, No. 8, 1964); Diane Dickinson, Norbury, London, writes that 'I heard on the good ol' London Transport the other day: "That Paul Macwhatsit is the most ansome feller out"'. She continues to reveal her nose fetish: 'the other one with the kissable konk (i.e. RINGO ... don't mind me, I've got a thing about noses' (*Beatles Monthly*, No. 16, 1964). Letters would usually start with 'Dear gorgeous, lovable Beatles' and end with 'lots of love and kisses', Gillian and Lynn (*Beatles Monthly*, No. 20, 1964). Issue No. 4 has a fan describing herself as a 'complete Beatles parasite' (*Beatles Monthly*, No. 4, 1964); the language is so heavily charged with repressed sexuality that in my notes for this issue I wrote about a 'double-centre spread of Porn'; this was in fact a Freudian slip, I meant to write 'double page centre spread of Paul'.

The letters page is full of fans' stories of falling and bumping into inanimate objects in their excitement when a Beatles song comes on the radio. Leslie Bryce's photographs seriously scrutinize the band with very detailed close-ups of each band member's face. The text is littered with exclamation marks and upper-case lettering to denote excitement, especially when the fans are 'ordering' the band to cut their hair or shave their moustaches. The text is a structuralist web of total fan devotion, absorption and sexual longing for a boy band by transgressive proto-feminist fans. The photographs most beloved by fans in *Beatles Monthly* were taken by Leslie Bryce, the magazine's in-house photographer. Leslie was a significant conduit between the fans and the band in the years 1963 to 1969 and his shots frame the Beatles in very down-to-earth domestic spheres: drinking tea, placing the stylus on a record, Paul pretending to comb Dusty Springfield's hair and Ringo at the wheel of his car. Again we see that Bryce's work constructs a performance from 'the boys' as smiling, carefree pop stars, which obfuscates the louche lives of musicians who drank and smoked marijuana immoderately. These beautiful portraits are a ghostly simulacra demonstrating the hyperrealist nature of Beatles fame, *Beatles Monthly* gave the fans what they wanted, good-looking pop stars: pin-ups that were demanded by girl fans.

The magazine is affirmed on the consumer boom of the 1950s and 1960s; it is all about consumption. In the fanzine, the Beatles are advertisements for the consumer society: the pictures fetishize clothes and musical instruments, and the magazine is a pictorial equivalent of one of their songs: easily affordable, standardized, selling love. The pages of the magazine are advertising 'Swinging London', and the fans are consuming and appropriating this fantasy into their own personal lives. The fanzine aims to promulgate optimism and love: the pictures are of smiling and happy Beatles. *Beatles Monthly* inherits the pop art style of *A Hard Day's Night* cover, the Beatles' pictures in Warholesque squares is a recurrent conceit. The fanzine includes tour itineraries, posters for sale, adverts for merchandizing: it is a magazine for neophiliacs seeking new excitement.

Every inch of the Beatles' personal lives and appearances is scrutinized here. The Beatles are under pressure from their fans to conform to certain looks: the Beatles are marketed as lovable and infantile, but it is important to stress that *Beatles Monthly* is not 'standardized rubbish' (Adorno, 'The Cultural Industry') that manipulates 'parasitic' fans: the fans in the Beatlemania years 1963–5 are more feminist than the later countercultural period as they call the shots. The counterculture Beatles from 1966 to 1969 – while on the surface politically progressive – are stereotyping women as dream eroticized others in songs like 'Lucy in the Sky with Diamonds'. In *Beatles Monthly* the girl fans are eroticizing the Beatles as dream objects. The fans' voices here are adoring, sexual, ironic, witty, emotional and overwhelmingly feminine. *Beatles Monthly* captures youth and beauty and is a publication of high quality.

Beatles Monthly is a trailblazer for pop magazines such as *Smash Hits* and the *History of the Beatles* written by Billy Shepherd enshrined the Beatles story and mythology before Hunter Davies and Philip Norman (and perhaps more truthful and more accurate than either journalist). The fanzine was also very global and it sold swinging London to an international market: *Beatles Monthly* is a product of Atlantic history and Anglo-American individualism: neo-colonialism selling the Beatles, London and feminism to the world. The Beatles are sold as nice, approachable, fun-loving, wacky boys; they are often depicted as cute insects in line drawings. The letters pages are teeming with bad poetry celebrating the Beatles by repeating their song titles *ad nauseum*. It is a fora where proto-feminist fans treat men as objects of desire, feminized men with long hair; the Beatles look is the antithesis of 1950s music and sports stars who were depicted as macho, whereas in *Beatles Monthly*, the Beatles are young, skinny, long-haired fashionable fops in Carnaby Street corduroy, Cuban-heeled boots with roll-neck sweaters.

Beatles fans' letters and double entendre

In *Beatles Monthly* the sexuality is sublimated by the twee language and double entendre. For instance, Jean Denmark, a Beatles fan from Elmhurst, Illinois, writes, 'Also John, please remember to bring your mouth organ to your next recording session. I'm still waiting to hear your beautiful mouth puffing out beautiful chords on a new song' (*Beatles Monthly*, No. 31, 1966). The fans often put their demands in upper case: 'And **PLEASE**, will you and the rest of the Beatles wear your hair as long as George's was on the last Ed Sullivan show? I've **NEVER** seen him look so fantastically gorgeous. Beatle hair was **MEANT** to be long' (*Beatles Monthly*, No. 32, 1966). Jan

Wade from Bethesda, Maryland, ends her hirsute plea with 'love love love love'. The language in *Beatles Monthly* is lascivious, focusing on hair, mouths and even noses! The fans could also be incredibly critical of the Beatles appearance. In February 1966, Annabel Lee complained in verse that the cover of *Rubber Soul* makes the Beatles look like 'freaks': 'I tried to work it out but could not, Why such a photogenic lot, should want to see yourselves portrayed as freak, You look as if you have been dead for weeks.' She describes John as 'the late', Paul as wearing a 'graveyard guise', Ringo as 'grey yellow' and 'Dracula like', George as 'cadaverous'. The rhyme ends with Annabel employing the un-feminist term 'bird' to express her disappointment in the Beatles looks: 'What bird who over Beatle picture drools/Can want to see her idols look like ghouls?' (*Beatles Monthly*, No. 31, 1966). If Annabel was shocked by the *Rubber Soul* cover, it's a shame her reaction to *Abbey Road*'s hippie look wasn't recorded for posterity.

Discounting the sexist symbolic order of some of the fans' language, *Beatles Monthly* illustrates that early 1960s Beatles fandom was nascent and incipient feminism. Ehrenreich, Hess and Jacobs identify the sexual repression in Beatlemania; sexual aggression is 'sublimated':

> In the decade that followed Beatlemania, the girls who had inhabited the magical, obsessive world of fandom would edge closer and closer to center stage. Sublimation would give way to more literal, and sometimes sordid forms of fixation: by the late sixties, the most zealous fans, no longer content with sobbing in virginal frustration, would become groupies and 'go all the way' with any accessible rock musician. One briefly notorious group of girl fans, the Chicago Plaster Casters, distinguished itself by making plaster moulds of rock stars penises, thus memorializing, among others, Jimi Hendrix. (Ehrenreich, Hess and Jacobs 1992: 104)

In *Beatles Monthly* the fans' sexual aggression is hidden behind juvenile language and metaphors for sex, 'konks' and 'puffing mouth organs'.

In this seven-year history, the fanzine also commoditized the Beatles as four lovable mop tops or boys next door, but from issue one the girls were aggressive fans and considered the Beatles as sex objects. The meanings created by girl fans were all to do with a sexual participation in this image: even the most asinine comments or letters from the fans had a highly sexualized subtext. For instance, in the section 'Letters from Beatle People', 'Marie Selander from Hasselquistvagen 1, Johanneshov, Stockholm' describes the fan hysteria surrounding the Beatles. In the letter entitled 'Beatles in Sweden', Selander's letter describes Beatlemania in a sexualized manner:

> I sat there calmly talking to my friends. Then suddenly they came up on the stage! I found myself jumping into the air, then crawling on the floor with my tongue hanging out of my mouth like a red tie and my eyes nearly fell out of my head! (recognise yourself girls?) After the show I flew home singing 'You really got a hold on me'. (Dean 1995: 78–9)

This is a typical letter from a girl fan in 1963–4: the Beatles are objects of amorous fixation; however, an explicit expression of female sexuality was impossible in the censoriously patriarchal 1960s. It was the 1990s before Beatles scholarship caught up in the feminist work of Barbara Ehrenreich, Elizabeth Hess and Gloria Jacobs. And as we shall see, this is tame stuff compared to online Beatles slash fiction in the noughties. Ehrenreich, Hess and Jacobs show the extent to which girl fans made their own erotic agenda when it came to their idols:

> For the girls who participated in Beatlemania, sex was an obvious part of the excitement. One of the most common responses to reporters' queries on the sources of Beatlemania was, 'Because they're sexy.' And this explanation was in itself a small act of defiance. It was rebellious (especially for the very young fans) to lay claim to sexual feelings. It was even rebellious to lay claim to the active desiring side of sexual attraction: the Beatles were the objects; the girls were their pursuers. (Ehrenreich, Hess and Jacobs 1992: 90)

Here the girl fans are described as active pursuers, and without them the Beatles' music and art cease to have significant meaning. As *Beatles Monthly* demonstrates, artistic credibility always has to be tempered with the chase for an audience. Once the audience is found, the audience chases back and the pursuers begin to produce their own work and responses to the Beatles.

Beatles Monthly from 1967 to 1969 demonstrates how determined the fans were to maintain their own ideas concerning the Beatles. Issue No. 46 from May 1967, for instance, has pictures of the band in their psychedelic regalia from the *Sgt. Pepper* sessions. In the face of strong evidence to the contrary Mary Watson from Macclesfield writes,

> I love the Beatles very much ... there's a hundred reasons to be proud of them for, but these are two which I've realised a lot recently. Firstly we've NEVER heard of any of the drugs business. I've nothing against other stars but if they have been taking drugs, they're very foolish, and also very selfish. Besides if their families worrying, they are forgetting their fans. I know if Paul took drugs, I'd be worried sick for him, but I know he's too sensible. The other thing is that we NEVER hear of the Beatles leaving their wives or girlfriends, or getting divorces. They are true to the ones that love them. (Although I'm very envious of the four females in their lives. I'm proud that they are so loyal.) I couldn't imagine Paul with anyone but Jane Asher, and he's being so loyal to her, even in the middle of all these pop romances breaking up. So, I just like to say, thank you, Paul, George, John and Ringo, for being so sensible, and so wonderful with it. (*Beatles Monthly*, No. 46)

Jan and Chris write in the same issue, 'What is a fish and finger pie?' an observation that completely misses the sexual innuendo in 'Penny Lane'. Both comments demonstrate that the Beatles fans both deliberately and inadvertently appropriate eccentric meanings from the Beatles' image.

The first *Beatles Monthly* was published in August 1963 to create a forum for fans (mostly girls) to scrutinize every detail about the Beatles' lives: their clothes, hair styles, musical tastes, touring itinerary, interviews, wit, holidays and praise for Ringo's drumming, 'He's the best drummer we've ever had' (*Beatles Monthly*, 1963). However, what is most noticeable about the August and September issues is the language that is directed at young girl fans. The Beatles are infantilized throughout in order to sell their image: they are 'the boys' and 'the four boys' and 'Britain's top pop stars' and are depicted as goofy, childish and incapable of taking anything seriously. In a short piece entitled 'Beatles Break' in the September issue, 'All four boys fly off … for two weeks' well-earned break' and the fans are informed that 'Paul and Ringo have gone to Greece. Paul "to have all my teeth out" and Ringo "to get my toenails tattooed"' (*Beatles Monthly*, 1963). On the surface the book is a shiny, shallow veneer to sell this boy band to preadolescents, but this marketing tactic is almost immediately reversed with the fans' letters appropriating the most banal details about the band into the web and weft of their own lives. The tone of these early books is to control the Beatles' image and to put into effect an image of four sexless, cuddly mop tops whose only interests are chip butties and music, and who are bewildered at their colossal fame; but the status inversion is evident even at this early stage: the Beatles' management seeks to control this phenomenon, but the fans' desire for the minutiae about their heroes is already transgressive in its sexuality and its brazenness. In fact the naivety of the language employed here is extremely patronizing and it isn't too long before the fans' language is demanding and interrogative.

It is already evident from the first edition that conversation and colloquial tone employed by Johnny Dean is catering to a romantic fantasy for the girl fans. The first magazine uses the term 'Beatlemania', the word 'frenzy' recurs and the fans' reaction is described as 'ecstatic'. Exclamation marks are dropped into the text like confetti which has the effect of stimulating excitement; in fact, the language is deliberately demotic to appeal directly to the fans. The whole tone is tabloid journalese which is a thinly veiled veneer to obscure sexual frisson. The pictures in this issue are of a smiling, identically attired foursome sporting the famous fringed Beatle haircut and in sharp mohair suits. The clear intention is to promulgate a standardized boy band look that appeals to girl fans, and when this is coupled with short frivolous pieces that promote their singles 'She Loves You' and 'I Want to Hold Your Hand' under the heading 'What a Month!', the intention is clear that image, tabloid language and hyperbole such as 'fans screamed for a glimpse of their idols' (*Beatles Monthly*, 1963) capture a feminist sexual phenomenon emanating from the fans.

Beatlemania was an emancipatory sexual experience for girl fans. The subtext of the words 'mania', 'frenzy' and 'screaming' is that in fact the fans were giving voice to repressed sexuality. Ehrenreich et al. have argued,

> The Beatles were sexy; the girls were the ones who perceived them as sexy and acknowledged the force of the ungovernable, if somewhat disembodied lust. To assert an active, powerful sexuality by the tens of thousands and to do so in a way calculated to attract maximum attention was more than rebellious. It was in

its own unformulated way, dizzy way, and revolutionary. (Ehrenreich, Hess and Jacobs 1992: 90)

Of course this is a reference to fans' behaviour at concerts, but the sexuality expressed in *Beatles Monthly* was revolutionary, albeit in a more understated manner. In fact Johnny Dean was so keen to promote a sexy version of the Beatles that was demanded by the fans that he began to doctor their photographs to waylay complaints about the Beatles' hirsute stylings in the psychedelic period from 1967 to their break-up in 1970: 'February and March 1967 issues carried rather different pictures of moustachioed Beatles. They appeared to be contemporary pictures of the band with facial hair, but upon closer inspection it is evident that hair has been added to previously existing photographs, mainly from photo sessions in late 1964' (Kirkup 2015: 75).

The rationale behind this was to accustom the fans to the new hairy fab four and to cater to pressure from the fans who didn't want their good-looking idols obscuring their handsome features behind beards, long hair and, in John Lennon's case, NHS granny glasses. O'Mahony is capitulating to the fans' sexual fantasies: the fans wanted an infantilized, pretty boy group that was perennially winsome, and if that took some artistic licence, then O'Mahony felt compelled to cave in to their pressure.

This pampering to the fans' demands emphasizes their revolutionary sexual power, which is refreshing as the music industry in the 1960s was incredibly misogynist. O'Mahony is explicit concerning his own prejudices about the band; his fandom preferred the lovable mop top Beatles, and he felt so pressured by the burden of Beatlemania that he argued vehemently for the young, clean-cut Beatles:

> The final issue of the original *Beatles Monthly* was published in December 1969. It featured a valedictory article concerned with the subject of The Beatles' transformation from mop-topped entertainers to long-haired experimentalists. 'The End of an Era', which was written by publisher Sean O'Mahony under his own by-line and addressed directly to the fans, discussed how the magazine started and brought together several strands of opinion about the group, their career, their image and the press. O'Mahony was refreshingly honest about each Beatle, acknowledging for example that Harrison disliked the magazine. O'Mahony admitted that he preferred The Beatles before what he called 'their hairy period', stating that they were 'tremendously photogenic, or at least they were in the days when you could see all of their faces'. (O'Mahony 1969: 14)

O'Mahony disliked the 'fabulous freak brother' Beatles and his defensive editorial accords with Ehrenreich that the Beatles were most revolutionary when they appeared innocent, 'the appeal lay in the vision of sexuality ... that was guileless, ebullient and fun' (Ehrenreich, Hess and Jacobs 1992: 102–3). Ehrenreich cites an interview where an anonymous Beatles fan asserts that the Beatles' image inverted machismo and sexual oppression:

I mean I liked their independence and sexuality and wanted the things for myself ... girls didn't get to be that way when I was a teenager – we got to be the limp, passive object of some guy's sexual interest. We were so stifled and they made us meek, giggly creatures think, oh, if only I could act that way and be sexy, and doing what you want. (Ehrenreich, Hess and Jacobs 1992: 102–3)

Beatles Monthly is similarly transgressive for girl fans. The pages are full of letters asking the Beatles to shave and to cut their hair, and this fanzine is so liberating as the girls know the fanzine is the way it is because their demands shaped it, in a profound sense, the fans sculpted it. An analogy between the screaming at concerts and ogling over glossy pictures of the Fab Four shows how the tail begins to wag the dog, 'And the louder you screamed, the less likely anyone would forget the power of the fans. When the screams died drowned out the music, as they invariably did, then it was the fans, and not the band who were the show' (Ehrenreich, Hess and Jacobs 1992: 104).

In concert the Beatles were subsumed in a sound vortex of screams; in *Beatles Monthly* the band were swamped in the language of teen titillation and the visual imagery of adolescent pin-up fantasy. In *Beatles Monthly* the fans have agency, they are not the passive mass audience of Adorno's theories, but are conversely a product of the fans' aggressive mania and sexual appetites. Tom Wolfe was stunned watching the fans in concert and he describes them as helpless onlookers of their own fame:

The Beatles cheese and mince at them [the fans] in the dumb show, utterly helpless to ripple them or anything else now, with no control left – ... *Ghhhhhwooooooooowwwww,* thousands of teeny bodies hurtling toward the stage and a fence there and a solid line of cops, fighting to hurl the assault back, while the Beatles keep moving their chops and switching their hips around sunk like a dumb show under the universal scream. In that surge, just when you would have thought not another sound in the universe could break through, it starts – *thwaaaac\-thwaaaac* ... CANCER – Kesey has only to look and it is perfectly obvious – all of them, the teeny freaks and the Beatles, are one creature, caught in a state of sheer poison mad cancer. The Beatles are the creature's head. The teeny freaks are the body. But the head has lost control of the body and the body rebels and goes amok and that is what cancer is. (Wolfe 1989: 183–4)

Beatles concerts and *Beatles Monthly* swallow the band up in the fans' demands: in concert the music is drowned out by screaming and in print the Beatles are swamped by the fans' hyperbolic language and highly constructed photography. Both these examples demonstrate that to a certain extent the Beatles phenomenon was affirmed on social, historical and cultural forces beyond their music and talent. Of course to a great extent the Beatles were authors of their fame: talented, hard-working (according to Malcolm Gladwell the Beatles achieved success after putting in ten thousand hours of work in the sleazy clubs of Hamburg), but cultural theory also shows that grand narrative of history collides with the mini-narratives of their lives and it is this collision that creates success. The national grids started in the UK in the 1930s; the Butler

Education Act in 1944; the NHS in 1948; and Conscription was abolished in 1960. These significant historical moments impacted on the Beatles to the extent that they were better educated, better fed, healthier, had access to record players and televisions through electricity and they weren't sent on a colonial adventure to be shot at and possibly killed. Their fans had broadly the same baby boom backgrounds, the Beatles and their fans were products of this affluent society and a consumer boom which saw young people indulge their fantasies (sexual and otherwise) in the pages of a teen magazine which is a shiny testament to the power of the consumer to put idols of *their* choice on a pedestal. In a very profound sense the Beatles' success was nothing to do with them, but with historical and technological determinism. It was the capitalist machinery that was in part responsible for producing the Beatles and their fans, and nowhere is this more prevalent than in the sexual frenzy of a concert hall or in the embellished glamour and garnish of *Beatles Monthly*. Concerts and *Beatles Monthly* were an indispensable part of their success and both showcased the fans' needs and desires, so much so that screams drowned out the music and photographic 'shiny barbarism' (Hoggart 1957: 193) commodified the Beatles as adolescent sex objects. *Beatles Monthly* and concerts were fora where they were subsumed in the desires of Beatles fans who were from the demographic of '13–17, a girl, middle class, white, Christian, a B-student, weighed 105–150 pounds, owned a transistor radio with ear plug attachment and had Beatles photographs all over her walls' (Makela 2004).

Beatles Monthly was a conduit to young fans that was appropriated into their lives in a transgressive feminist manner. What is so fascinating about this is that the fans have created affinity spaces where they can share their knowledge (and fantasies) about the Beatles in a demotic and informal manner: the letters in *Beatles Monthly* are a space where the most discourteous comment is consistent. One of the most radical features of this fan activity is that it places the misogyny of the late 1960s – the counterculture from 1966 to 1970 – into sharp relief. The image of women in the late 1960s was a very crude stereotype. In fact most of the popular songs in this period exoticized the feminine other, or as Kathy Acker puts it, 'Woman is dehumanised by being represent as kind of automaton, a "living doll"' (Acker, *Guardian*, 1997; cited in Whiteley). Shelia Whiteley discusses this repressive in songs such as Donovan's 'Jennifer Juniper' and the Beatles' 'Lucy in the Sky with Diamonds' and 'Julia':

> The idealisation of the image is subtle in effect. Lucy, Julia, Jennifer ... is a sense of deceptive fascination in this particular genre, in that the image of the woman is enhanced by illusion. She is etherealised and inscribed with a dreamlike and unreal world, detached from reality. The significance of this representation can be seen in the ways in which the idealised image was displaced onto the style of period. The long hair, the emphasis on eyes and the use of body make-up reaffirmed the' made-up-ness' of the image of the woman herself, as one composed of surfaces, defined by appearance. They are 'made-up' in the immediate sense in that the images are constructed by the songs and written by male singer songwriters. (Whiteley 2000: 35)

Of course *Beatles Monthly* is constructing a highly controlled and standardized image of the Beatles, but the *quid pro quo* of a fanzine is that fans in a very real sense have a more strident say about the content. The fans can use *Beatles Monthly* to comment on the songs, and they could stop buying sexist Beatles Records, but the exoticism of songs is more repressive as they were conceived and recorded in studios remote from the fans' reach, and exoticism insidiously controls and represses subtlety, 'what is manifestly different' (Said 1978: 12). Dream girl songs interpolate the female subject into a male symbolic order. In stark contrast to the eroticized sexism of the later 1960s counterculture, *Beatles Monthly* is an emancipatory feminist space predicated on fan appropriation. To Sheila Whiteley, the lyrics of the late-1960s counterculture create a feminine eroticized other in songs such as 'Lucy' and 'Julia', whereas *Beatles Monthly* demonstrates the agency of female fans. It is strangely counterintuitive that the supposedly radical late-1960s acid rock was in fact much more sexist than the Beatles teen pop magazine.

The Beatles songs and recording in this period, when they stopped touring on 29 August 1966, were remote from fans' interrogation the way their image in *Beatles Monthly* wasn't (see the controversy over the Beatles' facial hair). In contrast to the Beatles' self-absorbed counterculture late songs often predicated on 'dream exotic others', *Beatles Monthly* is an affinity space where the fans have room to breathe and to interact and to appropriate the Beatles' image. Challenging the image of 'Lucy' and 'Julia' is more difficult as the hard shell of exoticism is a carapace that is hard to crack because the machinery of the music industry is predicted on this type of institutional sexism. *Beatles Monthly* is the antithesis of this 'male gaze': instead of women as male fetish objects, in the glossy pages of *Beatles Monthly* the Beatles are a feminine fetish object in a manner similar to later boy bands such as Take That and One Direction, so the Beatles pin-ups are the subject of a female gaze, and as a result *Beatles Monthly* is a cultural moment which is less sexist than the exoticized feminine other in late-1960s counterculture.

The female fetishization of male pop stars is only one aspect of the female gaze: as fans have very different and heterogeneous experiences, and each individual fan has a mess of contradictory psychological feelings when viewing a visual sign, young fans make 'a series of identifications' that are 'shifting and mobile' (Dyer 1981: 5). One spoke on the wheel of this complex and 'shifting' fan consciousness is a series of pin-ups that can be transgressed by the very nature of their interactive forum. It is also important to note that 'the image that the viewer looks at is not summoned up by his or her act of looking but in collaboration of those who have put the image there' (Dyer 1981: 66); however, the image is *collaboration* in the context of *Beatles Monthly*, whereas the dream songs of 'Lucy' and 'Julia' are products of a sexist music industry. They are verbal visual fantasies that are 'socially defined and constructed categories of male and female' (Neale 1983: 5) and that are supported by a male language symbolic code, affirmed on a sexist 1960s music industry and which flicker in a liminal psychological space between the artist and the fan. In many ways *Beatles Monthly* makes it easier to appropriate new meanings: its imagery is bold and obvious in comparison with the amorphous psychedelic exoticism of Beatles lyrics. The Beatles' image in this period is feminized subverting macho stereotypes of masculinity.

The Beatles and feminism

The fact that during Beatlemania Beatles fans were mainly female was a significant pop cultural moment that recurs throughout this book, especially in this chapter on *Beatles Monthly* where the letters page was dominated by female fans:

> The novelist Linda Grant was a 12-year-old in Liverpool when she first heard Love Me Do. 'Everybody was a Beatles fan in Liverpool,' she remembers. 'You just knew you were in the centre of the universe. I still feel that Cliff and Elvis fans were from an earlier generation even though there was only a couple of years in it. The Beatles belonged to every teenage girl. I feel like I was there at the birth of pop music. The Beatles are the Book of Genesis'. (Lynskey 2013, *The Observer*)

Beatles Monthly is a teenage girls' perspective on fandom and because of this has been ridiculed by sexist writers, the most famous example is Paul Johnson's 'The Menace of Beatlism' essay. Aca-fandom is a way of addressing this snobbery,

> Teenage girl fans are still patronised by the press today. As Grant says, 'Teenage girls are perceived as a mindless horde: one huge, undifferentiated emerging hormone.' In an influential 1992 essay, Fandom as Pathology, US academic Joli Jensen observed: 'Fandom is seen as a psychological symptom of a presumed social dysfunction ... Once fans are characterised as a deviant, they can be treated as disreputable, even dangerous "others". (Lynskey 2013, *The Observer*)

If there is one overall unifying theme in this book it is that my book rejects the idea of young female Beatles fans as a homogenous mass, which is precisely what Tom Wolfe does:

> *And now – the Beatles –* what else could he say? – and out they come on stage – *them* – John and George and Ringo and uh the other one – it might as well have been four imported vinyl dolls for all it was going to matter – that sound he thinks cannot get higher, it doubles, his eardrums ring like stamped metal with it and suddenly *Ghhhhhhwoooooooooowwwwww,* it is like the whole thing has snapped, and the whole front section of the arena becomes a writhing, seething mass of little girls waving their arms in the air, this mass of pink arms, it is all you can see, it is like a single colonial animal with a thousand waving pink tentacles – it *is* a single colonial animal with a thousand waving pink tentacles, – vibrating poison madness and filling the universe with the teeny agony torn out of them. It dawns on Kesey: it is *one being.* They have all been transformed into one being. One of the Beatles, John, George, Paul, dips his long electric guitar handle in one direction

and the whole teeny horde ripples precisely along the line of energy he set off – and then in the other direction, precisely along that line. It causes them to grin, John and Paul and George and Ringo, rippling the poor huge freaked teeny beast this way and that – *Control* – it is perfectly obvious – they have brought this whole mass of human beings to the point where they are one, out of their skulls, one psyche, and they have utter control over them – but they don't know what in the hell to do with it, they haven't the first idea, and they will lose it. In Kesey the vibration is an awful anticipation of the snap. (Wolfe 1989: 182–3)

In a manner similar to Adorno's dismissal of mass audiences in 'The Cultural Industry', Wolfe's writing reveals the inherent sexism of the counterculture which was largely a male affair predicted on the institutional sexism of the music business and book publishing. The audience are characterized patronizingly as 'little girls' who are 'waving their pink arms' and, in a further dehumanization, describes them as 'one being' and a 'freaked teeny beast' that is controlled by the head, a euphemism for the Beatles and their corporate capitalist structure. The Beatles and their organization do not have 'total control' over the fans; the fans are appropriating the Beatles concerts to their own needs. The concert Wolfe is describing is a forum where female fans are releasing sexual tension and transgressing patriarchal oppression by making the Beatles the object of the female gaze: the Beatles are objectified teen sex objects. Ryan Moore in *Sells Like Teen Spirit* (2010) points out that it is impossible to discern what is happening in a fan's mind during a concert, and he demonstrates that fandom is empowering:

> Journalists and casual observers have typically believed that these male performers wield extraordinary power over their teenybopper audiences, which causes them to go into a physical frenzy. Some feminist scholars, however, have alternatively proposed that musicians are objects ... in other words that female audiences use their idols to actively construct their desire rather than being passively manipulated by them. (Moore 2010: 110)

Moore goes on to argue that fandom is about 'identification' which is emancipatory, again eschewing Adorno's mass audience theory: 'For many young women, the musical performer may be just as much an object of identification as of desire, as they (similar to male fans) crave the creativity, power and independence that musicians embody' (Moore 2010: 110). This is an acute observation; any ideology that reduces a mass audience to an unthinking monoculture is missing the cussedness and contrariness of the human psyche whether in a huge audience or penning a letter alone in a suburban bedroom.

This idea of the empowered and proto-feminist fan is not acknowledged in Wolfe's macho description of a Beatles concert, but the screams in concerts, the letters in *Beatles Monthly*, the whimsical sex of slash fiction and the all-female tribute bands tell a different narrative: a story of the sovereignty of fans.

A discussion of gender is one of the central themes in this book. As Leonard says, the Beatles mothers especially were responsible for encouraging their love of music, and as I said earlier in the introduction, their mothers were their first fans. The rock machinery tends to write about the band in a very male way marginalizing a female fan history: mothers, screaming fans, the sexual subtext in *Beatles Monthly* provided by girl fans, slash pornography which is largely written and enjoyed by female writers and consumers, girl tribute bands such as the Funkles who reimagine the Beatles canon into new songs; girl fan-vidders on YouTube who produce new nostalgia, love vids, which take old footage and make it new. Their parents give them the self-esteem and the confidence to not give up and make this (the Beatles phenomenon) happen. Their parents don't get enough credit. When Paul received his award at Buckingham Palace (Companion of Order for Services to Music) on 4 May 2018, he thanked his mother. *The Beatles and Fandom* is about sex: fans' sexual fantasies, screaming orgasms at concerts, sexual double entendre in *Beatles Monthly* and about sex meaning gender, and in a sense this book is a history of the fans, specifically female fans who appropriated the Beatles into a feminine consciousness, an Eros object, which takes the phenomenon into areas of gender bending androgyny and challenges the male institutions of the music industry; fandom is that powerful, the Beatles are feminized by the first scream at the concerts, and from that moment on the girl fans appropriated the band into a sexually amorphous sphere where the sexist music industry was reimagined by fans. A *leitmotif* of the book is the extent to which the Beatles feminized rock music: Elvis Presley and the 1950s rock and rollers promulgated a more macho culture until this was changed by the Beatles long hair and their three-way harmonies on songs such as the Marvelettes' 'Please Mr Postman'; Beatles fans intuited that here was a band (at least their performances) that was more sympathetic to women: the deaths of John and Paul's mothers when they were young shaped their art for the rest of their lives: Paul's 'Let It Be' and John's 'Julia'. Fans can extrapolate what they want from the Beatles and one of the main strands that run through *Sex, Death and Progressive Nostalgia* is that girl fans appropriated and turned the Beatles phenomenon into their own fantasy: the Beatles were feminized by fans but the fans recognized an androgynous band that was different to previous rock stars. It is important, however, to point out that behind the performative stage craft of the Beatle appearance and act was a history of chauvinist behaviour that wasn't scrutinized until after the band's break-up in 1970. In spite of the Beatles promiscuity and sexist behaviour on tour by the mid-1960s they represented a metrosexual sensibility to female fans:

> Mark Simpson's 1994 'identification' of the metrosexual has its roots firmly in the mid-1960s. Simpson describes the typical metrosexual as a young man with money to spend, living in or within easy reach of the metropolis, which could be gay, straight or bisexual. The Beatles in Help! Undoubtedly fit these criteria: they dramatize the increasing feminization of men's visual appearance, characterized by increased hair length and an ever more dandified dress sense. (King 2015)

Candy Leonard describes the girl fans as being in subordinate position at concerts, but she also recognizes that the girls' screams drowned out the band and were the first fission of emancipated sexual freedom where the boys are the appropriated love object (Leonard 2018).

Leonard describes seeing the Beatles on *The Ed Sullivan Show* for the first time and 'seeing' is as important as 'listening', something that *Beatles Monthly* was very keen to capitalize on:

> John, Paul and George affectionately communicate with each other through grins and knowing smiles, while performing masterly. At the same time they communicated a new proposition about maleness. They showed a generation of viewers that a softer more feminine male is attractive to women. They put forth the idea that warm affection between male friends is okay, and that men can work as a collaborative group. As the song concludes, two young girls in the front row, maybe eight and ten, wildly clap with their whole bodies. (Leonard 2014: 33)

Beatles Monthly uses this teen worship to sell magazines, 'the spectacle has succeeded in colonising *teen* (my italics) life' (Debord 1984: 21), but the teenagers and pre-teens appropriate these spectacles and glossy images into their own inner lives that are dependent on their age, class and gender and not on the machinations of big companies: *Beatles Monthly* is a transgressive text because of the fans' individualized perspectives and subversive expressions.

The letters pages in late period Beatles Monthlies 1967–9 are much more serious in content than the 1963–6 Beatlemania period, although the fans often pepper a thoughtful letter about 'Paul's marriage' or 'Criticism of Paul' with a remark about his good looks. *Beatles Monthly*, No. 69 from April 1969 has four presumably girl fans – S. M., C. K., L. M. and M. S. – write that the press should stop criticizing Paul because 'he is fantastically intelligent and creative, and actually, everything he's produced has come off very well, even if a few people are left too far behind to catch on right away.' The letter then changes tack into a typical fan letter about Paul McCartney's good looks: 'To top it off, Paul is very well assembled above and below his handsome face … none of us gas ever seen him look bad-**EVER**.' On the next page another serious letter about Paul's marriage to Linda Eastman by Anna Renton, Galashiels, Selkirk, changes into a comment on his winsomeness:

> Will anyone desert Paul to punish him for getting married? Not a genuine fan, anyway. Meditation didn't really make him happy; family life is much more likely to do so. He has given his fans so much happiness that they surely can only be glad that he now has the chance of happiness himself. Any road, what difference will his marriage make to us? Far from deserting us, he's working harder than ever on his records. He looks as appealing as ever and marriage won't alter his voice or gift of song. As for him being out of reach, wasn't he always. (*Beatles Monthly*, No. 69)

The gender ratio in 'Letters from Beatles People' in issue No. 1 (August 1963) was 100 per cent female. The Beatles metamorphosis from boy band to serious progressive rock artists is borne out in the letters page. In issue No. 72 from July 1969, the letter page is possibly 100 per cent male (I write 'possibly' as one of the fans doesn't supply his/her name and only provides the vague American College Student). This demonstrates that the Beatles were not losing girl fans who like the Beatles' looks, but what it shows is that male fans had different ideas about their expression of love for the band which had to be measured through serious enquiry about their art, and they could only express their fandom in this detached supposedly non-sexual manner. So the Beatles demographic according to the evidence from *Beatles Monthly* shows that exponentially the Beatles were attracting a diverse interest in their work. The letters from female fans in this period are also increasingly on 'grown-up' and 'serious' subjects, but these 'girl' letters are often punctuated with references to the Beatles' looks as in the letters cited in the last paragraph from issue No. 69, April 1969.

As issue No. 72 illustrates, *Beatles Monthly* was not the sole preserve of female fans. Male, female, heterosexual and gay fans were obviously part of the demographic of *Beatles Monthly*. I theorize that *Beatles Monthly* was not by any means solely for (or comprised of) girl fans as Duffett posits, 'If the cultural world is seen entirely through the prism of gender, there is a danger that we will think in that the ways in which male and female – or for that matter gay and straight – fans pursue their fandom are *inherently* different' (Duffett 2013: 193).

Issue No. 72 has particularly nerdy enquiries from male fans; Peter Wrigley and Geoff Wilson discuss the mono and stereo versions of the song 'Helter Skelter'; American College Student atomizes John and Yoko's Peace campaign, 'John and Yoko, instead, represent the highest and truest form of dedication to an ideal, for theirs is an appeal to the intellect rather than to the aggressive instincts of man.' Bob Carpenter discusses John and Yoko's *Two Virgins*, 'Only John could produce something like Two Virgins, call it art, and cart his money to the bank laughing.' D. Dicks, male, criticizes Revolution No. 9; Ricarda Gutt from Rio de Janeiro, Brazil, bemoans that *Beatles Monthly* overlooks George Harrison's solo album *Wonderwall Music*, and Glyndwr Chambers from Kent also quixotically praises John and Yoko's Peace Campaign, 'Love is the key word and it seems that the only two people who are truly human in the world today, are Big Uncle John and Auntie Yoko.' In spite of this highbrow timbre, *Beatles Monthly* is overwhelmingly a magazine that expressed fans' repressed sexuality; and although a more serious and sombre tone certainly crept in during the period 1967–9, levity and an obsession with the Beatles good looks frequently bubble to the surface, for instance, in the last issue, No. 77, December 1969, letters concerning Paul is dead rumours, the *Abbey Road* album giving 'happiness and meaning in life' (this kind of hyperbole is also relevant in a discussion of Beatles fan convention post-Beatles split trauma, fans really were culturally traumatized!); the joy at the Beatles' return to basic rock and roll with the 'Get Back' record is juxtaposed with a letter from Miss Linda Lakey, Essex, on the Beatles hair:

> Dear Sir, Although I am still a faithful member of the Beatles Fan Club and have every monthly issue of 'their' book from No. 1, and generally like the Beatles records enough to buy them, I find it very disheartening to think how rapidly the original four, clean, handsome lads suddenly changed their image the four scruffy

messes they have now become. What went wrong? Their so-called 'appearance' definitely does them far from justice, and I am sure a razor would 'turn tail' if it were faced with the hairy mob. And when I read in the September issue of the B.B about George apparently walking around Regent's Park Zoo and not being recognized, and you putting it down to the fact that so many youngsters have the same similar haircut these days, I think: **WHAT** haircut? But congratulations Paul to your more modest hairstyle, and I hope the rest of the group follow suit.

Even as the Beatles embraced the counterculture in 1968: mediation, drugs, songs about revolution, experimental Stockhausen pieces, the fans were stubbornly forging the Beatles in their own image, for instance, as late as the June 1968 issue (No. 59), Maureen Smith dedicates a truly awful poem to Paul, but it is notable for its repressed sexuality; entitled 'A Song for a Beatle', Smith writes,

> Let me tell you how it will be / Between my idol Paul and me / His music and his dark-brown hair / Make hippy's (sic) jealous with despair. That tender look I love to see / Is from my idol unto me / His groovy clothes, his kinky tie / His crocheted pullover on his thigh. That boyish smile tells me he's near / His loving voice I like to hear / His kindness is so great you see / Oh Paul you are the man for me. So now you know how it will be / Between my Beatle Paul and me / I hope you have a long last look / And print my poem in your book.

In the June 1968, No. 60 edition of *Beatles Monthly*, Eileen Read from Gosport in Hants is more concerned about John's 'good looks' than his artistic/political interests, 'I opened this month's B.M. and WOW! There was fabulous looking John looking as dreamy as ever.'

Both of these are examples of fans' seduction fantasies that are emancipatory: Eileen Read and Maureen Smith are engaged in 'affective play' and that this sexual innuendo is psychoanalytically healthy. Hills writes,

> It is important to view fans in the sense that they become immersed in non-competitive and affective play. I have suggested that what is distinctive about this view of play is that (i) it deals with the emotional attachment of the fan and (ii) it suggests that play is not always caught up in pre-established 'boundedness' or set cultural boundaries, but may be imitatively create its own set of boundaries and its own auto context. (Hills 2002: 112)

The fans' letters in *Beatles Monthly* are fantasies of the culturally active and the content of these letters is a site of free play where, 'Our emotional attachments within culture, or "little madnesses", continue throughout our lives as a way of maintaining mental/psychical health.' In this reading, fandom is neither pathologized nor viewed as deficient; instead it can be theorized psychoanalytically as a form of 'good health' (Hills 2002: 212–13). Reading a letter from Joan Gallagher in N. Ireland, which appeared in the last *Beatles Monthly* (No. 77, December 1969), in this context, her 'little madnesses' will strike a chord with fans of every stripe, aca-fans, slash fans will appreciate the sentiment here:

> I, as a Beatle person, live very day in thoughts of you, as musicians and people. On the release of each new single and L.P. I grow more devoted and appreciative. This has happened all over again on listening to Abbey Road. It surprised me on first hearing, because it wasn't at all what I was expecting to hear – so different – mature, as you are now – and just beautiful to understand. I'm thankful to be one of those people who understand you in all you do. Praise goes to each of you, on my behalf, on your work on a truly wonderful Abbey Road. It has given me, and I know, many others so much more happiness and meaning in life. Without you, here, may I refer to the letter of Nawal Gadalla, October edition, who thinks as I do, 'where would we be, and what could we do?' I wouldn't like to think of that.

Many scholars would read this letter and see the obsessiveness 'as a compensation for personal lack generated by psychological processes such as anxiety. There may be scope however to view the emotions manifest in fans' lives as more of boost than a lack, something productively added rather than intrinsically needed' (Duffett 2013: 120). *Beatles Monthly* is a space where healthy obsession (sexual and otherwise) is revealed. The fanzine is a communal space, in a manner similar to tourist walks and conventions, where fans 'are given happiness and meaning in life' (Duffett 2013: 120).

Beatles fans were empowered by *Beatles Monthly*: a cultural space where the original meanings of the Beatles' image and music are translated into a series of sexual meanings beyond the intentions of original text. Taking the Beatles' work and changing it is a feature that has recurred throughout the Beatles' career (the Paul is dead rumours that were read into the *Abbey Road* and the *Sgt. Pepper's* albums are an example of this).[1] In *Textual Poachers*, Henry Jenkins described this process as 'poaching', meaning away from the creators to the audience, 'Fans construct their cultural and social identity through borrowing and inflecting mass culture images' (Jenkins 1992: 23). *Beatles Monthly* was a forum where the fans appropriated the Beatles into their own private sexual fantasy.

As early as 1963, teenage girl fandom was recirculating the Beatles' image and work into the fans' own products such as *Beatles Monthly*, magazines and subcultural groups. From the beginning, the teenage girl hysteria surrounding the Beatles wrested control from the Beatles organization:

> In its intensity, as well as its scale, Beatlemania surpassed all previous outbreaks of star-centred hysteria. Young women have swooned over Frank Sinatra in the forties and screamed for Elvis Presley in the immediate pre-Beatle years, but the Fab Four inspired an extremity of feeling usually reserved for football games or natural disasters. (Ehrenreich, Hess and Jacobs 1992: 86)

The screaming of Beatlemania was the sound of teenage girl fans creating their own identity, and *Beatles Monthly*, especially Letters from Beatles People, was the written expression of this fan intensity. Ehrenreich et al. recognized the social and cultural implications of this expression:

> Yet, if it was not the 'movement', or a clear-cut protest of any kind, Beatlemania was the first mass outburst of 1960s to feature women – in this case girls ... To abandon control – to scream, faint, dash about in mobs – was, in form if not in conscious intent, to protest the sexual repressiveness, the rigid double standard of female teen culture. It was the first and most dramatic uprising of *women's* sexual revolution. (Ehrenreich, Hess and Jacobs 1992: 85)

And what is most notable about *Beatles Monthly* fandom is that it occurs within the Beatles' marketing machine: in a particular socio-economic framework. Lennon and McCartney deliberately wrote 'She Loves You' to appeal to teenage girl fans, and their manager Brian Epstein dressed the Beatles in suits to tidy up the image for girl fans. *Beatles Monthly* was about the fans appropriating the Beatles for sex. Epstein's image at the time was a clean safe take-me-home-to dad, but the fans usurp this with sex. In a sense, the fans were targeted by the Beatles and machinery of music business, and it is, therefore, ironic that female empowerment is visible in the pages of *Beatles Monthly*. The fanzine is a site of fan emancipation, as

> Empowerment of textual poachers ... does not occur within a transhistorical or essentialist space. Rather, it occurs quite precisely within the economic and cultural parameters of niche marketing whereby fan-consumers and producers are more closely aligned with a common 'reception sphere' or interpretative community. (Hills 2002: 40)

Beatles Monthly was the first significant step that Beatles fans took to interpret the Beatles in the context of their own lives. In the next five decades, there would be many more strategies fans would adopt to weave the music, films and image of the Beatles into the web and weft of their own lives. The next attempt at Beatles appropriation came after *Beatles Monthly* had been discontinued and the band had broken up in 1970; there were fan conventions which attempted to fill the gap left by *Beatles Monthly* and more importantly conventions provided a sense of fan community once provided by the fanzine. The trauma of the Beatles' break-up meant that fans came together in a support network where they could socialize with like-minded people and interact in a friendly physical space in a manner to the simulacra of *Beatles Monthly*.

Beatles Monthly was a proto-feminist fanzine because the Beatles and their long hair and falsetto screams undermined stereotypical male gender roles:

> Unlike many of their musical predecessors, the Beatles, at least at the onset of their career, were a clean-cut group without any rebellious or overtly masculine overtones. Brian Epstein, their manager, orchestrated this image for the group by putting them in matching collarless suits, boxy short jackets, heeled boots and dark sweaters. Combined with their relatively long hair, the Beatles' overall appearance

deviated from a traditional masculine image. This moderated type of masculinity made audiences equally interested in the group's appearance and music, and also added to the band members' allure among young female fans. As Stark argues, girls were able to see the Beatles as a reflection of themselves – a phenomenon that would be imitated in the future by androgynous stars such as David Bowie and Michael Jackson. (Cura 2009: 106)

The Fanzine conveys in print a sublimated sexuality that is radical when compared to previous pop phenomena such as Elvis Presley and Frank Sinatra. The language and playful tone of the letters in *Beatles Monthly* enshrine an emancipatory feminism:

> The Beatles created a rush of excitement for America's youth. Young teenage girls who had not fully reached adulthood yet were screaming at the top of their lungs for their music they loved. By doing so, they were breaking out of these very same gender identities that Adrienne Rich criticizes. These young girls were ripping and tearing apart the normalized belief that they had to be 'good'. These young girls were no longer behaving as 'good' girls. They were screaming, crying, dancing, and relating to each other in large groups of other girls who were just as hysterical as they were. These girls proved that they no longer wanted to be oppressed into this image of being 'good'. In a sense, these young girls were protesting against sexual oppressiveness. Through this cultural movement, women were given the opportunity to band together and express their repressed sexuality. It's no coincidence that Beatlemania and the second-wave feminist movement occurred around the same time. Both of these musical and social movements empowered each other and created a new, distinct American culture. If it weren't for the Beatles, would the second-wave feminist movement have been as successful in challenging oppressed female sexuality? (Echoi 2014)

Beatles Monthly is a fora where female fans could obsess about the Beatles looks, clothes and music in a highly critical manner; and for that reason, the fanzine is a social and cultural document of the first internationally successful boy band who had every aspect of their appearance deconstructed by female fans:

> Of course anything constructed by society may be deconstructed. The Fabs dared to challenge of masculinity and femininity of their time. The most obvious example, wearing long hair, considered a feminine trait then. But, more importantly, their music contained interplay of masculine and feminine traits. Their music explored previously unexplored ranges of and intensities of emotions considered unseemly for men at the time. Anxiety, uncertainty and loss of control. Prominent in the Beatles' early repertoire were covers of songs by women performers, such as Please Mr Postman (the Marvellettes). These they reinterpreted and demonstrated that types of inner experience thought to be limited to women are actually human experiences, true for both sexes. The main theme of the Beatles' early songs – the emotional intensity of romantic infatuation – resonated with their adolescent

and young adult audiences. Of course this theme is as old as the tradition of songwriting. What the Beatles did was to desexualize this theme. They got to the core of humanity of infatuation, its aspects that transcend biological sex. This isn't to say that the Beatles' music, at times, didn't reinforce conventional gender stereotypes. Sometimes it was even sexist and misogynistic. But they managed to break out of this box and upturn received conventions of gender identification and difference. This liberated both sexes. And infused the new genre they created – rock music – with a spirit of healthy rebellion. (Material Sounds 2014)

The magazine is a glossy, tabloid fora where fans' feminism and sexual desire is disseminated in letter pages that shudder with euphemistic, sexual transgression; it is a platform where the British vernacular of popular magazines obfuscates the sexual id.

Importantly the Beatles' image in *Beatles Monthly* was the precursor of gender bender rock stars such as David Bowie and Marc Bolan. The Beatles long hair was seen as feminine in the early 1960s and the group dynamic eschews machismo:

> In addition to their music, the Beatles' image, orchestrated by their manage Brian Epstein, increased their appeal to female audiences. The first thing he did, of course, … was to second their decision to refuse to conform to existing musical practice by making one of the four leader. This helped the Beatles later on to help change how men thought of masculinity. Academics such as Deborah Tannen and Carol Gilligan have described the different leadership styles of men and women. Men tend to lead by creating hierarchies with strict lines of authority, typically with one person in charge. Women more often create collaborative structures, or 'webs', in which people are more connected and the goal is consensus. Thus, when they eventually hit it big, the Beatles not only sounded and looked more feminine because of their style and their hair; they were more feminine in their group dynamic. (Armstrong Material Sounds 2014)

Beatles Monthly was popular for these reasons, the Beatles were 'a collaborative web' of democratic creativity and they looked outrageously feminine to an early 1960s female teen audience.

An addendum to sanitized and asexual image promulgated in *Beatles Monthly* is that, firstly, the fans' letters are highly sexual texts that shudder with a sublimated sexual tension, and, secondly, if the fans were hiding behind double entendre such as 'Ringo's kissable conk', the Beatles boy next door image of *Beatles Monthly* similarly obfuscated the real facts about their sex lives. Far from the cuddly asexual mop tops, the Beatles were leading highly debauched sex lives at the height of Beatlemania, and yet, *Beatles Monthly* disseminated an image of four 'wholesome' lads who prefer drinking coke and eating jelly babies to sex. The reality was that,

> The Beatles has hordes of screaming women throwing themselves at them. The women groupies would do anything to get close and once close the fab four had their pick of the girls. But it emerged instead of having to indulge in small talk

with star struck music fans the band instead opted for a more straight forward way of getting girls – paying for them. … at airports across America, four pre-paid high class hookers would be part of their welcoming party. The disc jockey Larry Kane vividly describes the first day at the band's hotel by being invited up to the Beatles' suite to witness a line of prostitutes in low cut dresses. 'Take your pick' were the words directed to him by John Lennon. (Myall 2016: http://www.mirror.co.uk/3am/celebrity-news/beatles-pre-paid-prostitutes-waiting-7830459)

It is clear that *Beatles Monthly* was a forum for fans to euphemistically imply their sexual desires, whereas the reality of Beatles tours offers a stark juxtaposition to the faux innocence of *Beatles Monthly*. In the Jann Wenner Rolling Stone Interview from 1970, John Lennon famously debunked the cuddly Beatles myth, a year after the last *Beatles Monthly*, emphasizing their sexual adventures and eschewing their boy next door image, speaking about groupies he said,

We had that image, but man our tours were like something else, if you could get on our tours you were in … wherever we went, there was always a whole scene going, we had our four bedrooms separate from – tried to keep them out of room, and Derek and Neil's rooms were always full of junk and fuck knows what. (Wenner 2000: 61)

Beatles Monthly was an indispensable cog in the Beatles public relations machine and the Beatles suits and choreographed bowing in the stage shows obfuscated the sexual depravity backstage; likewise the linguistic sexual metaphors of *Beatles Monthly* hid sexual frustration and the strident interrogative tone of the fans' words hinted a feminist sexual revolution that the Beatles sexual behaviour and the misogyny of the counterculture tried its best to suppress.

Beatles Monthly is an important forum where proto-feminist fans are emancipated and it is an alternative to the prevalent hoary male of the mid-1960s counterculture; 'fan devotion' in *Beatles Monthly* is a cultural moment of equality between the sexes (Feldman-Barrett 2014), and the girl fans are not an unthinking mass audience of passive consumers. Surprisingly early Beatlemania was much more liberated than supposedly radical late-1960s work by the Beatles, the Rolling Stones and Hendrix, 'Generally, mid-1960s beat was less overtly "macho" and, thus, accessible to young women. This is not simply because the Beatles, the Searchers, or Gerry and the Pacemakers sang about love, or that male, beat fashions were then-perceived as "androgynous"' (Bradby 2005: 359), but also because 'the "rock-as-masculine" concept was not yet a common assumption among music fans, journalists, or scholars. Though the majority of these bands were still all-male, young women were not dissuaded from forming their own beat groups' (Stanley 2004: 16).

Beatles Monthly opens a window of the sexual politics of the early 1960s; the fanzine was a space where fans could appropriate the Beatles into a proto-feminist paradigm and this ran concurrently with girl fans who formed bands, and an important area for future Beatles research is for scholars to quantify the girls who expanded upon their 'magazine reading' by forming bands (Stanley 2004: 16).

The letters *in Beatles Monthly* are highly sexualized texts, and the girl fans welcomed this new freedom. Andre Millard explains,

> It does not take a Freudian psychologist to suspect a sexual underpinning to the Beatlemania phenomenon, with hysterical young women generating all that emotional energy. Many of the psychologists and sociologists called in by the popular press to explain Beatlemania stressed the sexual attraction between fans and the band. They reasoned with all the stresses and strains that accompanied the spurts of rapid physical and emotional growth in the teenage years, there was a need for expression and release: boys had sports and gang violence (and later garage bands) as an outlet, but girls were much more restricted in what adult society would let them do. Beatlemania gave them the opportunity to reverse their roles and become more assertive. (Millard 2012: 132)

The word 'assertive' is key here; *Beatles Monthly* and the screaming fans at concerts were a feminist watershed in post-war culture as girls rejected their prescribed roles, 'There was more than an undercurrent of rebellion in Beatlemania, as thousands of middle-class girls took time off from being nice and instead assaulted policemen or slammed their heads against glass doors' (Millard 2012: 133). This sexual passion of fans is ubiquitous in the history of pop music; Fred Vermorel in his *Starlust: The Secret Fantasies of Fans* surveys this sexual desire and comes to the conclusion that fans' fantasies are wedded to capitalist music industry. For example, a Barry Manilow fan is so hooked to Manilow's image that her own sex life and relationship with her husband is suffering as a result. Rosie expands in a chapter entitled Rosie: Barry and God: 'Me and my husband only live together now as brother and sister. Because – and this may seem rather silly and stupid – but I just feel unclean with any other man apart from Barry. If I can't have sexual intercourse with Barry, I'll go without. I'll never be unfaithful to Barry' (Vermorel 2011: 80). The fans of *Beatles Monthly* are expressing similar fantasies (although a more conservative era and judicious editing by Johnny Dean ensured that letters of this type were cleaned up sufficiently before going to print). Nevertheless, the sexual frisson is obvious in this fanzine and these fantasies are predicated on the culture industry: capitalism so to speak, Vermorel calls this the

> 'psychohistory of fans' ... There is an intriguing development linking the history of consumerism to the mutations of hysteria, a development from the first fan suicide (for Valentino) of Peggy Scott above a London hat shop, to Chapman's Hawaii Five O style execution of John Lennon. A story of phantom horizons and fantastic expectations, discharging into a spiralling logic of desire which the economist Schumper prophesied would spell the death of capitalism itself. (Vermorel 2011: 147)

The ghostly spectre of capitalism is now visible in the boxes of the British Library where *Beatles Monthly* is a dusty shadowy reminder of a publication which at its height sold 350,000 subscribers. This capitalist Beatles love fetish was part of fans' lives because of the capitalist machine and its wraith-like presence is the forum where Beatles fans could collect the pictures and adorn their bedroom walls with fantasies; *Beatles Monthly* is the most germane place to begin the history of Beatles fandom as this glossy product furnished bedroom and furnished minds with imaginative flights of fancy that were caused by commerce. *Beatles Monthly* is the place to start as these sexually charged pages contain a psychohistory of Beatles fandom in shiny pictures and euphemistic sexual language:

> Beatlemania promoted the publishing business, but these highly illustrated magazines also provided much of the raw material for fan mania. The fans kept scrapbooks of pictures of their favorite band, along with newspaper cuttings and other mementoes, such as concert tickets and flyers – the printed paper that played such an important part in maintaining the presence of pop stars in their lives. Beatles fans built shrines of memorabilia, pictures and records in their bedrooms and covered walls with images of the band. Teen magazines were the major source of image for the recontextualisation of the Beatles. (Millard 2012: 124)

Recontextualization is the word that sets up the next seven chapters in this book. The fan conventions are the fans appropriating the Beatles' music and image ten years after the original Beatlemania. Every convention will have a stall selling *Beatles Monthly* to new fans. Pictures, it seems, fuel fantasies, especially sexual ones. By the 1970s, fans were more comfortable being explicit about their fandom and their sexual fantasies. So in a very real sense *Beatles Monthly* and fan conventions are the products of commerce, and fans are emancipated by the availability of mementoes such as fanzines. Matt Hills expresses how fans appropriate the cultural industry to their own ends, 'the dialectic of value … considers fans to be simultaneously inside and outside processes of commodification, experiencing an intensely personal "use value" in relation to their object of fandom, and then being re-positioned within more general and systematic processes of "exchange value"' (Hills 2002: 44). Sexual fantasies are one key area where commerce and personal appropriation coalesce; and *Beatles Monthly* is a commercial product that freed fans and stirred their imaginations. Pete Townsend's introduction to the much more explicit letters of contemporary fandom, Vermorel's *Starlust*, could well have been written about the dreamers of *Beatles Monthly*: 'But the letters collected here are benign, heart –warming and occasionally erotic. It's good to know that ordinary human beings are capable of such passion, imagination and creativity' (Vermorel 2011: 8). *Beatles Monthly* is a fanzine that is the template for the frenzied whimsy of modern slash writing, YouTube transgression and the creativity of fans at Mark Lapidos's fan conventions, all of which moved the Beatles' image forward to the present day. *Beatles Monthly* and fan conventions look back to look forward and an amalgam of technology, commerce and fans' caprices gives Beatles fandom its future. The physical space of conventions and the print form magazines are unanchored by new technology to be used imaginatively by Beatles fans online and in new exciting technological forums.

Mark Lewisohn told me that he was a fan of *Beatles Monthly* as were the Beatles themselves:

> They (the Beatles) were very happy that the magazine existed; they were very pleased to have something of quality that they could provide photographs for. It was deemed to be a good idea by the Beatles, and it was, because they were always about quality and that magazine delivered quality at a very affordable price. The Beatles would not let advertising in it because they wouldn't want to be seen to be endorsing any product. They denied O'Mahony the opportunity to take advertising … Leslie Bryce, the photographer had exclusive access; it was two and sixpence a month, not unaffordable, so it had a broad reach, private school dorms as well as council estates, it was read by boys as well as girls. (Lewisohn 2018)

Although the technology was old print media, *Beatles Monthly* provided an imaginative forum for fans to interact with the Beatles and raises profound questions regarding the imaginative capabilities provided and predicated on technology. Old print media spread the magazine widely and gave the fans artistic freedom in a manner that is commensurate with the huge changes ushered in by YouTube. YouTube has given fans the opportunity to create fan vids bricolage art with the corporate envelope of 2018; *Beatles Monthly* gave fans the chance to make transgressive art within the confines of print media. Beatles fandom is couched in corporate machinery but the Beatles' sense of humour and the fans' iconoclastic and licentious language strained against the standardized template of *Beatles Monthly*, just as YouTubers and slash writers find agency within increasingly corporate-owned cyberspace. Lewisohn argues that there were 'pretty strong quotes from the Beatles' (*in print my emphasis*) as early as 1963 and, although the format of *Beatles Monthly* didn't change in its six-year history, the Beatles words pushed against their happy-go-lucky image: Lewisohn says that the Beatles words were 'edgy … even if they were couched in a bright up tempo piece in Jackie' (Lewisohn 2018) (a British teenage girls magazine popular in 1960s Britain). So *Beatles Monthly* is an important example of fan literature that was popular with 13-year-old girls and boys, but often the language and tone of both fans and Beatles were slightly incongruous in the pages of a teen magazine. *Beatles Monthly* provided a space where thoughts may grow; and two of these most significant ideas were sexual liberation and feminism.

2

(Un)conventional: Beatles fan conventions

The home of Beatles fandom in the 1960s was *Beatles Monthly*, and apart from screaming at concerts, it was one of the few cultural spaces where fans could express their opinions on the Beatles. In 1974 fan conventions replaced the magazine as a space where Beatles fandom continued to flourish. The continuing popularity of the band in this decade was due, in large part, to these fans who met, created and performed all manner of Beatles-related activities including fancy dress, trivia quizzes, art exhibitions, hosting Battle of the Bands and fan art.

The founder of the Beatlefest, Mark Lapidos, in an interview with Susan Lewis from Continental Cable television in 1998, defined the Beatlefest as a collective where fans share a love of the Beatles and, 'come and celebrate our common love for the Beatles regardless of what age' (Beatlefest 1998). The main feature of this documentary, even as late as 1998, is palpable grief and trauma at the Beatles' break-up and the death of John Lennon. Lewis interviewed two middle-aged American women called Cherie and Nancy who said that their favourite Beatle was 'John', and Lewis replied that 'You can't say that without getting choked up' (Beatlefest 1998). The interview is very maudlin and sentimental, with Cherie stating that 'he [John] is never gone as long as he lives in my heart' (Beatlefest 1998). In a sense, this quote is key to understanding the Fest. Fans are motivated by a sense of loss: the fans have a deep emotional connection to the band and are impelled to come together in a forum where they can openly display their obsession.

Lapidos talks about the idea for a Beatlefest in March 2014 in 'Road to Damascus' terms, as he says that over a dish of ice cream at Thanksgiving 1973: 'I had this vision of a convention in a hotel that people get together, who are Beatle maniacs like me, who want to celebrate our common love for the Beatles' (How Mark Lapidos Met John Lennon, 2014). The words 'common' and 'love' recur in interviews with fans which makes the Chicago Beatles Convention a celebration cum support group. In this interview Lapidos's voice cracks with emotion when he talks about the genesis of the convention:

> So I took most of my life savings actually and booked this hotel, the Commodore Hotel, and booked it in 1974 for the weekend of September 7th and 8th. I proceeded to write all the Beatle letters, it was actually cassette letters, it was letters written and I put it on a cassette. So if they didn't want to read it they could listen to it.

This is strange logic as listening to a letter wouldn't be less time-consuming and onerous than reading a letter. Lapidos perhaps felt that a cassette would be a gimmick to pique the Beatles' interest. On 28 April, Mark Lapidos met John Lennon at the Sherry-Netherland hotel on Central Park. Lapidos found out from a fan that Lennon was staying in room 1019; Lapidos knocked on Lennon's door, which was answered by Harry Nilsson (a guest at thirty-five consecutive fests), who introduced Lapidos to Lennon. Lennon invited Lapidos back to the suite the following Tuesday. Lennon was so taken with the idea that he gave Lapidos one of Paul's guitars, signed by McCartney, a signed tabla used by George Harrison on *Sgt. Pepper*, a signed Lennon guitar and photographs signed by Ringo. On the day of the first Fest, John Lennon was interviewed by Lisa Robinson of *Circus* magazine, and when he was asked about the Fest, he said enigmatically, 'It sort of Smacks of Rudolph Valentino', alluding to the mass hysteria female fans felt over the death of Valentino in 1926, and the mourning catapulted Valentino to iconic status. This analogy is similar to Beatles fans, and the posthumous break-up cult status that the Beatles enjoy to this day is sparked by their grief over their premature break-up in 1970 and by the death of John Lennon on 8 December 1980. Both events ensured that Beatles mythology had messianic events that were similar to religious fervour: the death of the founding fathers of the cult and then resurrection by the fans. Each of these interviewees stresses the words 'common' and 'love', and there is little doubt that the fans congregate to not only exchange Beatle memorabilia and Beatle religious relics but also share their strong emotional ties to the band. In fact throughout the Beatles' career, they have been dogged with Christian/religious parallelism, from Lennon's 'bigger than Jesus' remark to Maureen Cleave of the *Evening Standard* on 4 March 1966 and finally to Lennon's murder by a religious zealot in 1980; the religious homology had elevated the Beatles to a quasi-religious status similar to the hysteria imbued on Rudolph Valentino, Elvis Presley and Princess Diana after their deaths. The opportunity for posthumous grieving recurs in the Beatles story: the break-up of the band; Lennon, Harrison and Epstein's death offering opportunities for mass hysteria; and as I write this piece, it is impossible to predict the outpouring of grief when Paul McCartney dies – it is only safe to say that mass hysteria is a conservative estimation of the cultural impact his death will have.

The Beatles are treated as 'divine' by fans: these communal gatherings at conventions are evangelical with fans emphasizing the words 'love' and 'community'. Lapidos speaks like a religious zealot when discussing the Fest, he described the convention as 'Thanksgiving without the arguments' (In the Loop, 2016); and 'We all (fans) have this common love the Beatles' (In the Loop, 2016). Lapidos is especially evangelical when he describes the future of the Fest. He boasts, 'We get new people every year, eight years-olds enjoying it' (In the Loop, 2016); he describes a fan who is 'bringing my grandchildren for the first time ... aged four to seven', and he is bubbling over with fervour when describing the Beatle heaven on earth to come: 'Passing the greatest music of all time on the next generation and the next generation and the next generation' (In the Loop, 2016). There are two considerations here; firstly, Lapidos is expressing 'Communitas: an idea proposed by the anthropologist Victor Turner which suggest that individuals can feel blissfully united at large, festive public events' (Duffett

2013: 291). Duffett also explains that iconic pop stars are totems, which he describes as 'the capacity for a star to acquire, guide and lead their fan base. In lay terms, totemic star is one who has charisma to magnetise a committed audience. Totemism is a term that emerges from Emile Durkheim's classic sociological work on religion' (Duffett 2013: 300). Pop stars and religion are wedded because of mass hysteria, 'The Beatles were neither the first nor last pop celebrities to undergo this process of becoming divine' (Stark 2006: 272). As Timothy Leary wrote, 'I declare that the Beatles are mutants. Prototypes of evolutionary agents sent by God, endowed with a mysterious power to create a new human species, a young race of laughing freemen' (Quotable Quotes, 2017). Stark continues his religious analogy,

> They were their own Trinity plus one. Their followers were fanatics, in the true sense of the word. Their muse was music, which has always been a key part of religion and unlike, say, the movies, is internalised in a way impossible with other genres. 1960s counterreligion, with its own music, festivals, and sacraments such as the use of marijuana. At the time, Harvey Cox, a scholar of religion, even described hippies as the founders of a new theology. 'It has evangelists, its sacred grottoes, its exuberant converts ... Scholar Camille Paglia has written in a similar vein about the "evangelical fervour" in which 1960s, "earth cult", as she described it, developed its own costumes, hymns, icons, holy texts, and mystical traditions'. (Stark 2006: 272)

Conventions are a space where Beatles fans indulge in this religiosity. The (quasi-religious) Beatles conventions began in 1974 when Mark and Carol Lapidos created America's first Beatles celebration in New York. It had the blessing of John Lennon who said to the couple, 'I'm all for it, I'm a Beatle fan too' (Lennon 1974). Beatles conventions form an important part of Beatles fandom. The conventions started in 1974 as part of a grieving process. Fans wanted more Beatles, but were so traumatized by their break-up in 1970 that they felt they had to organize together for two reasons: firstly, to keep the Beatles phenomenon in the public eye and, secondly, to come together collectively and put into effect a fan infrastructure as support for fans who felt loss and grief at the band's demise. Fan conventions are a network to protect fans in moments of crisis such as the band's break-up or the sudden death of a member. The outcome of these conventions is that fans can maintain and review a sense of identity with the band through fan artefacts and interaction with family members, friends and ex-band members. Fan conventions are coping mechanisms that help fans deal with their grief and the role that memorabilia at conventions play in minimizing that sense of loss. When the object of fans' devotion vanishes (no more albums, public appearances, concerts, films), they need to be replaced. Fan conventions fulfil this process. Conventions fill the gap left by the Beatles' break-up. An analogy with celebrity death is relevant here. On a slightly less dramatic scale the Beatles' break-up stirred emotions that were similar to the death of John Lennon and Princess Diana. Both these deaths are extreme versions of the Beatles' break-up in 1970: there was anger, outpouring of grief, hysteria which was akin to collective trauma, as well as press hyperbole surrounding the death (Philip

Norman's deification of Lennon after his death is an example of this press hyperbole, see Chapter Three on journalists/fans). Fan conventions became a panacea for the loss of the Beatles (it is worth noting that nostalgia is relevant here; instead of moving on to new music and genres, fans became obsessed with the Beatles' mythology through an attachment to conventions; however, an attachment to conventions does not mean that fans can be homogenized into a reactionary mass, as the fan questionnaire shows, fans often look back and move forward at the same time).

Grief surrounding the Beatles break-up is also a cultural grief directed at a media simulacra: people they haven't met and most likely haven't seen perform live (the last Beatles concert was 29 August 1966 and conventions are a post-Beatles phenomenon). My thesis that journalists are fans is supported by the fact that Hunter Davies is an avid collector and hoarder of Beatles memorabilia; Norman mythologized John Lennon as an act of post-trauma loss of the devotional object, and MacDonald was a consistent proselytizer for the 1960s as the golden age of popular music (*The People's Music* 2003).

The fannish object as a material substitute for new Beatles product goes some way to explaining fan conventions, and that includes people who have had close contact to the Beatles. A network of fans gathering to collect memorabilia or speak to Pete Best or Geoff Emerick is a corporeal experience that a group can experience to appease the grief of the loss of the original Beatles. Conventions are fora for concrete interactions; Bob Rehak's description of San Diego's Comic Con captures my experience of the conventions at International Beatleweek in 2017:

> [The Comic Con] walks a line between tongue-in-cheek exoticization and earnest celebration: cosplayers strike poses amid merchandise-packed halls while artists, actors, and directors hold panel discussions before standing-room-only crowds. The symbiotic interdependence of studios and audiences crystallizes in costumes and collectibles, shrines and pilgrimages, whose choreography is far more complex than any reductive notion of culture industries and their willing dupes/resistant reworkers can fully capture. Studying the physical habitus of contemporary fandom means moving beyond such binaries – along with those separating the 'software' of media content from the 'hardware' of their physical incarnations, or indeed the animate from the inanimate: close encounters with celebrity 'objects' like Joss Whedon or William Shatner, indexed in an autograph or snapped in a selfie, become yet another kind of artifact, fandom's manifestations spawning and respawning in an endless chain of items. (Rehak 2014)

The diverse manifestations of fandom at conventions is an emotional reliving of the lost object of affection (the Beatles); their break-up is 'a wounding intrusion from the outside' (Luckhurst 2008: 9) that is 'repressed and becomes available by reliving or repeating the repressed material as a contemporary experience instead of … remembering it as something belonging to the past' (Freud 1920: 18). Conventions are forums for repetition compulsion that stretches far back and for healing (breaking this repetitive cycle) that stretches far forward. The cultural grief at the loss of the Beatles stimulates a desire not to let go and to keep them alive, a convention is grief at the fissure with the past because a band's break-up or a celebrity death is a desire to hang on to the past with the knowledge of the ephemeral: 'so wired that when we mourn our losses we also mourn, for better or for worse, ourselves. As we were. As we are no longer. As we will one day not be at all' (Didion 2012: 198). Fan conventions are sites where the past, present and future collide in a repetition compulsion and where fans indulge in nostalgia but also join together to break out of this repetitive cycle, creating new social networks and attachments to tribute bands and memorabilia. However, although grief and trauma at conventions are often vicarious cultural grief, there is also real sentiment and real grief at the passing of John Lennon and George Harrison, and for fans this is a simulated cultural mourning for people they didn't know personally. Again the social dimension is important for fans as they are communities where they can mourn collectively.

Fan conventions are forward-looking and living cultural spaces, but they can be nostalgic arenas where fans mourn 'As we will one day not be at all' (198); for instance, a Las Vegas convention's line up from 2007 commemorates retrospective Beatles anniversaries, and the guests, such as Victor Spinetti and Pete Best, were 77 and 66, respectively. Since the 1970s, these events have become generic and a typical convention will have major and minor players in Beatles history who give talks and sign autographs for the fans at annual Beatles conventions all over the world. Las Vegas has run the longest Beatles fan convention since 1974: The running order of the Las Vegas event on 21 May 2007 is typical of Beatles fan conventions.

Highlighting the virtually round-the-clock activities are several set-piece events commemorating the Fab Four anniversaries:

- A special live performance of the entire *Sgt. Pepper* album
- A re-enactment of the legendary 'All You Need Is Love' happening
- Performance of songs John and Paul played the day they met
- Live performance of songs from the *Love* show and album

> The other Beatles-related activities in several ballrooms include concerts, photo & art exhibits, reminiscences by close pals and associates of the Beatles, Q&A panels, autograph sessions, talent contests for bands and individuals, trivia gameshows, Beatles memorabilia assessment (by a top 'Antiques Roadshow' appraiser), merchandise marketplace, screenings of rare Beatles videos, exhibit and sales of fine art created and signed by the Beatles. There will also be the first-ever Vegas online Beatles auction – conducted by famed auctioneers ItsOnlyRocknRoll.com The Mirage is set to become a veritable treasure trove for Beatles fans!
>
> Nine of the Beatles' friends who socialized and worked with them have already signed-on to be Special Guests throughout the three days. They will be reminiscing in special on-stage discussion sessions, performing concerts, signing autographs and interacting with the fans:
>
> Peter & Gordon – Good friends of the Beatles who also had 10 US Top 40 hits! ('Peter' is legendary record producer Peter Asher – whose sister Jane was Paul McCartney's mid-1960s girlfriend.)

Pete Best – The Beatles' first drummer will attend with his own band

Victor Spinetti – Actor & very close Beatles pal – co-starred in three of their films!

Denny Laine • Laurence Juber • Denny Seiwell – three members of Paul McCartney's band Wings. Also played music and socialized with the other Beatles.

Mark Hudson – Beatles pal who became record producer for Ringo Starr (as well as Aerosmith, Bon Jovi & Ozzy Osbourne)

Larry Kane – The only US broadcaster/journalist to have accompanied the Beatles on BOTH their 1964 & 1965 US tours – becoming a trusted road companion. (Beatle News 2014)

However, these generic and typical conventions self-consciously incorporate new Beatles material such as the Cirque de Soleil *Love* show, to intersperse the old with the new and to reimagine Beatles texts in a modern context.

The significance of fan conventions is that consumers have control over the presentation and dissemination of Beatles-related activity, which is ironic as the Beatles organization, from the early 1970s to the 1990s, was struggling to exert a semblance of control over their franchise, their finances and their publishing. Fan conventions represent a cultural shift away from the Beatles to their fans; and the fans have equal autonomy over the Beatles' music and image as the band themselves. The conventions are similar to *Beatles Monthly*, in that the meaning of the Beatles' legacy resides with the fans as much as it does with Apple. It is also important to note that the Beatles' 'friends' and ex-colleagues such as Pete Best, Victor Spinetti and Denny Laine and tribute acts emphasize this paradigm shift away from the band to everybody who ever had any involvement with the band, no matter how tenuous the link. Fan conventions are important in the history of Beatles fandom as they demonstrate the extent to which the caesura of the Beatles split caused such trauma and shock and opened up such a gap in people's lives that ex-colleagues, fans and business associates all felt a need to fill this Beatle-shaped hole with a constant supply of Beatles tribute acts, Beatles musicals, Beatles art and Beatles memorabilia.

The Fest for Beatles Fans, Chicago, 2018

I attended the Fest for Beatles Fans from 10 to 12 August 2008, and the Fest followed a similar template. I spoke to fans, tribute bands and special guests. Many fans I spoke to had been to every convention and others such as 13-year-old Dylan Dawson told me that he had been at thirteen conventions; his father John Dawson had taken him to a convention since he was a baby. John's 15-year-old daughter, Cassidy, told me she was a huge fan of the Beatles. Speaking to children at the Fest was not unusual, for instance, the Mohs family, Erica and Shannon, had brought their 11-year-old daughter Stella (named after Stella McCartney) and 7-year-old son Julian (Julian Lennon). Erica and Shannon both had Paul McCartney signatures on their forearms, which they had tattooed into a permanent reminder of meeting and indeed dancing with

McCartney onstage. The Mohs felt that fandom was forward-looking nostalgia as they mostly told me of their plans to see McCartney in the future. Julian and Stella were both wearing John Lennon-esque caps circa *A Hard Day's Night* and seemed not to be suffering any ill effects of this Beatles conditioning. Nevertheless the demographic of the Fest for Beatles Fans comprised mostly of first-generation fans in their sixties and seventies, and Chuck Gunderson, who has attended Beatles conventions since the 1970s and is the author of the definitive historical book on the Beatles US tours, told me that the Fest was a private world remote from everyday problems and for three days the outside world and its problems were forgotten. Debra Garver-Dewalt (60), a fan who has attended twenty plus conventions, repeated a similar theme, telling that after the weekend was over most of the fans had a Beatles-hangover and depression going back to work on the Monday morning after the Fest: This was a Beatles mantra that recurred throughout the weekend.

Tom Frangione is a DJ who features as a Beatles expert on *The Fab Forum* on the Beatles Channel 18 on SiriusXM; Tom has worked at the Fest for decades and provided a fascinating insight into its development over the years. Tom told me that the Fests in the 1970s and 1980s were better attended and much busier because of two reasons, firstly, first-generation fans, and celebrity guests for that matter, are dying off and, secondly, technology has contributed to the decline in numbers as fans in the 1970s, before VHS, Betamax and consequently the internet, had to come to see Beatles films and videos at a Fest; if they didn't, the films were only available once a year on television and pre-MTV and pre-video, Beatles videos were very difficult to access. Al Sussman, Beatles author, fan and regular at the Fest since the first convention in 1974, agreed with this observation and gesturing around the foyer suggested that it would be crammed with three times as many people in the 1970s and it was very difficult to move around.

Aca-fan Kenneth Womack launched his second volume of *The Life of George Martin* at the 2018 Fest, and this blend of writers, academics, celebrities and fan emotionalism was a very seductive mix: micro-narrative subjective, personal fan stories colliding with objective academic historiography. The Beatles' hairdresser Leslie Cavendish is an example of this bottom-up mini-narrative history; for example, he tells of the press fabricating a story about John Lennon going bald based on some very tenuous information gleaned from an interview with Cavendish; this may seem frivolous minutiae, but Cavendish's storytelling is incredibly revealing about the press in 1960s London: it is personal history. The writer/fan Jude S. Kessler interviews fans who met John Lennon and a story of a fan partying with Lennon in Key West in 1964 reveals attitudes to race as the party was an integrated gathering with the Beatles' support band the Exciters; the fan's observation that it was the first time he had partied with a celebrity, and with black girls, reveals the importance of personal reminiscence to history. This mélange of eclectic Beatles fans created an entertaining forum which combined acquiring musical and historical knowledge with show business; a convention is part rock concert, historical mini-narratives and part academic conference.

Of course celebrity guests are the main attraction at a Beatles Fest, and their insights are invaluable as Beatles fans who witnessed Beatles history. For instance,

Roy Orbison Jr told this writer that his father was the first American Beatles fan as Roy Orbison toured with them in 1963 before they became famous in America. Such personal reminiscences demonstrate the extent to which the Beatles phenomenon can be atomized, reappraised and how perspectives on the band are illuminated by such minutiae: the fact that a rock and roll icon such as Orbison was a Beatles fan conveys the phenomenon in a personal manner: it is nostalgia which reveals new information, which is a serviceable definition of progressive nostalgia.

The celebrity guests at the 2018 Beatles Fest included Peter Asher, a very close friend of Paul McCartney and star of 1960s pop duo Peter and Gordon; Peter felt that conventions were predicated on 'nostalgia, and were also a living culture' and when I asked what he thought of Beatles tribute bands he said 'that anything that kept the music alive was good, but he preferred the original records' (Asher 2018); again Asher was delineating the paradox of conventions: they look back to look forward and nostalgia has a part to play in keeping Beatles' music out there. Peter Asher's singing partner, Jeremy Clyde, who shared the limelight with Peter Asher in the 1960s with his duo Jeremy and Clyde, now sang at conventions with Peter Asher, and had similar feeling about conventions: 'Conventions are a nostalgia exercise, but there is also something happening beneath that with much younger people, they are going back to something they heard through their parents or grandparents' (Clyde 2018). Young bands are going back and taking 1960s music forward, which is fans using the past to transform nostalgic music into an updated art form.

Billy J. Kramer doesn't like tribute bands that 'sing Beatles songs all night and never come up with anything original, but [tribute bands] that make their own interpretation are good' (Kramer 2018). What interested me about talking to acts like Billy J. Kramer who were big in the 1960s was that they loved singing their old songs, but were keen to stress that interpretation was key to a successful song. Kramer said that 'John Lennon played me 'Bad to Me' (a number one UK hit for Kramer) on a piano and that it was my song' (Kramer 2018), again emphasizing that nostalgia is artistically interesting and creative when it is wedded to reinterpretation and progressiveness.

John Lennon's engineer and producer, Jack Douglas, said 'That I'm happy that the Beatles continue to be popular and it's good to see young people here today (Chicago Fest) and that's inspiring, and if you think ahead a hundred years, there will still be a memory of Beatles music'. Douglas played down the image, the iconography and the conventions, suggesting that if the Beatles were 'just songwriters they would still be remembered, like Gershwin, Cole Porter, they are in the same class, and as long as their music is played and it will be played forever. And covered! I'm building a studio in LA, and my guide is using old Beatles recording equipment and I have to have every piece of gear that's in there' (Douglas 2018). Here Jack is fetishizing Beatles recording equipment and its practical application; he is taking old equipment and applying it to new artists in a progressive and intelligent manner.

Leslie Cavendish, the Beatles hairdresser in the 1960s, and Nicola 'Little Nikki' Hale, who was the little girl on John Lennon's knee in the Magical Mystery Tour film, also spoke to me about their impressions of the Chicago Beatles Fest. Nicola Hale told me it was her first convention and that for her they were transformatively happy occasions: 'It's the joy I see when I speak to fans and it's not necessarily nostalgia; it's a moving forwards of what they want' (Hale 2018). Leslie agreed, saying that when he attended the New York convention the people were jamming in the foyer and it was a joyful feeling, and was that living in the past or the future? It depends on how they interpret the songs. The one that got me at a convention in Liverpool was a Japanese band that played Beatles songs punk style. What a great way of interpreting it: it's going forward! I'm not going to turn round and say 'I don't like it! I love the new way!' (Cavendish 2018).

Gary Astridge, the historian and curator of Ringo's drum gear, said,

> I was a fan. I started playing and collecting drums because of Ringo. I have the privilege of documenting history. Ringo's people called me to arrange and document Ringo's kits for the future. My role is (a) having the privilege of documenting history ... other people who were around in 1960s, whether it was working at drum city shop in London. People who are still alive; I'm having contact with them and the basic theme is I want to give you information before it's too late and so the golden nuggets they are giving me ... and I'm giving a picture that is totally different to information in books because I'm finding that there's people who insert themselves into Beatles history ... and when you dial in, you find they are inserting themselves in Beatles history. My purpose is to document Ringo's drum kits for future generations and to get things right. (Astridge 2018)

This is another important aspect of fandom, Astridge is a fan and also curates Ringo's drum for future generations: it is a sexy history outside the museum that is being experienced by generations of fans who can sit behind Ringo's iconic Ludwig drum kits, as I did, in a warm and convivial convention atmosphere.

Tribute bands are discussed in greater depth in Chapter Seven, but these acts were well represented at the 2018 Beatles Fest. John Merjave, the lead guitarist of the tribute bands The Weeklings and Liverpool, said, 'The thing about our band is that we don't focus on the dressing up aspect, but more on the music. Liverpool is more of a note perfect tribute band, but The Weeklings have old Beatles demos that they didn't finish, and we finish them. We went to Abbey Road in London to play them' (Merjave 2018). For Merjave, playing on stage was a combination of nostalgia and progressiveness, and that each performance was different and often their gigs were 'spontaneous and new. And things go off the rails in a good way'. Merjave talks about the bands in an excited and progressive manner: The Weeklings play at 'Daryl Hall's house and with the Nashville Symphony Orchestra'. He describes himself as 'a fan first and a musician second' (Merjave 2018). When The Weeklings played their set at the Fest they interspersed the Beatles cover versions with their own material and the sound of both covers and their own material was raucous and visceral that was more in style of punchy rock bands and punk icon Iggy Pop and the Stooges' *Raw Power*. Watching The Weeklings was all about the performance in the here and now, a thesis which Georgina Gregory builds on in Chapter Seven of this book: their performance was a hybrid of the old and new and their set felt in the contemporary vanguard of rock music.

Tony Giangreco, a 26-year-old multi-instrumentalist who plays Ringo in Meet the Beatles and bass in another Beatles tribute band The Time Bandits, is the spitting image of Ringo. Tony spent the last year building an exact replica of Ringo drum kit from the *Ed Sullivan* appearance of 9 February 1964. He says,

> In order to be in a tribute band you have to really enjoy it. You're giving the people a live concert experience. My mom was a huge Beatles fan. I mainly listen to the Beatles and classic rock. The Beatles keep going down from generation to generation and I think music today is nowhere as good as music back in 1960s and seventies. It feels new every show. It's a whole different experience every show. (Giangreco 2018)

Giangreco pointed out that tribute acts learn from each other and that he had learned from Beatles tribute acts American English, British Export and Liverpool Legends; and this shows that artistically tribute acts are constantly developing and changing. The literary critic – Harold Bloom – contends that artists have an anxiety of influence and have to create new material to metaphorically kill their influences in a Freudian sense: tribute bands may not exactly break Oedipally with their father, but there is certainly a strain and tension that makes them morph into something new: Tony looks and dresses like Ringo but he is taking Beatles' music to new younger fans and he is reinterpreting the song canon every night he plays live, and Tony is providing healing for first-generation fans traumatized by the death of John Lennon, for instance, while providing Beatles' music for the first time to young fans such as Stella and Julian Mohs.

Terri Hemmert, a Chicago DJ, was attending her forty-third Beatles Fest, and when I asked how the Fest had changed over the years, she said,

> It has gotten younger, but part of the charm of it is that the kids are up with the jam sessions. It's like a community because some of these people come their whole life. It's a twelve step, but we don't want to be cured. I do a breakfast radio show and it's anything but nostalgia because I'll incorporate new version of songs, and this Sunday I'll go from The Vipers' *Maggie May*, that's ancient, and then I'll play punk versions of a Beatles songs, and a jazz version by Pat Metheny, *And I Love Her*, and a German version of *You Know My Name (Look Up the Number)*. I'll be playing Paul's new album: so it's about what's going on now. Chicago a Cappella do their songs. Jay Z's The Grey Album, Kanye West and Paul McCartney. (Hemmert 2018)

It seems obvious that the Beatles songs are so good and so ubiquitous that they will last for two hundred years, but all the interviewees at the Fest also stressed that fandom is a living culture that contributes to the Beatles' forward trajectory. This is true with all fan cultures, but Beatles fans are so dedicated and creative that the fan art is a transformative nostalgia that embraces the new.

Bruce Spizer, author and fan, who has attended twenty-one Fests, feels that 'some fans have a strange unhealthy obsession with the past, but I think people enjoy coming because they learn a lot of new things about the group, I think it's healthy' (Spizer

2018). What is progressive about conventions to Spizer is the constant stream of new information about the Beatles which informs the future scholarship. Roy Silva, a Beatles tribute musician and fan, who has been attending conventions since 1996, describes the convention as 'Magic' and agrees with Bruce Spizer that they are progressive and not solely exercises in nostalgia, 'You get everything from little kids to grandparents' (Silva 2018). John Lennon expert Judith Southerland Kessler quoted The Eagles' 'Hotel California' when I asked her about fan conventions:

> Some dance to remember and some dance to forget, fans come remember how they were, in the lobby someone shouted 'Hey Lennon chick, I wasn't offended because that's who I really am; others come to forget the anger and problems in the world, to be happy, to come together: it's a family!' Kessler agreed that fans came together as support after the band's break-up and John Lennon's death, and she said that fan convention were 'a celebration, like Thanksgiving'. (Kessler 2018)

Jeff Alan Ross says that bands such as 'the Beatles and the Beach Boys are so iconic that they keep regenerating' and he told that when he played with Al Jardine from the Beach Boys that the audience were young and ecstatic about the music (Ross 2018). Susan Shumsky, author of *Maharishi and Me: Seeking Enlightenment*, 'You feel that you are part of something, especially people who are lonely' and that community aspect is a vital ingredient to the Fest. Ross, Kessler and Shumsky are repeating the fan mantra that the Beatles' music keeps being reappropriated, changed and regenerated and that it provides an important social function of bringing people together in a community, which they all agree can't be a bad thing in an increasingly atomized and individualized culture. And Jorie Gracen and Mario Novelli of the Pond Hawks think this sense of community will continue when conventions 'go digital in two hundred years' time' (Gracen and Novelli 2018). Big D Unplugged, whose real name is Daniel Philips from Indiana, has been playing at conventions for twenty years, drawn by friendliness and sense of community; he says that conventions 'have the vibe as twenty years ago but they are nowhere near as crowded because of EBay and YouTube' (Philips 2018), which is an observation very similar to that of Gracen and Novelli. Technology is the way forward and it is very obvious that conventions will be increasingly convivial and social because of the ubiquity and speed of technology: no one will need to come to the Fest to watch videos or to buy memorabilia. In the future, conventions will be able to access more people via technology and with the resurgence of young people buying vinyl and the need for social interaction and community it is likely that conventions will benefit from technological advancement just as Beatles' music was disseminated globally because of electricity and satellite links. In the spirit of quixotic and utopian Fest goers, to borrow the title of Rob Young's book on English folk music, conventions have the potential to be *Electric Edens* for Beatles fans, a weekend escape into a Beatles Fest of bells and whistles.

When the 2018 Chicago Fest was over the fans felt a significant loss. The forty plus interviews I conducted over the three days elicited very similar reactions. Nearly all interviewees said that they felt depressed that they had to leave the Beatles Fest bubble and go back to their lives. My own experience of the Fest was of a sense of community and there were certainly moments of sentiment and cloying, sickly nostalgia, but the Fest is a forward-looking event which acts as a Beatles Support Group for fans who miss the band and who lament the deaths of John Lennon and George Harrison. The fans were tearful when Jack Douglas talked of making Ringo Starr cry after telling him that John Lennon 'really loved him' (Douglas 2018), Gary Astridge getting emotional when describing his friendship with Ringo Starr, fans singing along with Peter Asher and Jeremy Clyde's nostalgic reinterpretations of their 1960s hits; but as all happiness studies show, people live longer, happier lives if they have a wide circle of social networks: and this support network seems to mix nostalgia and progressiveness in a potent mix of forward thinking and backward yearning, so my memories of sentimental stories and 1960s music was also tempered with an interview with Shannon and Erica Mohs who showed me their matching forearm tattoos inked over Paul McCartney's signature from a 2017 concert; their children Stella and Julian were Beatles obsessed, Julian telling me he was a Beatles fan since the age of 4 and that this was his third convention. Both had danced on stage with Paul McCartney, Stella twice!

As I checked out of the Regency Hyatt O'Hare, I was thinking that fan conventions were a consolation for a defunct band and a positive affirmation after the deaths of half the Beatles; as an American breakfast television company strapline seemed to sum up the feeling of community and offered another definition of progressive nostalgia: 'good new memories!' was the company's phrase and these words demonstrate how seemingly mawkish conventions help people forget their problems for a short while, and in 1974, the Fest gave fans a focus post-Beatles break-up as did the Fest post John Lennon's death in 1980. In a sense, conventions transform nostalgia and transform grief.

Beatles fan conventions are a vital stage in the development of Beatles fan cultures. The conventions sprang up at a moment of cultural grief for Beatles fans after the break-up in 1970, and the continuation of conventions ensures that Beatles phenomenon is a site of contemporary interaction for fans. In a sense, conventions perform shaping and 'an important function in activating and shaping the entire grieving process'. Conventions are predicted on 'the conservative impulse, the instinctive drive to preserve continuity'. For example, Grateful Dead fans in the aftermath of lead singer Jerry Garcia's death structured the grief through communal activity in a similar manner to Beatles fans:

> So although some Deadheads perceived Jerry's death as an irreconcilable loss that led them to withdraw from the community or as an opportunity for growth that led them to focus on other aspects of their life, some Deadheads demonstrated the conservative impulse and sought ways to preserve continuity in their Deadhead identity and community. ... Understanding how the Deadhead community survived Jerry's death will lead to an understanding of how other geographically dispersed fan communities might persist in the face of similar changes. (Adams, Ernst and Lucey 2014: 187)

As Beatles conventions started in 1974 before emails and the internet, an analysis of the Beatles fan convention community is also a history of technological change in the period 1974 to 2017.

International Beatleweek Festival, Liverpool

The most well-known Beatles convention is the International Beatleweek Festival which has run in Liverpool every August since 1981. I attended the convention from 23 to 29 August 2017 to undertake participant research into Beatles conventions. My research was based on a questionnaire that I gave to Beatles fans (see Appendix 1 of the book). This chapter will cover the findings of this questionnaire and other significant areas of Beatle fandom such as international Beatles fans, the Beatle cultural events at the convention and the sense of community that permeates an event such as this; the most notable feature of this type of occasion is the togetherness and community spirit in Liverpool. Most of the fans seemed to know each other after attending the event since its inception in 1981. There was also a palpable feeling of grieving for the past at this event. Many fans needed the communal atmosphere to share their love of the band, in fact, cultural trauma and grief are two of the most prevalent emotions at Beatleweek (it is significant that International Beatleweek started the year after John Lennon was murdered); fortunately as we will see, these two emotions are tempered with youthful enthusiasm and optimism: young tribute bands and fans across the generations.

My first sample of thirty questionnaires (see Appendix 1) was very revealing about the demographic of Beatles fans. Twenty-one fans in this sample showed that they had been Beatles fans for 20+ years; four revealed that they had been fans for 11–20 years; two for 1–5 years; one for 1–5- years; and, finally, two fans indicated that they had been Beatles fans for less than one year. The first significant finding here is that popular music fandom cannot be dismissed as juvenilia: Beatles fans are not young and impressionable. The 20+ Beatles fans often modified the questionnaire by adding that they had been Beatles fans since 1962 or for forty years! Their answers demonstrate that fandom is a serious adult preoccupation and these fans share a real sense of long-lasting community with other fans who want to keep the band's memory alive and vital. Out of thirty sample questionnaires, the age group of Beatles fans was thirteen in the 40–49 age group; six in the 50–59 age group; three in the 30–39 age group; also three in the 60–69 age group; two in the 16–21 age group and one fan was in the 22–29 age group. The second question on the questionnaire revealed that these 20+ fans had attended conventions 'since 1984', 'for thirty-four years', 'twenty-two years' and 'twenty-five years'. This entire sample of twenty-one 20+ Beatles fans ticked that the main reason for attending Beatles conventions was to 'Meet other Beatles fans'. A convention was almost like a Beatles support group for fans whose obsession left them feeling like outsiders. My sense was that in this convention environment fans felt comfortable with their fandom and conversations were flowing easily as the fans knew each other from previous years and anytime there was the danger of a lull in the conversation a discussion of Beatles songs, Beatles chords and Beatles memorabilia broke the ice.

Question three, 'What are the main reasons for attending the Beatles Conventions?' backs up this support group thesis: four questionnaires in this sample supplemented the questions with comments in capital letters such as 'Re-meet (stet) old friends', 'Meet old friends', 'Was a huge fan as a child – many years ago. Now come back mostly to catch up with old friends', 'Love that there are other people who share the same passion', 'Beatles merch! Be myself and live out my Beatlemania. Listen to Beatles music. Charge my inner batteries'. The questionnaire showed that this Beatles support group/community spirit was passionately interested in experiencing new interpretations of the Beatles' work with like-minded friends. Four questionnaires answered question three by stating other reasons for attending the conventions. Two named a specific Beatles tribute act as their main reason for attending the convention: The Belittles, a Japanese tribute act from Yokohama. One wrote that they wanted 'to see bands who interpret their music in different ways' and another 'to listen to bands', which again makes a very persuasive argument that Beatles fandom eschews the easy stereotype of backwards-looking, old-fashioned hippies who are only interested in the music of the past. 3Q3, for example, are a Spanish Jazz trio who reinterpret Beatles classics in the style of Miles Davies, John Coltrane and Herbie Hancock with Latin Jazz, New Orleans Trad and Alex Clinton-style Funk thrown into the mix. They are also notable as Beatles tribute acts that don't use a guitar. The Funkles too are another woman Spanish Beatles tribute act that appropriates the Beatles' work into the rhythms of new funk and soul. Two of my questionnaires had fans who replied with 'Less than one year', and one of these respondents markedly circled part 'c.' of the third question in black felt tip, highlighting that her fandom was in part due to 'Keeping the Beatles alive for the future'. 3Q3 and The Funkles are band/fans who do this through music; the attendees at conventions keep the Beatles alive through community: and what a huge international community it is. The ethnicity of Beatles fans at Beatleweek in my survey was seven British (two Northern Irish British included in this), one Northern Irish, four English, two Irish, one Finnish, six Japanese, three Swedish, one Scottish, one Polish, one UK and three declined to answer.

I spoke to a Polish Beatles fan, Joanna Kozlowska (aged 32), on 28 August at the Beatleweek convention. Joanna told me that Beatles fans come to conventions 'because they have a certain sense of identity as a true fan'. These fans use conventions as vehicles for meeting other obsessives and creating 'a sense of community' (Kozlowska 2017). Joanna also saw similarities between conventions and YouTube: both keep fandom fresh and vital and as she told me that YouTube is 'more about the account: it is coming from the people who regularly visit it (subscribers) and maybe post a video themselves'. To Joanna, conventions and YouTube were 'about the movement and flow of expression' (Kozlowska 2017). By this, I think she means community interaction and group behaviour keep the Beatles canon fresh and burgeoning. Joanna used the word 'community' when she described how fanzines such as *Beatles Monthly* have been replaced by Facebook groups and the extent to which such networks have taken over from fan clubs and how Facebook groups impact on physical communal gathering such as conventions and McCartney concerts:

Also the communities like Facebook groups or message boards took over the relevance that fan clubs once had, also typical for these times where people prefer informal gatherings. I belong to FB group pa svenska (Beatles in Swedish) (Joanna is Polish but lives in Sweden) and we even organized a meeting before a Macca concert in Stockholm where anybody could perform, and we had crisps, cola, a mini market for exchanging beatler merch we didn't need. And we even designed t-shirts for that FB group. (Kozlowska 2017)

My interview with Joanna provided a counterargument to the findings of my questionnaire, where the majority of Beatles fans had been attending conventions for twenty plus years. Joanna told me that Beatles fandom is a very wide demographic, and that an online survey would provide a very different indication of fans' age groups than a convention or a concert. 'Another interesting thing I thought about when it comes to Beatles online communities like Tumblr or Instagram is that a huge percent is made up for the youngest generation of fans, of teenagers, especially girls' (ibid.). It was fascinating to hear that young teenagers who are obsessed by the Beatles also had retro mania for retro that they were too young to experience: neophiliac Retromania! She said,

And many of them (young teenage girls) are drawn to the retro forms of communication and devices – so acquiring an LP player is a goal for many (I remember a whole wave, a trend to get the awesome looking Crosley turntable. I actually was affected too, and am also planning on buying it, although it is a very bad LP player, but it looks very sixties and is cheap for a turntable – one after another posts around Christmas time showed these young people that asked their parents to get a Crosley. (Kozlowska 2017)

Joanna was very expansive on this fetishization of 1960s:

Also – a typing machine was a thing, and of course – many of the young fans want to have actual old-fashioned pen pals from around the world. When I was growing up, I as had pen-pals, people whom I contacted through notification in magazines like Mojo, as that was just before the Internet became a thing. But nowadays, this is more interesting, because young people who are 'fed' on the Internet and all modern ways of communication, do recognize the value of writing by hand, of making one's message more personal, being able to attach a gift or maybe draw something etc. And the joy of receiving a real letter. But my guess is that the inspiration comes from letter writing coming from the 'older times', so it's reliving the older ways, making them relevant today. It's like nostalgia, but none of those people LIVED through those times, so it's nostalgia in another sense of the word, and also – it's bringing BACK that way of listening to music/communicating to the present, so it is kind of "unnostalgising" in a way. (Kozlowska 2017)

After Liverpool's Beatleweek, the Fest for Beatles Fans is the biggest convention in the world, and the attendance of a diverse demographic of fans is very revealing about second- and third-generation fans. The online *Rebeat* magazine makes two very important points about 'new' Beatles fans. Firstly, second- and third-generation Beatles fans have the distinction that their fandom is always tainted with the death of John Lennon and George Harrison. One of the spokes on the wheel that comprises conventions is grief:

> If you became a fan after 1980, the Beatles' story inevitably included John Lennon's horrific murder. Kids learn about it as soon once they start asking adults about the Beatles ('Can we see them live?' 'What are they doing now?'). It was heartbreaking to learn that the cheeky Beatle standing stage left at *The Ed Sullivan Show* is not only gone but met such a gruesome end.
>
> For me, a new fan at eight years old, it was the first time I learned about such a tragic event happening anywhere to anyone. As the years have gone on, more events have compounded this sadness for fans of all ages. Perhaps we're lucky to have never felt the innocence-shattering sorrow that so many first-generationers describe on that tragic day. But we didn't know that innocent time either. (Rebeat 2017)

This piece of writing contextualizes Beatles fandom in 2017, a phenomenon that grows exponentially year by year; this is one of the most fascinating of Beatles fandom, that it is constantly reimagined into something fresh:

> The way fans express Beatlemania has changed with the time and the power of global communication, and many second- and third-gen fans now consider themselves part of a fandom, much like those who are devoted to *Doctor Who* or *Harry Potter*. Creative extensions of the Beatles, like cover bands, original music, visual art, and even fan fiction (go on, search 'McLennon' … I dare you) aren't relegated to someone's garage or journal.
>
> They're shared with the world through social media, Tumblr, SoundCloud, and so many other outlets. Beatles-themed music and art are appearing more and more at Comic Cons alongside traditional 'nerd' culture – check out Vivek Tiwary's *Fifth Beatle* graphic novel about Brian Epstein for one – and with the Fest and similar gatherings, Beatles fans have their own dedicated cons. (Rebeat 2017)

The fact that Beatles fandom is mentioned alongside Harry Potter signifies its breadth.

In August 2017, the Fest for Beatles Fans continues to grow exponentially. Fans gather in Chicago's Hyatt Regency O'Hare Hotel to create enterprising new types of fandom, the Fest has a 'Fabatory' that invites fans to appropriate and transgress Beatles phenomenon and 'invent the future of being a Beatles fan' (Facebook, The Fest for Beatles Fans). The Fest for Beatles Fans looks far back to look far forward. Conventions are cultural industries that continue to attract new fans who demand fresh and innovative approaches to the Fabs.

Beatles conventions are an arena where fantasy brings the band back together; in a sense most of the fan behaviour in this book ranges from harmless fantasies such as conventions and fan fiction to the psychotic reactions of Chapman and Abram. Conventions are magical thinking or creative fantasies of fans:

> Where do all these fictional Beatles fantasies come from? Just off the top of my head, there's the musical Beatlemania, the Seventies TV movie The Birth of the Beatles, the early Robert Zemeckis film I Want to Hold Your Hand, recent films like The Hours and Times and Backbeat, Beatle fan-fiction Web sites, and Austin Powers, which goofs on the Beatles even more than it goofs on Bond. Nobody makes movies about Dylan or the Stones or Zeppelin. And if memory serves, none of these Beatles fantasies is entirely rubbish, either – not even Beatlemania, which rocked me and my little sisters just fine in fourth grade. I guess the dream of a Beatles reunion dies hard, even twenty years after tragedy settled that question. There's a bond we hear in the Beatles' music, as the lads start off celebrating their friendship (the joy of 'Boys') and end up remembering it mournfully (the ache of 'Two of Us'). Movies like Two of Us tap into a fantasy that we Beatles fans have shared since long before John died: Because the Beatles can't bring themselves back together, the job falls to us. In our dreams, John and Paul are still on their way back home. (Sheffield 2017 http://web.b.ebscohost.com/ehost/detail/detail)

When I interviewed Candy Leonard on fan conventions she agreed that it was a sense of community that brought fans together and that these communities were mushrooming everywhere; two examples she used to illustrate this were Abbey Road on the River in Jeffersonville, Indiana, and Beatles at the Ridge, Walnut Ridge, Arkansas. Both conventions began in the early noughties and continue to grow exponentially, however, and their existence illustrates that Beatle fandom or as Leonard calls it 'Beatleness' has become a 'secular religion' (Leonard 2018) where fans find a like-minded community who are 'magical thinkers', that is, they buy memorabilia and watch tribute bands, and this informs their fandom in the here and now; and this is an experience of Beatleness in real time. The Walnut Ridge Festival is a good example of the secular religiosity of Beatle fandom; its formation is predicated on the flimsiest of rationales, that the Beatles changed planes here on 18 September 1964, for a brief holiday between engagements in Dallas, Texas, and New York City. They arrived on a light aircraft chartered by Reed Pigman, who lent them his ranch for the weekend. The fact that such a flying visit offered a very spurious opportunity to stage a festival emphasizes that conventions are quasi-religious sites where fans can use locale to indulge their fantasies about the band; and a festival such as Walnut Ridge demonstrates that fans have created a limitless transgressive site that can appropriate fandom into new psychological areas.

The links between fan conventions and celebrity death are very strong; in both instances, fan forums are set up as support groups for loss of the love object. The reactions to the deaths of John Lennon and George Harrison are a simulated media trauma, meaning the death of a beloved rock star or the break-up of a favourite band is a vicarious shock. Princess Diana's death in 1997 is analogous to the psychological mix of magical thinking and trauma that motivated people such as Mark Lapidos to start conventions where a community can share their loss with a like-minded community. Candy Leonard has spoken of Diana-mania, that 'Diana was very Beatle-like, the image and the presentation are so important. We are a very visual culture' (Leonard 2018). It is these visual stimuli which are so widely disseminated that conventions are places where fans can indulge with icons of grief and feel a common bond while they are so doing. At conventions, a high proportion of the event is purely visual: album covers, T-shirts, posters, mugs and key rings; and these conventions are a fora where fans resurrect the dead in their heads through a sophisticated social network which is affirmed on the visual: no matter if that stimuli is four identical Pierre Cardin Beatles with uniformed length mop top haircuts or Princess Diana gazing out from under her Beatle fringe in her wedding photographs after her marriage to Prince Charles in 1981. Conventions are spaces where dead bands are enlivened in fans' heads because the fans' minds were colonized by the ubiquitous media of band break-ups and celebrity death; and these images add potency and emotion to fandom; as a social species we do not want to grieve alone. In a sense, commodification and packaging is the seam that runs through all eight chapters of this book. Band break-ups are packaged; funerals are now consumerist, fanzines, books, online bangs and whistles. Conventions are just one spoke on this consumerist wheel and fans' innovations are entrepreneurial and unconventional yet streamlined and appealing because they are a reaction to a brilliant Beatles marketing phenomenon. And you don't have flesh and blood Beatles to do the selling when the image is out there. Once the package is in place it grows exponentially in every recess: Apple continues without Steve Jobs and the Beatles continue without the band. In fact Apple copied Beatle packaging; Steve Jobs was a Beatles fan, he went to India, he lived the conspicuous life of a hippie and Apple modelled its packaging on the Beatles, 'It is totally Beatle-esque he [Jobs] learned as young Beatle fan the importance of the packaging' (Leonard 2018). Conventions are spaces where fans pore over carefully curated Beatles relics and these *object d'art* furnish our lives, whether that is the glossy pictures of *Beatles Monthly* or the seductive and lavish Beatles biographies of Davies, Norman and MacDonald.

It is important to end on the caveat that fans at conventions are not parasocial fantasists; they do indulge in magical thinking and interact with a community to make them feel better about celebrity death or the death of a beloved band, but this type of fandom should not be pathologized into anything unusual; most fans I spoke to used conventions as a space to interact with other enthusiasts. Mark Duffett's description of numerous Elvis fans he has met at conventions, in over twenty years of research, epitomizes the psychological portrait of Beatles fan I have spoken to at Beatles conventions and his definition of fandom demonstrates that fan conventions are sites of a 'living culture' populated by enthusiasts who didn't feel that 'fandom was a waiting room for a real relationship with the celebrity, it was instead a living culture that give people a communal life based on a shared focus' (Duffett 2018). Candy Leonard agrees, suggesting that conventions are about 'community … and people like to be around like minded people and when you are a Beatles fan you immediately have something in common with other Beatles fans' (Leonard 2018): Leonard's and Duffett's Occam's razor analyses, meaning the simplest explanation is the best, is a convincing summation of fan conventions; an artistic living stream which is enjoyed by diverse people with a common interest in the Beatles phenomenon.

Mark Lapidos and I spoke about the commodification of Beatle Fest in Chicago. He told me it had mushroomed from a whimsical folly in 1974 to a huge event in 2018 which is sponsored by Hyatt Regency O'Hare in Chicago, Q104.3 New York's Classic Rock Station, 93 XRT: Chicago's Finest Rock, The Beatles Channel on Sirius FM and Modern Drummer. The 2018 Fest has the world's largest Beatles shop and, as in previous years, a line-up of classic acts and guests including fellow Mersey beat star, Billy J. Kramer, John Lennon's producer Jack Douglas, the Beatles hairdresser Leslie Cavendish. There is a giant Beatles marketplace – which has rare recordings, vinyl, books, photographs, posters and art; and a line-up of Beatle-related imaginative activities such as a Battle of the Beatles Bands, Beatle Sound Alike Contest, Beatles Museum and Art Contest, Look Alike and Dress Up Contests, Trivia competitions. For the little child, activities include yoga for the under-12, Guest Author Discussions, Beatles Ashram, Deeper Beatles Cuts and a Beatles Poetry Jam. What is so notable about these diverse activities, apart from the fact that anything related to the Beatles is marketed and sold, is that they are a mix of nostalgia and progressiveness. For example, the 'classic' acts and the 'classic' rock stations seem unhealthily obsessed with the past, but when seen in conjunction with art competitions, children's yoga and young tribute acts, we have a convention that is looking back to look forward. More importantly we cannot homogenize fans at a Beatles Fest, many fans I spoke to enjoyed it in an ironic and self-conscious way. For children it is fresh and new, an event that has no shared cultural capital: gender, class and nationalities receive their Beatles product according to their own cultural biases. The authoritative voices here are the voices of the fans; the fans at conventions, aided and abetted by Beatles cultural tourism institutions and machinery, are not bounded by nostalgia: these are progressive voices which transform nostalgia into something proactive and transforming: Beatles fans at conventions are not fossilized by memory and ossified by heritage conservatism, they are looking forward in the Deleuzian sense: that is, 'Becoming is an anti-memory' (Deleuze and Guattari 1987: 16). Mieke Bal contends that exhibitions can be considered 'utterances' of 'productive tension' (Bal 1996: 128); this is true of conventions such as Beatle Fest, on the surface the glitzy websites and the sponsors hint at a conservative and retrospective ideology, but the reality of the fans' appropriation of the commodity on offer with 'visual motifs and juxtaposition of objects … that are "innately polysemic and open ended"' (K. Johnson 2015: 14). And not all of this activity is escapist and apolitical; the event has an overtly political side: an advertisement for the liberal America and hope for a more progressive body politic in the States, for example, the event is not hidebound by the past as it raised over $6,000,000 for various charities including *Spirit Foundation* (set up by John and Yoko to donate to charities anonymously) and *The Coalition to Stop Gun Violence*. The Beatle Fest, in a manner similar to Richard Porter's Beatles walks in London, is heterogeneous fans enjoying music and memorabilia in a psychologically progressive manner, that is, employing Beatles merchandise and tribute bands by looking back to look forward and using the Beatles as a platform for creative multiple readings of their music and image.

Two final considerations to sum up fan conventions. Firstly, as Mark Lapidos contends, the 'fastest increasing demographic at the Chicago Beatle Fest is teenagers and fans in their early twenties' (Lapidos 2018); secondly, conventions are cultural spaces, like Beatles walks and cultural tourism, where fans use the past as material to shape their future fandom, and the death of beloved mop top pop idols is no impediment to the spectral longevity of the Beatles' cultural phenomenon:

> In institutional frameworks established for pop culture (commemorative events, its integration into museums, etc.), in behaviours and fashion styles (the increasing number of 'retro' movements), in visual as well as symbolic spheres, pop always refers to its history and increasingly relies on it. With a past being reinvented, remixed, idealised or made ever 'kitscher', bygone days have become the raw material for novelty. Sound ghosts – whose presence simultaneously follows an aesthetic, existential, social and commercial logic – increasingly invade the present and make their mark across styles in the way of a memory kaleidoscope whose spectres, like samples of samples, keep multiplying exponentially. (Guesdon and Le Guern 2014: 70)

Institutional frameworks such as Beatleweek in Liverpool, Mark and Carol Lapidos's Chicago Beatle Fests and Richard Porter's Beatle Walks in London are examples of cultural tourist space where fans' memories are a non-linear progressive nostalgia that morphs the death of John Lennon and George Harrison and the trauma of the Beatles break-up into new unexpected corporeal and ghostly spaces: and all this imaginative creativity is predicated on what at first seem to be conservative heritage movements.

The question here is how do first-generation Beatles fans make a nostalgic visual or a nostalgic sound seem new? These stimuli, experienced at conventions or encountered on the Beatles' cultural industry trail, are appropriated by fans coming at an object, or songs, through adult eyes and adult ears. For new fans such as children and adolescents, conventions and Beatles heritage are new. Capitalist machinery, commodification and technology (YouTube constantly creates new Beatles art) are institutions that illustrate that art is a profound negotiation with the marketplace: conventions are electronic and global spaces that breathe life into the Beatles body politic.

Mark Lewisohn asserted that the beginning of Beatles conventions was very unglamorous, 'in 1977 it was hard to be a Beatles fan; no one wanted to talk about the Beatles'. Lewisohn was at the first Liverpool convention in 1977 where 'we knew each other by name' and he estimated 'that there were about one hundred people there'. The Liverpool convention was started by Bob Wooler (the DJ for the Beatles in the Cavern) and Alan Williams (their first manager). It was held 'at Mr Pickwick's club in Liverpool ... and inside the programme they included the English Tourist Board's guide to Liverpool. Considering Williams' and Wooler's experience in organising events, starting late and sometimes offering no more than a video for entertainment' (Leigh 2016: 187).

Lewisohn had been at the very first UK convention organized by Dave Chisnell in Norwich in 1976. To Lewisohn, it was 'very low key, small and English, but it was the first time that Lewisohn had heard Alan Williams speak and saw Stuart Sutcliffe's painting for the first time' (Lewisohn 2018). Lewisohn also points out that pre-Lennon's death (8 December 1980), Beatles fandom was very niche and that only after Lennon's murder did interest in the Beatles begin to mushroom. As we will see, such inauspicious beginnings led to a huge cultural tourist industry in Liverpool and London.

A coda here is that fan conventions are a support group for fans who love the Beatles. I asked the writer and Beatles fan Paolo Hewitt if he felt that conventions provide support, social networking and solace for Beatles fans and commented to him that he looked very sad when discussing the Beatles break-up; his reply was very revealing about the importance of the Beatles in fans' lives and the need for Beatles companionship:

> I was five years old when I heard She Loves You on the radio on a Sunday morning. It filled my body with ecstasy, and growing up the Beatles were as much part of the world as food, air, water, school, all the things that were solid, that's what they were. When I heard they split in April 1970, I was in a post office in Cobham, I just couldn't believe it, they can't, that's just not allowed. (Hewitt 2018)

3

'Paperback Writer', journalists as superfans: Hunter Davis, Ian MacDonald and Philip Norman

The Beatles phenomenon has produced a curious hybrid which I will call the journalist/fan. The three main obsessives in this category are: Hunter Davies (the only authorized Beatles biographer), Ian McDonald (1960s proselytizer, who has written an obsessive book which has an essay on every Beatles song ever released) and Philip Norman (a Lennon obsessive, who has courted controversy with his opinionated work on the Beatles). Music journalists are subjective fans, Steven Stark concurs, arguing that biographies and journalism are fan literature: 'To a certain extent, almost all books about the Beatles – even the so-called objective histories – are a form of fan literature' (Stark 2006: 1). Davies, Norman and MacDonald are 'writers who look at the Beatles and tend to see themselves' (Stark 2006: 7): the real theme of their most significant Beatles book is themselves and their entirely partial opinions.

Norman and Davies are superfans and have clear agendas in their writing. Davies, when researching *The Beatles: The Authorised Biography* (1968), found John Lennon an uncooperative subject and produced a book that heavily favoured McCartney, in short, a highly impressionistic and subjective take on the Beatles. Norman, too, fell into a similar trap, favouring Lennon in his opinions writing on the Beatles. The reason for this bias in both writers is the simple fact that they are fans just as much they are 'objective' journalists: their work is very subjective, hence the term journalist/fan. All three journalist superfans write about their own life and experiences as much as they do about the Beatles.

In a sense, Davies, Norman and MacDonald's work demonstrates that their writing is the highly subjective literary productions of the fan-journalists. Lindberg makes this point in *Rock Criticism from the Beginning* where he contends that the founding fathers of rock journalism (Greil Marcus, Lester Bangs, for example) were wholly opinionated 'fans' and all their writing was 'deeply rooted in personal experience' (Lindberg et al. 2005: 173). Lindberg shows that the 'Founding Fathers' of rock journalism were often opinionated, subjective and often narcissistic. Music writing is a history of bias, invective and highly impressionistic writing often based on emotion. Davies, Norman and MacDonald are in this tradition of subjective music writing, a tradition which saw Dave Marsh dismiss the band Toto without applying any objective professional journalistic criteria: 'Toto grows more popular every day, but then, cockroaches are supposed to outlast the human race' (Lindberg et al. 2005: 175). Lester Bangs took this subjectivity to the extreme: in a review of The Stooges he abdicated all journalistic ethics about responsibility to be a truth teller whose job is to provide only facts of a story, and went into a Jack Kerouac, New Journalist carnivalesque rant about himself; 'I hate myself. Same damn thing last year, this year, on and on till I'm an old fart if I love that long. Shit. Think I'll rape my wank-fantasy cunt dog-style tonight' (Lindberg et al. 2005: 175). This is an example of what all music writer superfans do: they write about themselves! Journalist are fans who 'slip into ravings about … experiences, traumas and phobias' (Lindberg et al. 2005: 183). Bangs provides a definition of superfan journalist. On one memorable occasion he played his typewriter onstage with the J. Geils Band: 'I started to play on the beat, grinning and nodding at the rest of the group who grinned and nodded back as the peanut galleries gawked, hawked and kfweed. The writing was coming out great too: VDKHEOQSNCHSHNELXIEN(+&-SXN+(E@JN?.' I heard one of the roadies, kneeling a few feet to my right, laconically drawl, 'Yer doing great man' (Lindberg et al. 2005: 184). So Davies, Norman and MacDonald are in this subjective and narcissistic tradition of music writing where their fandom constantly shines through the blinds of journalistic objectivity. All three journalist fans allay their idiosyncratic fandom to the Beatles story appropriating the Beatles into their lives and in the case of Ian MacDonald galvanizing the colourful, vivid and subjective prose of Hunter S. Thompson and Lester Bangs into what George Nelson calls *Retro-Neuvo*: MacDonald's *Revolution in the Head* is reminiscent of the opinionated carnival of the words of Lester Bangs and MacDonald's work 'embrace(s) the past to create passionate, fresh expressions' (2005: 184) on the Fab Four.

Hunter Davies and *The Beatles* (1968)

Davies was born in Johnstone in 1936 in Scotland to Scottish parents and moved to Carlisle when he was 11. He is four years older than the oldest Beatle Ringo Starr, which is very significant as he is slightly older than the Beatles which gives him a detached and mannered approach to their lives; in short, he doesn't put the band on a pedestal. He was also a working-class scholarship boy like John, Paul and George which meant he could relate well to his subject. Davies also has an avid fan mentality; he is a hoarder of Beatles memorabilia and has bequeathed some of his collection of Lennon and McCartney's handwritten lyrics to the British Museum. He has written over thirty books: travel writing, novels, biographies and children's books. He is a serious and dedicated researcher, but his style doesn't engage the emotions and *The Beatles* (1968) doesn't come fully alive because his detached reporting leaves the Beatles flat on the page. In many ways, it is an excellent book, but unfortunately his research has been overshadowed by Beatles historian Mark Lewisohn (his first part of a trilogy on the Beatles is already a thousand pages long and he has only reached 1962); John Harris describes Lewisohn as a Beatles oracle: he is the author of such exhaustive reference books as *The Complete Beatles Recording Sessions* and *The Complete Beatles Chronicle*, as well as reams of sleeve notes (*The Guardian*, 2013). As we shall see, Davies' journalese has also been eclipsed by MacDonald's prose-poetry *tour de force*, *Revolution in the Head* and his attention to detail by Mark Lewisohn. Lewisohn would have been included in this chapter, is a dedicated fan 'as a seven-year-old in his native Middlesex, so taken with *Sgt Pepper's Lonely Hearts Club Band* that he stood in his garden as it played, shaking his head wildly while trying not to dislodge the cardboard moustache lodged under his nose' (*The Guardian*, 2013); the reason for his occlusion is that his mammoth project is nowhere near completion. Even though Davies' book is the only authorized Beatles book, the four Beatles do come across as shadows as Davies's prose doesn't quite reveal their minds and the historical context. Lennon went as far as to describe the book as 'bullshit' (Wenner 2000: 61) in an interview in 1970. Davies's *The Beatles* has strengths, it is impeccably researched, Davies writes 'Confessions of a Collector' for *The Guardian*, and he has published a book on stamp collection called *The Joy of Stamps*. Davies is a self-confessed fan but his passionate fandom is hidden by a prosaic style that doesn't fire the imagination.

Hunter Davies found Lennon an uncooperative subject when he was researching his authorized biography, *The Beatles* (1968). In 1967–8, by all accounts, Lennon was in an LSD-induced torpor and could summon up very little interest in Davies's project. Davies writes,

> John was the hardest to talk to. I spent hours at his home in Weybridge in silence, swimming round his pool with him, eating a meal, sitting in his little living room, often without a sound, except a rotten television set flickering away in the corner. In the end, if conversation seemed impossible, I would pack up and come again another day … He seemed to be in a permanent state of abstraction. (Davies 2009: 58)

McCartney, on the other hand, was a much more willing and talkative participant: the result was a very flattering portrait of McCartney and a very negative and partial account of Lennon's contribution to the Beatles. Hunter Davies is a brilliant researcher, he has hoarded thousands of items of Beatle memorabilia including handwritten lyrics, letters and postcards from the Beatles, concert programmes, he is also an incredibly industrious writer, an appendix of his biographies is four pages long; however, there are two problems with his authorized biography of the Beatles (the only authorized biography) and that is the Beatles and Brian Epstein read the final drafts and forced Davies to make several changes including a passage which said that they didn't take drugs (this is 1967 Beatles at the height of their psychedelic period); more importantly Davies writes in a terse journalese, in a demotic voice that doesn't capture the inner lives of the Beatles and their families or the context of the 1960s.

Davies's *Beatles* comes out poorly when his work is compared to MacDonald's: Davies's common-sense voice often reads like hack work as opposed to MacDonald's literary style: the artisan versus the artist. There is no doubt that Davies's access to the Beatles and his superfan archive would suggest that his book would be the classic text of the Beatles, but this isn't so, and being a Beatles obsessive isn't enough; Davies's book is good source material and there are many valuable insights, mostly from family and friends and not the Beatles themselves; unfortunately, the book never comes alive as Davies's dry and objective method doesn't 'capture emotion, and as MacDonald's writing is very passionate adhering to Wolfe dictum about journalism being hot-blooded and requiring "emotional involvement", its "gripping" or "absorbing" quality' (Wolfe 1973: 46). Davies's biography is not a soul-stirring read, a point over the years that many critics have noticed. In a review of Davies's memoir, *The Beatles, Football and Me* (2006), *The Observer's* Anthony Quinn identifies the main problem, as a fan/hoarder/researcher Davies is more than up to the job, but his writing is not revealing:

> Hunter Davies writes in the foreword to this memoir that 'the very best' he hopes to achieve is to be 'vaguely interesting' and 'passably amusing'. The very best? I wonder how happy he would be to see those words quoted on the cover. It is only as you read further into the book that you realize that vague interest and passable amusement are, indeed, all that *The Beatles, Football and Me* could possibly aspire to, so plodding and savourless is his style. (*The Observer*, 2006)

Davies's tabloid voice and his 'man of the people rhetoric' does a disservice to his scrupulous research in *The Beatles* (1968). Davies's style should be inclusive and help the reader participate in his meanings, but his traditional narrative, his hackneyed characterizations and his popular tabloid colloquialisms do not make the reader feel, Quinn observes, that the writing in his memoir displays a 'remarkable instinct for the untelling anecdote and the commonplace observation' (*The Observer*, 2006).

Unfortunately the same can be said about *The Beatles*. Quinn again contends that 'A good memoir is not about how much you recall – it's about how you make it come alive' (*The Observer*, 2006). Wolfe inadvertently summarizes the difference between Davies and MacDonald: 'The idea was to give the full objective description, plus something that readers always had to go to novels and short stories for: namely, the subjective or emotional life of the characters', Wolfe feels that good writing had an 'interior monologue' and that prose should be able to 'enter people's minds' (Wolfe 1996: 35). And although Davies spent a year with the Beatles, he doesn't capture their interior lives, and MacDonald never met his central characters (the Beatles), but MacDonald's fiction creations come alive on the page: Davies's participatory research and 'real' documentary approach is much more prosaic and his style is dead compared to MacDonald's.

The three writers under consideration here are all fan-journalists whose fandom subsumes their supposed 'objective' journalistic integrity, although all three are excellently researched books. Their subjectivity shines through and is a perceived strength or weakness depending on the extent to which readers are credulous about their opinions. All three are fans as much as they are journalists; fans first who then gradually become experts. I call these three writers superfans because of their professional dedication to the Beatles. However, as we will see, Ian MacDonald's fandom is the most seductive to this writer than Davies's and Norman's, as his writing conveys personal fandom to a greater extent: he is a self-identified Beatles enthusiast.

MacDonald embodies Beatles super-fandom and he is often strident in his fandom, 'So obviously dazzling was the Beatles' achievement that few have questioned it. Agreement on them is all but universal: they were far and away the best-ever pop group and their music enriched the lives of millions' (MacDonald 2008: 1). Davies and Norman are more restrained in their fandom.

Philip Norman, *Shout!* (1981)

Philip Norman's book *Shout!* (1981) took the same basic facts as Hunter Davies and came to a vastly different conclusion. Throughout the text, Lennon is lauded as the errant artistic genius of the Beatles and McCartney is depicted as a Machiavellian schemer who rides to success on Lennon coat tails. The reasons for such a subjective account are that Norman's book was published a year after Lennon's murder and Norman deifies Lennon post-tragedy, as did most of the Western mainstream media. It is also quite clear from the book that Norman had been writing about the Beatles since the 1960s, and his copy had a tendency to hero-worship Lennon. James McGrath identifies Norman's subjectivity as very extreme: 'Norman's florid prose and disdain for McCartney render his narrative impressionistic and biased. Though he later retracted the statement, Norman commented upon the book's 1981 publication that "John was three-quarters of the Beatles"' (McGrath 2010: 309).

Philip Norman was born in 1943 and like Davies and MacDonald he is a baby boomer Beatles fan. Norman started his career with *The Sunday Times* in 1965 and in the 1970s was *The Times*' music critic. Norman doesn't possess the seductive prose of MacDonald, but he is as strongly opinionated. *Shout!* caused considerable controversy because of its attack on Paul McCartney (Harrison and Starr are relegated to bit players in the Beatles' drama). McCartney has been known to refer to the book as *Shite!* And he has a good point, as Norman has completely revised his opinions on the Beatles in his biography *McCartney* (2016). *The Guardian*'s John Harris demonstrates the shortcomings of *Shout!* Philip Norman's biography of the Beatles *Shout!* has sold more than a million copies. Published in 1981 soon after John Lennon's murder, it was buoyed by the wave of nostalgia that ensued – the first stirrings of the over-the-top Beatles worship that is now an immovable part of popular culture all over the world. Norman delivered arguably the first literary look at Beatledom: the book divided their career into four parts – Wishing, Getting, Having and Wasting – and told the story in gleaming prose. But *Shout!* has one big drawback: a glaring bias against Paul McCartney who was portrayed as a kind of simpering egomaniac, and a correspondingly overgenerous view of Lennon, who, Norman later claimed, represented 'three quarters of The Beatles' (*The Guardian*, 2016). In fact, Norman's text was so strident and partial that the whole *McCartney* project was an attempt to address his John Lennon bias. *Shout!* raises the debate of whether objectivity is even possible: 'there can in fact be no objectivity … there is a variety of potential journalistic accounts of events, corresponding to the plurality of viewpoints which exist in the world. More than one of these accounts may have validity' (McNair 2003: 38). Norman's *Shout!* and *McCartney* demonstrate that his work is highly subjective, opinionated and whimsical: both texts flatly contradict themselves, and to summarize McNair, both texts have an entirely different angle on the same story. In fact *McCartney* is an apologia for *Shout!*: 'this is a book that redresses a lingering imbalance – with the piquant twist that one of the people who so skewed things in the first place was the author himself' (*The Guardian*, 2016).

Norman makes a habit of impressionistic subjectivity, but his prose doesn't shoulder the weight of such strident outspokenness to the same extent as MacDonald's profligate élan. For example, Norman has argued that Ringo Starr is too addled with a lifetime of alcohol and drug abuse to remember 1960s; 'Paul rewrites history' (this is exactly what Norman has done) and that Harrison is a mediocre talent and junior member of the Beatles (Harrison 1987): both these statements on McCartney and Starr are unsubstantiated bias! So Norman's writing is untrustworthy opinion, and he has admitted this saying that his work has 'supplemented the methods of the investigative reporter with faculties I developed as a novelist' (Collins 2017); this is a very accurate description of his approach in *Shout!*, and it is also the manifesto of Tom Wolfe and the New Journalism movement; however, Norman's poetic prose is minimal, sparse and monochrome compared with the colourful expressive language of Ian MacDonald: MacDonald's work is partial and subject just like Norman's, but MacDonald's prose burst with warmth and passion which captures the quixotic nature of Beatles' music much more effectively than Norman's. MacDonald is the greater artist, the more impassioned fan and his musicologist's ear breathes life into the subject, whereas Norman's suppositions are dry, mannered and cold in comparison.

Josh Tyrangiel illustrates the strident subjectivity of his *McCartney* (2016) biography in a *New York Times* review in 2016 correctly arguing that he was 'overcompensating' for his unflattering portrait in *Shout!*

> It's at this point you suspect the ancient offenses in 'Shout!' have made the author too reverent. There's other evidence of overcompensation. Norman wrote a nuanced 2008 biography of John Lennon, but here John comes off as a farting, masturbating, Beluga-caviar-ordering infant. Comparing Lennon's and McCartney's reactions to the end of the Beatles, Norman even becomes cruel: 'Unlike John, he did not turn himself over to some modish therapist, but toughed it out'. 'Paul McCartney' is full of things that happened to Paul McCartney, and through absurd fame and a few tragedies he appears to be an unusually decent man with few regrets. But facts aren't insight, and readers won't emerge with any real idea what it was like to have lived one of modernity's most amazing lives. At least in that sense Norman's subject remains elusive. (*The New York Times*, 2016)

Norman's method in *McCartney* (2016) demonstrates that to a great extent his writing is no more than the (admittedly well-researched) opinions of a superfan imbued with all the fallibility of his fandom personality: 'Paul McCartney' opens with Norman's confession that, in hindsight, the offending passages in 'Shout!' were fuelled by a lifelong case of Paul envy: 'All those years I'd spent wishing to be him had left me feeling in some obscure way that I needed to get my own back. This is weird territory' (*The New York Times*, 2016).

Norman's attack on Paul McCartney in *Shout!* sparked a hostile reaction from McCartney. In an interview in 1984, the journalist Roy Leonard asked McCartney about Philip Norman and after referring to Norman as 'Norma Philips', McCartney, if you scrutinize the clip closely on YouTube at 7.39 minutes, under his breath calls *Shout! Shite!* And later in the interview he complains that Norman painted him as the villain of the Beatles story, 'the JR Ewing from Dallas character' (Leonard 1984, https://www.youtube.com/watch?v=QSebxaVz-I8).

Hunter Davies and Philip Norman employed conventional journalistic method to research and write *The Beatles* (1968) and *Shout!* (1981). Both texts have a veneer of documentary fact, that is, detailed research based on interviews with the Beatles, press cuttings, archives and, in Davies's case, participatory research, he spent a year watching the Beatles record, socialize and relax. However, MacDonald's book is based entirely on his subjective opinions, but because it is the most literary and lyrically expressed of the three books, it comes closer to revealing the emotional lives of the Beatles and also his florid style opens a window onto the 1960s counterculture with wistful and colourful prose poetry that is beyond the journalese of Davies and Norman.

Ian MacDonald, *Revolution in the Head: The Beatles' Records and the Sixties* (1994)

MacDonald's work is more evocative than the documentary and biographical evidence gathering approach of Davies and Norman. MacDonald's approach is very similar to the New Journalism movement of the 1960s. He uses techniques usually associated with the novel to make *Revolution in the Head* come alive. Each essay creates characters out of the four Beatles, and although his analysis and depiction of these characters is almost entirely a subjective invention, the novelist technique conveys a feel for the 1960s and its most famous sons that conventional journalism lacks: 'All New Journalists in his view employed four realistic techniques once the prerogative of fiction writers ... scene-by-scene construction ... accurate dialogue ... inserting a point of view ... using concrete descriptive details (such as behaviour, possessions, relationships with others in the story) to round out characters' (Cline and Gillies 2012: 12). MacDonald's writing is more exciting and more descriptive and makes the reader feel his emotional love for the subject matter. Davies's and Norman's cold, detached and objective writing is intended to impart a mannered and realistic description of events, but everything that they write is personal opinion that is obfuscated by pretence of impartiality. MacDonald makes no claims to be unbiased: he writes out his feeling in a mellifluous and persuasive manner that is obviously often his own invention but this method takes the reader very close to the Beatles cultural phenomenon. Tom Wolfe in his manifesto for the New Journalism movement comes close to describing MacDonald's style and approach. 'It was the discovery that it was possible in non-fiction, in journalism, to use any literary device, from the traditional dialogisms of the essay to streams of consciousness, and to use many different kinds simultaneously, or within a relatively short piece to excite the reader both intellectually and emotionally' (Wolfe 1996: 28).

Revolution in the Head also weaves the cultural, social and political mores of the 1960s into the personal lives of all four Beatles more effectively than Davies and Norman because he writes about the literature, music and political events in a manner that shows how the grand narratives of history collide with the micro-narrative of the Beatles' lives. In short, MacDonald uses cultural theory, his obsession of a superfan and his colourful prose to make a strong sentimental and emotional impact. MacDonald's fandom is much more intellectually rigorous than other writers: he uses evidence gathering (his days spent as editor of the NME); his musicology (he was a musician) and his literary bent (he studied English at Cambridge) to create literary non-fiction which should 'have all the elements of good fiction: intriguing characters, variety of condition, about the motives behind what people did and whether they were driven by emotions or by outside influences such as national events or the mores of the day' (Cline and Gillies 2012: 77).

Use of language is the key to the elevation of MacDonald's text to the status of literature beyond the demotic voice, the colloquialisms and the hackneyed journalese of Davies's and Norman's biographies. The language of daily speech that we find in Davies and Norman does not scale the emotional and imaginative heights of MacDonald's character building (Oedipal, mother-obsessed, drug-addicted Lennon; multitalented, workaholic McCartney; thoughtful, spiritual George; and funny ace musician Ringo). MacDonald creates spurious character stereotypes and writes as if he was present at every recording session and speaking from first-hand knowledge, but this subjectivity brings the time period alive, as Wolfe famously wrote in his introduction to the New Journalism, lyrical and subjective stylings are 'nice new fat Star Streamer Rockets that will light up the sky' (Wolfe 1996: 51). MacDonald's inventive use of language conveys his super fandom like no Beatles book. 'Central to the concept of excellence is the use of fine and polished language, which will show mastery of texture, colour, word choice, rhythm and voice. Literary non-fiction writers will also offer a way of looking at the world, as well as serious research, which makes the content credible and helps shape the material' (Cline and Gillies 2012: 8). MacDonald's book gives us not only insight into the Beatles and the 1960s counterculture but also a valuable insight into the inner life of a Beatles fan.

With *Revolution in the Head* (1995), Ian MacDonald has written the most scholarly mainstream book on the Beatles: it was instantly held up as classic by fans and critics alike. However, his account is again biased and partial. For example, MacDonald's interest in Hinduism and Buddhism coloured his account of the Beatles significantly. He believed passionately in an afterlife having read widely on Eastern religions. This bias is explicit when he writes about the Beatles', especially Harrison's, spiritual interests. In fact, before MacDonald's suicide in 2003, he was planning to rewrite *Revolution in the Head* to give more scholarly attention to Harrison's contribution to the Beatles canon. We get an insight into this unfinished project in his collected journalism *The*

People's Music (2003). In 'The Psychedelic Beatles: Love and Drugs', he suggests that it was 'Harrison who inspired the West's mainstream acquaintance with Hindu religion and created the late sixties spiritual revival' (MacDonald 2003: 96). It is this religious theme which informs most of his published work with an anti-materialist spiritual quality. MacDonald was a writer who was proselytizer for the 1960s counterculture and *Revolution in the Head* is as much a paean to 1960s idealism and spirituality as it is a work of praise for the Beatles. It is a book as much about MacDonald's religious convictions (which are similar to Harrison's) as it is a book about the Beatles. MacDonald's journalistic voice is often the argumentative tone of an opinionated Hippie: a 1960 evangelist for the counterculture.

MacDonald's essay on the Lennon song 'Glass Onion' epitomizes this tendency: his writing here is not objective journalism, but the hectoring of a superfan. In the essay, he overstates Lennon's taunting of the fans. He unrealistically suggests that this irresponsible teasing of his audience in the songs and his love of chaotic random wordplay led to his murder:

> Chaos draws psychopaths … Listeners were left to generate their own connections and make their own sense of what they were hearing, thereby increasing the chances of dangerous misinterpretation along Masonian lines. … The aleatory philosophy of derangement associated with 1960s counter-culture, obsessions such as those which beset Charles Manson, and later Lennon's assassin Mark Chapman, were inevitable. As prominent advocates of the free-associating state of mind, The Beatles attracted more crackpot fixations than anyone apart from Dylan. While, at eh time, they seemed like harmless fun for Lennon to make them the subject of the present sneeringly sarcastic song, in the end they returned to kill him. (MacDonald 2008: 313–14)

The 'Glass Onion' essay shows MacDonald's worst subjective traits. It is *his* contention that the Beatles' random and chaotic attitude to their art was in some way responsible for fan violence and murder. There is no way to quantify such a bold claim, in fact, if anyone is to blame, it is more likely to be journalists and the media for disseminating fantasy and myth. Nevertheless, a strength of this essay is that it underlines the special relationship between the Beatles and their fans. The song is addressed to the fans and acknowledges them in a similar manner to the camera to the *Hey Jude* and *A Hard Day's Night* films, but it is a thumping overstatement to suggest that Lennon's jokes led to his murder. James McGrath's words on MacDonald describe his biased tendencies accurately (and his words can be inadvertently applied to Hunter Davies and Philip Norman's partial writings). To McGrath, MacDonald is 'subjectively passionate' and 'asserts arguments without solidly constructing them' (McGrath 2010: 312).

MacDonald's writing is subjective, opinionated and partial because *Revolution in the Head* is a biography of his life, simmering with 1960s evangelism. This proselytism is a strength of his writing and one of the reasons that *Revolution in the Head* is such a robust apologia for 1960s idealism. MacDonald's fervent approach leads to valuable insights. He argues that the Beatles are the apotheosis of 1960s counterculture, more so than other 1960s icons such as Dylan or the Rolling Stones. In 'Within You Without You', Harrison sings the lines 'with our love we could change the world' (Beatles 1967). For a finite moment in 1966–7, the Beatles subscribed to the countercultural concerns of peace, love, psychological revolution more than their more seemingly rebellious contemporaries. As MacDonald puts it:

> The true revolution of 1960s – more powerful and decisive for Western society than any of its external by-products – was an inner one of feeling and assumption: a revolution in the head. Few were unaffected by this and, as a result of it, the world changed more thoroughly than it could ever have done under merely political direction. It was a revolution of and in the common man; a revolution ... whose manifesto – its vices as much as its virtues, its losses as well as it gains, its confusions together with its lucidities – is readable nowhere more vividly than the Beatles' records. (MacDonald 1998: 27)

The reason that MacDonald writes with such efficacy about this period is that he also believed passionately in the counterculture and he personified these diverse philosophical strains. MacDonald was a *nom de plume* adopted early in his career. In fact, *nom de guerre* may be apposite as he argued in print vigorously and passionately for the music he believed in. He briefly attended King's College, Cambridge where he studied English before transferring to archaeology and anthropology. He dropped out after a year and pursued a career as a music journalist with the New Musical Express and also a musician with his brother's band Quiet Sun. In 1972 he became assistant editor of the NME with Nick Logan and took the sales of the paper from 90,000 to 220,000. He released an album of his own songs entitled *Sub Rosa*.

MacDonald believed passionately in an afterlife having read widely on esoteric Buddhism and Hinduism. This interest is important when he writes about the Beatles and especially Harrison's spiritual interests. In fact before MacDonald's suicide in 2003, he was planning to rewrite *Revolution in the Head* to give more scholarly attention to Harrison's contribution to the Beatles canon.

We get a glimpse of this unfinished project in *The People's Music*. In his essay entitled *The Psychedelic Beatles: Love and Drugs*, he suggests that it was 'Harrison who inspired the West's mainstream acquaintance with Hindu religion and created the late sixties spiritual revival' (MacDonald 2003: 96). It is this religious theme which informs most of his published work with anti-materialist spiritual quality. In a sense his work adheres to Romanticism, that is, a reaction to rationality. Romanticism is concerned with the limitations of Rationalism rather than a rejection of reason *per se*. This sums up the philosophical outlook of the Beatles, the counterculture and MacDonald.

A recurrent *leitmotif* in MacDonald's work is the social milieu that formed the poetic lyricism of his writing and his strong opinions. About his university years he writes:

> During the academic year of 1968–9, Cambridge University felt an alien influence from beyond its sober curtain walls. Solemn flagstones frowned up at kaftans,

wooden beads and waist-length hair. Staid courtyards winced to the sounds of Beggars Banquet, The White Album, Big Pink and Dr John … drifting thorough leaded windows. The stately air was fragrant with marijuana and on one seemed to be doing a stroke of work. (Williams, *The Guardian*, www.guardian.co.uk/news/2003/sep/08/guardian-artobituaries)

Here are the seeds of a writer who was to become proselytizer for the 1960s in general and the Beatles in particular. MacDonald heaps such high praise on the 1960s because it was the decade that informed his nascent musical taste and his philosophical outlook. The book is suffused with the golden light of MacDonald's teenage years.

In his introduction to *The People's Music* (2003) he makes it clear that pop music is a social indicator that opens a window on the society that produced it: 'The creativity of rock music rides on a social background and takes much of its cut colour from what's going on in the wider world' (MacDonald 2003: 7). The 'social background' which manifests itself in MacDonald's work is that of 1960s idealism. MacDonald's writing is a melange of countercultural perspectives. He subscribes to these hippie ideals. He believed in reincarnation and the idea that a society is changed by an interior mental revolution. When this is wedded to a deep scepticism about politics and materialism we have a writer who ideally qualified to write about the Beatles and the 1960s. In fact his writing is littered with spiritual references; the word 'soul' recurs consistently in all of his three major publications.

In *Revolution in the Head* he writes that because of this 'spiritual aridity' the West is 'sinking as if into a babbling, twinkling, microelectronically pulsing quicksand' (MacDonald 2003: 7). MacDonald also suggests that the Western military industrial complex is a murder machine intent on killing our souls. In contrast,

> 1960s seem like a golden age to us because, relative to now, they were. At their heart, the countercultural revolt against acquisitive selfishness – and, in particular, the hippies' unfashionable perception that we can change the world only by changing ourselves – looks in retrospect like a last gasp of the Western soul. Now radically disunited, we live dominated by and addicted to gadgets, our raison d'etre and sense of community unfixably broken. While remnants of our once-stable core of religious faith survive, few are very edifying. (MacDonald 1998: 33)

Prose of such fragility and limpidity shudders with the weight of dogmatic assurance. The evangelical glint shines off the pages of his books. It is a mellifluous style of writing that does justice to the Beatles' most melodic songs. It is this opinionated and lush style that he uses to the same effect in *The People's Music* and *The New Shostakovich*. Writing about the English singer/songwriter Nick Drake he opens up both barrels on the modern world.

> The World Health Organisation predicts a vast upsurge in clinical depression in the first quarter of the coming century. Already, doctors report that half of their patients display signs of illness. Can it be that the materialist worldview, in which

there is no intrinsic meaning, is slowly murdering our souls? Nick Drake's reminds us that life is a predicament and that the world is an insoluble mystery.

It tells us that a 'magical', contemplative way of seeing can keep us aware of this, preventing us from destroying the world through the arrogant assumption that we know what it is. We do not. We're all exiled from heaven, though some of us don't realise it. But when magic reveals heaven to us in a wild flower, we remember. And then we hear the chime. (MacDonald 2003: 256–7)

Here there is a preoccupation with notions such as 'soul', 'heaven' and 'magic'. The philosophical underpinning of such vehement assertion is decidedly anti-materialist. He is religious in a non-denominational sense, mirroring the Beatles' dalliance with Eastern mysticism circa 1966–7. He is also sceptical about conventional approaches to politics and, in turn, describes both the Beatles and Shostakovich as apolitical. He puts an emphasis on a sense of community, but which has a bourgeois libertarian individualist sensibility as opposed to a more doctrinal socialist collectivism. His work is a eulogy for the optimism of 1960s' dream.

MacDonald's work is a Wordsworthian and Yeatsian celebration of nature and a Romantic recognition of the limits of rationality. Wordsworth's *Lyrical Ballads* are the seeds of MacDonald's sensitivity to the natural world and his rejection of technology, rationalism and the material. It is clear that the psychedelic period of Beatles (1966–7) and MacDonald's writing is a blooming of late Romanticism: the causality from Wordsworth's nature poetry through Yeats's early Romantic poetry to the psychedelic Beatles is clear.[1]

MacDonald's interest in both classical music and popular music is typical of a time when classical music collided with popular music. In *The New Shostakovich* MacDonald frames his music criticism in similar spiritual terms to his Beatles scholarship, developing his theme of materialism which crushes the individual. Anderson (2003, www.independent.co.uk/news/obituaries/ian-macdonald) suggests this book 'changed Shostakovich studies forever' and that MacDonald saw Shostakovich as a 'courageous anti-Stalinist' and rejects that long preconceived attitude held in the West that the composer was a Soviet puppet.

In fact MacDonald seriously believes that the spirit of Shostakovich, physically manifested, poked him in the back and pleaded with him to write the book. To MacDonald the most malign characteristic of the Bolshevik Revolution was

> the ... abolition of the soul. Identifying the Church as more than anything else responsible for the pre-revolutionary status quo, the Bolsheviks set about severing its grip on the Russian mind within weeks of achieving power. As a supplement to shooting priests and razing monasteries, propaganda was set in motion to discredit the idea that human beings possessed a spiritual aspect that survived death. (MacDonald 2006 [1990]: 47)

To MacDonald, the USSR's official figurehead (Shostakovich) was a secret dissident whose music showed parodic contempt for the Bolshevik Revolution. It was this theme of cultural resistance that MacDonald perceived in the Beatles' music and which led to his most evocative writing and ideological outbursts about their music.

MacDonald's essay on the sound collage ' 'Revolution No 9' puts the song in a wider 1960s cultural context while at the same time affirming a subjective individualist art. The sound collage of the song represents the synthesis of the popular and the classical *avant-garde*. The essay is one of the most important for his thesis (which as we see recurs in most of his published work) that political revolution is predicated on psychological revolution and not the other way around.

> On one level, Revolution No 9 is another Lennonian evocation of the domain between sleeping and waking, its wavelength-wandering radio-babble resembling the sound an infant might have apprehended in a suburban garden during a typical post-war summer. On another, it is a sarcastic homage to cliché so impartially targeted that even its fade – on the sound of chanting crowds – becomes ambiguous, if not actively ironic. The common factor is consciousness itself; indeed, if Revolution 9 can be said to be about one thing it would be the abiding concern of 1960s counterculture: quality awareness. 'Do not adjust your brain, there is a fault in reality', ran a hippie slogan of the time. Revolution 9 restates that slogan in sound. (MacDonald 1998: 253)

MacDonald recognized in the work of the Beatles and Shostakovich a psychoanalytical individuality which is at odds with mechanized conformity.

Theodor Adorno's work can be applied to this aspect of the music and illuminate the radical individualistic art of Shostakovich and the Beatles:

> Their music gives form to that anxiety, that terror, that insight into the catastrophic situation which others merely evade by regressing. They are called individualists, and yet their work is nothing but a single dialogue with the powers which destroy individuality – powers whose 'formless shadows' fall gigantically on their music. (Adorno 2002: 303)

MacDonald's individualistic rebuttal of Soviet totalitarianism and the worst excesses of Western capitalism invoke Adorno's theories on commodified mass culture. Of course, Adorno thought pop culture was inauthentic, exploitative and a mass deception that destroyed individuality, whereas MacDonald found the pop culture of the 1960s authentic, individualistic and subversive. Adorno's writing on popular culture prefigures MacDonald's disenchantment with contemporary commodified, manufactured and repetitive pop songs. MacDonald seems to agree with Adorno's critique of the Cultural Industry[2] when writing about contemporary pop music, especially dance culture.

MacDonald's philosophy was concerned with pacifism and with one's mental furniture. To MacDonald's generation the Blue Meanies could be defeated by a change in consciousness itself: A Revolution in the Head. MacDonald was also influenced by Herbert Marcuse and Norman O. Brown's ideas about the scientific repression of individuals. Marcuse and Brown's psychoanalytical reading of history influenced 1960s radicals Angela Davis and Abbie Hoffman,³ and humanist literature such as Erich Fromm and Wilhelm Reich, who suggest that revolution is linked to psychological freedom. In the song 'Revolution No 1' Lennon sings, 'we'd all love to change your head' and 'you'd better free your mind instead' (*The Beatles*, 1968).

The reason for delineating MacDonald's character in the context of the 1960s is that his cultural and political sensibility is ideal for examining the Beatles' songs and for placing them in their correct social and economic context. The writer Mark Kurlansky in his book *1968* also captures the mood of the mid-1960s; and his idealistic outlook on that decade is startlingly similar to that of MacDonald. His words are illuminating about the Beatles' songs and the social upheavals of the period; and his words also illuminate Ian MacDonald's cultural origins:

> What was unique about 1968 was that people were rebelling over disparate issues and had in common only that desire to rebel, ideas about how to do it, a sense of alienation from the established order, and a profound distaste for authoritarianism in any form. Where there was communism they rebelled against communism, where there was capitalism the turned against that. The rebels rejected most institutions, political leaders and political parties. (Kurlansky 2005: 17)

One of MacDonald's themes is the individual pitted against the State. His essay on *I Am the Walrus* is a case in point. As well as discussing the musicality of the piece, he places the song in its countercultural context, the height of the hippie dream, 1967 the summer of love. His essay makes references to several icons of the counterculture (R. D. Laing, the radical psychologist, and Lewis Carroll, author of *Alice in Wonderland*). The analysis of the song makes a great deal of the hippie context:

> I am the Walrus became its author's ultimate anti-institution rant – a damn-you-England tirade that blasts education, art, culture, law, order, class, religion, and even sense itself. The hurt teenager's revenge on his 'expert textpert' schoolmasters (I'm crying') ... A trace of the peaceably philosophical Lennon remains in the song's opening line, but the rest is pure invective. (MacDonald 1998: 234)

It is one of the more revealing essays in the book concerning MacDonald's own views: the sensitive artist estranged from society (Nick Drake, John Lennon and Shostavokich). Writing about Soviet totalitarianism he characterizes the Soviet goal as 'a social experiment into the adaptability of human nature with the ultimate goal of producing a nation of human robots programmed to the love only state' (MacDonald 1990: 147); taken in isolation, this is an accurate description of Stalin's Russia, but it also applies to England in the 1960s.

MacDonald's freethinking is also an exercise in McCartney revisionism. He rejects the media bias which has sprung up in recent years of Lennon as the tortured genius and innovator of the Beatles. While in no way downplaying Lennon's role and contribution to the band, he is at pains to show McCartney's brilliance; *Revolution in the Head* was published four years before *Paul McCartney: Many Years from Now*

(1997) where McCartney's friend Barry Miles pointed out how McCartney's interest in the avant-garde predated Lennon's. Chronologically, however, it was MacDonald who was first to address the anti-McCartney bias in most of the music press, writing in 1994 on the subject.

This bias was due in part to the fact that most rock writers do not write about music per se. The John Lennon cult is a result of two trends: he is deified after his death and music journalists prefer to concentrate on lyrical content as opposed to musical analysis. MacDonald does not downplay Lennon's huge contribution but he cuts through the narrow-mindedness of critics who have dismissed McCartney. In an article for *Mojo* he hits the right chord about their working relationship:

> They worked together as usual on 50–50 co-compositions but also made sure they strove to match each other independently, at which effort Lennon, seemingly by design, was demonstrably more effective for about 12 months (I.e., February 1964 to February 1965). Thereafter, McCartney came increasingly into his own, eventually dominating the partnership in terms of quantity of compositions, whether independently or collaboratively done. (MacDonald 2003: 46)

Cultural historians have built on this insight, most notably Dominic Sandbrook in his book on 1960s *White Heat*, published in 2006. He suggests that McCartney was as adventurous as Lennon, citing his interest in the contemporary art scene in London. The 'Vivaldi strings' for Eleanor Rigby; the 'high baroque trumpet' (Sandbrook 2006: 207) for 'Penny Lane' was influenced by Bach's *Brandenburg Concertos* but McCartney's work with tape loops and electronica on *Revolver* and *Sgt Pepper* was also impacted by the experimental work of Berio's *Sequenza V*, Cage's *Variations VI* and Stockhausen's *Hymnen* (for a full discussion of classical influences of the Beatles see Kenneth Womack's magisterial two-volume biography of George Martin published in 2017 and 2018, respectively). He goes on to take a few swipes at Lennon suggesting that he had a 'self-pitying, self-indulgent and pretentious personality' (Sandbrook 2006: 204–5). He argues, taking MacDonald's cue, 'Not only was Lennon effectively beatified in the minds of many after his murder in 1980, but he was given full credit for anything the Beatles did that was supposedly risky, dark or adventurous, while anything gentler or more populist was blamed on McCartney' (Sandbrook 2006: 207).

A biased journalistic approach to the Lennon/McCartney songwriting team has been fairly typical in most readings about the group. Even two of the best books on the Beatles – Philip Norman's *Shout: The True Story of the Beatles* (1981) and Hunter Davies's authorized biography *The Beatles* (1968) – have promulgated in Norman's case a Lennon bias while Davies favoured McCartney. The debate is still fresh with the Beatles' engineer Geoff Emerick's 2007 memoir *Here, There and Everywhere* suggesting that McCartney was the leader of the Beatles. However, MacDonald writes evenly about their respective work with the clarity of a musicologist.

For example, his writing on 'Blackbird' demonstrates his ability to concentrate on music itself. In this piece he laments the loss of the finger-picking style in contemporary popular music (a theme in most of his major music criticism). MacDonald feels that Punk revolution in British music effectively stamped out the folk idiom and produced music, as Adorno puts it, of the 'always identical' (Adorno: 2002: 302), or in MacDonald's words,

> Nowadays we live in a loud shin, mechanised musical ethos of shallow excitement: glamour and clamour. On the one hand, titanic drum-sounds shudder the ground with the massive Metropolis of robo-fours of club culture; on the other hand, post-Punk Indie-rockers scrub their guitars like crazed archaeologists grubbing for expression beneath the coarse signal distortion they're generating. (MacDonald 2003: 212–13)

The finger-picking style of Davey Graham's *Anjii* (1963), Archie Fisher's *Reynardine* (1968), John Renbourn's *Mist on the Mountain* (1965), Bert Jansch's *Needle of Death* (1965) and Donovan's *Catch the Wind* (1965) influenced the Beatles to play arpeggio style on the songs 'Julia, Mother Nature's Son' and 'Dear Prudence'. To McDonald this style finds its most perfect expression in 'Blackbird':

> This haunting thing was taped and mixed, including a warbling blackbird from the Abbey Road effects library, in six hours. Inspired by the experience of being woken by a blackbird bursting into song before sunrise, McCartney's lyric translates this into a succinct metaphor for an awakening on a deeper level – in its quiet way, one of his finest pieces. (MacDonald 1998: 256)

MacDonald's work is also enlivened by the notion that contemporary music is 'of such a low standard compared to that of 1960s and the Seventies' (Colli 2003: 4). MacDonald is never more convincing than when he is in his stride evangelically denouncing contemporary pop culture. Taking his cue from Theodor Adorno, he feels that the 'the purposes of mechanical reproduction surpasses the rigor and general currency of any "real" style' (Adorno and Horkheimer 1997: 127) or as MacDonald characterizes modern pop culture, especially techno/dance music, as 'the creative equivalent of Frankenstein's monster' (MacDonald 1998: 342). He feels that the popular music industry has degenerated into an all-consuming production line that churns out mass-produced, inferior cultural commodities: it has ceased to be a genuine art form: it is a standardized drone.

He is also surprising in his assessment of his songs, selecting 'Long, Long, Long' of *The White Album* and 'Something' of *Abbey Road* as his favourites and dismissing 'Here Comes the Sun' and 'While My Guitar Gently Weeps'. He feels that 'Long, Long, Long', 'with its simultaneous suggestion of death, a new beginning, and an enigmatic question, is one of the most resonant in the Beatles discography' (MacDonald 1998: 238). This opinion is linked very strongly to his spiritual insights. He writes, 'This touching token of exhausted, relieved reconciliation with God is Harrison's finest moment of *The Beatles*: simple, direct, and in its sighing, self-annihilating coda, devastatingly expressive' (MacDonald 1998: 238). Overall, MacDonald's light and flowing prose and his spiritual and cultural interests made him ideal for capturing the inherent musicality of the Beatles' songs and for delineating the cultural context that produced John, Paul, George and Ringo's finest recorded moments.

The Christian writer Christopher Booker adopts a cultural and political conservative tone which is very similar to Dominic Sandbrook. Booker (1992: 80) calls 1960s a 'collective fantasy' that was caused by a post-Suez and postcolonial crisis. No doubt to Booker, MacDonald has been beguiled by 1960s' dream. MacDonald sees 1960s as the halcyon days of British popular music and as a more spiritual time. MacDonald also sees little wrong with fantasies as they are the antithesis of the materialism he despises.

Regardless, the Beatles fantasy resonates to the present day in a constant metamorphosis into something new. Whether it is their image or their songs or grainy 'images of broken light' (*The Beatles*, 1970) from YouTube or their songs being mashed and reinterpreted by Jay Z and Danger Mouse, the Beatles' fantasy still furnishes our lives and exists in what MacDonald would call spirit.

MacDonald's experiences hardened into the dogmatic assertion that 1960s was the most exciting period for popular music. He writes in the introduction to *The People's Music*, 'the best popular music ... was made during 1960s, when at its peak both as a new, half invented art form and as a receptacle for rebellious social impulses' (MacDonald 2003: 8). He argues that pop music of the 1960s (particularly the Beatles) has declined from a genuine, albeit nascent art form to a low-standard, mass-produced commodity.

There is a quixotic emotional honesty and a persuasive lyricism at the core of MacDonald's worldview. In his essay on Nick Drake, *Exiled from Heaven: The Unheard Message of Nick Drake*, he writes so convincingly about Drake's depression because of his own struggle with the illness that eventually killed him. And yet, there is also a faith in the power of the individual to change society through artistic endeavour. Writing in *The New Shostakovich*, he inadvertently puts his finger on the Beatles message and on his own *raison d'être* as a writer: the Beatles and MacDonald were 'fated to follow an individualistic metier in a militantly collectivistic environment' (MacDonald 1990: 296). In MacDonald, Beatles scholarship finally found a writer who could do justice to the Beatles' songs: there is mellifluous, lyrical quality and iridescent shudder to his prose style that matches the Beatles' most melodic songs. Moreover, the optimism of the Beatles' message remains evocative to MacDonald: 'Far away from us on the other side of the sun-flooded chasm of 1960s – where courtesy of scientific technology, The Beatles can still be heard singing their buoyant, poignant, hopeful, love-advocating songs' (MacDonald 1998: 33).

MacDonald is a superfan whose work is entirely subjective and biased. His work is a desire to return to the past which makes him very dogmatic about new music. His bias is, however, a yearning for the past which is predicated on engaging with new technology. Niemeyer describes MacDonald's 'nostalgia' as simultaneously backward looking and forward looking nostalgic expressions or the creation of nostalgic worlds could indicate a twofold phenomenon: a reaction to fast technologies, despite using them, in desiring to slow down, and/or an escape from this crisis into a state of wanderlust (*Fernweh*) and nostalgia 'in the sense of (*Heimweh*) that could be "cured", or encouraged, by media use and consumption' (Niemeyer 2014: 2). MacDonald's nostalgia may be 'cured' by the fact that he is constantly interfacing with new media, but the fact that his opinions are subjective truth liberates his work from the Beatles phenomenon: MacDonald is a fan who has appropriated his own valid meanings and interpretations of 1960s culture and Beatles' music.

John or Paul?

Philip Norman's and Hunter Davies's supposedly objective writing style avowedly aspires to the central principle of journalism which is 'Do Not Add' (Kovach and Rosentiel 2003: 79); they elucidate that all truthful and documentary journalism should be predicated on the truth, and not embellishing the truth:

> Do not add simply means do not add things that did not happen. This goes further than 'never invent' or make things up, for it also encompasses rearranging events in time and place or conflating characters or events. If a siren rang out during the taping of a TV story, and for dramatic effect it is moved from scene to another, it had been added to that second place. What was once fact becomes a fiction. (2003: 79)

Their work is impeccably researched and based on thousands of interviews, but the fan in these two writers keeps shining through the seeming impartiality and which ultimately leads to very partial truth of an opinionated Beatles fan. For instance, Philip Norman admits that his work is based on the opinion of a fan (a well-researched fan) in his introduction to *Shout!* He writes:

> Others felt my judgements of Paul McCartney were too harsh, perhaps even motivated by personal dislike. In the Beatles subculture one inevitably finds oneself tagged either as a 'John' person or a 'Paul' person. I cannot pretend to be other than the former. Just the same, it was wrong of me – though it won me my initial access to Yoko-to say, as I did on an American TV programme that 'John was three-quarters of the Beatles'. (Norman 2005: xxviii)

Norman's book is indeed a fan's subjective piece which belittles Paul's contribution to the Beatles.

Davies, on the other hand, is a 'Paul' person. When writing *The Beatles* (1968) Paul and Linda holidayed with the Davies family in Portugal, and his fanaticism is constantly belied by his writing: 'Paul was the mainstay of group ... keeping them going as composers, pushing them into new ideas' (Davies 2009: 481). Like Norman, the journalist/fan Davies has an ostensibly detached style that attempts to convey documentary fact, and this supposed objectivity is very debatable. Davies is quite fond of pointing out the shortcomings in his work: 'If I were writing it again now, I would try to improve the style, smooth out the wrinkles, polish the prose' (Davies 2009: 74). As the New Journalist movement would also argue, Davies's objectivity is a myth with many occlusions and aporia throughout including a weak denial of their drug-taking: 'I had included quite a few references to drugs, including them taking LSD, which was rather daring for 1968, though I always referred to it in the past, sometimes saying that they did not take pot *now*, though, I'm sure I made the truth fairly obvious' (Davies 2009: 67). In fact Davies obfuscates the truth here helping to disseminate an anachronistic picture of the Beatles as four cuddly mop tops. Davies admits changing the book to appease John's (childhood guardian and de facto parent) Aunt Mimi: 'You will notice in the book that Chapter 1 ends rather abruptly with the phrase "John was as happy as the day was long". This was at Mimi's insistence. I gave in, a compromise; in order to keep in John's other stories. She thought this would soften them' (Davies 2009: 69).

Davies's and Norman's books are works of the devoted fan: strong opinions that are not always grounded in fact. Both books are written in a vernacular and popular tabloid voice that conveys the facts but doesn't engage the emotions, and the popular common sense of their rhetoric doesn't fly to the imaginative height of MacDonald. Unfortunately, Philip Norman's *Shout!* and Hunter Davies's *The Beatles* are books by obsessive journalist fans that lack the stylistic flair of MacDonald's prose.

All three texts are linguistic performances which give a partial truth, but MacDonald makes the reader see and feel exactly because he dispenses with the conventional journalistic method of Davies and Norman (cold, detached, truthful). MacDonald's style is not bounded by conventional journalese and by the despotism of 'fact'. As a musician and 1960s hippie, he writes with a florid style that at times reads like extravagant fiction (he makes the Beatles into fictional characters too). *Revolution in the Head* succeeds because it is stylistically ambitious and subjectively opinionated, it is documentary fiction. Wolfe's description of New Journalism describes MacDonald's type of prose that is writing which combines fictional elements (invented characters, expressive language, subjective opinion and, at times, a cavalier attitude to the truth): 'it just might be possible to write journalism that would ... read like a novel' (Wolfe 1996: 22). MacDonald is a fan and also a literary artist who raises *Revolution in the Head* to the status of literature, something that Davies and Norman don't quite achieve. *The Beatles, Shout!* and *Revolution in the Head* are literary/journalistic productions that demonstrate the partial and subjective fandom of all three writers, but MacDonald is the only one to raise his writing to the level worthy of capturing the Beatles and their immense achievement.

Another commonality between all three writers is that they have an unhealthy obsession with the past. In all three books there is only the cursory acknowledgement of the Beatles' influence on younger artists: there are a few short sections on Britpop; but all three tend to promulgate reactionary nostalgia when discussing the Beatles: no YouTube, mashing of the canon by fans and hip-hop artists or participatory slash fiction is mentioned.

Another point about Beatles books is that they are a peculiarly masculine affair; that is why *Beatles Monthly* and slash fiction are important, they are feminist ripostes to the male rock writing. Sibbie O'Sullivan points out that male Beatles books are now canonical, despite many spurious claims (Philip Norman, for example, seriously contends in *Shout!* that Brian Epstein was murdered without presenting any convincing evidence). O'Sullivan argues that we are almost exclusively offered a male understanding of Beatlemania:

> Girls may have created Beatlemania, but male writers have always dominated journalism and scholarship about the Beatles. I know of no full-length book written by a woman that offers a serious treatment of Beatles songs. No female authors appear on any of the top-10 listings of essential books about the Beatles ... If any book by a wife belongs on these lists, it's Cynthia Lennon's *John*, a heartfelt but bittersweet account about loving a musical icon. (O'Sullivan 2017 www.washingtonpost.com/entertainment/books)

The porn fantasy of slash fiction and the sublimated sexuality of *Beatles Monthly* may not possess the persuasive, although often erroneous, 'documentary' fact and the cultural capital of Davies and Norman's work, again O'Sullivan pokes gaping holes in Davies's and Norman's male rock hagiography and their ilk; she exempts MacDonald though because 'he places the songs in an "exciting narrative" and he places the song in "a cultural context" ' (O'Sullivan 2017). She argues,

> Once journalists lost interest in weeping female fans and turned their attention to the sophistication of the band's evolving compositions, the conversation became far more intellectual, if at times combative. (Is there really much difference between male critics strenuously debating which is better, 'Revolver' or 'Sgt. Pepper', and two teenage girls debating why one loves Paul and the other John? Both require deep knowledge, judgment – and a bit of frenzy). (O'Sullivan 2017)

In other words, Davies's and Norman's work is subjectivity dressed up as detached criticism and their work is cultural capital of the last vestiges of the sexist 1960s music industry.

Davies and Norman mythicize the Beatles' story in terms of individualized rags-to-riches story, whereas MacDonald's subjective new journalist approach is expressive and emotional and his colourfully expressed fandom approximates the resistive desire of *Beatles Monthly* and slash. MacDonald too exhibits progressive nostalgia sexing up Beatles songs: they become Day-Glo curiosities that demonstrate the modernist and experimental nature of their work (see the essay on *Revolution No 9*). Reading *Revolution in the Head*, we can understand McCartney remark that 'I feel like 1960s is about to happen. It feels like a period in the future to me, rather than a period in the past' (Miles 1997: 3). In contrast to MacDonald's and McCartney's glorification of 1960s, Davies and Norman feel that 1960s is a bygone age of English heritage culture. Their work is couched in the past by the clichés of the mythologizing baby boomer of biographers: Davies's and Norman's work is detailed and fascinating research, but in their books, the Beatles are not the love objects of resistive desire that jump off the pages of *Revolution in the Head* and *Beatles Monthly*, and progressive Eros of the blinking electronic dreams of slash fiction. MacDonald's writing may on the surface be anachronistic: he is spiritual, he had a dalliance with 1960s pharmaceuticals, his appearance was that of a counterculture hippie (long hair and a beard), but his prose possesses a transformative openness, a resistive 1960s radicalism and a fan's love that renders Davies's and Norman's work arid, anaemic and asexual compared to his passionate evangelical rhetoric that makes the 1960s breathe with life and potential: the poetic evanescence of his work is a rebuttal of the conventional biographical approach which is wedded to nostalgia, the *mal d'archive* and Thanatos. Davies's and Norman's work is cogent research, but their prose does not aspire to the biographers' as the art of making the reader feel. The best journalist fan epitomizes the resistive sexuality of female fans and transformative nostalgia of slash.

Norman's style at its best is lucid, limpid and colourful, but he has the tendency to wallow in nostalgia, he sees the Beatles story as a cautionary tale of four gilded Jay Gatsbys. In Norman's work, the reader looks back and the backwards is focused on the past: like Davies his prose can occasionally spin gold, and this writer ranks both Davies's and Norman's biographies highly, for expressing the Beatles phenomenon so well:

> Only in ancient times, when boy emperors and pharaohs were clothed, even fed with pure gold, had very young men commanded an equivalent adoration, fascination and constant, expectant scrutiny. Nor could anyone suppose that to be thus – to have such youth, and wealth, such clothes and cars and servants and cars – made for any state other than inconceivable happiness. For no one since the boy pharaohs … had known, as the Beatles now knew, how it felt to have felt everything, done everything, tasted everything, had a surfeit of everything; to live on that blinding, deadening, numbing surfeit which made each, on bad days, think he was ageing at twice the usual rate. (Harris, *The Guardian*, 2012)

Here we have a wonderful evocation of the past: MacDonald, however, is a superfan of a different stripe: there is a progressive nostalgia at the heart of *Revolution in the Head*, a quixotic fan-boy energy which presses forwards while looking back for inspiration. It is ironic that of the three Beatles journalist fans mentioned here, he is dead, survived by Davies and Norman, but his fandom hauntingly transformative and progressive as it sees the Beatles and 1960s as futurist, post-humanist even because their image and music is kept constantly alive by technology. The Beatles to Norman and Davies, on the other hand, are forever 'boy pharaohs' entombed in the past.

Although it is clear that MacDonald's writing is more emotional than that of Davies and perhaps even more strident than Norman, one of his important contributions is his foregrounding of the Beatles' classical musical influences. In an interview with Aaron Krerowicz, author of *The Beatles and the Avant Garde*, Krerowicz told me that he didn't like MacDonald's *Revolution in the Head*, 'not because it was opinionated, but because many of these opinions were unsubstantiated' (Krerowicz 2018). Nevertheless, as our conversation continued he acknowledged that the book did at least analyse experimental music well because 'MacDonald was a musician' (Krerowicz 2018), and that he was a proselytizer for contemporary *avant-garde* music. MacDonald's evangelism and proselytizing is important as Krerowicz told me that in 2018, the fiftieth anniversary of *The White Album*, he was travelling across the United States with his *Carte Blanche White Album Discussion*, where he spoke about all thirty *White Album* tracks and then invited the fans to vote which fifteen tracks to keep if it was a single album. The innate conservatism of the fans' choices meant that he tried to 'convince the audience why all thirty tracks should be kept, but at the end they (the fans) have to vote which fifteen tracks to keep and which fifteen tracks to get rid of, and *Revolution No 9* never makes the cut, not once does it make the cut, which I think is a shame' (Krerowicz 2018). This is another reason that MacDonald's evangelical poetic and strident new journalism has a critical methodology (admittedly an idiosyncratic colloquial and personal methodology) that Davies's and Norman's work lacks. MacDonald demonstrates the Beatles importance as artists and their attempt to bring radical ideas into the mainstream. *Revolution in the Head* shows that, the Beatles' experimentation in tracks such as 'Revolution No 9' ensured that they were constantly looking forwards in their art and MacDonald's evocative, vivid and colourful prose matches their inventiveness. MacDonald's essays on the experimental Beatles' work are the longest pieces in the book: 'Strawberry Fields Forever' is ten pages and 'Revolution No 9' is five pages long in the 2008 Vintage edition; the essay on 'Revolution No 9' gives the book its title and, to paraphrase MacDonald, experimental music stimulates a revolution in the head; and Krerowicz's participatory and empirical fan research (he has given over five hundred talks where he asks fans to vote for a single *White Album*) finds that 'Revolution No 9 never makes the cut'. However, quantitative data could quite easily be found that supports the contrary argument, that Beatles' dalliance with twentieth-century *avant-garde* music had a significant impact on fans.

Krerowicz contends that 'Revolution No 9' is also an autobiographical Lennon song which is critical and resentful of Beatles fans. The song moves through three stages: early child of a baby crying, through the noisy chaos of Beatlemania (violence and screaming) to his 'reward, the pot of gold at the end of the rainbow, John finding Yoko as the last minute and half of the song is all Yoko and she is entirely absent from the first eight minutes' (Krerowicz 2018). Of the three superfan journalists discussed in this chapter, MacDonald is the most devoted fanboy, the most dedicated fan and the most powerfully strident in his opinions. Speaking to Krerowicz, he highlights the progressiveness and intellectualism in MacDonald's writing that makes his work transformative and inventive ideas that are predicated on nostalgia yet not hidebound by nostalgia as Davies's and Norman's writing so often is. Krerowicz argues that 'Revolution No 9' is 'one of the most interesting pieces of music ever made' (Krerowicz 2018). And if MacDonald conveys this love of the Beatles *avant-garde* period it is because he is a journalist fan, and, for that matter, Krerowicz is an aca-fan. Krerowicz points out MacDonald's new journalistic subjectivity by saying that,

> I try to be objective and I try to get at what is good about any given song even if I personally don't like it, but MacDonald is very set in his ways and not open to considering anything other than he already thinks, and it strikes me as an extremely closed mind style of writing, but there are things I really like about it,

MacDonald is a musician and most Beatles authors are not musicians and you can tell, but the downside is that he is very opinionated and doesn't back up any of his assertions. (Krerowicz 2018)

Here Krerowicz has described MacDonald as a journalist fan who has subjectively appropriated the Beatles into his own worldview. The MacDonald Krerowicz evokes is similar to the young teen readers of *Beatles Monthly* and the traumatized fans at conventions and the highly sexualized writers of slash; MacDonald has weaved the Beatles into his own fantasy fandom and appropriated their art into his life where it is charged with the subjectivity of the fan, making it inventive, unique to the fan and a consistently forward-looking and transgressive energy.

Krerowicz describes Philip Norman's *Shout!* as 'John heavy' and that he has been 'harsh on Paul', but he enjoyed all three writers discussed here, and as Krerowicz is an aca-fan and a classical trained musician and music theorist, he describes the historiography of Mark Lewisohn's study as the 'gold standard' of Beatles books and 'as his favourite Beatles book ever' (Krerowicz 2018); indeed the research in Lewisohn's books is stunning; the detailed minutiae of his historical method puts Davies and Norman to shame. In an interview with Mark Lewisohn on 23 July 2018, I asked him if he considered Hunter Davies and Philip Norman to be Beatles fans:

I wouldn't use the word fan for Philip, or necessarily for Hunter; they are professional journalists who at different times came to the Beatles and used what they felt to be a natural understanding of it all; both good journalists of the right generation; they thought it was fair game to write about them, they hadn't necessarily been out and bought every record; they may have bought one or two along the way; but they were certainly open to learning about the Beatles and writing about them. They were positive about their subject, but when it came to *Shout!* Philip took it upon himself to positively dislike one of the four: McCartney. That's a tactic, if you like, a journalist's position. (Lewisohn 2018)

So Davies and Norman are 'fans' of a type, but they don't write with the enthusiasm, knowledge and passion for the subject that Ian MacDonald has. Lewisohn goes on to say 'that I've been a fan in a way that Hunter Davies and Philip Norman never were ... they are not looking as true biographers or historians at the subject; their opinion is kind of forefront' (Lewisohn 2018); with both Davies and Norman we get a biased and subjective 'fan' account but their work does not have the élan of MacDonald's: the term 'superfan' is more relevant to MacDonald than it is to Davies and Norman. In fact you could call all three writers superfans, but MacDonald is a superfan in terms of passion, while Davies and Norman are superfans in careerist terms. Lewisohn says that 'fan is a three letter word but it covers a vast spectrum, a gamut, of human approach' which is a succinct summary of the differences in these three writers, and also cogent description of Beatles fandom. Lewisohn points out that it is being a Beatles fan that keeps him motivated, 'being a fan gives me the impetus to go forward, if I wasn't a fan, I'd be in trouble' (Lewisohn 2018); it is revealing that Lewisohn describes Beatles writers as fans: which all the people mentioned in this chapter are, but there is a gulf in terms of passion: a fervency that MacDonald and Lewisohn share.

Each of these fan/journalists also has a fictional feel to their writing. In MacDonald's case his mellifluous style is seductive and persuasive conveying emotion and feeling, but like Davies and Norman, he uses devices we would normally associate with the novel: dialogue, metaphor and characterization. Characterization is the aspect of their writing where documentary and fiction blur to the greatest extent. Under the auspices of 'documentary fact' Davies, Norman and MacDonald are creating fictional characters: they are combining reporting and fiction so that 'reality' reads like an invented narrative. These three Beatles superfans create character and dialogue that wouldn't be out of place in the page of Mark Shipper's *Paperback Writer* and the fan erotica of slash. Slash is fiction which is based in reality and Beatles journalism is fact that is heavily fictionalized.

Krerowicz feels that one of the plus points of MacDonald's work is that he is a musician and Krerowicz discusses MacDonald's work in the same context as Walter Everett (the author of *The Beatles as Musicians*), and who like Krerowicz is a serious musician who applies music theory to his discussion of the Beatles. My preference is for MacDonald's work over and above that of Davies's and Norman's. MacDonald's musicology, his evangelical zeal for the Beatles and his fecund prose positioning make his work fan journalism of a different stripe, but that is only a fan's opinion.

4

'Fanaticism' and the Beatles

The dark side of Beatles fandom, and any fandom, is fans who become dangerous fanatics. Two fans that found themselves at this extreme were the infamous Mark Chapman, John Lennon's murderer, and Michael Abram, who attempted to murder George Harrison in a knife attack in 1999. Both were dangerous Beatles obsessives, and both felt that they were on missions from God. In fact each 'fan' explained their obsession in religious terms. Mark Chapman suggested that 'a small part of me must be the Devil' (Jones 1992: 98).

Using press coverage (newspapers, television documentaries, films and biographies of the killers) of Chapman and Abram, this chapter will problematize the media's description of them as 'fans'. It is clear that they initially loved the Beatles, but by the time of their attacks, they had ceased to be fans, and instead of being Beatles fans they were eccentric outsiders erroneously categorized as 'obsessive fans', 'extreme fans' and 'dangerous fans' by the media: this terminology is typical of media discourses that mistake far outliers as representative of fandom in general. In this chapter I will discuss the extent to which the lives of Chapman and Abram have been used by the media to create a negative stereotype of fan in general. As Duffett contends, Chapman was not a fan when he shot Lennon, 'he was already seriously ill' (Duffett 2013: 108) and a shallow media categorized him as a fan when, in fact, he 'suffered from a personality disorder that did not spring from his fandom' (2013: 108).

These Beatles 'fans' give us an insight into schizophrenia, mental illness and the inability of fans to distinguish between fantasy and reality. The Beatles became such a huge cultural phenomenon that they attracted very extreme reactions to their celebrity. By 1966, their tours had become dangerous and when they had to flee the Philippines, after snubbing First Lady Imelda Marcos, they were attacked in the airport and bullet holes were found in the rear of their plane. Chapman and Abram are just two examples of the frenzy the Beatles attracted.

Mark Chapman is currently serving twenty years to life in Attica Correction Facility in New York City. Denied parole for the sixth time in 2010, he told the *Guardian*, 'I felt that by killing John Lennon I would become somebody and instead of that I became a murderer, and murderers are not somebodies' (*The Daily Telegraph*, 2010). In 1980, his celebrity hit list included David Bowie, Elizabeth Taylor and Johnny Carson.

The Michael Abram story is equally upsetting and tragic. Abram (from Huyton on Merseyside) broke into George Harrison's home in 1999, brutally stabbing him seven times in front of his wife Olivia and son Dhani. Bizarrely, and miraculously, press reports of the attack convey that post-assault, Harrison managed to retain his sense of humour:

> Nonetheless, according to police, at about 3:30 a.m. on Dec. 30 Abram broke through a kitchen window and attacked the couple with a six- or seven-inch knife, stabbing **Harrison** in the chest until Olivia clubbed the attacker with a lamp. The bloody scuffle tracked through three rooms before the couple managed to subdue Abram. **Harrison** suffered a punctured lung, Arias a minor head wound. From his hospital room, the **Beatle** joked that his attacker 'wasn't a burglar, but … he certainly wasn't auditioning for the Traveling Wilburys', the singer's late-1980s band. (Leland, Newsweek, 2000)

In 2000, Abram was cleared of attempted murder and served nineteen months in a mental health facility. After his release, Harrison's widow was distraught at the release and implied that the attack hastened her husband's death (November 2001) from cancer: the attack sapping his will and physical strength to fight the disease. In both examples, celebrity fandom has led to delusion, obsession, violent attack and murder.

However, there is an important caveat about over-simplifying the unhinged fan thesis. Mark Duffett correctly points out that Mark Chapman's fandom was

> far more complex than those of a supposedly normal fan … Chapman suffered from a major personality disorder which did not spring from his fandom. By the time he began to think about killing John Lennon, Chapman had been sectioned in a psychiatric hospital, prayed to Satan in the nude … When Chapman became fixated on the singer he then posed as a fan in order to get close. By that time he was therefore not a fan driven insane, but an insane man pretending to be a fan in order to meet John Lennon. (Duffett 2013: 108)

It seems likely that the violence of Mark Chapman and Michael Abram is a complex psychological cocktail of religious fundamentalism, envy and paranoia. However, it is very difficult to build a psychological profile of Chapman and Abram without understanding that their identification with Lennon is not simply 'a psychical process whereby dangerous or disavowed aspects of the self are projected onto somebody else', this is a complicated mental process where 'inner and outer self' exist 'at the level of unconscious fantasy: we are not aware of their dynamics' (Hills 2002: 97). Even with access to the psychological reports it is nigh on impossible to understand the motivations of Chapman and Abram. Perhaps it is a moot point whether they were fans or not when they carried out their murderous intentions. What is clear, however, is that both 'fans' represent fandom when it tips from harmless obsession into psychotic narcissism and violence. And Chapman was not always the 'scary monster' fan media stereotype. At his first job as a Camp Counsellor in South DeKalb County, Georgia, he was so popular with the children that they nicknamed him Captain Nemo because of his kindness and his leadership qualities. This continued throughout his professional life and everyone he encountered in a work capacity considered him an outstanding worker.

Duffett raises a very important point when he contends that Chapman was not a 'fan'; Duffett sees Chapman's personality being reduced by the media into a stereotype of the stalker archetype. This cliché of the deranged fan fits easily into media narratives concerning the death of the 1960s dream and it also lends itself to the low-grade biographical press which enshrined Lennon as a romantic hero of the Beatles story (to the press a story with a neat beginning, middle and tragic end). However, Duffett makes it clear that the truth is more tangled: that Chapman's personality was a mix of paranoia, fixation, obsession and music fan, which was just one strand in an intricate psychological make-up. Mark Chapman was a mix of all these mess of contradictions but the media post-death simplified him and also the Beatles story (see my comments on Philip Norman's *Shout!* for numerous examples of how pulp novelistic invention replaced serious analysis in many Beatles books and in the press).

Scary monster fan

To Duffett, Chapman became a 'scary monster fan' which made him easy to categorize as an insane fan: 'In a sense the phantom behind Lennon's killing represents an archetypally large, ugly and frightening imaginary creature whose role in the public imagination is to associate monstrosity, celebrity and "deranged" fandom' (Duffett 2013: 110). Duffett's work also raises the issue of anti-fans. There is an argument to be made that Chapman and Abram display traits of the non-fan or anti-fan:

> Studying the anti-fan could also provide further insight into the nature of affective involvement, for many of us care as deeply (if not more so) about those texts that we dislike as we do about those that we like. To offer a famous example, Salman Rushdie will forever be in danger because of a strong anti-fan reaction to his novel *The Satanic Verses*. Thousands, perhaps even millions, of these anti-fans care enough about a text they have not read that they would call for its author's assassination. Certainly this is an exaggerated example, but it nevertheless points out that dislike is as potentially powerful an emotion and reaction as is like. (Gray 2003: 73)

In my discussion of Chapman and Abram it is worth acknowledging that a fan is a kaleidoscopic mix of many contradictory impulses and 'that any analysis of the obsessions and motivations of fans has to be predicated on the knowledge that any work on the area of fandom in relation to psychology is partial, provisional and deeply wedded to cultural and historical context: a context which is also constantly changing' (2003: 73).

In this chapter I will contend that the spokes on the wheel of Chapman's and Abram's personalities were religious fanaticism, envy, paranoia, and fandom is one of these many spokes. As Duffett argues, fandom is often subsumed by more important psychological personality traits. In the case of Chapman and Abram a warped religious fundamentalism played a significant part in their actions.

Chapman's friends describe his conversion from 'LSD freak' to 'Jesus freak' (Jones 1992). Chapman's conversion was characterized by intolerance and fundamentalism; his high school friend Miles McManus told Jack Jones, 'When Mark was in the ninth and tenth grades, he was doing drugs very heavily, then he went into his Jesus stage and his whole identity changed. It was like he had to be the best Christian in the world' (Jones 1992: 117). Jones's book starts to build a complex picture of Chapman. An essential part of his psychological make-up comprises of being a Beatles fan, but is just one colour in the palette of his personality. Duffett may be throwing the baby out with the bathwater when he downplays Chapman's fandom: Chapman was a Beatles fan, but other psychological factors come into play. For instance, one of the most famous descriptions of Chapman shows how his fundamentalist approach to Christianity was predicated on his fascination with Lennon and the Beatles:

> Members of church groups that Chapman joined after his instant spiritual conversion, recall that he engaged in a vendetta against 'Imagine', warning that Lennon's message – to imagine a world with no heaven or religion – was blasphemy. At prayer meetings and rallies he attended, often several times a week, ('God is a concept by which we measure our pain' 'God', *Plastic Ono Band, 1970*) comes to mind here as Chapman was obviously experiencing deep psychological trauma, friends remember that he would sing his own foreboding lyrics to the Lennon tune: 'Imagine John Lennon is dead'. (Jones 2002: 117)

A caveat about psychological approaches to fan studies is relevant here. As Sandvoss argues 'psychological to fandom explore processes and motivations that remain concealed from the researcher as much as the researched' (Sandvoss 2005: 67). Admittedly this argument has some validity when discussing Chapman and Abram, but there is such a surfeit of archival material including psychiatric reports that a profile begins to form; and one of the psychological strands that does recur in both men is a religious obsession. When asked about attempted murder of George Harrison, Abram said that 'he had been sent on a mission by God to kill him' (*The Guardian*, 2002). Both these violent fantasies are example of the ego being flooded by the id and the resulting inability to control the 'bad parts of self ... and the "imagined control" over the "projective identification" (Lennon in both these cases) breaks down "whereby the boundaries between self and object are increasing blurred"' (Sandvoss 2005: 83). In Chapman's case, his

> projective identification, in which Lennon ultimately fails to live up to the violent idealisation in Chapman's projective fantasies. Chapman engaged in a range of introjective processes imitating and copying Lennon, such as learning to play the guitar, and even marrying an older Japanese-American woman. However, when Lennon seeks to align his public image with the transformations in his personal life and makes a series of statements regarding music, religion, and politics that run

against Chapman's values and reading of Lennon, he can no longer accommodate Chapman's projective fantasies. As a result, the fragile stability of Chapman's ego collapses as he loses control over the external projected object and his dislocated 'bad' elements return in force. (Sandvoss 2005: 84)

On the Larry King Show in 1992, speaking about Lennon murder, Chapman said that he couldn't differentiate between the simulated media image of John Lennon and the real person: 'I realise that I really ended a man's life, then he was an album cover' (Larry King 1992). Chapman tells King that even after meeting Lennon and his son, Sean, he still couldn't perceive Lennon as a real person, 'I just saw him as a two dimensional celebrity with no real feelings' (Larry King 1992). Describing the moments immediately after he'd shot Lennon, Chapman describes his feelings using a 'film' simile: 'Then afterwards it was like the film strip broke. I fell in upon myself' (Larry King 1992). Chapman reveals his religious faith in the interview. When Larry King asks Chapman how he was cured from 'What he believed was his schizophrenia', Chapman iterates his Christianity:

Not medication and not doctors but the Lord; I've walked in the power of the Lord now for a number of years ... I think the Lord has a tender spot in his heart for prisoners. He said so, the rest of the Bible said so in many different places, and I've leaned on Him ... He told my heart, 'don't kill; I don't want you to kill. He doesn't like murder'.

Throughout the interview Chapman alludes to a personal relationship with God. The interview takes a bizarre turn when Larry Kings asks Chapman if he has 'fans'. Chapman's response is as follows:

I don't call them fans but there are people that write to me, I got a letter yesterday, I guess you wouldn't call this fellow a fan, but he said I hereby declare on this date that you will not die a natural death; and then another fellow sent me a package, a book, a Christian book ... and it's a book on healing ... so I'm getting both ends of the spectrum, extreme hate, which I understand, and the compassion, the understanding ... this was a monstrous act, but perhaps not done by a monster. (Larry King 1992)

Chapman then reveals that he gets romantic letters from 'fans', and when asked why people stalk celebrities he says, 'People stalk celebrities ... because they have nothing inside of them; their esteem is rock bottom, and they feel that by writing fan letters or actually coming in close contact with a celebrity, they feel important, I know I did those sort of things' (Larry King 1992).

The effect of John Lennon's death on Beatles fans was monumental; Beatles fans were grief stricken and traumatized by the band's break-up in 1970, but the shock was nothing compared to Lennon's murder. Immediately fans gathered outside the Dakota building singing Lennon's songs and crying inconsolably. The news networks in the

United States and the UK suspended their planned schedules to give blanket coverage of Lennon's death. The day after John's murder, Yoko was told that a fan had committed suicide after hearing about John's death:

> Yoko is informed that because of John's death one fan has already committed suicide. She immediately issues a statement requesting fans not to turn against themselves in their anguish. Shortly before this, Ringo and Barbara arrive at the Dakota to comfort Yoko and play with Sean, their entrance to the building blocked by hundreds of still hysterical weeping fans. (Badman 2001: 274)

Time magazine described the fans' turning the Dakota building into a shrine to Lennon's memory:

> In the days after Mark David Chapman shot John Lennon on Dec. 8, 1980, the area around the gates of the Dakota, Lennon's apartment building in New York City, quickly turned into a makeshift memorial. Flowers and signs from fans quoting Beatles lyrics were displayed alongside the more official remembrances, as world leaders made their way to honor an artist whose life had been ended too early. (*Time* 1980)

The reaction to Lennon's death was a watershed moment for the Beatles, just as the band's break-up prompted fans to create conventions to keep the band alive in their memories, the grief at Lennon's murder engendered interest in the band for a new generation of younger fans. The effect of the tragedy was tumultuous: fans became more posthumously obsessed with the band and the murder generated a legendary status comparable with JFK's, Marilyn Monroe's and James Dean's deaths.

> Time discussed frightening grieving process, also mentioning fans' suicides, In Los Angeles, more than 2,000 people joined in a candlelight vigil at Century City; in Washington, D.C., several hundred crowded the steps of the Lincoln Memorial in a 'silent tribute' that recalled the sit-ins of the '60s. Record stores all over the country reported sellouts on the new Lennon-Ono album, Double Fantasy, their first record in five years, as well as the back stock of Lennon's previous records. Some reaction was tragic. A teenage girl in Florida and a man of 30 in Utah killed themselves, leaving notes that spoke of depression over Lennon's death. (*Time* 1980)

These suicides echo the extreme act of Lennon's murder. Beatles fandom is an arena of intense overreaction to artists and their art. In a sense, fans are vicariously reacting to media structures of grief as they didn't personally know Lennon (this describes Chapman and Abram as well, their obsession was a simulation of the real Lennon). Fans are performative traumatic subjects:

> A morbid cult of sentimentality and victimhood turns out on closer inspection to be a viable historically situated technology of the self that integrates an identity

around the void of the wound. Trauma becomes the ground on which an identity is constructed ... Rappaport refers to this process in an essay on Judith Butler when he censures the 'metaphysical trait' of the automatic presumption of 'a community that emphasizes and makes common cause with the supposed authenticity of the experience of injury'. (Carville 2011: 34)

Fans created a community around 'a void of the wound' and put into effect a grieving process that is a 'cult of sentimentality'. The fans' pain is real, but the event (the murder of Lennon) is mediated through the media and the fans reaction is to a simulated and structured media event. They share this with Chapman and Abram: their extreme emotions are second-hand reactions to the structures of media institutions: the trauma is real, but the message was received through the cold light of television and numbing sharpness of the printed word.

'The void of wound' created after Lennon's death has also been a cash cow for the Beatles phenomenon. Fans are eager to buy any product that is associated with him: even relics of his death are sought after:

> The last album he autographed – *Double Fantasy*, inscribed at the request of Mark Chapman a couple of hours before the 25-year-old returned to the Dakota building to make himself famous – went for $525,000 seven years ago. One of last year's most successful British films was *Nowhere Boy*, Sam Taylor-Wood's scrupulous and sensitive account of his early days. John Lennon's name is hardly one that needs to be artificially hoisted into the public gaze. But that hasn't stopped his widow exploiting it in fields that have nothing to do with music. In the last couple of weeks, the Montblanc Company has been promoting a John Lennon special-edition fountain pen, with a clip shaped like a guitar fretboard. The newspaper ad has a CND symbol in the background and a slogan: 'To John, with love.' An earlier pen was dedicated to the memory of Mahatma Gandhi, with a picture of the spiritual leader engraved on its 16-carat gold nib. John would have laughed at that, wouldn't he? Perhaps with scorn, certainly with amusement at the incongruity of the project. But only diehard Beatles fans seem to be upset. The rest of the world accepts it as part of a new culture in which everything – particularly if it evokes a set of desirable values – is for sale, everything is negotiable, everything is there to be sampled and remixed and put to some new purpose. (Williams, *The Guardian*, 2010)

John Lennon's death resonates through the ghostly spectres of capitalist enterprise and fans are attracted to ghoulish reminders of his death: Many aspects of Beatles fandom are affirmed on memories of Lennon's murder and George Harrison's assault.

Abram seems to have undergone a similar breakdown to Chapman between his projective fantasies and the reality of his object's life (in Abram's case, Harrison). Abram's profile fits that of Chapman, a Beatles obsession, voices of God in his head and a history of drug abuse. His mother was quoted in the *Liverpool Echo* at the time of the attack in 1999:

Mrs. Abram, 52, described how her son was a former heroin addict who had been treated at a psychiatric unit. Recently he had become obsessed with the music of the Beatles. 'It is the Beatles at the moment but a few weeks ago it was Oasis. He has been running in pubs shouting about the Beatles. He started to wear a Walkman to play music to stop the voices in his head'. (*The Guardian*, 1999)

Abram's was clearly someone who was mentally ill first and a Beatles fan second, although the police reports demonstrate that an obsession with George Harrison was Abram's tipping point:

The investigation determined that this was not a simple burglary gone wrong, but a planned attack on Harrison. The prosecutor said that Abram 'believed that The Beatles were witches who flew around on broomsticks. Subsequently, George Harrison possessed him and that he had been sent on a mission by God to kill him. He saw George as a sorcerer and a devil.' The attack drew parallels to Mark David Chapman's killing of John Lennon on Dec. 8, 1980. Abram was found not guilty by reason of insanity and committed to a psychiatric hospital, where he stayed until mid-2002. With his customary dry wit, Harrison said that his would-be assassin 'wasn't a burglar, and he certainly wasn't auditioning for the Traveling Wilburys'. (Ultimate Classic Rock, 2014)

Duffett's thesis then is that a fan cannot be essentialized into a 'scary monster' stereotype, arguing that Chapman is not strictly a fan, but has (with Abram) undergone a psychological trauma in which he is trapped in an impasse of obsession that he can't transcend. Fandom is the manifestation of their violence, the problem is not that of a music fan, but of individuals who are trapped in a cycle of trauma that haunts them and their devotional objects, Chapman and Abram can't transcend the media ghosts of Lennon and Harrison that they have created, they are defeated subjects stuck in their traumatic pasts of which the Beatles are one fractured shard of their shattered psyche.

So, it is important to make the distinction that the 'scary monster' stereotype of a fan comes about because the media conflates mental illness and fandom. Abram had been suffering from schizophrenia since 1991, according to press reports, and yet his attack on George Harrison was eight years later on 30 November 1999. Chapman, too, was ill before he was interested in the Beatles, as a child he spoke to his country of little people that lived in a drawer in his bedroom. Only later did he become a Beatles fan. Beatles fandom was one part of two deeply troubled men. Abram and Chapman used Harrison and Lennon, respectively, as a focus for their illnesses. Abram had attacked a male nurse on 17 November 1999; he had spoken of killing Noel and Liam Gallagher of Oasis; and 28 August 1999, Abram had told medical workers that he had 'sold his soul' and 'was going to burn' and 'two months later he was complaining of stigmata on his hands and forehead, and being visited by good and bad spirits' (*The Daily Telegraph*, 2001). Chapman prayed to Satan for the strength to murder John Lennon, he convened a council of little people and asked for them to vote on whether he should assassinate the Beatle or not. His court of 'little people' told him not to go ahead with his murder plan. In 1980, there were already plenty of red flags about Chapman's mental stability. Working as a security guard in Hawaii, Chapman was drinking heavily (Budweisers for breakfast), he was worrying his wife, Gloria Hiroko, who described his rocking back and forth naked while listening to Beatles records, convening a council of the 'little people' who lived in his walls. Profligate spending, plans to read every book in the local library, picking fights with everyone he came into contact with and violent tantrums, in which he once threatened the Hare Krishnas – the evidence is overwhelming that Chapman was damaged well before shooting John Lennon. This therefore problematizes his pigeon-holing as a 'deranged fan': he was ill and just happened to like the Beatles; in fact, he was more of a superfan of Todd Rundgren. In New York he thought about killing David Bowie, George C. Scott and Todd Rundgren and eventually settled on Lennon because of his accessibility: Lennon would come and go from the Dakota without any security. Chapman was so delusional by the time of the murder that he felt he would dissolve into the pages of the *Catcher in the Rye* in a pool of ink, and that John Lennon would vanish into the ether immediately after the bullets hit his body. It is clear that Chapman was mentally ill and that his fandom was just one aspect of a very complex person. In fact years of psychiatric reports have proved inconclusive to find out his condition. He was convicted of the murder after refusing to plead insanity, and the thirty-six years of psychiatric reports have variously found Chapman to be autistic, schizophrenic and psychopathic. In 2016, he told journalists that he was sane and his reason for killing Lennon was solely for the publicity and the attention. This is a man who had 'little people' living in his apartment walls and to whom Chapman would sing Beatles songs and insist that they address him as their monarch, King Mark! If they didn't comply with his wishes, he would kill them all; weirdly in the weeks leading up to Lennon's murder, the 'little people' returned and rebelled against their creator; but the fact remains that whether Chapman was insane or not, he was used by the media as a stereotypical obsessed 'fanatic'. Headlines around the world on 9 October 1980 promulgated this stereotype: The *LA Times* referred to him as a 'screwball' and the *Liverpool Echo* called him a 'crazed gunman': these papers are typical of the reaction to Lennon's murder, and more importantly they conflate these descriptions of Chapman with the word 'fan'. So to pathologize Abram and Chapman as deranged fans is erroneous, the most comprehensive conclusion about both is that their fantasy lives are incomprehensible; as Duffett argues, 'Mark Chapman's incomprehensible motivation for assassinating Lennon can only be understood if we see it as the result of Chapman's inner fantasies' (Duffett 2013: 116). And being a fan is just one aspect of their troubled psyches and why would theorists want to relate this action to 'fans, rather than to other groups or individuals'? (2013: 116). I have used Derrida's terms 'hauntology' to illustrate why first-generation Beatles fans at a convention wish to repeat memories of their youth; but they transcend the cycle and turn cultural hauntings of the past (the Beatles' break-up, Lennon's death and Harrison's death) into a positive psychological phenomenon: 'magical thinking' that accentuates the positivity of communal sharing. Abram and Chapman, on the other hand, are trapped in a *Groundhog Day* of negative compulsion; they are isolated individuals who cannot break the compulsion to repeat; in a Derridian sense, their mental illnesses 'remains effective as a virtuality (the traumatic compulsion to repeat, a fatal pattern)' (Fisher 2014: 16). Abram and Chapman were trapped in a negative spiral and they found it impossible to envision an alternative to their dreadful actions, and fandom was only one of these virtual ghosts that reverberated in their heads.

Cultural and psychic wound

As we have seen in Chapter 2, the Beatles break-up caused a cultural psychic wound in fans and the only way to deal with this wound was to restage trauma in order to master or control it. Beatles fans at conventions used the progressive nostalgia (i.e. conventions informed by the here and now) of a communal gathering to move forward: to master and control the cultural and vicarious upset caused by the band's break-up and transform the nostalgia into something new (admittedly fans' 'wound' is cultural as opposed to a deep psychological damage). Chapman and Abram never manage this, especially Chapman who claimed that growing up, he and his mother were abused by his emotionally distant father; in fact, he and his sister were terrified of his father. Freud argued in *Beyond the Pleasure Principal* (1920) and *Moses and Monotheism* (1939) that the individual's response to a traumatic childhood involved three stages: the first, which he described in *Beyond the Pleasure Principal*, was 'the piercing of the individual's mental apparatus form the outside' (Freud 1920: 29); the image of the mind being penetrated graphically illustrates that the mind is overcome with shock and is so overwhelmed that it cannot process this experience. So instead of the mind managing the traumatic episode, the event instead becomes repressed in the unconscious: this is the second stage of trauma. After an incubation stage, the third stage is the return of the repressed memory, which causes the victim flashbacks, nightmares and panic attacks. This 'compulsion to repeat' (Freud 1920: 19), according to Freud, 'overrides the pleasure principle' (Freud 1920: 22) and the only way to escape entrapment in the traumatic episode is by restaging the trauma, and in this way the psyche would be able to assimilate this event and so find a way of controlling it.

The trauma felt by fans at the Beatles' break-up is hardly commensurate with Chapman's childhood abuse, but the same rule applies; an individual can manage trauma by overcoming the haunting by facing up to the traumatic episode. Chapman, unlike fans in a communal environment, is trapped or haunted by his abusive childhood. Chapman never managed to outrun the shadow of his depression; he attempted suicide by gassing himself in his car, but the plastic pipe melted, saving him. Throughout his life he never managed to break the repetition compulsion cycle; he fought with his parents, took LSD and went on obsessive spending sprees that left him in serious debt. He never managed a talking cure or a testimony and the ghosts of traumatic childhood were a 'haunting that does not initiate a story; it is the sign of blockage of a story, a hurt that has not been honoured by a memorializing narrative' (Luckhurst 2008: 93). When Chapman shot Lennon four times in the back outside the Dakota at 10.50 pm on Monday, 8 December 1980, he was a mentally ill subject and not a fan: a sick man who was a 'phantom' caused by the 'consequences of silence' (Abraham and Torok 1994: 168).

Chapman was also deeply sexually repressed, and in a re-enactment of Holden Caulfield's scene with the prostitute in *The Catcher in the Rye*, Chapman on the eve of Lennon's murder gave a prostitute a massage, insisting that she wear a green dress, again like *The Catcher in the Rye*, and spoke to her without sex taking place. Chapman's repression is very similar to the mechanics of power concerning the girl fans' sexuality in *Beatles Monthly*; Chapman's repression and *Beatles Monthly* demonstrate that because our sexuality has been inscribed into discourses of power since the rise of capitalism and the Industrial Revolution, this discourse 'put into operation an entire machinery for producing true discourses about it' and so sex became 'an economy of pleasure' and an 'ordered system of knowledge'. Beatles fans in *Beatles Monthly* have discovered 'pleasure of the true discourse of pleasure' and have, in a manner similar to fans at conventions, talked out repression and become liberated from the machinery of 'the uniform truth of sex' (Foucault 1980: 69–71). Chapman never banished his childhood traumas, or his sexual repression through a talking cure, and this resulted in his taking revenge on society by killing one of its icons to make a name for himself and to give meaning to his life. The trauma of death is central to fans' stories. Abram and Chapman are the dark side of the Beatles story. Death has usually been treated in a productive manner by fans: celebrity-styled funerals, tribute bands and conventions are a humorous, ironic and progressive way of reacting to trauma; and these expressions of fandom are remote to the Abram/Chapman tragedies.

'The dark side of Beatles fandom' is a phrase used by Richard Porter in reference to Yoko Ono, when I interviewed him about London Beatles Walks. Porter told me that he had spoken on numerous occasions over the years, and if he mentioned her in a Facebook post, she would receive 'misogynist and sexist abuse from Beatles fans' (Porter 2018). It is important to mention this in a chapter on 'fanaticism' and violence because this abuse of Yoko demonstrates an innate conservatism in fans who cannot move forward and accept change, whether that change is Yoko Ono leading John to embrace the *avant-garde* or to force fans into the realization that the boys' club (the Beatles) had to fragment and change. This *mal d'archive* had the fans of *Beatles Monthly* complaining in 1967 that the Beatles should stick to singing 'She Loves You'. This is the same stasis that Aaron Krerowicz speaks about when he asks fans to vote on the songs that would make the cut on to *The White Album* if it was only fifteen tracks: so far 'Revolution No 9' has never been voted on the single album. It is a deep inflexibility and unreconstructed bigotry and conservatism that leads to a refusal to accept change. The sexist and racist treatment of Yoko Ono by fans demonstrates this dark side of fandom as does the psychotic paralysis that kept Chapman and Abram mired in mental illnesses that went untreated and which they never mastered.

Mark Duffett told me that Chapman/Abram were suffering from mental illness and that is the best description of their psychological predicament, and they also happened to be Beatles fans. Duffett argues that it is practically impossible to know the paradoxes, psychological motivations and the kaleidoscopic mess of contradictory impulses that comprise a fan's mental furniture. The methodology for accessing any truth about what fans are thinking is through empirical research and participatory observation, even this has its limitations. However, in these cases, all the evidence points to two mentally ill men who have been pigeonholed by the media as a scary monster archetype. Both men were fans, but Beatles fandom was only a fractional part of their troubled psyches and complex make-up; and at the time of their breakdowns and violent attacks, they were simply sick men who were trapped in a *mal d'archive* and repetitive compulsion of violence. As Duffett argues, 'at this point of their psychological disintegration, and at the apex of their traumatic stasis, it is very dubious that they can even be considered Beatles fans' (Duffett 2018).

A discussion of Chapman's murder of John Lennon also links to the discussion of cultural tourism in Chapter 8. Fan spaces can be considered as toxic reminders of tragedy and are an unhealthy *mal d'archive*; fans who visit the Dakota Hotel where Chapman murdered Lennon, according to Lincoln Geraghty, indulge in these types of 'fan pilgrimages' which are 'geographic spaces in which, and through which, fans travel to get closer to their object of fandom. But it also about how those spaces can become toxic, acting as painful reminders of the object turned bad, tragic failure' (Geraghty 2018: http://www.participations.org/Volume%2015/Issue%201/19.pdf). Spencer Leigh, the author of *The Cavern Club: Rise of the Beatles and Merseybeat*, interviewed the Cavern's DJ Bob Wooler about the effect John Lennon's death had on the Beatles; he agrees that Lennon's murder was the key moment in the birth of fan conventions:

> One catastrophic event changed the city's attitude to the Beatles. Bob Wooler: 'The death of John Lennon at the end of 1980 transformed everything with regards to the Beatles. Everything became Beatleised. Sam Leach organised a very big candlelight vigil on St George's Plateau in Lime Street. David Shepherd, the Bishop of Liverpool, was there with other luminaries. The weather was kind to us: the event was free and extremely well attended, and it was very touching. I felt then there was a rebirth, a renaissance of the Beatles. It's extraordinary really but from the moment that John Lennon was shot by a crackpot, the whole attitude towards the Beatles changed. Beatles conventions have done very well since that date.' (Leigh 2016: 188)

John Lennon's assassination changed attitudes to the Beatles worldwide, and writing about John Lennon's death, Keith Badman agrees with Wooler, when he wrote in his Beatles Diary for the entry Tuesday, 9 December 1980: 'all around the world, the image, legend and devotion surrounding the Beatles will never be the same' (Badman 2001: 276).

And one of the aspects of this devotion is that Beatles fandom has the capacity to transform and appropriate death, trauma and toxic 'fan pilgrimages' into a positive living culture.

The legacy of Chapman and Abram is that we cannot have a fulfilled life without others and communities, fans or otherwise are essential to well-being; Carrielynn Reinhard summarizes Ting-Tommey's work on *Communicating Across Cultures* and makes the argument for connection and shoe swapping in her 'The Dark Side of Fandom', 'we need communication practices that facilitate self-expression and meaningful connection, especially across our differences and disagreements. ... Dialogue becomes the means to solve problem, but only if people can step out of the entrapment of adversarial individualism and argument culture' (Reinhard 2018: 18). Reinhard's work demonstrates that 'communication is fundamental to being human, as is having disagreements' and 'dialogue cannot be forced from the outside but nurtured, moment-to-moment, from the inside'. 'Fans' such as Chapman and Abram show the importance of 'dialogic communication ... an openness to new ideas, perspectives and willingness to change' (Reinhard 2018: 19).

5

'Images of broken light': The Beatles on YouTube

In the 1960s, the media, the Beatles' management and their record company EMI/Parlophone disseminated a carefully calculated image to Beatles fans. The Beatles canon was a top-down phenomenon with the fans in a subordinate position to the culture industry that grew up around the Beatles. The fans' reception and reaction to the Beatles was different before participatory culture such as YouTube was available to all. This chapter will investigate to what extent YouTube has radically altered the way fans receive, interact and disseminate the Beatles' music and image. Writing about Lincoln Geraghty's work, Michel S. Duffy suggests,

> Geraghty's most compelling riffs concentrate on how specific fandoms help generate and construct modes of behavior for individuals. Collecting and interactive fandom increasingly help consumers develop and maintain an 'endlessly-deferred narrative' (176) about the universe they're playing in, yet also allow them to maintain a 'transformative nostalgia' for their own personal connection to beloved characters and worlds. (Duffy 2014: 178, http://journal.transformativeworks.org/index.php/twc/article/view/584/444)

YouTube is an interactive forum where fans can make bricolage art melding together the memories of the past to create fan vids for the present. Geraghty's ideas about transformative nostalgia allow fans to create fresh, progressive texts which combine the old and the new, and YouTube transgresses the machinery of the music business to create bespoke fandom, though admittedly this interactive fandom remains couched in the economic envelope of big corporations and capitalism.

The Beatles' image was carefully guided and contrived by their manager Brian Epstein. With little objection from the Beatles, he changed their onstage demeanour. They stopped swearing, smoking and eating on stage and their Hamburg leather jackets and leather trousers were replaced with Pierre Cardin collarless suits. The Beatles were packaged and felt a process of commoditization was necessary to attain success in an age of capitalism and consumerism. The Beatles tailored their act to the pop industry of the day and in so doing compromised their personalities and their image.

The nascent popular music press of circa 1963 to 1964 bought into this image and called it Beatlemania. Beatlemania spread throughout the media, creating an image of the Swinging Sixties which was a media construction. The press clippings and the television clips from the period were used to create a series of hackneyed images representing 1960s.

As the decade progressed, the Beatles, buoyed up the countercultural politics of the period, became increasingly uncomfortable with their cuddly boy band image. By 1966, the image that had been created was slipping, as the band themselves began to deconstruct it. In a 1966 interview with Maureen Cleave of the *Evening Standard*, John Lennon suggested that the Beatles 'were more popular than Jesus now' (Maureen Cleave, 'How does a Beatle live? John Lennon lives like this', *Evening Standard*, 4 March 1966, p. 10), causing an uproar which almost led to their 1966 tour of the United States being cancelled. Paul McCartney also broke ranks in the *Summer of Love* (itself a media creation) to confess he had taken LSD. The Beatles look by this period has altered considerably. Gone were the identical pudding bowl haircuts and in their place were hippie moustaches and gypsy clothes that were *de rigueur* in the counterculture.

By the end of the decade, the Beatles deconstructed their image even further; John Lennon in an angry interview for the Rolling Stone (1970) called the Beatles' image and music a myth:

> I don't believe in the Beatles myth. I don't believe in the Beatles … I don't believe in them, whatever they were supposed to be in everybody's head, and including our own for a period. It was a dream. That's all. I don't believe in the dream anymore. (Wenner 2000: 134)

Lennon felt that aggressive marketing had promulgated a false image of the Beatles. He felt that their music and image were sanitized when they became successful. Despite all his efforts, the Beatles' iconography was synonymous with the 1960s and a top-down model of their image and music was put into effect with the fans in a subordinate position. In a sense, there was a pyramidal structure with the Beatles at the top, the press next and the fans at the bottom. It is only with the advent of interactive technology that this pyramid has been effectively challenged.

The iconography of the Beatles' records also puts a myth into effect. Their original British LPs are a visual chronology of the 1960s. Their first British album *Please Please Me* has the four musicians gazing down from the EMI offices in Manchester Square; the Beatles' attire is dark brown suits and identical fringe haircuts. Their second album *With the Beatles* is a photograph by Robert Freeman that captures the four faces in silhouette. *A Hard Day's Night*, *Beatles for Sale* (has there ever been a more ironic comment on the music industry), *Help* and *Rubber Soul* albums all have a cover shot of the four individuals as *gestalt*. The later albums *Sgt Pepper's Lonely Hearts Club Band*, *The White Album*, *Abbey Road* and *Let It Be* are equally as iconic, capturing the Beatles' image as it morphs into long-haired personifications of the counterculture. The album cover art is as powerful at creating and cementing an image as the music. Here we have the Beatles' image frozen in aspic: it is a visual history of the 1960s: a prescriptive visual gallery which saddles the Beatles audience with immutable pictorial imaginings of the decade.

The music is also constrained within these cultural commodities: the journey from two-minute pop songs on *Please Please Me* to the experimental sound collages on *The White Album* is again an exercise in popular historical chronology. The music and the cover art are a series of implacable texts that serve to create a visual and aural construction that the media and cultural historians have been able to assemble into a seamless line of cultural production.

It is easy to delineate a series of 'facts' about the cultural period if all Beatles product is viewed, listened to and read about through the lens of the culture industry. We are left with a series of cultural artefacts that represent the Beatles' music and career and which also bleed into a series of contrived media clichés about the Beatles.

The power of this image building by the music industry and the press tends to ignore one very important point. That is, the music, the DVDs and the cover art are a very carefully chosen, highly selected process. This selection process is made by big record companies, management, television and the press.

The art of the Beatles is disseminated from above and trickles down to the consumers. All the power comes from the media's big mouth and the consumer has no alternative but to listen. The image is so powerful that historians and a lazy media spread an image of a golden sunrise of creativity. Incidentally, Apple Records propagated this image further after the Beatles' break-up in the 1970s by releasing the *Red* and *Blue* albums: both compilations of their greatest that neatly confine the Beatles' image and music to succinct historical periods.

However, there have been exceptions to this orthodoxy. The Christian writer Christopher Booker saw the 1960s as a society in moral decline and the Beatles symbolized this decline by putting a fantasy into effect; and a fantasy which was aided and abetted by technology, 'Technology has re-shaped society, breaking up the organic unity in all directions. It has cut man off from nature, distorted the scale and pace off his life, and deprived him of the chance to make meaningful patterns out of his work' (Booker 1992: 346).

Booker felt that the Beatles' music and the industry was a machine which manipulated teenagers into buying shallow ephemera: Beatles records, films and fanzines; and that this acquisitiveness was a symptom of a society in sharp moral decline. Booker is also prescient about the influence of YouTube and fan vid culture, that is, YouTube 'breaking up organic unity' of the Beatles' image and emancipating the fans to participate in the cultural meanings of Beatles texts, but his writing on technology is entirely pejorative and he fails to predict the participatory possibilities of technology. Historian David Fowler in his book *Youth Culture in Modern Britain* sees the Beatles as capitalist opportunists who are the antithesis of the countercultural values. Fowler felt that university students represented 1960s radicalism, not pop stars like the Beatles. To Fowler, 'the key groups that could have generated a Youth Culture were not pop stars but university students' (Fowler 2008: 177). To Fowler, the Beatles represented the conservative values of the music industry and, like Booker, he doesn't feel their work can break free from its capitalist and hegemonic context.

However, neither critic has engaged with the new technology which has been instrumental in deconstructing the Beatles' manufactured image: first as lovable pop stars in the years 1962–5 and then as hippie idealists in the years 1966–70. If either Booker or Fowler had been aware of the new technology, their thesis that the Beatles' canon was an irrelevant fantasy would have had much more weight. YouTube has deconstructed, reappropriated and de-historicized the Beatles' cultural monolith more effectively than Booker and Fowler's work. The fans also show a sensitivity and intelligence to the Beatles art that is completely missing in Fowler and Booker's dismissal of the Beatles' work.

Nevertheless, the significance of Booker and Fowler's retrospective analysis of the Beatles' cultural significance is that their work chipped away at the monolith in a similar manner to the YouTube generation. In a sense fans, journalists and academics have a commonality. That is, deconstructing, translating and reconfiguring accepted canons into new shapes.

In 1995, Apple released a DVD of all the remaining Beatles archives. The difference with other media constructions, such as the press and television, was that the Beatles, their producer George Martin and assorted friends and colleagues reminisced on their own experience of the 1960s. The first and most startling aspect of this attempt to tell their own story was the fact that they contradicted themselves from start to finish. To the Beatles themselves the chronology of their work was not a seamless series of albums and films but a kaleidoscope of contradictory memories. Added to this mess of opposing impulses was the fact the DVD, which seemed to point to another exercise in Beatle canon building, included many out-takes and alternative versions of their songs as well as previously unseen footage.

So technology and unreliable memory had inadvertently set off a process of deconstruction. The technology is fundamental for setting these wheels in motion. For the first time the viewer is offered a non-linear and piecemeal version of history. We have access to never before seen clips that are framed in a celluloid shudder, the very ethereality of which eschew fixed historical positions, totality and any sense of grand narrative. We have micro-narratives that have been possible by a technological collage. This is only the first stage in deconstruction as the DVD is not interactive: we are getting an alternative version of the Beatles' canon, but it is still filtered by Apple Corps. However, with the advent of new media all this changed when the audience began interrogating the canon of the Beatles' work on their own terms. The moment when the carefully prescribed version of history was challenged was when YouTube began in 2005.

Before we look at the effect new technology has had on the Beatles' image and music it is apposite to look at the history of YouTube. DIY television, what became YouTube, was started in 2005 by Chad Hurley, Steve Chen and Jawed Karim who were employees of PayPal. It grew rapidly, becoming the third most used internet site after Google and Yahoo. By July 2006, the site was receiving 65,000 new videos every day and 100 million video views per day. YouTube now has a market share of approximately 44 per cent and more than 5 billion videos were viewed in July 2008. On 13 November 2006, Google bought YouTube for a reported 1.65 billion dollars.

The important cultural ramifications of this were that for the first time there was a forum where ordinary consumers could post and share their own videos. In a very real sense cultural clout now lay with the consumer and nowhere did this pay more dividend than with the image and music of the Beatles. A very carefully controlled and packaged cultural phenomenon was now virtually unrecognizable.

The free exchange of videos has kept the music and images fresh. Not only are pieces of music augmented with video and comment, but the forum has provided a wealth of original material that has not been seen or heard before. YouTube also broadcasts rehearsals and out-takes that mainstream media organizations have not broadcast. The amateur nature of much of this previously unreleased material also raises profound questions about the nature of celebrity. Here we have rehearsals of songs and lyrics that do not sound polished and are not ready to be presented to the world. As Lennon said discussing the *Let It Be* project with Jann Wenner in 1970, we now have the Beatles 'with no trousers on and no glossy paint over the cover and no sort of hype' (Wenner 2000: 102). YouTube videos show the Beatles rehearsing, arguing in the studio, out-takes and fans' videos with 'no glossy paint'.

So 'The Beatles with their trousers down' is due to technological innovation. Just as the social phenomenon of the Beatles in the early 1960s would not have happened without a certain technological determinism: since the 1930s Britain had been on the national grid giving electricity to every home and this gives the general public access, through technology, to the image and music of the Beatles. It was technology that contributed hugely to their initial success through electricity, record players and then television, but it was an image that was possible to control and market in specific ways. This totalitarian aspect of the music industry and capitalism, in general, is something that Herbert Marcuse identified in *One-Dimensional Man*, first published in 1964:

> The incessant dynamic of technical progress has become permeated with political content, and the Logos of technics has been made into the Logos of continued servitude. The liberating force of technology, the instrumentalization of all things, turns into a fetter of liberation; the instrumentalization of man. (Marcuse 2002 [1964]: 163)

Here Marcuse's words could be describing the top-down music industry of the 1960s: a totalitarian industry where technology enslaves instead of liberating fans. YouTube changed this, giving us a highly interactive and fragmented view of the Beatles phenomenon. Until the ubiquity of new technology, consumers and Beatles fans were in a subordinate position to the culture spread by the music industry. With YouTube, they experienced 'the technical impossibility of being autonomous, of determining one's own life' (Herbert Marcuse, *One-Dimensional Man*, 2002: 162).

The development of the new technology has made this possible, elevating to the role of cultural producer and also changing the very essence of creativity. In the 1960s, 1970s and even the 1980s the consumer held onto the vestige of a post-romantic and individualistic concept of genius as the repository of a group or individuals.

The technological revolution of the latter part of the twentieth century has changed all this. Art is now seen as collaboration: a group effort. Nowhere is this truer than the

Beatles. It is a collective effort of managers, producers, song writers, arrangers, press officers, film directors and sleeve designers. We would be forgiven for not noticing this until the advent of YouTube which brings the strings of the puppets into sharp relief. This is not to diminish the core of the Beatles art and music, which is still Lennon, McCartney, Harrison and Starr, but to paraphrase Roland Barthes, the 'Death of the Author' is the birth of the consumer.

Walter Benjamin in 'The Work of Art in the Age of Mechanical Reproduction' (1935) quotes from Paul Valery's 'Aesthetics: The Conquest of Ubiquity'. Here we have prescient words that help clarify my argument about the effect YouTube has had on art. Valey suggested, 'We must expect great innovations to transform the entire technique of the arts, thereby affecting artistic invention itself and perhaps even bringing about an amazing change in our very notion of art' (Benjamin 1999: 211). He goes on to capture the ubiquity of technology, which applies as easily to YouTube today: just as water, gas, electricity are brought into our houses from far off to satisfy our needs in response to a minimal effort, so we shall be supplied with visual or auditory images, which will appear and disappear at a simple movement of the hand, hardly more than a sign (Benjamin 1999: 212).

In a profound sense reality is reconfigured and the artistic object is loosed from stolid and fixed meanings. Traditional media has been transgressed to such an extent that we (the audience) are cultural producers. YouTube has given the audience the freedom to resist the commoditization of culture. The Beatles' music and image breaks free from the constraints of big record companies and global producers: fans become creative consumers. They produce sound collages, parodies, versions of songs and post interviews and clips that were presumed lost and, more importantly, fans customize this as their own hybrid product. As Walter Benjamin puts it, 'the technique of reproduction detaches the reproduced object from the domain of tradition' (Benjamin 1999: 125).

As far as the Beatles and their image are concerned, two significant paradigmatic shifts in how we disseminate and receive information have been influential in our understanding of their work. It was a technological determinism (first the national grid and television) that put an image in the public consciousness: albeit a simulation of the real, but a simulation that was difficult to challenge. Something John Lennon recognized in his infamous *Rolling Stone* Jan Wenner interview: the Beatles' image continued because people wanted a fixed image to continue. The Beatles, their entourage and the fans had been seduced by a simulation, and the Beatles were afraid to break away from such a powerful consensus. Lennon felt their image was so sanitized and commoditized that success had ruined the Beatles, 'But as soon as we made it the edges we knocked off. Brian Epstein put us in suits and that, and we made it very, very big. We sold out. The music was dead before we even went on the theatre tour of Britain' (Wenner 2000: 20).

In an organic sense, the Beatles' music was marketed into a cultural product and Lennon realized this; and expressed bitterness that their art had been compromised to a money-making capitalist machine. However, this interview is prescient as it deconstructs the Beatles' work, an act of self-deconstruction. In this interview, he also alluded to the acceptance of the Beatles as a national institution when they received their MBEs from the Queen: the Beatles had become institutionalized.

Lennon's interview is important as it delineates the point at which a relatively fixed media construction was about to change. Television and the national grid promoted a dominant image which came from above and was mediated through record companies. In 2002 with YouTube the basic character of top-down information had changed. Art now came from the bottom-up, that is, from the consumer. The fans were no longer in a subordinate and reactive role, they were proactive.

Benjamin addressed the idea that a seemingly unbreakable nexus between artist and fan had been broken. 'The distinction between author and public is about to lose its basic character' (Benjamin 1999: 225), he wrote in 1935. In 2002 his words proved to apply to the changes in the manner in which we receive information and broadcast information.

The main revelation about the Beatles on YouTube is twofold. The wealth of original material that hasn't been seen or heard before by the Beatles themselves and the new hybrid forms produced by the consumer. Fans have posted out-takes and unreleased performances of songs on YouTube. It is, for example, the first time that the song 'India' has been available to a mass of people. The same goes for experimental music such as 'Carnival of Light'. There are out-takes from the Maharishi's ashram in Rishikesh. In 1968 in Rishikesh, the Beatles recorded songs such as 'Brian Epstein's Blues', 'Child of Nature' and 'Spiritual Regeneration' which had never been heard beyond a niche of hard-core Beatles fans. On YouTube, their songs had also been augmented by the fans' own creativity: they had posted video images to accompany these songs.

The same process has been applied to unseen material such as The Mad Day Out session on 28 July 1968 and to rarely seen images of the Beatles backstage at their 1966 concerts at the Budokan in Japan. The result of these minutiae of Beatles imagery is a changed perception of their lives and work, diverging from the music and image that previously comprised the Beatles canon for two reasons. Firstly, we get a hybrid of Beatle texts, fan vids that use the Beatles' image and music to create a new work of art, for instance, an innovative collage of Beatles photographs and video created by the fans. Secondly, there is unseen Beatles material on YouTube that fans have unearthed for the first time.

The creative consumerism of YouTube has resulted in the Beatles' work being reinvigorated by the fans' input. The numerous reworking of their songs is seemingly endless. The consequence of this is a celebration of the transitory. Their canon is removed from its old signature in space and time. Their work has been cut loose from its 1960s event and context. Fans and musicians have radically altered the Beatles canon. In fact the postings are so diverse in quality and range that they have a very ephemeral life on YouTube.

The work on YouTube has an ethereal and insubstantial quality: there is impermanence to the 'art' posted on YouTube. It is a fragility that adds poignancy to the Beatles art.

Many contemporary musicians such as Jay Z and Danger Mouse have posted their own reworking of classic Beatles songs. They have famously mashed the Beatles canon adding a hip-hop and dance dimension to their music. They and many other contemporary artists use innovative techniques to produce 'new' material and in fact so much of it is so convincing that it is often difficult to distinguish the imitators and the satirists from the Beatles themselves. So at the heart of the developments in the new media is a paradox. The Beatles' music and image are a text that is on one hand wedded to the 1960s. Their songs and image are a text that opens a window on the society that produced it: just like a Dickens novel tells us about Victorian Britain and a Shakespeare play gives us insight into Renaissance England. However, new technology and particularly YouTube translates their work in a variety of texts which tell us about 2010. As Benjamin puts it, 'The mass is a matrix from which all traditional behaviour toward work of art issues today in a new form' (Benjamin 1999: 232). We have a dual interpretation of old and classic works of art. The traditional canon of the Beatles' songs opens a vista on the 1960s while a reinterpretation of their work by a contemporary audience conveys society as it is today and also creates a new consumer-led form of art. The ramifications of this are immense, the empowerment of the audience and their ability to control Beatles product for a new audience and to keep alive the optimism and power of those beautiful songs. The songs are now our property: they are the product of the consumer. This is a good thing depending on our aesthetic perception. If we are precious about Beatles art it is possible that YouTube sacrifices the quality of the Beatles' music. To some, no doubt, the dubious quality of mashing the Beatles canon is a sunless chasm of imaginative dearth which has sacrificed the original context and meanings of their art. This is not true.

The original canon is there to be appreciated and still informs us about the art, politics and culture of this decade. However, YouTubers now 'brush aside a number of outmoded concepts, such as creativity and genius, eternal value and mystery-concepts whose uncontrolled application would lead to a processing of data in the Fascist sense' (Benjamin 1999: 212).

In a sense YouTube is a golden sunrise of imaginative possibility. The multifarious rare out-takes, rare press conferences, lost studio tapes, Beatles parodies (The Rutles, Peter Serafinowicz; a slew of spoofs by unknown fans such as The Teables and the Rutbeats and even a Sesame Street parody) along with posting of the home videos of John, Paul, George and Ringo demonstrate how technological innovation has translated the Beatles' work anew and how this material is a necessary resource for Beatles scholars and a riposte to Beatles mythology. YouTube refutes Beatles mythology because it offers fans an interactive smattering of new and dynamic Beatles-related material.

The user-generated content on YouTube has permanently dented the monolith of the Beatles cultural industry. It has promulgated an interactive forum that deconstructs and translates the Beatles' image and music anew. Simultaneously it puts an alternative cyber canon into effect. A canon that does not exist physically the way the previous cultural artefacts of the 1960s and 1970s did; but it is an alternative canon nonetheless. Jean Burgess and Joshua Green discussed the archival possibilities of YouTube in 2009. 'In fact, if YouTube remains in existence for long enough, the result will be not only a repository of vintage video content but also something more significant: a record of contemporary global popular culture (including vernacular and everyday culture) in video form, produced and evaluated according to the logics of cultural value that emerge from the collective choices of the distributed YouTube user community. YouTube is thus evolving into a massive heterogeneous, but for the most part accidental and disordered, public archive' (Burgess and Green 2009: 88).

Although there is the creation of an archive it differs in many significant ways to the traditional Beatles canon. The user participates in the meanings of the text and when the canon is reviewed, changed and updated, it doesn't have to go through the official of the music business. In the case of the Beatles that is the Apple organization. In a real sense, we have a constantly shifting archive, the pace of which is dictated by the audience interaction and not established record companies. The way the Beatles' work is disseminated has been completely reconfigured by YouTube. Their work is now more random, more fragmentary and creatively evolving into a public sphere that is dictated by the audience. YouTube has radically changed how we spread and receive information.

YouTube is predicated on individualism and entrepreneurism like the 1960s counterculture which produced the Beatles and their work. Subcultures in the 1960s and the noughties were the result of 'doing your own thing. ... they were uninhibited examples of private enterprise' (Marwick 1998: 17).

Moreover, there is also a technological determinism at work here. Just as the national grid and the affluent society created a ready and eager audience for the Beatles, so new technology has morphed into individualistic and technical realm where institutional control is difficult to maintain. Technology, and the more innovative the better, keeps the Beatles' work in the stream of contemporary digital culture. The importance of technology to maintaining and expanding the Beatles art is recognized by Ian MacDonald, writing about the 1960s: 'Far away from us on the other side of the sun-flooded chasm of 1960s – where courtesy of technology, The Beatles can still be heard singing their buoyant, poignant, hopeful, love-advocating songs' (MacDonald 2008: 37). Technology keeps their work alive and keeps it flexible. It is an essential paradox: YouTube creates an archive and at the same time shatters it into subversive fragments.

Although technology is a great enabler, it is important to state that new media exacerbated, and gave a forum to, a tendency in fan culture that had always existed: that is, reappropriating the dominant cultural meanings of a text. In the case of Beatlemania, fans always participated aggressively. There were two elements to this. Firstly, the hysteria surrounding the Beatles was on a scale that had been previously unknown in pop history; secondly, fans were empowered by creating fanzines: cultural spaces where the original meanings of the Beatles' image and music are translated into a series of meaning beyond the original text. Taking the Beatles' work and changing it is a feature that has recurred throughout the Beatles' career (the Paul is dead rumours that were read into the *Abbey Road* and the *Sgt Pepper's* album are an example of this).[1] As Henry Jenkins has suggested in his book *Textual Poachers*, 'Fans construct their cultural and social identity through borrowing and inflecting mass culture images, articulating concerns which often go unvoiced within the dominant media' (Jenkins 1992: 23).

As early as 1963, fandom was recirculating the Beatles' image and work into the fans' own products: magazines and subcultural groups. From the beginning, the hysteria surrounding the Beatles wrested control from the Beatles themselves and their organizations; and this was predicated on the ferocity of fan worship. 'In its intensity, as well as its scale, Beatlemania surpassed all previous outbreaks of star-centred hysteria. Young women has swooned over Frank Sinatra in the forties and screamed for Elvis Presley in the immediate pre-Beatle years, but the Fab Four inspired an extremity of feeling usually reserved for football games or natural disasters' (Ehrenreich, Hess and Jacobs 1992: 86).

The level of hysteria that was directed at the Beatles from the beginning of their career resulted in one of the biggest social and cultural phenomenon of the twentieth century. As their press officer Derek Taylor puts it, the Beatles relationship to their audience was 'the twentieth century's greatest romance' (Derek Taylor, The Beatles Anthology DVD Sleeve notes to episodes 7 & 8, 'July '68 to the End').

However, like many romances it turned sour. George Harrison was brutally attacked by a fan in 1999 and was lucky to survive the assault. John Lennon was stalked and eventually murdered by a deranged fan in 1980. The social contract between the Beatles and their fans was always very tense and obsessive, so the ubiquity of user-generated content concerning the Beatles was no surprise. A forum where all the content is created by the audience is a suitable coda to their career.

The ramification of this *volte-face* away from the creators and towards the audience is that any top-down prescriptive dissemination of the Beatles' image and music is unlikely in the future: the essence of how information is spread and shared has been radically changed by YouTube. New cultural products have been created by this participatory culture:

> This development takes us toward an interesting future where the ratio between the amount of professionally generated content and the amount of user-generated content available online is asymptotically approaching zero. In other words, almost all content available online is user-generated and only a small fraction is created by those people who actually write texts, make movies or sing songs professionally. In a world coloured by virtues of the remix culture it will become virtually impossible to charge users for simple access to content. It is interesting to speculate how such a development will affect the professional development of popular culture. Probably it will be increasingly difficult to create profitable entertainment projects such as full-length motion pictures or traditional music albums. In order to survive, the producers should rather focus on providing tools and building blocks for users to create their own material. (Wikstrom 2009: 159)

Given the mass insanity that surrounded the Beatles, the fans aggressively 'poached' the Beatles' work. Before digital technology, the Beatles fame was predicated on a technological determinism that reacted to and spread their image. Technological determinism means the Beatles' music spread so rapidly because society's infrastructure disseminating the Beatles' work on television, though records and the print and visual media; without this platform, it is likely that they would have remained in obscurity, and because of this technological infrastructure, if the Beatles hadn't taken advantage of this environment, another band would have taken their place. This technological *quid pro quo* was the basis for obsessive mania that eventually was to result in the YouTube generation. Beatles' texts had been transgressed and 'mashed' early on in their career. This idolatry was a phenomenon, although not unique to the Beatles, but in the case of twentieth-century popular phenomena, it is the most extreme example. The fan and press reaction to the Beatles was unprecedented:

> By 1966 the Beatles' longevity-unprecedented for pop stars at the time-had made them and their music objects of a kind of scrutiny and study previously reserved for venerated religious leaders and sacred texts. Their every move was chronicled by fan magazines, music trade publications, and even the mainstream press. The daily newspapers of every city on the 1966 U.S. tour printed a front-page story about the Beatles on the day after their appearance. (Schneider 2008: 169)

What is most notable about this obsessive fandom is the rejection of prescriptive and hegemonic cultural industries such as the Beatles' marketing machine. Here the fans and the press are participating in shared cultural meaning. The totalistic meanings of Adorno's culture industry are rejected by this obsessive fan madness:

> Today every monster close-up of a star is an advertisement for her name, and every hit song a plug for its tune. Advertising and the culture industry merge technically as well as economically. In both cases the same thing can be seen in innumerable places, and the mechanical repetition of the same culture product has come to be the same as the propaganda slogan. In both cases the insistence demand for effectiveness makes technology into psycho-technology for manipulating men. (Adorno and Horkheimer 1997: 163)

Adorno's argument presupposes that fans are obedient and an unenlightened mass, but fan forums from the early 1960s to YouTube have distinguished to what extent fan cultures are empowered and own culture (here the Beatles' image and music). It is also important to note that this cultural empowerment occurs in a particular socio-economic framework: 'Empowerment of textual poachers who are able to turn "textual gamekeepers" does not occur within a transhistorical or essentialist space. Rather, it occurs quite precisely within the economic and cultural parameters of niche marketing whereby fan-consumers and producers are more closely aligned with a common "reception sphere" or interpretative community' (Hills 2002: 40).

In other words, fans have been appropriating the products of the cultural industry (in the specific case of the Beatles) since the early 1960s; however, it is an important point that fan culture is an enabler only when couched in a very particular historical and social group. Fans cannot be homogenized and the history of fan participation is predicated on clear technological and historical factors. Without technology to spread product, there is no product; and these products (Beatles merchandise) cease to have prescriptive meaning when the audience interprets these works in the context of their own lives. So the digital generation will mix, mash and superimpose new meanings on old texts.

In a very real sense, the Beatles' music is transformed by YouTube. In this fan forum we get an accommodation between the traditional products of the old top-down music industry colliding with the new technological world. This has to be a good thing, although not all critics are as happy with electronic and digital hybrids. The music critic Ian MacDonald writes,

> As software, sequencing is the controlling technology in almost everything recorded in popular music in the last fifteen years. In a nutshell, it allows anyone, however unmusical, to organise musical material into a semblance of composed and performed sound – the ultimate democratising technology of our time. Moreover, this technology is employed throughout modern popular music, almost all chart pop being built up on a sequenced chassis, its parts controlled for offline, EQ and mixing purposes by the sequencer, using MIDI protocol. As such, the sequencer constitutes the final step in the shift from popular music industry to the industry of the people's music. This is particularly true of dance music. Using the technology of sequencer, sampler and synthesiser, anyone can organise the basis of a dance record in their bedroom within minutes. When this fact is combined with limited pressing of twelve-inch white labels to be distributed to club DJs, the music industry made its final transition from popular music returned to where it had all started in the mid-eighteenth-century, the orbital 'raves' of the late eighties paralleling the evening jaunts to the pleasure gardens of Kew and Vauxhall. (MacDonald 2003: 202)

Although writing about electronic music, MacDonald is repeating Adorno's theories about a highly commoditized culture manipulating an ignorant and gullible population. His words are pejorative about sampled dance music, he sees sequenced music as unmusical. In fact, it is anti-music:

> Pop and is shatteringly sensationalistic cousins rock, disco, and 'rave' music have been as much colonised by technology as any other are of modern life. Its once flexible human rhythms replaced by the mass-production regularity of the drum-machine, its structures corporatized by the factory ethic of the sequencer, its vitality disguised to death and buried in multi-layered syntheticism, pop is now little more than soundtrack for physical jerks. (MacDonald 1998: 30–1)

The hybrid videos of Jay Z mashing the Beatles would be a crime comparable to the rise of amateur dance music in the eyes of MacDonald. MacDonald didn't write explicitly about YouTube, but the digital hybrid text of remixed Beatles' music would not be to his taste: too amateur and too disrespectful of the canon.

YouTube, then, is a hybrid of the cultural monolithic canon of Beatles' film clips and music combined with amateurish poaching mentality that creates a new text.

It has also put into effect an archive of rare and never seen before material for fans and researchers. It has de-historicized the shallow media chronology of 1960s Beatles albums: the Beatles myth has been deconstructed and reworked into a twenty-first-century mongrel text.

The nature of art has also been radically altered by YouTube: post-Romantic notions of creativity. The work of art is no longer seen as a repository of individual genius but creativity is a bricolage composed by a group effort: the diverse group of fans participating in the Beatles monolith in a highly subversive manner.

A trawl through YouTube gives us access to a kaleidoscopic slew of diverse Beatles texts. Every song, film, interview or public appearance is available online in a new form. YouTube quite simply changes any preconception about the Beatles or their work. It is a digital cubism capturing the Beatles from many new angles. A project to list, review and archive this material would be a life's work and, unlike the old canon, it is a constantly shifting visual text.

The ephemeral quality of much of this material coupled with the subversive participatory nature of YouTube has replaced experts with amateurs:

> Thus far the commercial media and entertainment industries have pursued an industrial or expert-system model of production, where professionals manufacture stories, experiences and identities for the rest of us to consume. This system is representative, both in the sense that 'we' are represented onscreen and in the sense that a tiny band of professionals 'represents' us all. The productivity of the system is measured not by the number of ideas propagated or stories told, but by the number of dollars earned per story. Thus, over the past century, cinema, radio, and television have all organized and scaled human storytelling into an industrial system, where millions watch but mere hundreds do the writing. Broadcast media speak to and on behalf of us all in anonymous cultures. (Burgess and Green 2009: 132–3)

So we get a dynamic process where experts and amateurs collide and this collision results in a fora where, 'bottom-up (DIY consumer-based) and top-down' (industrial expert based) knowledge generation connects and interacts' (Burgess and Green 2009: 133). The innovation of YouTube represents the growth of 'the mediated world, one of signs and symbols, meanings and understandings' and this 'semiotic system ... has real economic and political power'. In the specific example of the Beatles words and lyrics, YouTube is technology that 'can create a gesture that is magical, unique, poetic, but that can change and transform the very nature of power' (Burgess and Green 2009: 133). But not forgetting that it is still owned by one of the biggest multinationals in the world: the epitome of the capitalist machine.

For instance, a song such as 'Across the Universe' is supplemented with the fans' own collage of images changing the context and meaning of the song. It is cut free from bonds that tie it to Beatles and their cultural monolith, but words and music remain intact: here is a synthesis of the amateur and professional hybrid which change the reception and dissemination of a text. Texts are created by the audience for the audience.

'Across the Universe' appeared on the Beatles' final album, *Let It Be*, released in 1970. The song's lyrics are typical of a 1960s countercultural text (indeed the song was written in 1968 in Maharishi's ashram) as Eastern concepts of ego-death and the fragmented nature of human essence are the song's narrative (She Loves You, it is not). The song challenges the notion of an immutable human essence with hippie countercultural lyrics: 'Images of broken light which dance before like a million eyes, They call me on and on across the universe' (The Beatles, *Let It Be*: 1970). The gist of this text is a Buddhistic ego death, the contingency of all knowledge and the seeming randomness and flux of reality. The song recognizes the impermanence of being and contrasts this with 'eternal undying love'. Fixity is challenged in this song and in a similar manner YouTubers and fan vids interrogate notions of the inflexibility in the Beatles' canon. On YouTube, 'images of broken light' resonate with the Beatles' song and image reinterpreting their work for a contemporary audience.

YouTube's fan cultures are the antithesis theorists, like Adorno and Fowler, who feel that fans of popular culture are passive consumers. YouTubers also challenge official culture as their fan vids are affirmed on production and participation in cultural texts. Technology such as YouTube creates hybrid Beatles 'fan artists' ... who 'rework industrial texts according to self-proclaimed priorities' (Lewis 1992: 5).

Beatles fandom is such a sharp *volte-face* away from the creators and towards the audience that any top-down prescriptive dissemination of the Beatles' image and music is very unlikely in the future. The essence of how information is spread and shared has been radically changed by YouTube. New cultural products have been created by this participatory culture:

> This development takes us toward an interesting future where the ratio between the amount of professionally generated content and the amount of user-generated content available online is asymptotically approaching zero. In other words, almost all content available online is user-generated and only a small fraction is created by those people who actually write texts, make movies or sing songs professionally. In a world coloured by virtues of the remix culture it will become virtually impossible to charge users for simple access to content. It is interesting to speculate how such a development will affect the professional development of popular culture. Probably it will be increasingly difficult to create profitable entertainment projects such as full-length motion pictures or traditional music albums. In order to survive, the producers should rather focus on providing tools and building blocks for users to create their own material. (Wikstrom 2009: 159)

YouTube is the forum where fans have aggressively 'poached' (Jenkins 1992) the Beatles' work. Here through fan vids, the fans have radically mashed the Beatles' songs, film, interviews and still photography into new texts. Fan vids is the phenomenon of fans making their own tribute videos of the Beatles and posting them on YouTube.

For the first time there was a forum where ordinary consumers could post and share their own videos. In a very real sense cultural clout now lay with the consumer and nowhere did this pay more dividend than with the image and music of the Beatles.

A very carefully controlled and packaged cultural phenomenon was now virtually unrecognizable.

The free exchange of videos has kept the music and images fresh. Not only are pieces of music augmented with video and comment, but the forum has provided a wealth of original material that has not been seen or heard before. YouTube also broadcasts rehearsals and out-takes that mainstream media organizations have not broadcast.

YouTube gives us access to a dizzying variety of 'new' Beatles texts. Every song, film, interview or public appearance is available online in a new form. YouTube quite simply changes any preconception about the Beatles or their work. It is a digital cubism capturing the Beatles from many new angles. A project to list, review and archive this material would be a life's work and, unlike the old canon, it is a constantly shifting visual text. The participatory nature of YouTube has replaced experts with amateurs:

> Thus far the commercial media and entertainment industries have pursued an industrial or expert-system model of production, where professionals manufacture stories, experiences and identities for the rest of us to consume. This system is representative, both in the sense that 'we' are represented onscreen and in the sense that a tiny band of professionals 'represents' us all. The productivity of the system is measured not by the number of ideas propagated or stories told, but by the number of dollars earned per story. Thus, over the past century, cinema, radio, and television have all organised and scaled human storytelling into an industrial system, where millions watch but mere hundreds do the writing. Broadcast media speak to and on behalf of us all in anonymous cultures. (Burgess and Green 2009: 132–3)

The result of the YouTube generation is a dynamic process where fans (amateurs) have offered an alternative to an 'industrial system' of experts. YouTube is a forum where a 'bottom-up (DIY consumer-based)' fan activity has superseded 'top-down industrial expert based knowledge' (Burgess and Green 2009: 132–3). The creation of YouTube signals a period in history where experts have been replaced by fans.

YouTube and reimagining the old

YouTube cannot be dismissed as *Retromania*; it makes the old new, and not just in a cosmetic way. Beatles texts are so comprehensively mashed that they are barely recognizable and the transgressive, and often abusive, comments by subscribers are instant cannibalism creating new psychological perspectives. So YouTube is retrospection, but not the mainstream retrospection of most pop culture: Oasis, Robbie Williams and Harry Styles who all recycle Beatles riffs. Mark Fisher sees this type of music as a feature of 'late capitalism':

> The other explanation for the link between late capitalism and retrospection centres on production. Despite all its rhetoric of novelty and innovation, neoliberalism

capitalism has gradually but systematically deprived artists of the resources necessary to produce the new. In the UK, the post-war welfare state and higher education maintenance grants constituted an indirect source of funding for of the experiments in popular culture between the 1960s and the 80s. The subsequent ideological and practical attack on public services meant that one of the spaces where artists could be sheltered from the pressure to produce something that was immediately successful was severely circumscribed. As public service became 'marketised', there was an increased tendency to turn out cultural productions that resembled what was already successful. The result of all this is that social time available for withdrawing from work and immersing oneself in cultural production drastically declined. (Fisher 2014: 15)

This 'pressure' and scarcity of time has meant that digital cultures such as YouTube are a forum where we have bricolage: that is, retrospective texts (Beatles films) that are mashed with new sounds, and we also have a bricolage of the artist fan, who uses the new digital spaces to reimagine the old. So we have 'novelty and innovation' online circumscribing the old materiality for instant gratification and artistic fan expression: that is fan vid art and ribald fan commentary. In a sense fans are animating a cadaver with their digital experiments, and these ghostly presences are 'throwing up anxieties about issues of media authority and control' (Burgess and Green 2009: 36–7); and fan vid ghosts 'oscillate between two dominant explanatory frameworks for the website – YouTube as a player in the commercial new media landscape on the one hand (the top-down view) and YouTube as a site of vernacular creativity and lawless disruption on the other (the bottom up view)' (Burgess and Green 2009: 37). I subscribe this 'vernacular creativity' view, as the Beatles vids (Danger Mouse's mash-ups) and the accompanying Rabelais-esque, Marquis de Sade-esque comments are transgressive and fan vids take the past and make it forward-looking, Fisher I feel is demonstrating through his writing that Beatles fan vids are an 'impersonal melancholy' (2009: 156); their shuddering ghostly simulations of the past are a Janus-faced hauntology: while looking back we indulge in nostalgia but then we create knew meaning by refurbishing the old with new visual, fresh sounds and indiscrete comments:

'Here you see old sunlight from other times and other lives' … To leaf through other people's family photos, to see moments that were of intense emotional significance for them but which mean nothing to you, is, necessarily, to reflect on the times of high drama in your own life, and to achieve a kind of distance that is at once dispassionate and powerfully affecting. That is why the – beautifully, painfully – dilated moment in Tarkovsky's Stalker where the camera lingers over talismanic objects that were once saturated with meaning, but are now only saturated with water is me the most moving scene in cinema. It is as if we are seeing urgencies of our lives through the eyes of an Alien-God. Otto claims that the sense of the numinous is associated with feelings of our fundamental worthlessness, experienced with a 'piercing acuteness [and] accompanied by the most uncompromising judgement of self-deprecation'. But contrary to today's ego psychology, which hectors us into reinforcing our sense of self (all the better to 'sell ourselves'); the awareness of our own Nothingness is of course a pre-requisite for a feeling of grace. There is a melancholy dimension to this grace precisely because it involves a radical distanciation from what is ordinarily most important to us. (Fisher 2014 : 157)

The Paul McCartney song 'I Want to Come Home' on YouTube is an example of bricolage; a McCartney song is bound to a series of nostalgic ghostly images of the Beatles, the melancholy music accompanies a video which is a God-eye, omniscient snapshot of the Beatles' career. The moves through a series of iconic images made new and sad by the incongruous McCartney song: there are the black-and-white Pierre Cardin-suited Beatles, wide-eyed and smiling beneficently on the psycho-drama of the new fame; the psychedelic Beatles frolicking beneath the Giacometti, stark Gothic tree from the *Strawberry Fields Forever* video; the outgrown mop tops of the 'Rain' video, matching each other's gazes while performing and giggling the absurdity of their fame; the Shea Stadium Beatles blinking myopically in the dark crowd who are illuminated only by the studded light of thousands of press flash bulbs; the gig on the Apple rooftop infused with a real melancholy as we know we are looking at their gig together: Ringo's raincoat is preternaturally red, John's cold red nose and unPC fur coat is a bleak contrast with George's lime green trousers and Paul's dark Mr Fish suit, a bleak premonition of the demise of the band and his Pavarotti beard obscures the deep hurt of the Beatles' imminent break-up. As we watch these rapid images flip past our eye, the pathos of the McCartney song makes us mourn for our own lost past and fear for our new unknown futures; McCartney's singing transforming clichés about sun and moon into Yeatsian symbols of loss (see *The Song of Wandering Aengus*), 'And pluck to time and times are done/the silver apples of the moon/the golden apples of the sun' (Yeats 2008: 30); 'For so long/I was out in the cold/And I taught myself to believe/ Every story I told/It was fun hanging onto the moon/Heading into the sun/But it's been too long/Now I want to come home/' (McCartney, 'I Want to Go Home', https://www. youtube.com/watch?v=8aWFIHcYwlo).

This minor McCartney track is very constructive about fandom because it is an example of how sentimental nostalgia can morph into progressive nostalgia by the inventive art of collage which creates a bricolage text that takes old images and mixes them with a contemporary McCartney song to make a new fan vid, and such fan creativity is the apotheosis of a fan, 'Fans feel for feelings sake. They build identities and experiences, and make artistic creations of their own to share with others' (Baym 2018: 81).

As one unnamed YouTube fan comments, 'Weird as Hell, but also cute'. 'Weird' because these insect shadows remind us of our lost youth and our departed loved ones; and 'cute' because the optimistic warmth these images stimulate makes the future seem sanguine. Fisher's work is concerned with YouTube ghosts:

It is clear to me that now the period from roughly 2003 to the present will be recognised – not in the far distant future, but very soon – as the worst period for (popular) culture since the 1950s. To say that the culture was desolate is not to say that there weren't traces of other possibilities. *Ghosts of My Life* is an attempt to engage with these traces. (Fisher 2014: 29)

Fisher's contentious and subjective argument that '2003 to the present … is the worst period for popular culture' is impossible to quantify, but it may be true; however, YouTube remains in 2017 a space where there remains 'traces of possibility' (2014: 29). Henry Jenkins comes to similar conclusions about the democratic nature of YouTube; and the manner in which this relates in Beatles media mythology promulgated by Apple, lazy journalism, biased journalists such as Philip Norman (often apocryphal stories disseminated by the Beatles themselves, see the hilariously contradictory interviews the Beatles gave for the *Anthology* project), 'Fans reject the idea of a definitive version produced, authorised, and regulated by some media conglomerate. Instead fans envision a world where all of us can participate in the creation and circulation of central cultural myths' (Jenkins 2008: 267). And although it is now owned by Google, YouTube remains a space of imagination and guerrilla citizen art where the studios, record companies and stars' PR are translated into something new; whether that has the professionalism and sheen of artist-led/company aesthetics is another question, but the fans on YouTube are bricoleurs who 'reject the studio's assumption that intellectual property is "limited good", to be tightly controlled lest it dilute its value. Instead they embrace intellectual property as "shareware", something that accrue value as it moves across different contexts, get retold in various ways, attracts multiple audiences, and opens itself up to a proliferation of alternative meanings' (Jenkins 2008: 267). From Beatlemania to tribute bands to YouTube we have a history of Beatles fandom which takes the Beatles' image, music and lyrics and twists them into new shapes which are sometimes ugly and sometimes beautiful, but always retaining the trace of their original artistic creation: memes of broken light that reconfigure into fresh and unusual but still familiar shapes.

Vidders on YouTube are remixing and mashing the Beatles video archive; archon comes from the Greek meaning ruler, and with YouTube the archive is untethered from the Apple CEO or archon and released into a digital space where old videos become transformed into hybrid texts, living cultures, progressive bricolage where the past and the future collide and mingle in a confusion of strains that look back to progress forward. YouTube is a fan community which is shifting, progressing and transforming. YouTube is a transgressive and messy space where videos, carnivalesque comment and surreal, and often absurd debates coexist in a strange palette of the old and new. Writing about Tumblr Paul Booth's words are relevant to YouTube; the radical mimicking and alloying of the old and the new Booth calls 'transformative fandom' and this appellation is a synonym of progressive fandom, 'Whereas affirmative fandom tends to uphold the text and its creator, transformative fandom tends to take the text and mould it, to create something new with it' (Booth 2016: 238–9). The vidders on YouTube remould the Beatles video archive and in so doing are creating messy spaces of hybrid fan visual art. It is important to note, however, that it is the second biggest website in the world and is a subsidiary of Google; and so the playfulness of vidding and comment is couched in the machinery of a multibillion-dollar company which relies on advertisement revenue to pay creators; although its subversive nature remains extant as the company relies on crowdsourcing and fans to monitor controversial content by clicking the Report button. However, the primary concern of Beatles fans on YouTube is to take pleasure in the act of fandom, engaging with the Beatles phenomenon for enjoyment, or as Duffett contends,

> Evidently, as fans, we are not stooges. We are human beings with the full range of human capabilities. This does not mean, however, that our primary aim is *always* political in the traditional sense: to poach, subvert or negate corporate culture or intellectual property. In reality, fandom is inspired by media output but not restricted to it. Its concerns escape the matrix of corporate production by raising more humanist issue; seeking pleasure, exploring creativity and making social connections. (Duffett 2013: 285)

Baby boomer Beatles fans engage with Twitter accounts or Facebook groups as well as YouTube. Fandom has moved into the era of web 2.0 and ageing fans have connected and this is also empirically and theoretically interesting as YouTube and Tumblr mean that Beatles fans from boomers to millennials 'curate their own personal journey through fandoms' (Booth 2016: 236). Twitter, Facebook, YouTube and Tumblr offer 'multiple interdisciplinary conversations with other academic areas and developing connections with areas that might appear disparate; for instance, links between fan studies and political science might reveal civic commonalities, or between fan studies and history could help nuance discussions of fans through time' (Booth 2016: 236).

YouTube is a site of play and although it has radically challenged the hegemony of Apple and its corporate tentacles, and has given fans more agency to create links and to nurture a communities of fans, critics such as Henrik Linden and Sara Linden argue that YouTube's site of utopian play remains 'settled in ways that promote and reinforce neoliberal attitudes and ideologies. While a neoliberal system and its free marker approach encourages agency, it is an agency without self-reflexion, and the question of dominant structures that is favoured' (Linden and Linden 2017: 68). In terms that rather echo Adorno's dismissal of standardized art as 'rubbish' and mass culture as 'propaganda'; Linden and Linden contend that 'the "good" fan accepts that he or she can affect the production of media content by establishing himself or herself as part of a visible and vocal market segment – without openly questioning the "rules" of the free market' (Linden and Linden 2017: 68–9). This entrepreneurial and individualistic quality to social media argues that social media including YouTube (it's called YouTube after all; and not We Tube) is a social sphere of 'microcelebrity' and 'neo-liberal values' (Linden and Linden 2017). As I have argued YouTube interrogates the monolith of Apple, but in an individualistic manner: 'In the age of social media, we are meant to operate as self-interested subjects, not civic minded citizens' (Linden and Linden 2017: 69).

I have argued that YouTube is a space of liberation from the big voice of Apple, and in an artistic sense this is true; we now have emancipatory spaces where individuals and communities are creating remix and mashed content that moves Beatles art in a new realm of bricolage and citizen art, but concurrently a practical engagement with politics and society has to Linden and Linden become severed. They posit that 'in the Web 2.0 era bands and artists are increasingly expected to market themselves via Twitter and Facebook' (Baym 2017), and for younger-generation musicians this is seen a natural component of being an artist (Linden and Linden 2017: 72). Also fans are incorporated into high consumerism:

> For brands, it is important to keep track of fan communities and learn about their consumer behaviour … The recommending function is a central part of what businesses such as Amazon are doing, and through increasingly sophisticated software, online companies are able to steer potential customers in a certain direction. Consumers seem to like this, as they do not mind buying what others have bought. Perhaps, rather than convergence culture, as we are increasingly being 'spoon-fed' by the company trying to sell us products. (Linden and Linden 2017: 72)

So YouTube is an innovation that offers a certain agency and autonomy for the individual, but praxis or practical uses of knowledge (political application for example); in fact Debord's words on the deconstruction of art are germane to YouTube: that is a cultural form that takes fragments and reconstructs the old Beatles art into bricolage of past and present: 'When art, which was the common language of social inaction, develops into independent art in the modern sense, emerging from its original religious universe and becoming individual production of separate works, it too becomes subject to the movements governing history of all separate culture. Its declaration of independence is the beginning of its end' (Debord 1994: 103). YouTube is a technological fragmentary bricolage art form that makes the old new, but its transgressive play is couched in individualistic consumerism and the YouTube Company is part of a web or paradigm of profit making. For this writer, YouTube is obviously a multibillion-dollar business concern, but it is also a dazzling people's guerrilla art and its brilliance lies in the fact that is a collage and bricolage form which remixes, mashes, reimagines, re-boots and appropriates the Beatles archive into a new expression of old and new technological strains: it takes the canon of 'great' Beatles art and shifts it into texts of forward motion which are affirmed on looking back; Debord describes the process when art is in need of customization, 'When art becomes independent and paints its world in dazzling colours, a moment of life has grown old. Such a moment cannot be rejuvenated by dazzling colours; it can only be evoked in memory. The greatness of art only emerges at the dusk of life' (Debord 1994: 104). YouTube is progressive fandom in the sense that it moves the old forward into new hybrid texts; it takes nostalgia and memory and creates new mental landscapes of imagery which are in turn the birth of memories out of old nostalgia memory. The ownership of YouTube keeps it as a slick cog in the machinery and institutions of the corporate world, but the strange new videos which amalgamate and wed the Beatles Apples archons to the new: YouTube may not be 'dusk of life' but a colourful golden dawn of carnivalesque and surrealist art that creates new fan communities and identities in cyberspace. However, as I have argued, participatory cultures such as YouTube are no longer to be understood in terms of emancipatory fan cultures versus the hegemony of big media; Henry Jenkins elucidated the complexity of online fandom as early as 2007: 'The old categories of resistance and co-optation seem quaint compared to the complex and uncharted terrain that we are now exploring' (Jenkins 2007: 362). Beatles online participatory cultures are transgressive, energetically revised, annotated, remixed and mashed, and theory on these shifting sands is cognizant of issues such as crowdfunding which is an opposition position to big companies such as the Beatles' Apple; and conversely, the future of online fans studies scrutinizes the extent to which the creative industries commodify, co-opt and monetarize fan cultures, as Jenkins explains:

> We now need to accept that what we used to call co-optation also involves a complex set of negotiations during which media industries change to accommodate the demands of consumer even as they seek to train consumers to behave in ways that are beneficial to their interests. Media companies act differently today because they have been shaped by the increased visibility of participatory culture: they are generating new kinds of content and forming new kinds of relationships with their consumers. (2007: 362)

In sum, then, the Beatles on YouTube represents progressive nostalgia because 'under the influence of technology, the human race is morphing into something new and strange' (Buckley 2012: 267): YouTube is constantly transforming the past into the new. However, one final caveat about participatory spaces such as YouTube, the rationale of capitalism is weaved into new technologies and artists are using technology in imaginative ways to make more money and simultaneously giving fans more access to stars. For instance, Taylor Swift, whose label is called Big Machine, is particularly adept at this; her The Swift Life (TSL) app is a mixture of Instagram, Tumblr and Pokémon Go. TSL is the latest launch from Glu (the developer of mobile games for smartphones) and it is responsible for Kim Kardashian Hollywood and Katy Perry Pop. TSL is a photo-sharing opportunity with the goal of being noticed by Taylor Swift. The app is a billion dollar concern predicated on the hope that fans will be noticed by Taylor Swift herself. The corollary with Apple and YouTube is that it is a forum that either gives fans new boundaries to transgress or to the opportunity to luxuriate in electronic aspic. Most academics abhor this corporate world, but it does give fans access to stars and it also gives them platforms which they can change, as dana boyd posits: 'Having worked inside and around corporations for the better part of a decade, I've come to accept that corporate interests are part of the ecosystem and that's healthier to engage them than to pretend they don't exist' (Jenkins, Mizuko, boyd 2016: 145). It is important to add that these innovations in technology, such as YouTube, TSL, Rock Band and MagiQuest, also give fans innovative tools to rework the Beatles back canon in their imaginations; it is a 'transformative nostalgia [that] helps fans in their quest to imaginatively inhabit the past' (Duffett 2013). When YouTube interacts with fans' minds the exchange is a non-linear engagement with the past which creates mosaic memories where past and present collide to create new imaginative futures; and fans' minds are colonized by the Beatles and affected deeply by capitalism. Nevertheless, the fans' negotiations with technology and capitalism eschew *mal d'archive* and retrospective nostalgia.

Mark Duffett feels that pre-internet Beatles fans enjoyed an immersive and transgressive experience of Beatles fandom which in many way is as liberating as functioning within the YouTube/capitalist/technological envelope (Duffett 2018); the experience of buying vinyl in a record shop, for instance, is as psychologically and imaginatively liberating as making a fan vid and interfacing with YouTube, but what cannot be gainsaid is that YouTube disseminates information faster and that a post-human cyborg experience is changing fandom into the creation of new technological aesthetically pleasing texts. In a review of Lincoln Geraghty's *Cult Collectors* (2014), Michael S. Duffy demonstrates the extent to which YouTube has brought nostalgia into the present in the form of bricolage YouTube art:

> *Cult Collectors* arrives at just the right time to explore how the roles of fans and the nature of memorialized objects are shifting thanks to the expansion of the Internet; the World Wide Web has allowed collectors of previously obscure material to become more sophisticated both in their knowledge of media and object histories and in their ability to discuss and reobtain precious items of–or representing–their youth. For Geraghty, the Web, and our access to it, has made 'history more accessible, our memories more tangible, thus bringing the past into the present' (2). Now, with the Internet, 'collecting enables fans to connect with the histories of their favorite media texts in ways they just could not achieve twenty or thirty years ago'. (Duffy 2014, http://journal.transformativeworks.org/index.php/twc/article/view/584/444)

Writers such as DiPetro and Stephen O'Neill have discussed the YouTube aesthetic of making the past present as Presentism. The Presentism of Beatles fan posts on YouTube is 'a site of productive tension between the homogenizing effects of mass culture and new forms of individual vernacular expression' (O'Neill 2014: 18). O'Neill's description of You Tube as a form of progressive nostalgia is closely linked to memory and technology. As Worcman and Garde-Hansen suggest the technology of YouTube demonstrates 'that our memories are dynamic and the narratives we construct come from the present moment in which we construct the memory as a story we tell ourselves and others' (Worcman and Garde-Hansen 2016: 54). In this manner the mashing of Beatles images on YouTube is a 'process of constructing narratives on behalf of the self or of the group's members, and sharing those selves amongst the group and beyond' (Worcman and Garde-Hansen 2016: 55). The Beatles mashed and bricolage videos on YouTube are Presentism, which is historical spectral images combined with music to produce a fan-generated progressive nostalgia predicated on technological innovation and fans' creativity. Old clips of the Beatles are nostalgic memories translated anew. 'Memory has become rogue in the sense that it has come loose from its fixed place in the production cycle' (Kosnik 2016: 4). YouTube is affirmed on a remix culture which starts as an act of memory, with a user remembering a loved (or hated) mass culture text and isolating, then manipulating, revising, and reworking ... At present, each media commodity becomes, in the instant of its release, an archive to be plundered, an original to be memorized, copied, and manipulated – a starting point or springboard for receivers' creativity rather than an end unto itself. (Kosnik 2016: 4)

The 'memories' on YouTube are progressive nostalgia as they transform 'traditional memory institutions' (2016: 4) into rogue digital archives created by Beatles fans.

6

Paul Is Undead: Fan fiction, slash fiction and literary fiction

Fan fiction grew out of *Spockanalia*, a fanzine started in 1967 by *Star Trek* obsessives. The first edition had a letter of encouragement from Leonard Nimoy (Spock from the television series). Here is the birth of fan fiction as genre, by definition, amateur works of fiction. Of course it didn't take Beatles fans long to catch up. Girl fans had been writing romantic stories in notebooks since 1963. Beatles fan fiction evolved from this science fiction genre, and by 2006 Rooftop Sessions (one of the main online forums) had collated thousands of stories. This has become known as 'slash fiction': highly eroticized sexual fantasies by fans, which often stars the Beatles in homoerotic stories.

Slash fiction and fan fiction do have much in common: both fulfil their fans' wildest fantasies and both completely re-appropriate the Beatles' work, image and personalities to the fans' needs. Notable classics of the genre are Mark Shipper's *Paperback Writer* (1979), *Beatles* by Lars Saabye (1984) and zombie Beatle fiction *Paul Is Undead* by Alan Goldsher (2010). In Alan Goldsher's novel, Jesus agrees with John Lennon that the Beatles are bigger than him. The 'plot' of the novel develops with the Beatles being attacked and turned into zombies. *Paul Is Undead* epitomizes slash, and for that matter fan fiction. The Beatles are placed in fantastic circumstances (this could be the romantic, pornographic or horror genre) and these fan spaces completely transgress and re-interpret the Beatles' music and image.

There are hundreds of online forums which have thousands of stories with the four Beatles as the central characters. For instance, *Across the Universe: Fan Fiction Archive* produces unprofessional work published by the fans for the fans, titles such as *Going to the Moon* and *Meeting an Alien Beatles*. The internet teems with sites of this type: Angelfire, stories, poetry and essays about the Beatles, Bungalow Bill's Beatle Fan Fiction, Nothing Is Real (a Beatles fan fiction site) and Beatlegirl's World.

The manner in which gender is altered by fans is addressed in this chapter where fans use Jenkins's phrase 'perform a kind of "intellectual transvestism", identifying their own cultural experiences and constructing countertexts to express their own desires' (Jenkins 2006: 44) cited in Duffett 2013. In slash 'women ... habitually find themselves identifying with characters of the opposite sex' (Duffett 2013: 2002).

There are three serious considerations to be made concerning fan fiction. Fan fiction is often predicated on a series of what ifs, or 'magical thinking' as Joan Didion calls it. What if the Beatles were zombies? What if the Beatles reformed in the 1970s? What if John Lennon visited the island he bought in Ireland? What would it be like if all the Beatles slept together? The second consideration is that the 'what if/magical thinking' phenomenon has close links to the fans' desire to appropriate the Beatles phenomenon into their own lives and to be transgressive concerning the Beatles public relations machinery; the third consideration here is that fan fiction often problematizes documentary and biographical fact, in a manner akin to Ian MacDonald's emotional new journalism technique which can be factually inaccurate, but what it lacks in fidelity to the truth, it more than makes up for by evoking a strong feeling for the Beatles art. Slash, Shipper, Barry and McLeod's fan fiction is whimsical, eccentric and counterfactual, but it feels as 'real' as Davies's and Norman's 'facts'. Fan fiction evokes powerful emotion and we can find Beatles 'truth' in fiction writing. In fact Norman, originally a novelist, invents characters in his work: John, the lovable rogue and errant genius of the band; Paul, the Machiavellian, sneaky PR, opportunist Beatle; George, a religious bore and untalented musician who was jealous of Lennon and McCartney; and Ringo, the everyman clown, who was lucky to be in the right place at the right time. Fan fiction conveys nuance and inventiveness and uses novelistic techniques to make readers experience the Beatles phenomenon. Documentary 'fact' is often spurious and biographical material is often erroneous. Often biography is heavily fictionalized and fiction contains much documentary 'fact'.

Mark Shipper, *The Life and Times of the Beatles* (1978)

There is a need in fan books and slash fictions to take control of the Beatles phenomenon. Mark Shipper's book *The Life and Times of the Beatles*, published in 1978, presents an alternative Beatles history. The book's subtitle, *The Spurious Chronicle of Their Rise to Stardom, the Triumphs & Disasters Plus the Amazing Story of Their Ultimate Reunion*, shows that the intention of many Beatles fans is to control the Beatles story to such an extent that they force the band to reform.

The novel *Paperback Writer* is very well written and has a modicum of respect for the Beatles legacy that is entirely absent from sites such as Beatles Slash and Beatles Sex. However, both fan fiction and slash fiction share a commonality, that is, a desire to appropriate the Beatles phenomenon into a private and personal fantasy. Paperback Writer is the whim of Mark Shipper, who was 27 at the time of writing this novel, and in a nostalgic whimsical manner similar to the desire of fan conventions, Shipper's intention was to keep the Beatles fantasy alive, the novel imagines the Beatles reforming in the early 1970s for a new album, *Get Back*, and a concert with the Sex Pistols and Peter Frampton. This conceit is developed in three chapters at the end of the novel: 'Get Back', 'Not a Second Time' and 'Tomorrow Never Knows'. Shipper makes the Beatles' comeback album and their concert artistic failures to drive home his point that a much heralded comeback may not be a good idea of the real Beatles, as the McCartney character says at the end of the book, 'you can't live in someone's past and in their future too' (Shipper 1979: 252).

Although ostensibly the novel's theme is a warning against resorting to nostalgia, this is exactly what the book does. The comeback album and the concert indulge Shipper's fantasy of enjoying the Beatles one more time (of course all four Beatles were alive at the time of writing). The novel mixes anti-nostalgia and nostalgia; the new Beatles album and concert (although a failure in the text) are playing on Beatles fans' expectations that an album and concert would be a good idea. But what makes this book progressive and subversive (something it has in common with Beatles slash) is that Shipper's sense of humour stamps all over the Beatles myth. The acknowledgements may end with the line, 'And thanks to John, Paul, George and Ringo for the excitement and magic and that was the Beatles' (Shipper 1979: 253), but this sentiment is absent in the Beatles reunion section of the book.

The Beatles reunion album *Get Back* is recorded in April/May of 1977. It comprises nine songs, six new Lennon/McCartney originals: 'Gilligan's Island', 'Yoko's Going Broke-o', 'Son of a Pizza Man', 'Hold on to Your Dream', 'Please Freeze Me' and 'Maybe I'm Amazed, Maybe I'm Not (It's None of Your Business)', and two Harrison's originals, 'Disco Jesus' and 'Bring the Captain in to Kneel (Before the Altar)'. The final track is a cover of David Crosby's 'I Almost Cut My Hair'. The song titles are comic in themselves, but the comedy kicks in when the head of Columbia Records hears the album for the first time without knowing the authors of the songs: Lee Soption (head of Columbia) describes it as the 'worst piece of unadulterated shit I've heard in twenty years in this business' before Ronald Number, the Beatles' PR, reveals that as well as being shit, 'It is something else too, It's the new Beatles album' (Shipper 1979: 225). From this point on the comedy gathers pace and it has a subversive carnivalesque quality. Yoko's art is ridiculed: 'They don't buy her bags, Don't buy her blintzes, don't buy milk bottles in the snow-ko/Perhaps they'll change/When they get the news that/Yoko's going broke-o' (Shipper 1979: 227). Harrison's spirituality is lampooned in 'Disco Jesus': 'Yeah, Jesus gets down/When it comes to boogie, he's the boss/You ought to see him do the hustle/ Up there on that funky cross' (Shipper 1979: 231). Of course when the album is released it totally bombs with fans demanding refunds. Shipper writes a mock review of the album, 'Rolling Stone pans Get Back, June 19, 1979'. He writes, 'The Beatles are back and we all wish they'd stayed away. … A final love letter to the Beatles: Get Back to where you once belong – to our hopes and dreams and our memories. May they rest in pieces' (Shipper 1979: 237). And then there is the concert supporting Peter Frampton and coming on stage after the Sex Pistols.

The Sex Pistols open for the Beatles and Johnny Rotten's introduction is a carnivalesque dismissal of nostalgia: 'You'll get Peter Frampton, all right. You'll get him. You idiots deserve him! But first, you'll have to sit through that bunch of exiles from the old-age home, The Beatles, I heard those old farts at rehearsal this afternoon and they bored the shit out of me. But since all fifty thousand of you bore the shit out of me, you'll probably like them' (Shipper 1979: 245). When the Beatles take to the stage at the Dodger Stadium, Los Angeles, on 2 August 1979, the band undergo the indignity of fans using the Beatles set 'to go to the snack bar, to the bathroom' (Shipper 1979: 248). The comeback concert ends with John and Ringo backstage atomizing the nostalgia impulse: 'They never really did want us to come back Ringo,' John said. 'We were just symbols of things they did want back – their youth – their innocence.' '1960s,' Ringo added. 'Right,' Lennon continued. 'That's all we mean to them. They only want us when we remind them of the good old days. As long as we sing She Loves You, everything's alright. For three minutes, they're back in high school in 1960s when they had no responsibilities, no worries, no obligations' (Shipper 1979: 251). For pulp fiction, this is a serviceable definition of Derrida's *mal d'archive*, an unhealthy obsession with the past that prevents forward movement both artistically and emotionally. The reformed Beatles are a media spectacle that is regressive, backwards and represents conservative nostalgia: 'the spectacle is a bad dream of a society in chains and ultimately expresses nothing more than its wish for sleep' (Debord 1984: 12): Shipper's novel vacillates between two contradictory positions: celebrating the 'bad dream' of spectacle nostalgia and subverting the past through Bakhtin comedy.

Shipper is a novelist/fan who appropriates the Beatles for his own nostalgic fantasy, but ends up ridiculing their legacy by creating new and inventive fan fiction, but his subversion is conservative and safe compared to Beatles slash. As we will see, slash or sex fiction gloriously and offensively negates 'sleepy' nostalgia. Slash fiction is a form of 'nomad thought' that does not 'respect the artificial division between the three domains of representation, subject, concept and being … The concepts it creates … do not reflect upon the world but are immersed in the changing state of things' (Massumi 2016: xi). Unlike Shipper's fan fiction, slash is immersive because of interactive technology and because of fluid, ever-changing, highly sexualized content.

Beatles slash fiction

Mark Duffett has suggested that slash fiction is important to academics because we 'seek out creative and resistant activity' (Duffett 2013: 178) and he points out that although this is now something of a cliché, there is mileage in the transgressive argument of this 'nomad genre'. My reading of Beatles slash is that it is subversive (constantly changing because of interactivity) and because slash is transgressive about ideas of fixed identity: 'Character bodies provide a shared space where queer and straight fans can discuss their desires outside the polarizing realm of identity politics' (2013: 178).

Firstly the interactive element of slash is vitally important to an appreciation of this genre of fandom. Every slash website is overflowing with bespoke sexual choice. The prosumer can choose any configuration of Beatles group sex. Here the fans display the minutiae of their Beatles knowledge. Storylines about aspects of the Beatles' career are available online. There is every configuration of Beatles sex: not only John with Paul and so on but also with every player in Beatles history: Brian Epstein, Pete Best and Stu Sutcliffe. For instance, a fan fiction guide on 'Beatles Sex' has recommendations for all four Beatles, and a section on *Others* such as Stuart Sutcliffe (*Others*, http://missmcharrison.tumblr.com/slash).

Beatles slash is very explicit, it is hastily written and the sexual dream scenarios are an aspect of fandom in which sexual identity is fluid and malleable. For instance, we often don't know the gender of the author or their sexual orientation. The ambiguity of this writing is immersed in the changing state of things. Sexual identity, gender, authorship are all subsumed to the act of reading. It is an I. A. Richards reading exercise where the text is a self-contained aesthetic object. Beatles characters are unmoored into a realm of personal fantasy: a self-contained imaginative world where fixity is rejected. For example, the story 'Who Knows How Long I've Loved You' by sherlocked221 shifts John Lennon into a performative personal fantasy that transgresses any sense of control from the machinery of the music industry:

> This morning, I wake up naked. It's a little more surprising than it probably should be, but I haven't slept in the nude for quite a while. Moreover, I haven't slept beside John in about a week. His naked body is draped over mine. I feel his breath curling against the back of my neck. Maybe he thinks my back is an extension of the mattress, judging by the way he practically has me pinned by the shoulders. I nuzzle the back of my head into his mess of fair hair. (sherlocked221 http://missmcharrison.tumblr.com/slash)

Predictably the story develops into a graphic pornographic fantasy that is highly personal, it is an 'oppositional subculture' that is not deliberately setting out to be oppositional, as Hills suggests attempting to be subversive 'restricts possibilities for expressing personal significance' (Hills 2002: 93). In fact what we have here is 'nomadic writing' which is a site of play where identities are unmoored (Lennon, author, reader) into a sphere of writing where identities blur into a fluid Rabelaisian orgy of words that express fan emotions in an indeterminate space of play: slash fiction is 'play that is not always caught up in a pre-established "boundedness" or set of cultural boundaries, but may instead imaginatively create its own set of boundaries and its own auto-context' (Hills 2002: 112). It is also significant that interactive technology is remote from being couched in a paperback.

After reading thousands of Beatles slash stories, recurrent leitmotifs begin to become apparent. Again taking another example from Beatles slash/tumblr.com, *Evasion* by quietprofanity ticks many of the slash fiction boxes. Each story often has a detailed home page which has a guide; in this instance, 'Rating: Explicit. Category: M/M. Fandom: The Beatles. Relationships: Paul McCartney/George Harrison, John Lennon /Brian Epstein/George Harrison, John Lennon/Ringo Starr. Characters: George Harrison, John Lennon, Brian Epstein, Paul McCartney, Ringo Starr, Bob Wooler, Billy J. Kramer, Pete Shotton, Cynthia Lennon, Gerry Marsden' (Beatles slash/tumblr.com). There is also a statistics section: 'Stats: Words: 20,808, Chapters: 3/3, Comments: 25, Kudos: 90. Bookmarks: 17. Hits: 2,971' (Beatles slash/tumblr.com). The stories are very well written, character and dialogue are convincing and the detail about Beatles history is scrupulously researched. *Evasion* is set at Paul's twenty-first birthday party at his Auntie Jin's: a real event where John Lennon in a violent rage beat up the Cavern disc jockey Bob Wooler after Wooler had insinuated that John had had an affair with Brian Epstein while on holiday together in Barcelona. After the party, and John disgracing himself, the Beatles make up in the usual predictable manner for this type of fiction. Nearly all these stories end in an orgy and, in this case, a foursome:

George wiped his mouth, trying to clean it, although the taste of Paul's come lingered in his mouth despite his efforts. He raised his head to look at the others. Paul had collapsed back in the chair, his trouser tangled about his ankles and his cock mostly limp in his lap. Ringo looked back at him, his eyes wide and confused. George had no idea what was going through his mind, wasn't sure if it was arousal or pity. Then there was John, smiling triumphant John. His eyes made George want to sink into the floor. George was still incredibly horny, his cock fully erect inside his clothes, and even though he was on his hands and knees on the floor, crouched so John probably couldn't see him well, it seemed like John nevertheless knew everything he felt. (Beatles slash/tumblr.com)

The desire to appropriate the Beatles into a sexual fantasy which the audience 'controls' is based in early childhood. Freud contends that the unborn child is unable to distinguish between him/herself and the external world, and so the child 'feels' in control of everything. Sandvoss elaborates this point:

In this state of omnipotence the child engages in a form of pleasurable 'autoeroticism'. External objects such as the mother's breast are experiences as a pleasurable form of nurture. ... Yet the experienced unity ... is soon disrupted by the child's realisation of its lack of control over external objects. At this point the child's sense of wholeness and the pleasure that arise form it are lost. The self is henceforth a construct of lack, marked by a profound sense of loss of (sexual) pleasure, and the resulting attempts to fill this void through fantasies and action are the basis of Freud (1923/1984) labels the pleasure principal. (Sandvoss 2005: 70–1)

In a sense Beatles fandom is predicated on the loss of the 'transitional object', as we have seen, whether that is the suppressed sexuality of *Beatles Monthly*, the band's breakup and therefore the obsession with fan conventions, biased superfan journalists who devote their writing to their devotional object (and much of what they write is erroneous fantasy), the violent fantasies of Chapman, who desperately wants to be a part of Beatles mythology, YouTubers who translate the Beatles into a mashed bricolage, tribute bands who see performative fandom as a way of inhabiting the Beatles' skin and also crossing the breach of separation from their 'transitional object' and cultural tourism in which fans use heritage sites as a geographical space to reimagine the Beatles phenomenon and so filling the Beatles-shaped hole in their lives.

Of course the play of slash fiction is a pre-Oedipal realm where nomadic play reimagines the Beatles into fans' lives in the most intimate way. Guests can send messages and leave replies anonymously, which heightens the comedy, the play and the carnivalesque aspects of these stories. The sexual content rapidly becomes predictable, but the unusual expressions and nom de plumes are endlessly creative; for instance, slash fans of *Evasion* are called shydeer, deerlike, Lezbot, tootsiemupet, slashrfan, Lady McLennon (a John/Paul coupling obviously), wowlennon, ringolovesjoj. Slash fiction is a site of play based on technology where fans can configure the Beatles into whichever shape they want. This type of pornography 'underlines the important function of fandom as a realm of negotiation between inner and external realities, and thus as a source of both pleasure and security' (Sandvoss 2005: 94). This highly sexualized play takes the tiller of the Beatles phenomenon and steers it in stormy waters of personal fantasy.

Beatles fan fiction is part of the genre of writing that has transformed the literary world as it is unregulated, interactive and outside the literary mainstream of publishing houses and reviewers: 'Before the modern era of copyright and intellectual property, stories were things held in common, to be passed from hand to hand and from narrator to narrator. ... fanfiction represents the swinging back of the pendulum to that older way of thinking' (Grossman 2013: xiv). Beatles fan fiction 'has pried open the door, allowing fans a chance to participate in the continuing storylines of the characters they love' (Benson 2013: 388).

And slash has benefitted the most from lack of regulation and participatory aspect as Beatles fans have weaved the iconography of their heroes into transgressive storylines that are the written equivalent of Duchamp drawing a moustache and goatee beard on the *Mona Lisa* to save it from bland reproduction; similarly slash fiction rescues Beatles iconography from banal standardization by creating a fresh perspective on clichéd icons. Beatles slash is important as it makes us view the old (Beatles iconography) in a new way (Beatles slash). Slash's speed also makes it difficult to keep pace with the huge diversity of ever-changing material; fans can anonymously post instantly whatever they imagine, and as slash demonstrates its imagination is very fertile:

> fanfiction has become wildly more biodiverse than the canonical works that it springs from. It encompasses male pregnancy, centaurification, body swapping, apocalypses, reincarnation, and every sexual fetish, kink combination, position, and inversion you can imagination and a lot you could but would probably prefer not to. It breaks down walls between genders and genres and races and canons and bodies and species and past and future and conscious and unconscious fiction and reality. (Grossman 2013: xiii)

Beatles slash is RPF (Real Person Fiction)/fanfic that takes real people and real events that 'can be enjoyed in a new way if they are appropriated in imaginative writing' (Duffett 2013: 170).

Beatles slash fiction is a sexually explicit Mills & Boon; the writing is much more graphic than that series of 'romance' novels, but like Mills & Boon, it recycles the same standardized plot ad nauseam. However, as Duffett demonstrates RPF is the most befitting category for Beatles slash. The fan studies scholar and writer of fan fiction, V. Arrow, embellishes this:

> Real Person Fic, or RPF, is a world in some ways completely apart from the rest of fanfiction subculture. While all fanfiction suffers from a stigma in the mainstream, RPF is something even other fanfiction writers often mock and deride as 'creepy' and often juvenile. Why? RPF, as its name suggests, is fanfiction written about 'real people'-celebrities. Written, almost solely, about – well, cute boys. And nothing

but cute boys, essentially – despite the persuasive idea among other fans that RPF readers and writers want to imagine themselves with their favourite stars, RPF thrives on fans imagining their favourite cute boys with other cute boys. (Jamison 2013: 323)

However, in terms of stylistics and aesthetics, RPF is of a high quality. Its cultural capital should be higher but the Mills & Boon plots make it is easy to compare unfavourably to Beatles fan fiction and Beatles literary fiction. But who reads solely for plot or narrative these days? The most significant aspect of slash is that it transgresses the Beatles canon, creating an alternative fanon. The imaginative alacrity of this process is dizzying:

An increasingly connected world – particularly via twitter – has changed the lens through which 'real' history, and real people are viewed. Historians work by interweaving primary documents to create their version of the truth – historiography being, essentially, a larger framework of Humanity Fanon – and RPF writers do the same. With every new piece of evidence, every day, every tweet, the canon evolves and changes. (Jamison 2013: 323)

With RPF we have an audacious and disrespectful art form that transmutes with a swiftness which was denied to the writers of *Beatles Monthly*. RPF is a naughty and mirthful electronic porn version of *Beatles Monthly* which is predicated on technology and a 1960s sexual revolution in the head, to paraphrase Ian MacDonald.

Fans wanting to control or to appropriate the Beatles legend is key to understanding fandom, and this is especially true in the case of such unregulated activity as slash fiction. *Beatles! Slash: All You Need Is Love* is a fan site dedicated to slash. The site is described as 'a community for writers and fans of Beatles slash (fan fiction featuring male/male romantic pairings, though we also welcome female/female pairings)' (Beatles Slash 2014). The site recognizes that fans feel so passionately about the Beatles that even in such an unrestrained and liberal online environment, fans still manage to go too far: personal attacks, cyber-bullying and generally extreme behaviour. It has become such a problem that in September 2014, the site issued a warning to all participants about 'trolling': the site 'has experienced a lot of trolls and drama recently ... measures must be taken to protect the rest of the members'. The site also gives warning of the explicit nature of the postings: 'All Adult / R-rated / NC-17 rated posts (whether they are pictures, fic, stories, etc.) *must* be flagged as "Explicit Adult Concepts" when you post them' (Beatles Slash 2014).

The highly sexualized fiction available in Beatles Slash is an electronic version of the Beatles as a fetishized love object that we saw earlier in my description of *Beatles Monthly*. This online participatory culture has the same sensual intimacy and ego-driven narcissism as *Beatles Monthly* (an Oedipal desire for the Beatles which we saw in the murderous urges of Mark Chapman and Michael Abram) with the main difference being that this technology is an 'affinity space ... a world where knowledge is shared and where critical activity is ongoing and lifelong' (Jenkins 1992: 192–3) and where the exchanges between fans are fast, urgent and almost immediate unlike the 'snail mail' print media of *Beatles Monthly*. Beatles slash fiction is what Fathallah calls 'derivative writing' that can escape containment and become 'as the legitimacy of authorship itself begins to be questioned' (Fathallah 2017: 10). Writing about George R. R. Martin's *Game of Thrones*, she uses quantitative data to argue that fanfic 'generates new statements,' that 'characters in fanfic enact transformation of the system by and through traditional forms of authority,' and that 'fanfic transforms the discourse through self-conscious appropriation of Martin's text' (Fathallah 2017: 13). So, Beatles slash or fanfic is, like Lester Bang's subjective and subversive writing on music, a carnivalesque site where 'discourse formations are always malleable and subject to change' (Fathallah 2017: 15). Fanfic is potentially 'progressive nostalgia': fans' heads, whether they are journalists or tribute acts, are sites where memories are triggered by the empirical world into creating new fan activity in art, performance and progressive fan consumption.

Kevin Barry and Ian McLeod: Literary Beatles fan fiction

Beatles literary fan fiction is an upmarket version of fandom, receiving intellectual approbation unlike Shipper's pulp fiction which is considered the bottom of the literati's pecking order. Two fan fictions which have received much praise and reviews in *The Guardian* and the 'broadsheet press' are Kevin Barry's novel about John Lennon, *Beatlebone* (2015), and Ian McLeod's short story about Lennon, 'Snodgrass', which was published in his collection of short stories, *Snodgrass and Other Illusions* (2013). Barry's and McLeod's fan fictions have the cultural capital of literary fiction, which Shipper's pulp and slash totally lack. In fact an aesthetic comparison of Shipper and slash with Barry's *Beatlebone* and McCleod's 'Snodgrass' problematizes the sharp distinctions between literary and pulp/slash. The characterization, dialogue and prose poetry are as robust in the 'lower' literary forms. A relativistic comparison of the three genres – slash, pulp and literary – refutes the argument that slash/pulp fan fiction is bad and literary fan fiction is good. Admittedly slash's porn carnivalesques often have standardized plots and predictable sexual excesses (think the Marquis de Sade combined with Rabelais), but there is an élan and mellifluousness in the rococo sexual perversion which means its eccentric aesthetics can rival literary fiction's more conventional and literary approach. As we have seen, pulp and slash are well-written stories and the language is comedic and very expressive. So all three genres have many commonalities in terms of language and storytelling, and they share the one thing that all Beatles fan culture has in common: they appropriate the Beatles onto dream fictional scenarios that are whimsical and autonomous imaginaries remote from the Beatles' cultural industry, Apple's PR spin and the machinery of the music business.

Slash fiction opposes and transgresses the Beatle canon, but as we have seen, slash is not in opposition when compared to mainstream fiction. It certainly has its roots in the romance fiction of Mills & Boon, but Elizabeth Woledge draws a distinction between slash and mainstream romance and porn literature. Woledge calls this distinction intimatopia. She writes, 'The subset of slash fiction ... takes part in a fantasy world I dub intimatopia, because its central defining feature is the exploitation of intimacy'

(Woledge 2006: 111). Beatles slash is an example of intimatopia, and intimacy is a salient feature of literary fiction and slash: 'Mass media, much advertising, pornography and popular psychology, as well as a proportion of popular literary texts on homosexual themes, work to foreground the centrality of sex within interpersonal relationships. In opposition to this, and striking a contrastingly subversive note, intimatopic texts insist that intimacy, not sex, drives human interaction' (2006: 111). Beatles slash is predicated on notions of friendship; so aesthetically the writing in Beatles slash is often as good as literary fandom (Kevin Barry's *Beatlebone*, for instance) but slash shares with mainstream literature a *leitmotif* of companionship and love, as we shall see this is the main theme of *Beatlebone*, the intimacy between the John Lennon character and his driver Cornelius O'Grady. Cornelius is constantly remarking on John Lennon's looks and the book is part love story between John and Cornelius: 'Cornelius considers him carefully and for a slow, held moment – You have the longish nose, he says. Like a particular type of dog I can't place' (Barry 2015: 47). The novel's gay subtext is concerned with intimacy and not sex: 'In this way, it can be seen that intimatopic slash fiction shares with professionally published intimatopic literature a desire to foreground an ideology that restores the links between love, friendship and intimacy' (Woledge 2006: 111).

Slash, fan fiction and literary fan fiction are fiction concerned with intimacy and friendship, even if the plots and content are often pornographic. The links between all three genres are very strong:

> Considering what fan fiction can tell us about the intimacy of romance and pornography, I place fan fiction in a history of literacy, popular culture, and private self, concluding that pornography is structured in relation to the conventions of romance, and romance fiction is sustained by porn's ecstatic relationship to exposure. Fan fiction, belonging to the categories of both porn and romance and yet to neither, allows us to rethink their form, content and significance. (Driscoll 2006: 79)

A comparison between Barry, *Evasion*, and Shipper's work demonstrates that fan fiction is breaking down the demarcation between 'high' literary culture and 'low' popular culture.

Aesthetically and romantically, Barry, slash and Shipper have commonality, but it is worth making a distinction about technology and form. Online work, such as slash, is constantly commented upon, edited and revised by fans: electronic fan fictions are 'writerly texts':

> Work in progress is a term used in the fan fiction world to describe a piece of fiction still in the process of being written but not yet complete. This notion of intersects with the intertextuality of fannish discourse, with the ultimate erasure of a single author as it combines to create a shared space, fandom, that we might also refer to as community. The appeal of works in progress lies in part in the way fans can engage with an open text: it invites responses, permits shared authorship, and enjoins a

sense of community. In S/Z, Roland Barthes (1974) distinguishes between readerly and writerly text, with the former denoting a text whose interpretation is solidified with little room for the reader to enter the text. In contrast, the latter is 'a perpetual present ... is ourselves writing, before the infinite play of the world (the world as function) is traversed, intersected, stopped, ... which reduces the plurality of entrances, the opening of networks, the infinity of languages' (5). If the fan is a reader in the Barthesian sense, then serial production is the ultimate writerly text. In so doing, the open-source text in particular invites fans engagement where the fan not only analyses the text but also must constantly renegotiate her analysis. (Busse and Hellekson 2006: 6)

Beta-readers or Beatles-readers (my neologism for providers of online fan content) create writerly texts, for instance, Beatles Sex (missmcharison.tumblr.com) is blog that has stories which are constantly commented on, such as Boy, You've Been A Naughty Girl: 'Paulie in a skirt is the best'; Red Sky: 'I really like this one because Stuart's in it and you what happens when Paul and Stuart or in a fic together'; Cuddling to Sleep: 'damn. This one's ... just damn ... Paul/George and Back Ally/sore Wrists – Hot Hot Hot! Paul/George'. The stories are consistently morphing into a new text, and they are interactive as the tag suggests:

Beatles Sex. Every girl has her own sexual needs. And this blog is all about the possible needs of a Beatles fangirl hopefully we can help you! Message us if you have questions or a request for a specific kind of post. So, here are some examples of what this blog is all about. Lots of Beatles slash. Your confessions about the Fab Four. (https://missmcharrison.tumblr.com/)

'Slash stories posit a same-sex relationship, usually one imposed by the author and based on a perceived homoerotic subtext' (Busse and Heleekson 2006: 10). Kevin Barry's *Beatlebone* is literary fan fiction which is all subtext: a novel where a real character, John Lennon, becomes Barry's fictional plaything. The novel has no sex, but a slash version would be electronically open to appropriation of a gay relationship between the two characters Lennon and Cornelius: *Beatlebone* is a readerly text with a gay subtext.

In Kevin Barry's *Beatlebone*,

The Lennon of *Beatlebone* is 37. The story opens as he arrives by night and incognito on the west coast of Ireland in May 1978; 'all he asks' is to 'spend three days alone on his island'. The island in question is Dorinish in Clew Bay, County Mayo, which the real-life Lennon bought in 1967 at 'the knock-down price of £1,550' – and which he briefly visited with his first wife, Cynthia, and then with Yoko Ono. Barry's Lennon has returned nine years later in search of solitude and in order to 'scream his fucking lungs out' and 'at last to be over himself'. (*The Guardian*, 2015)

Barry's fictional Lennon is delineated with the love and passion of a fan: Lennon is sentimentalized and idealized with an emotional gusto that girl fans from *Beatles Monthly* would recognize. The Lennon in *Beatlebone* has been appropriated to Barry's ends; and Barry uses this agency to its full extent and creates a character that conforms to his prejudices and bias. Barry takes poetic creative license to extremes (the entire plot of *Beatlebone* is fiction) in a manner similar to slash and Shipper. However, the characterizations of Lennon here have as much fidelity as Davies' and Norman's 'real' Lennons. Moreover after reading Shipper, slash, Barry and McLeod, the mosaic of Lennon that comes of these pages has a candour and honesty that matches the veracity of biographical accounts. I reread Ray Coleman's sycophantic, hero-worship hagiography, *Lennon: The Definitive Biography* (1995), and Albert Goldman's condemnatory *The Lives of John Lennon* (1988) while writing this chapter and I can say that the line between the categories 'fiction' and 'documentary' is blurred: fan fiction's inventions convey an impressionistic Lennon which problematizes the authentic Lennon of biography. The fictional Lennon in slash, pulp and literary fiction is as complex, nuanced and naturalistic as biographical truth. In the case of Beatles fandom, biography has many elements of fiction (reductive character types; see my discussion of Norman's Lennon in Chapter 3) and fiction has biographical elements, the slash story *Evasion* has impeccably researched the historical context and social milieu of Paul McCartney's twenty-first birthday party, for example, while combining this documentary fact with a fantastical sex orgy including all four Beatles. Slash problematizes the documentary fact of biographers.

Evasion has permutations of sex between Paul McCartney/George Harrison, John Lennon/Brian Epstein, Brian Epstein/George Harrison, John Lennon/Starr. 'quietprofanity' writes with a scrupulous historical accuracy about the 1960s. As well as knowing the period inside out, the writer has an in-depth knowledge of the Beatles' entourage, here for example, Bob Wooler (the Cavern DJ), Billy J Kramer, John Lennon's best friend from school, Peter Shotton, Cynthia Lennon and Gerry Marsden all feature. Chapter 3 of *Evasion* is typical of slash; George goes into Abbey Road recording studios late at night: 'George entered the sound recording booth from the back way. He peered over the audio console, looking through the glass and down into the recording below, knowing what he would see' (quietprofanity, 2010). George Harrison pruriently watches Brian Epstein and John Lennon have sex:

John had Brian sprawled out on his back on the brown paneled floor of the studio. They were already naked; the only thing that John wore were his glasses. John crouched over Brian, one hand wrapped in his hair and the other round his shoulders. Brian's legs hitched up near his hips. John was kissing him, too – wet, sloppy kisses with his mouth open and tongue out, kisses that Brian returned just as eagerly. (quietprofanity, 2010)

In a sense, this scene appropriates the heritage cultural shrine, Abbey Road, into the imagination of the slashwriter: that is warped cultural tourism; and the carnivalesque and comedic porn fiction (John is only wearing his famous NHS granny glasses) subverts the iconic Beatles and their manager into the writer's mellifluous sexual creativity.

The fictional Lennon in *Beatlebone* is reminiscent of the John Lennon that comes off the pages of Jann Wenner's Rolling Stone interview in 1970: In Wenner's interview Lennon is angry, bilious, bitter and giving full vent to his frustrations thanks to his sessions with Dr Arthur Janov (the founder of Primal Scream therapy) opening him up emotionally. *Beatlebone* fictionalizes this Lennon showing him attempting to outrun his past and retreat to Dorinish, where his screaming cure will exorcize his demons and also his writers' block. Barry's vernacular suits Lennon. Lennon's angst and outpourings of grief are couched in Lennon's own emotional vernacular. On the way to Dorinish island retreat, a binge in a local pub unravels Lennon's tortured psyche and grief over his dead mother:

> He is called a stoaty cunt and a lying cross-eyed cunt and a Jew nosed-nosed cunt and an English cunt, an English cunt, English cunt. The night folds in. He drinks the white spirit and he smokes and he sings. And now he is among the trees. He believes that he can talk to her across the night and trees. He tells her that he loves her. He says he sees her sometimes in faces that pass by. He says that near the sea he thinks of her most of all. He tells her what might have become of us together. He says that he misses her still and badly and that he will miss her always. He says you were younger that I am now. He says that he thinks of her as a girl still. *my blue-veined love, my Julia*. (Barry 2015: 73)

Fan fiction, literary or otherwise, disseminates a voice that evokes real people with a fidelity that matches documentary or journalese. Lennon's voice has such veracity because Barry is a fan. Speaking to Barry, he revealed his fandom by saying that he was particularly fond of Lennon's confession songs on *The White Album* (this album contains the song 'Julia' about his dead mother) and his first solo album *John Lennon/Plastic Ono Band*. It is this caustic and cynic voice that fills the pages of *Beatlebone*. Barry's fandom is revealed explicitly by his autobiographical intrusion in part six of the novel. It is this chapter which reveals his fan devotion and a healthy suspicion concerning efficacy of the usual clichéd research material, 'Fictional and biographical treatment of John Lennon have tended either towards hagiography or character assassination, and I felt the wisest practice was not to do any traditional research among the texts. I did listen to the music: the *Plastic Ono Band* album repeatedly – his primal scream album – and The White Album, as ever, a great deal' (Barry 2015: 181). The conceit of inserting a biographical essay in the middle of the fiction was inspired. By doing this Barry blurs the boundaries between fiction and autobiography, as well as playing a narrative game with the reader worthy of Roland Barthes's essay, *The Death of the Author* (1967). Barry subverts his own objective authorial voice by intruding in the text, in effect, his fandom transgressing the omnipotent author. This chapter discusses many details of Lennon's personal life, the history of Lennon's purchase of Dorinish and a history of the 1960s counterculture, 'Primal Scream had become popular by the 1970s ... There were a number of devoted groups in Ireland, and notorious among these was a collective in Burtonport, Donegal ... who named themselves the Atlantis Community but who were known, locally, as the Screamers' (2015: 181). Barry's Lennon fandom gives off a powerful scent of obsession in this chapter. It is a beautifully written piece, but for its mellifluous purple prose it is the paean of a fan and should be judged as such: no different to slash or pulp, apart from the literary cachet of Canongate and all the marketing finesse that they have provided; its poetic flights of fancy are matched by the humour of Shipper and the Gothic sexuality of slash. If I may intrude author stylee à la Barry, I am a huge fan of this piece of fandom, especially Barry's discussion of Lennon's speaking voice:

> He is quite nasal and often defensive. There is a haughtiness that can almost be princely but his moods are capricious – sometimes he is charming and light; at other times there is darkness evident, and an impatience that can bleed almost into bitterness. He can transition from fluffy to spiky very quickly, even in the course of the same sentence. Often during these interviews he was accompanied by Yoko Ono, who very clearly, from this distance, was the tethering fix in his life; lacking her presence, you get the feeling that he might have unspooled altogether. (Barry 2015: 178)

Here we have Barry's Lennon suitable for an edgy novel: the traumatized Lennon suits his fictional purpose, and Barry begins to conflate his own painful experiences with Lennon's:

> The sense of an ache or a wound just beneath the skin – almost impalpable but always there ... in my own long experience ... the ache can lie buried so deeply and so quietly it might seem not to exist, but it comes back, and it has a definite weight ... and the urge to Scream, I believe is by no means an unreasonable response to it. (Barry 2015: 180)

The Lennon character depicted in *Beatlebone* is angst ridden (which suits Barry's purpose) and obsessed with Ireland (singing rebel songs): *Beatlebone* is fan fiction and this novel creates an imaginative fantasy which conveys the 'real' Lennon with as much gusto and nuance as dozens of biographies including Davies, Goldman and Norman. The coup de grâce of *Beatlebone* is chapter 11 where Barry segues into autobiography. In this chapter, he writes of his trip to the Dakota building in New York. This is where Barry's narrative takes a very strange twist, he writes of experiencing occult forces while visiting Lennon's apartment building,

> I took out a pad and began to make a sketch of the scene. The building itself is Gothic folly, with dark stones, sombre turrets and an air of bespooked Victoriana, and as I drew I tried to imagine within it occult dreams, and the view across the trees, say on the night of a spring gale, in the soak of an insomniac sweat, as the trees shake out their fearful limbs, and the green shimmers of the treetop faeries move like gasses through the dark. The fact that I am myself tuned to occult

frequencies – and frankly I have come to the point in my life where there is no longer deniable – felt like half the battle, but still I had a nagging worry at the edges of my thought, and it was this: If I was going to make *Beatlebone* everything it should be, I had to get the island. (Barry 2015: 176)

Here Barry is writing autobiographically: in a manner similar to Ian MacDonald and he dispenses with any pretence of objectivity; his style in the chapter is first-person personal pronouns, he describes his travels in New York and Ireland researching the book, this is primarily the writing of a Beatle fan, it is fan fiction of a literary hue. Describing John Lennon's island Barry again juxtaposes his autobiography with fiction, having no pretence at capturing objective and empirical reality: Barry is concerned with his own truth appropriated from his knowledge of Beatles myth: this novel is fandom couched in prose poetry to engage the emotions, truth is the warmth of descriptive and colourful feeling, not the reporting of arid facts as in the journalism of Norman and Davies:

On a lit, clear morning, Clew Bay is an infinitely beautiful place – especially if it is seen from a height above Mulranny, with a springtime light coming slant-wise to pick out and give definition to the islands' shapes – but more often than not the Atlantic clouds swarm in from the west, moving like an invading force, or a slow disease, and the view is uncertain and in shifts; the islands appear to come and go in the mist. Among the islands are Freaghullanluggagh and Gobfadda and Muaherillan. There is Kid Island, a Rabbit Island, a Calf Island. Dornish is in fact a pair of islands – Dornish Beg and Dornish More – linked by a rocky causeway. The local pronunciation would be closer to Dur-nish than 'Dor-in-ish'. In the 1970s and 1980s this place was known as Beatle Island. (Barry 2015: 177)

This creative non-fiction chapter is a very bold conceit as Barry is revealing his inspiration and his research methods. In fact, Barry's tortured Lennon is informed by Barry's own autobiography, like many of the slash writers and Norman, Davies and MacDonald; Barry's theme is himself, and the primal-scream Lennon is based on the angst of Barry's 20s and 30s:

The sense of an ache or a wound just beneath the skin – almost impalpable but always there – is not uncommon as you move through the sobering ruts of your thirties. Psychedelic experimentation, in my own long experience, will tend to deepen or amplify this sense. Earlier, in the maelstrom rush of your twenties, in the campaign to selfhood and determination, in finding out who you are – the ache can lay buried so deeply and so quietly it might seem not to exist, but it comes back, and it has a definite weight – as though it has lain buried on the dark side of each passing moment, just there – and the urge to Scream, I believe, is by no means an unreasonable response to it. (Barry 2015: 180)

The reason Barry's autobiographical chapter is so engaging is that the writing here is 'proof indeed that a new literature halfway between reportage and fiction is being born' (Cline and Gillies 2012: 96). Barry is synthesizing documentary fact and mellifluous poetic prose to create a fictional Lennon whose rococo caricature conveys felt experience as much as any documentary are 'real' autobiography. Barry reveals this working method in the 'true' novel, 'Fictional and biographical treatments of John Lennon have tended towards hagiography or character assassination' (Barry 2015: 181); Barry avoids this trap by combining fiction, biography and autobiography in this novel. In fact Barry's writing in this chapter demonstrates the advantages of subjective, partial interpretations over conventional journalistic method. In a sense, Barry iterates the extent to which pornographic slash, biased and the opinionated lyricism of Ian MacDonald and mash-ups of YouTube have more fidelity than spurious testaments of truth such as newspaper reports and documentaries on the Beatles. If a subjective truth is bathed in the golden light of imagination, reality mediated through the human subject (and acknowledged by the writers to be so) trumps hackneyed repetitions of the Beatles myth. Barry's credo seems to be, I'll give you my truth, my Lennon from my fan's eye point of view, and the reader as fan can interpret this version of the Beatles and Lennon subjectively and translate into the web and weft of their own lives. So we have a fragmented reality informed by the perceiver's (the fan's) bias, that is, we create our own concept of the Beatles based on our own class, gender, sexual orientation and this idiosyncratic myriad version of reality has an emotional warmth and vitality that documentary fact lacks unless journalistic truth is mixed with art:

> True memory of the era – as in sense memory, as in the precise tang on the air of a new morning back then, or the throb and rumble of a great city rising from its fumes in the early morning back then, or the way a lover's dark hair might splay just so on the sheets, and she stretches – has now succumbed to time and distance, and what's left to us is mediated, and it can only be built up again in gimcrack reconstructions, with scenic façade, but if we can get the voices right, the fiction might hold for a while at last. (Barry 2015: 201)

Barry eschews definitive notions of truth in this novel, and citing John McGahern, in the epigraph, he emphasizes the problem with capturing the subject through documentary method: 'the most elusive island of all, the first person singular' (Barry 2015). Barry's 'novel' is a deep meditation on fandom and *Beatlebone* raises issues that are key to fandom, sexuality, trauma, bereavement and grief, and this novel shows that fanzines, letters, conventions, journalism, violent obsession, YouTube, cultural tourism, tribute bands and fan fiction are a grief of loss and an attempt to keep memories alive with the acceptance that memory is partial and ephemeral, and transgressive art is often more affecting than pious and conservative documentary fact and heritage. Beatles fandom is predicated on loss of a devotional object and the pain of this loss is alleviated by creative fan culture fantasies, which are mélange of 'open eye' documentary fact colliding with partial memory and fools' huckleberry. Emily Dickinson writes, 'There is a pain – so utter- It swallows substance up – Then covers the abyss with trance – So memory can step Around – across – upon it As one within a swoon-Goes safely – where an open eye Would drop him – bone by bone'

(Dickinson); her words evince that nostalgia is a mélange of fact and fiction, and that progressive nostalgia emphasizes a positive fantasy as grief, trauma and truth are too difficult to bear. Beatles fan fiction is nostalgia transformed and appropriated into an emotionally positive and forward-facing partial memory: 'it covers the abyss with trance' (Dickinson 2010 [1955]: 599).

A genre of fan fiction which indulges in nostalgia in a manner similar to Barry's whimsical literary nostalgia is Beatle time travel slash fiction. Time travel Beatle fiction is a romantic version of slash; there is sex and romance but nothing explicitly sexual. This sub-category is motivated by nostalgia and *Retromania*, and like many of the younger fans I met at Beatleweek in Liverpool in August 2107, the nostalgia and *Retromania* is for a period before they were born. The time travel fiction I researched idealized the 1960s and many elaborate conceits were dreamt up to fetishize the period. For instance, here is a typical biography of a time travel Beatle fan Camille:

> I'm just a 19 year old who likes **music, anime, books, and fandoms**~ I like to daydream endlessly; imagine things and turn them into a story.
>
> I also like all kinds of music, as long as it isn't mainstream. Just anything that catches my attention, whether it's old or modern, you name it. My top bands right now are Arctic Monkeys, Gorillaz, The Beatles <3, metalcore bands like Pierce the Veil/Sleeping with Sirens, and so much more. My fandoms change from time to time, but right now… I'm obsessing over. (**The Beatles** https://www.quotev.com/stories/)

Her story 'Go to Him' has the salient features of the genre; it is a story about Anna Thompson who finds a vintage 1960s pocket watch and travels back to 1965 to meet the Beatles. Like Barry, Camille is obsessed with a period she didn't experience firsthand. The writing in this story is adolescent purple prose, but it is fluent, expressive and the narrative zips along, and the story is predicated on 1960s nostalgia, 'If only I was from the same era as The Beatles as you were', Anna says at the beginning of the story before being whisked off into the 1960s, 'The darkness sent Anna spiraling into nothingness, and a bizarre feeling came over her, as if she was being sucked into a vortex.' Anna travels back to 1965 where she watches the Beatles record *Rubber Soul* and rejects a sexual advance by John Lennon, and the story ends predictably with her having a romance with Paul McCartney: 'Paul closes the distance between them and their lips finally meet. Anna tilts her head to fit their kiss better, and Paul cradles her head with his hands entangled in her long brown hair. Soon, their kiss deepens, and Paul closes the door behind him with his free hand. The two moves slowly towards the bed, not breaking the kiss.' Camille's time travel story reveals that the motivation of fans is affirmed on very basic principles: sexual fantasy and the tendency to idealize either a time period one remembers from adolescence or, as in Camille's case, a desire to escape the present by quixotically imbuing the 1960s Eden before the fall: these dual fantasies are present in the 1960s fans' obsession with *Beatles Monthly*, the nostalgia of conventions, the projection of fantasies onto the Beatles by journalist fans, the violence against Lennon and Harrison by 'fans' who saw the simulacra of the Beatles as a psychological panacea for their mental illness, the mash-up forward-thinking nostalgia of YouTube vids is also looking back to look forward, fan fiction, as we have seen, is constantly fetishizing the 1960s, cultural tourism and tribute bands inherit this romance about the 1960s. All these aspects of fandom are a mix of nostalgia and sex, but nostalgia/sex that looks back to look forward.

Beatles time travel stories express a desire to escape the present and to somehow grasp on to the ephemeral. This is largely the motivation of all fandom: a regret of missing the past of your youth or a desire to whimsically reject the present. Beatles time travel stories are all slight modifications of Camille's story: there is *Back in Time* by Jade, 'Lucy's family has been time travelling since any of them can remember. They can only go back in time, though, not forwards. What happens when Lucy travels back to 1959 and meets her favorite band, the Beatles, before they are officially a band?' There is Wholockmania by Wholockian38, 'A story of two girls who get taken away 221B Baker Street by a man in a blue box to meet their biggest idols – the Beatles!' This Doctor Who/Beatles cultural collision is popular, for example, *Across the Universe: A Beatles Dr Who Crossover* by Sophie. The fans who write Beatle time travel fan fiction are young and female and are a 2017 version of the *Beatles Monthly* demographic, for instance, Julia, who wrote Manifest Destiny, is '19 and a professional starving art student'. The bio in quotev.com fan fiction are girls aged between 16 and 19. This is also true of other fan fiction sites, and these fora are numerous and the stories are imaginative, although the trope of finding a magic totem such as watch recurs often, for instance, in *All in Good Time: A Time Travel Beatles Fan Fiction*, the magical antique time portal is a locket ring, 'Lainey scoffed at the words of the old gypsy fortuneteller. Then the woman handed her a locket ring revealing her grandmother's deepest secret, and the magical ride began' (https://www.wattpad.com/story/77550522-all-in-good-time-a-time-travel-beatles-fanfiction).

Fan fiction is constantly commented upon, annotated and written on request, which differentiates it from literary fiction. Violet Smith, author of Beatles time travel story *Love Is in the Air*, begins her biography on quote.v.com by stating, 'If you want me to write you a story, feel free to ask and I'll do my best.' This interactive approach to art is an anathema to literary fiction,

> Fic can be uncomfortable for writers who believe they create autonomously in a void. Fic lets its seams show in ways other works that also build from sources and predecessors may be at pains to hide – even apparently from their authors … [fanfiction] feeds on its predecessors and its contemporaries, interacts with them, make them new. It is in a constant state of conversation and exchange. It is often unclear where its boundaries are. It is often unclear who the writer is and who is the reader and what the difference is. It sometimes references actual 'real world' events; it sometimes custom-crafts fictional elements masquerading as real. It extracts what usually transpires over many texts and places them in a partly real, partly fictional virtual network it's also funny and romantic and erotic at times. It showcases complex relationships, which are sometimes fraught and angsty and sometimes very sweet'. (Jamison 2013: 14)

A survey of fan fiction is an impossible task because of the sheer volume of stories and writers: archive of our own.org has at the last count 1307 stories that are being changed according to fans' caprices. However, what I've tried to achieve in this chapter is demonstrate the main themes and tropes, and also the age group which suggests that in 2017 we have the same demographic as *Beatles Monthly* and similar interests, sex and romance, but this is a new generation whose writing is affirmed on technological expertise, and reaches an audiences instantaneously.

Ian MacLeod's 'Snodgrass' ruminates on the traumatized Lennon 'I recognize in the cracks in ye pavement. This one looks like a moon buggy. This one looks my dead mum's face after the car hit her outside Mendips. Not that I saw, but still yer dream, don't yer' (MacLeod 2013: 51) and damaged Lennon as its central character, 'nifty fifty with his whole death to look forward to' (MacLeod 2013: 48). The short story sees Lennon as a 50-year-old, long-term unemployed and sharing digs with a prostitute in Birmingham. He has walked out on the Beatles in 1962 over a row about recording 'How Do You Do It' (which they record without him) and has never managed to piece his life back together while the Beatles have gone on to moderate success without him: 'And whaddayouknow the Beatles are playing this very evening at the NEC. The Greatest Hits Tour, it says here on ye corrugated fence. I mean, Fab Gear Man. Give it Bloody Foive. Macca and Stu and George and Ringo' (MacLeod 2013: 48).

Lennon in 'Snodgrass' is 'a sad and bitter man' (MacLeod 2013: 50). MacLeod (who protests that he is not a fan, although he does write 'literary fan fiction') appropriates a Lennon who speaks caustic poetry when describing the scholastic, career and romantic failures in his life:

> When the clouds had cleared we bought fish fresh from the nets in the whitewashed harbour. Then we talked in firelight and the dolphins sang to the lobsters as the waves advanced. … But Formenta was a long way from anything. It was so timeless we knew it couldn't last. The tourists, the government, the locals, the police – every Snodgrass in the universe – moved in. Turned out Morwenna's parents had money so it was all just fine and dandy for the cunt … somehow I ended up in Paris, sleeping in a box. (MacLeod 2013: 50)

Here Lennon is a composite of his pubic self and the famous Beatles biographies, but MacLeod's story sequesters this Lennon and provides us with a cannibalized media hybrid that hijacks the documentary Lennon. The Lennon of 'Snodgrass' is a fan creation who rebels against biographical and media authorship; MacLeod's Lennon is bricolage of fragmentary journalistic pieces and interviews and even in these real historical documents Lennon adopts a performative role. In 'Snodgrass', MacLeod has created a polysemic Lennon who exemplifies 'the deconstructive potential of intertextual composition – a potent rhetoric of critical demolition, comic inversion and cultural provocation' (Hopper 2011: 24). In short, fan fiction has deconstructed popular Beatle stereotypes and clichés. MacLeod has called the story 'debunking' (Brooke 2013) and the novelette does commandeer the story to MacLeod's fictional cravings and bias. Reviewers of the Sky Arts film of 'Snodgrass' demonstrate the extent to which it is a subversive piece (that is usurping the legendary Lennon deified by Philip Norman, Ray Coleman and the media):

> 'Semi-detached houses, semi-detached people leading semi-detached lives', he muttered. 'Me auntie used to say "Oh guitar's all right, John, but you'll never earn a living at it."' F---ing hell, Mimi, you weren't wrong. This was an alternative reality in which Lennon had had an argument with Paul McCartney over a song in 1962 and walked out of the Beatles. The band carried on, performing McCartney songs like Mary Had a Little Lamb and Mull of Kintyre, but never breaking through. 'We could have been bigger than The Hollies', reflected Lennon. 'Snodgrass' was his word for a boring, suburban person. Looking out of the bus window, he saw a man in a suit with a mobile phone. 'You can do the yuppie walkie-talkie all you want, pal. You're still f---ing Snodgrass to me.' The drama was a gentle, admiring portrait of how the Lennon wit and surrealism might have survived in an average life. It also highlighted the fine line between becoming a legend and becoming a claimant. (*The Daily Telegraph*, 2013)

MacLeod's writing is an act of wresting the unreal Beatles Lennon of media myth into his fictional universe:

> but you cannot rationally argue for its predetermined reality through a deficient system of language. Reality is called into being by the process of naming, and it is contingent upon the songlines of discourse. ... language is not unified and monographicial, but multi vocal and dialogic. The point is that Humpty Dumpty was never really together in the first place, so it is disingenuous to pretend that we can really piece him together again. ... all literature is 'about' something – if only the self-conscious theme of the 'unreal' fractured reality. (Hopper 2011: 9)

MacLeod, like newspapers, television and film, is piecing together a mosaic of the simulated Lennon from the media and is no more capturing the flesh and blood Lennon than the YouTube ghostly hauntings of Beatles' image and sound echoing to our ears in 2017. What MacLeod, slash and fan fiction, does is put Humpty Dumpty Lennon/Beatles together in a new way that transgresses the supposed 'reality' of the press and journalist superfans. And MacLeod's 'Snodgrass' imagines Lennon as a failed artist and the Beatles as a very mediocre band:

> I nick a programme from the pile when no one's looking. Got so much gloss on it, feels like a sheet of glass. The Greatest Hits Tour. Two photos of the Fab Foursome then and now. George still looks like his mum and Ringo's Ringo. Stu is wasted, but he always was. And Macca is Cliff on steroids. ... 'And here we have the Beatles, still gigging, nearly a full house here at the NEC, almost as big as Phil Collins or the Bee Gees.' (MacLeod 2013: 52–5)

'Snodgrass' is comedic, parodic carnivalesque of Beatles of deconstructive fandom or given MacLeod's protestation about his fandom, can the text be considered anti-Beatles fandom?

It is important to make one final consideration about slash fiction's subversive and disruptive peculiarities. I have emphasized the inflammatory aspects of this type of writing, but the interactive and immersive elements of slash are as, perhaps even more, mutinous:

> The incorporation/resistance paradigm rests upon an understanding of the text as an inviolable and discrete semiotic surface, its 'preferred' or 'dominant' textual meanings are accepted, negotiated or opposed by the reader By this rationale, slash fiction, which contradicts the source text's preferred meaning of heterosexually, must be the product of subversive or 'deviant' reading. But the incorporation/resistance paradigm offers limited and clumsy models that do not account for the deeper textual strategies of cult television, for its engagements with the fantastic, its function as a species of virtual reality, its emphasis upon the implicit, or its invitation to immersive and interactive engagement. (Jones 2002: 81)

In a manner similar to YouTube, the resistant paradigm of slash is affirmed on technological participation, this is also what differentiates Barry and MacLeod's literary fiction and Shipper popular/fan fiction from slash. As McLuhan famously argues 'the medium is the message'; and slash's subversive elements are a mix of porn, intertextuality and interactivity. Jones contends that 'its extension across a variety of other media, its modes of self-reflexivity and constant play of interruption and excess, work together to overwhelm the processual order of cause and effect, enigma and resolution, extending story events and other narrative and textual elements across boundless networks of interconnected possibilities' (Jones 2002: 84).

Although Jones is writing about television, the same argument applies and differentiates slash from print fiction. The interconnectedness of slash has a transformative effect on Beatles fantasies; the fans' whimsy connects with other fans instantaneously and the online fiction eddies into an online vortex of cannibalized content which is a bricolage of disparate elements: biographical facts of the Beatles' lives meld with make-believe scenarios into stories which have lives of their own. Slash is an inheritor of literary modernism where once fiction was liberated by the wide dissemination by magazines and radio, now the internet creates imaginative worlds which flow together mudding the waters of authorship: often the writers of slash are unknown. Technology has made the Beatles phenomenon a moveable feast of subatomic electrons constantly morphing instantaneously with the warm finger pulse of fans' creativity.

In summary, slash fiction is at once transgressive and simultaneously has similarities to the mainstream literary culture it critiques. Paul Booth demonstrates this very cogently, 'slash fiction is a type of fanfiction textual production that depicts a homosexual relationship that did not exist overtly in the original text' (Booth 2015: 132). In the Beatles' case (apart from Epstein and Lennon's apocryphal affair;

for a detailed discussion of the Epstein/Lennon affair see Pete Shotton's book *My Life*) their sexual lives are a heterosexual text that is subverted by carnivalesque slash; however, these online texts are constantly fluctuating into different contexts and plural meanings:

> 'This balance between respecting the rules of the original and offering new, sexually explicit, noncanonical homosexual relationships is ... constantly shifting. One academic discourse of slash sees its transgressive potential as the most relevant factor in its writing; another acknowledges slash's ideological similarities to the text it references. These are not clear cut categories, however, and slash is inherently multifaceted'. (Booth 2015: 132)

Indeed, Beatles slash is a huge untamed beast that stalks every recess of the internet; if I attempted a survey of this material this chapter would run to hundreds of thousands of words. Booth's writing on slash demonstrates that no matter how subversive a material happens to be, it is dependent on the machinery of traditional publishing houses (Kevin Barry, Ian McLeod and Mark Shipper) or the convergence culture of the web: 'Media fandom is best understood as a continual, negotiation and dialogue within already extant industrial relations' (Booth 2015: 1); the fans' subversive play is structuralist, meaning that play exists 'in a network of intertextual connections'(Barry 2009: 48). For example, structuralism is explained in Literary Theory 101 as a chess set, you can make any move you like as long as it is in the parameters and rules of the game: be as playful and creative within the rules or as Booth puts it, 'play becomes a way of finding new methods of following the rules, using different shades to colour inside the lines, thinking inside the box but changing that box's shape' (Booth 2015: 7). This is a very pertinent definition of slash: The Beatles can be appropriated into any sexual scenario, the most carnivalesque sexual gymnastics and the most dizzying vortex of orgiastic throbbing gristle, but the authors of such imaginative flights are simply moving the pieces around a chess board: the work is existing within the paradigm of existing linguistic structures. Beatles slash is twisting the Beatles phenomenon into new exciting areas, but machinery of production and the linguistic palette is reshaped and not completely rejected.

Another aspect of slash fandom is humour: it appropriates the Beatles' image into a parodic and satirical space. The journalist David Barnett contends that 'There does, it has to be said, seem to be something inherently funny about writing erotic fiction based on established fictional characters. Like people who knit daleks or create huge model railway layouts, fan fiction writers are seen as gently mockable; slashwriters even more so' (*The Guardian*, 2013). In fact the majority of fandom is very humorous: colloquial letters to *Beatles Monthly* concerning 'kissing Ringo's conk'. Conventions where the Beatles phenomenon is celebrated with good-natured bonhomie and ironic obsession. Davies, Norman and McDonald are gently risible and self-deprecating about their own fandom, for instance, Norman's complete *volte-face* on his McCartney thesis; the transgressive fan vids on YouTube range from the sentimental to the outrageously comic (see the comedian Steve Riks for Beatles parody and humour). The Beatles walk in Liverpool and London run the full gamut from serious oration to stand-up comedy, depending on the tour guide that is!; and tribute bands' stage craft lends itself to spontaneous improvised humour which changes each night depending on audience reaction.

Play and humour are closely linked: the fact that slashhumour and slashplay is online is significant as the simulacra gives fans a fora to play, 'English psychoanalysis and theorist Donald Winnicot described play as a way for humans to articulate a meaningful connection between their creative selves and personal psychological development. Play has value because it allows the human mind to practice and experiment with change in a safe environment before approaching change in reality' (Booth 2015: 16). So the jouissance of text demonstrates that the good humour and irony exist in the Beatles fan community; fans recycle the Beatles and their work into subversive humour, which is a riposte to the threatening refashioning of the Beatles into murderous intent by Michael Abram, Charles Manson and Mark Chapman. Vermorel explains fan reactions that range from good humour to violence: 'Showbiz folklore likes to pretend there is an "acceptable norm" of fanhood, only occasionally transgressed by extremist deviants. Most fans, it asserts, are jolly sorts who only desire their idol's well-being, and the smooth operation of the industry. We met quite a few who desired rather more' (Vermorel 2011: 247).

It is important to note that although slashfan and literary fiction are an arena of subversive and transgressive laughter, this carnivalesque is nonetheless a game structured and couched within a conventional digital culture which gives fans permission to ridicule the Beatle phenomenon. Slash is a fringe and radical literary fora of a laughing chorus, but slash, fan and literacy Beatles texts help official Apple culture and Beatles merchandising by promoting the Beatles and encouraging fans to buy and sell a dizzying range of Beatles product. Paul Booth illuminates the extent to which radical slashwriting helps to promote official popular cultures: 'carnival becomes a force of regeneration for official culture, not the dynamic break with it hypothesized by Bakhtin' (Booth 2016: 73). In a discussion of slash, Booth demonstrates how fringe surrealistic and pornographic work is contained within a capitalist framework; just as the semiotic and structuralist language games operate in the manner of a chess game where pieces have symbolic value and are moved into numerous different configurations, however, the pieces are framed within the board and the regulations: a chess game can develop into millions of patterns, but these patterns remain framed within a network of symbols which are, in turn, contained within the rules of the game. The language in slash works along similar lines; it is a subversive use of words, but they are contained in a dominant paradigm and slash, fan and literary fiction are likewise contained in a media/capitalist framework form which they cannot break free. The carnivalesque sexual wordplay of slash strains at its leash but doesn't break free from a digital world based on advertising and promotion: Slash is a naughty capitalism grounded after school and dreaming of the school bell. Using *Star Trek* as an example, Paul Booth shows that slashwriters who often break copyright law (George Lucas and Star Wars are especially litigious with their fans' unofficial transgressions: see Mark Duffett 2013 for a full discussion of Lucas). Booth writes,

Both slash fiction and carnival are subversive acts that are supported by the same culture that is being subverted. Fan fiction subverts traditional or dominant readings of media products. For example, fans may subvert the intended relationship between Kirk and Spock in *Star Trek* and reread it as a homosexual bond, subverting cultural expectation. Or, fan fiction authors may use copyrighted materials for their own creative work, deliberately subverting the political power of the established media oligarchy. Of course, media producers may also support this behavior, as it encourages fans to buy more products and spread knowledge about the media product by word-of mouth- advertising. (Booth 2016: 73)

Even blogs that are playfully augmented by subversive comments are tethered to bigger media structures. Booth contends that 'livejournal.com/story' might direct to a document with both fiction and comment. While the fiction post may remain static, the comment may increase in number continually' (Booth 2016: 57). So fixed or static text is updated and commented upon constantly, as Booth argues: 'The blog is a Barthesian multi-worked text; a mash-up an object with more than one component that retains the unique character of each' (Booth 2016: 57). The progressive nostalgia of slash, and here I define progressive nostalgia as a melancholy longing for a past that paradoxically was before most slashfans were born, is a form of writing that 'is tangible and specific, as well as something that cannot be pinned down or defined, something that cannot be computed or figured out' (Booth 2016: 57). Slash, fan and literary fiction are subversive language games that are a beautifully warped and erotic poetry that are constantly trying to break free from media copyright and regulation and the digital paradigm that co-ops these imaginings. In short, fan writing is an attempt at subversion of literary norms, whether this is Kevin Barry's autobiographical fan fiction, online fan stories or pornographic slash; literary imagination unites with digital technologies to strain at the constraints of the print and online medias. All forms of fan writing attempt to outrun the shadow of their forums (blogs, printed books, etc.), and they are all a type of progressive nostalgia that at least tries to keep one step ahead of the media paradigms that frame their work, and this progressive nostalgia is a fascinating ongoing creative transformation that uses the past to attempt to move fan art forward, as Booth puts it: 'Carnival relishes the grotesque … Just a grotesque body continues to grow past its normal limits, to fatten with excess, so too does the carnival expand exponentially. The carnival grows to incorporate all' (Booth 2016: 74).

Beatles literary fiction, fan fiction and slash fiction are spaces where quixotic whimsy reimagines the Beatles in eccentric erotic dream scenarios. The most serviceable definition of the subversive humour and play of text is provided by David Barnett:

Fan fiction is written by amateur authors using characters from (usually) the published authors' works, TV shows or movies. Slash takes fan fiction to another level: it imagines relationships – often sexual – between those characters that were never intended by the original authors. Slash takes its name from the punctuation between characters' names to denote sexual content and probably dates back to the 1970s, when it came to prominence with Captain Kirk and Mr Spock, in the original Star Trek series. There's a possibly apocryphal tale, which I like to believe is true, purporting that William Shatner asked Spock actor Leonard Nimoy what this Kirk/Spock stuff was all about. Nimoy apparently replied: 'It's you and me, Bill. Fucking.' (*The Guardian*, 2013)

Uber Beatles fan Stephanie Hernandez (who works at The Beatles Story in Liverpool) asked Beatles fans on Twitter about 'stan, shipping and McLennon'. A stan is an 'obsessive' fan, shipping is imagining (and writing about) gay erotic dream scenarios between the Beatles, and McLennon is a predilection for a John and Paul pairing. Fans, who are also slashwriters, reveal subversive humour and illuminate a deep psychological understanding of the motivations of slashstorytellers. Their words demonstrate the extent to which fans who express their fandom through stories are motivated by Eros and these interviews reveal the extent to which our heads (aca-fans, slashfans, tribute band fans, journalist fans) are colonized by our fandom, how our fandom is couched in an 'electronic envelop' (McLuhan 1968). Twitter fans revealed the following about Beatles 'Stan' Twitter and shipping McLennon:

Why do you think the McLennon shipping is such a big thing in stan twitter? Do you think people really believe it/do you believe it?

Because stans can see how close Lennon and McCartney were they want to believe there was some kind of secret 'thing' going on between them. It also makes them current since 'Gay Culture' has become a big presence on social media outlets like Twitter. Also, all the other fandoms also have ships and fanfictions, so it's kind of to be inclusive. I don't believe it but it's nice to think that these boys from probably very conservative families in Liverpool would be accepting of gay relationships. – Bex, 20, Female, Gay: Does not ship McLennon.

Omygod here we GO! I have no idea how the McLennon shipping came about and how it became such a big thing. All I can say is that I think people just felt the strong connection between them, plus the little things that might hint to their relationship. I think people do believe it, and I do too. Maybe not to the extent some may believe, but I do think something happened between them. – Daph, 15, Female, Heterosexual: Ships McLennon.

Probably because shipping like that happens in every fandom and I believe people really do ship it but I don't personally – Ellen, 16, Female, Bisexual: Does not ship McLennon

I really do think people believe it. I think it's a bit creepy to think of these men, half of which are dead, in that way. The things that these people write in the fanfics are just … wow … – Lois, 15, Female, Bisexual: Does not ship McLennon.

I think because they had such a close connection with each other people immediately began to believe they were in a relationship. I definitely think people believe it but I personally don't have an opinion on mclennon as I can't decide if I believe it or not ☺ – Lois, 17, Female, Bisexual: Not sure about McLennon.

I think it's an interesting concept, I mean, if they were in a relationship there would be more proof of it I think. Some of the lyrics though … I mean, look at If

I Fell. Dunno, I don't know where I stand on it but I know people who really do believe it. – Dayna, 16, Female, Straight: Not sure about McLennon

I think people really do buy into it. And I'm really not sure about it myself. I think there may have been something going on, but I don't think we'll ever know for sure. They were experimental guys so they probably did at some point try gay relationships. I think the biggest piece of evidence for me (also a Beach Boys Stan) is Paul's song 'Here Today,' that he wrote for John. Paul would've been very aware of The Beach Boys' 'Here Today' on the Pet Sounds album which is all about a failed relationship and getting over it ... kinda ... – Kaila, 17, Female, Bisexual: Not sure about McLennon, leans towards shipping.

People really do believe it. I think for me, it helps me with my personal life. Being a gay girl I like to read about other gay things? So I like the fanfics. Sounds weird, but there hasn't really been much gay content until recently with like Love, Simon. So I know I'm probably projecting my gay tendencies on The Beatles, but I really do think that they were together at some point. Look at how jealous they were about each other's wives. And look at If I Fell, something was so up then lol – Michelle, 20, Female, Gay: Ships McLennon

I think these girls are just trying to find themselves through The Beatles, but I don't know. I personally don't think so, they were just really really good friends. You can see that in the way they look at each other and the way they took care of each other. It wasn't just John and Paul either, they all were like that with one another. Maybe it's just the fact that they like the way the name sounds together haha. I'm older than a lot of the people in this fandom, so maybe that has something to do with the fact that I don't believe in it. I grew up when they were ALL still releasing stuff, so I have a bit of a different memory of them, whereas all these girls don't, so they have to just make it up as they go. – Gen, 44, Female, Straight: Doesn't ship McLennon

Oh god, yes! People definitely believe it, I do for sure. There's so much evidence to back it up but of course it's all hidden because they had an image to keep up. But look at the way John treated women, all the beating. He was clearly overcompensating for feeling like less of a man, due to his gay feelings for Paul. 100%. – Gio, 18, Female, Straight: Ships McLennon

I asked Stephanie if she had any conclusions about slash writers, and she said,

> A bit of a conclusion: clearly there is a big presence of this in the twitter universe. There are some devout believers in it as I see probably 20 tweets a day pictures of John & Paul together with a 'McLennon' caption. There doesn't necessarily seem like a correlation between the person's sexuality and whether they believe it or not, which I find interesting. The people who aren't really sure about it seem to have some kind of evidence that they believe 'proves it' but ultimately they say they aren't certain. Therefore, the presence of those who do 'ship it' on twitter, likely influences those who say they do not. (Hernandez 2017)

Fan fiction, like all fiction, is a literary performance, and like sexuality is a complex and nuanced identity, a performed identity or, as Judith Butler puts it, 'identity categories', like 'gay' and 'straight', 'tend to be instruments of regulatory regimes, whether as the normalising categories of oppressive structures or as the rallying points for liberatory contestations of that very oppression' (Butler 2004: 15). This means that fan fiction is a carnivaelsque of enunciatory moments of deep fan love.

My discussion of fan, literary and slash fiction draws a distinction between literary and fan fiction which is liberal humanist nostalgia and slash fiction which is transgressive nostalgia. This means that 'good literature is of timeless significance; it somehow transcends the limitations of and peculiarities of the age it was written in, and thereby speaks to what is constant in human nature' (Barry 2009: 17). So Kevin Barry, Mark Shipper and Ian McLeod produce 'literary' works which convey nostalgia as representing universal 'truths' about the nature of memory, loss and trauma; slash combines this type of nostalgia with a transgressive élan that takes the past and reworks it into work that cannibalizes the Beatles myth, making it look forward and making the Beatles' image virtually unrecognizable because of its subversive pornographic strangeness. The Brooklyn-based writer Freddie Winnifred Moore surveys the literature which influenced the Beatles and the writers they in turn influenced. Her survey places the Beatles very much in this liberal humanist paradigm: 'Before The Beatles were inspiring writers – Haruki Murakami, Nick Hornby and, hell, even Kurt Vonnegut, to name a few – they were borrowing their fair share from literature, including the works of Lewis Carroll, James Joyce and Thomas Dekker' (Moore 2014). Her piece demonstrates the following about 'I Am the Walrus':

> In the spirit of Carroll's poem *Jabberwocky*, the song is infused with nonsensical, onomatopoeic language – but the chant 'goo goo g'joob' actually comes from James Joyce's *Finnegans Wake* (Joyce used a slightly different sound: 'googoo goosth'); *I am the Walrus* is also bricolage art preempting their fans' appropriations for the next fifty years, *I am the Walrus* incorporated literature on a subliminal level, as well. During the recording of their 1967 version of the song, the Beatles may have intentionally included two snippets from a static radio broadcast of William Shakespeare's *King Lear* (Edgar leading his blinded father, then killing Oswald). (Moore 2014)

As the Beatles morphed from teen pop stars to mature artists the literary references came thick and fast, The Beatles borrowed from more directly:

> Their song 'Golden Slumbers' took quite a bit from Thomas Dekker's lullaby of the same name. 'Tomorrow Never Knows' also practically copies *The Psychedelic Experience: A Manual Based on the Tibetan Book of the Dead* (Moore 2014); and as well as borrowing and appropriating themselves the Beatles inspired a huge diversity of writer-fans such as S. E. Hinton (in *The Outsiders*) included references to the Beatles' as a sort of timestamp to mark an era; the fictional record snob

Rob Fleming in Nick Hornby's novel *High Fidelity* conveys the band's healing powers after a brutal long-term break-up; But the writer to take the crown for the most Beatles references in their work must be Haruki Murakami. Not only has he named one of his most well-known novels after the *Rubber Soul* track *Norwegian Wood*, he's mentioned the band in passing in many of his other works and even named one of his short stories after another track, *Yesterday*. (Moore 2014)

Moore gives other examples including Kurt Vonnegut's *Timequake*: 'I say in speeches that a plausible mission of artists is to make people appreciate being alive at least a little bit. I am then asked if I know of any artists who pulled that off. I reply, The Beatles did' (Moore 2014). But the most interesting literary illusion is on the democracy of the Beatles art. The plurality and the ubiquity of their work, a combination that makes their songs open to appropriation:

In Jonathan Safran Foer's novel *Extremely Loud and Incredibly Close*, 'I am the Walrus' is the tune the protagonist Oskar Schell imagines his father whistling before he dies in the World Trade Center. At one point in the book, Oskar worries that he can't remember more about his father from that morning – how high his shirt was buttoned up or how exactly he was holding his copy of *The New York Times* – but the whistle of his father's favorite Beatles' melody sticks out. It is infectious; it fills the reader with its melody. The key to empathy right there in the first few lyrics: 'I am he as you are he as you are me and we are all together.' (Moore 2014)

The liberal humanist supposition that Beatles' music is 'timeless' is explored in Beatles fiction. Of course nothing is 'timeless', but what is perpetual and incessant is that Beatles fans take the Beatles' work and relocate it into electronic meme texts that are adaptable, pliable and regenerational as the Beatles patchwork songs themselves. As Moore writes, 'At the end of Foer's novel you want to hear Oskar's father whistle I am the Walrus backwards. That is the unyielding literary power of the Beatles: they connect us' (Moore 2014). Beatles fans instinctively knew from the first bars of 'Love Me Do' on 5 October 1963 to 'The End' on the flip side of *Abbey Road* that they can 'whistle' the Beatles forwards and backwards translating the old into the new: mixing ghostly traces and vestiges with their own personalities and the Beatles' songs continue to change depending on the age, gender, sexual orientation, nationality and temperament of the fans. Christine Scodari writes presciently in 2007 that cyberspace is a forum where Beatles fans 'labor to shape the canon and mythology of this group, its music, and its cast of personae so as to privilege their favored subjectivities, thereby implicating, among others, gendered power relations of sexuality, sociality and romance' (Scodari 2007: 49). In slashgender is a site where complex sexual performances are negotiated because technology is a space where slash can 'defy the neatly defined boundaries of a book, film, or television series' (Scodari 2007: 49): Sandvoss calls this 'space neutrosemy' (Sandvoss 2005: 832; cited in Scodari). In other words, it seems that removing the cultural capital of more traditional media stimulates a fluent type of expression that sidesteps the machinery of hidebound fan and literary fiction. Slash is the troubled delinquent teen of literary forms, and its accessibility (and interactivity) results in an élan of expression and a writerly brio that compensates for the more literary aesthetics of its more mannered parents (literary and fan fiction are better behaved because they are couched in artistic forms that are less open to constant incendiary electronic comment). No matter how avant-garde a paperback writer happens to be, it is not as open as slash to instantaneous appropriation and comment. In a manner similar to tribute bands, the performative moment is emancipatory and liberating: fan fiction whether of the literary or slash hue is an example of resistive sexual desire in an erotic form first glimpsed in the letter pages of *Beatles Monthly*.

Candy Leonard offers a fascinating take on the gendering of fandom and the fact that most slash fiction is written by women. Her analysis shines a light on the inherent sexism of the music business since the 1960s. She says that in 1964 it was not an option to form a band and play instrument like the Beatles; this was a male preserve, and it was 'not an option' to wear your hair or grow sideboards Beatles stylee, again, the boys did this, so girl fans hung pictures of the Beatles on their walls and eventually began to write fan fiction about the band as a result of being frozen out by the machinery of the music business. It is significant to Leonard that fan fiction written by teenage female writers often has stories with themselves in the fiction as helpers or caregivers to the Beatles, 'that was a very strong theme in fan fiction … she is there to help them deal with the crowds, it was a kind of caretaking of them' (Leonard 2018). It is significant that often the only role open to girl fans was not to form a group and play the music, but to write stories where they have a domestic role, although as we have seen, the pornographic imagination of the fans often places the Beatles in many compromising sexual permutations overseen and controlled by the female authors: domesticity here is giving way to appropriation and control of the image by the girl fans.

Leonard suggests that fan fic/slash is also very close to literary fiction and in fact slash and literary fiction are a continuum and very often the reason that literary fiction has greater cultural capital is that it is male. She points out that all serious writing about the Beatles up to the noughties was by men; the book-length treatises on Beatles are all male and this literary treatment of John Lennon (Kevin Barry's *Beatlebone*) is male, he is an established novelist, there is a higher bar for women to be taken seriously period, whether it's literary fiction or serious scholarship, I'm grouping those two together now. One cannot imagine a female graduate student in the late 1990s saying she wants to write her dissertation on the Beatles. Women were a very big part of what made the Beatles the Beatles and the female fan voice was critical to the phenomenon (Leonard 2018). Leonard is correct, these female scholars and novelists did not have an outlet and were ignored, to wit my chapter on journalists as fans, Davies, Norman and MacDonald, given more time I would incorporate Leonard in this discussion of Beatles scholarship.

As Leonard says 'screaming girl fans never really retained their dignity' in the eyes of serious rock critics and that being a girl fan in the 1960s was 'a very unempowered place' because 'women internalized a lot of the misogyny watching as they watched bands from a subordinate position'. In a sense slash fiction is a status inversion as in the 1960s 'for the most part they were powerless'. In fact most popular songs in the 1960s were about masculine heartache, as Leonard argues, 'men get their hearts broken and sing about it' and 'between 64 and 69 there were very few female voices at all'. She contends that 'Hearing Grace Slick break through … you realized that women could have cultural authority too'. The manner in which girl fans appropriated the Beatles phenomenon before Slash was by acting up at Beatles concerts, 'Screaming was the first "whisper" of the women's movement' to Leonard and 'We had never seen human being who looked like this before they were androgynous, but it was always the men who were doing the gender bending … hair and looser gender roles … girls could not behave in public like that' (Leonard 2018). There is a continuum between the highly sexualized letters in *Beatles Monthly*, the screaming at concerts and the subversion of slash: an appropriation which inverts media-dominated male power structures.

Big business and 'what ifs'

Apple and the Beatles organization had more control over product and image before increased fan participation in fora such as YouTube and slash fiction, but this 'radical' fan appropriation is constantly being incorporated into big business. Jenkins, Mizuko and boyd write that companies such as Fan Lib wanted 'to become the platform for fan fiction on the web' and the company began 'to make a profit off fan fiction writing without taking any legal responsibility to defend the community against any legal ramifications' and 'offering them space to publish their work in return for accepting lots of regulation over their content' (Jenkins, Mizuko and boyd 2016: 136). Chapters 5 and 6 of this book, the YouTube and slash chapters, demonstrate a paradigm shift facilitated by technology in which fans are becoming cyborg-like and this post-humanism creates new emancipatory spaces for fans, but these electronic playgrounds are being regulated and corporatized by big organizations in a manner that Apple controlled the Beatles' image and music in the 1960s and the 1970s. FanLib tried to 'aggressively undercut some platforms that had emerged from fandom itself' (Jenkins, Mizuko and boyd 2016: 136), but these simulations, sub-atomic electrons are 'images of broken light' that maintain a certain linguistic energy, invent unusual visual collages, strain for a political and economic autonomy, and fans employ this technology to twist the Beatles phenomenon into new shapes and nuanced shades of meaning that keep the Beatles art facing forwards. The Beatles' work is now palimpsests of new texts based on the old: building on the past to create new fan art.

What literary fiction, fan fiction and slash fiction have in common is that they are all open-ended and ask a series of 'what ifs' that are an invitation to fans to continue the narratives. This open-endedness 'is sometimes translated as "inconclusiveness" or "unfinalizability", referring to a kind of irresolution or lack of closure that reflects the unfinished nature of real life and suggests that the dialogue the text initiated can and should continue. The author's last word in the text is not the final word regarding the topic' (Marshall 2006: 23). That's what fan writers, whether they are literary or not, do; they create an open-ended 'what if' carnival of voices which are 'a celebration of the spirit and life of the people, a time of mischief and good humour, unpredictability, with a touch of madness to it all' (Marshall 2006: 26). As we saw in this chapter, fan fiction is a renewal of the Beatles' death as a band, and of Lennon's and Harrison's deaths: 'But carnival also engages serious themes, frequently involving the recognition of the reality of death and our fear of death in the midst of a celebration of life and the spirit of renewal and the possibility (or certainty, even) of revival' (2006: 26). The Beatles 'what if' stories also challenge the authority, they have a political importance, and 'carnival is an opportunity to challenge established authority. It is subversive and anti-establishment, breaking down codes of class and privilege. Carnival admits the voices of the lower class and allows them to talk back to officialdom' (2006: 26). Regardless of the cultural capital debate I have raised here between literary, fan and slash writing, all three types of literary production are carnivalesque what ifs.

Fan fiction is based on a series of what ifs: what if I could go back and save John Lennon? What if John Lennon visited Ireland? What if John had left the Beatles in 1962? What if I could have sex with Paul, George and Ringo? What if the Beatles had reunited in the late 1970s? Aaron Krerowicz contends that 'this the point of this genre: that you are able to do things that you are unable to do in real life, and often times fantasy is stronger than reality' (Krerowicz 2018); and Beatles fan fiction is a fantasy where fans appropriate and reconfigure the 'reality' of Beatles history into fan fantasies.

7

'I play the part so well': Beatles tribute bands

Beatles fan fiction provides a literary arena where the Beatles are re-energized and reborn through imaginative storytelling, creative characterization and carnivalesque language and description. Beatle conventions express a desire to bring the band back from the dead. Where this Lazarus desire to re-form the Beatles is at its most performative is Beatles tribute acts. Andy Bennett's description of the tribute band phenomenon expresses this Lazarus effect and retrospective urge as 'a postmodern landscape in which real and the hyperreal blur into one. An oft cited explanation for the origin of the tribute band phenomenon is that it began as a response to the perpetual unavailability of original acts' (Bennett 2006: 23). However, this resurrection of the dead bands is creative: as the live simulation is new and fresh depending on the interaction between band and performer on any given night. The key to understanding tribute acts according to Bennett is that tribute bands add a new dimension as they appropriate the image, history and style of the original band into a new live context and add a new forward-looking perspective to the retro:

> In the course of tribute band performances, dead rock stars are brought back to life, defunct bands are reassembled, and classic live performances of yesteryear are accurately reproduced ... Moreover, in revisiting a tribute group or artist's recording and performing history, tribute bands are in the privileged position of being able to creatively play around with that history. (Bennett 2006: 23)

A discussion of Beatles tribute bands is based on these two points: the Beatles are unavailable, so the corpse has to be reanimated and, in so doing, the audience gets to enjoy an eerily and haunting simulation of the Beatles, and the added value of experiencing a unique and singular performance based on the specific live context; in short, a creative copy of the original adding new stagecraft, songs never performed live by the band (that's almost everything from *Revolver* to *Abbey Road*); unrehearsed rapport between audience and band, in a sense, just like recorded music and image, tribute bands are the 'singing dead' (Ellis 2002). It is important to acknowledge, however, that a band being unavailable is not the sole motivation for seeing a tribute act; bands that are still going have tribute bands now and problematize this thesis, for example, Coldplace for Coldplay and Mused for Muse.

The Spring 2012 *Newsweek* published a special commemorative issue entitled *The Beatles! 50 Years since the Music Started*. It was a shiny and seductive publication that archived the most famous and iconic images of the Beatles. As well as a series of predictable pictures, the text included familiar and clichéd ruminations on the cultural impact of the fabled foursome. The selection of articles ranged from Beatles insider Peter Brown's reminiscences on Beatlemania, 'At the Height of the Insanity'; Abby Haglage and Sarah Durham Wilson wrote a human interest piece called 'The Wives and Sons'; Haglage also chronicled 'The Complete Discography': 'Every album, every song, every cover – and how they fit in the pantheon'; and stars such as Billy Joel, Norah Jones, Michael Caine and Jude Law picked their favourite Beatles songs. Albeit that this material is packaged sumptuously, it breaks no new ground. It is an exercise in canon building which follows a chronological history of the Beatles' lives and work. However, one piece that is included in this official canon is 'The Faux Beatles: In Praise of Tribute Bands around the Globe'. This is by far the most interesting section of the *Newsweek* Special. The reason that it is so striking is that it is about Beatles fans. In fact, tribute acts are the ultimate fans: they are so consumed by their heroes that they want to inhabit their skins and to be the Beatles 24/7. The Beatles cultural phenomenon has always been about the fans as much as the famous icons themselves. Here the super fans or ultimate fans are the tribute bands. Everything about the tribute bands connotes obsession and devotion. London's The Bootleg Beatles have been playing together since 1980, and with over four thousand performances they have devoted their whole artistic lives pretending to be other people. The British Invasion in the United States preformed at the EPCOT centre for fifteen years. This kind of obsession is typical of fans and has been delineated in quantitative depth and detailed by academia under the auspices of the philosophy know as fandom.

A fan's desire to write sexual fiction about the Beatles is an act of dedicated fan worship, but, in a sense, the tribute bands are the ultimate fan. The tribute acts inhabit the skins of the Beatles. They try their best to be the Beatles; they mimic their songs note for note and their personalities down to the last glottal stop. It is method acting, and they take the characters home at night. The website thewordislove.co.uk provides an archive on Beatles tribute bands. Like slash and fan fiction, the list is endless and it would take a lifetime of research to delineate the history of each group. The most successful tribute acts such as The Bootleg Beatles, The Kazakhstan Beatles, The Apple Pies, The Return, The Roaches, The Scarabs, The Cheatles, The Nowhere Men and Rain are so obsessed with the Beatles that they not only want to play their music but also want to speak in their accents, wear their clothes, adopt their mannerisms and devote their lives and careers to imitating the Beatles. The journalist Ian Herbert, reviewing the annual Beatleweek in Liverpool in 2000, shows the international flavour of the acts:

> Next year the Bombay Beatles, the convention's first Indian band, will be putting in an appearance (largely on the basis of their novelty factor).Both will have the most obscure band yet to live up to – the Kazakhstan Beatles, enigmatically known as Museum, who appeared two years ago. The band comprised four shepherds

who lived 70 miles from the nearest town. The founder member bought a guitar, formed a band and within a few years was covering 'Yesterday' and 'Hey Jude' in a local factory. The locals loved it. 'They weren't great, but they weren't awful', said Mr Heckle, ambiguously. He's taken a few punts on tribute bands in his time. 'At least they (the Kazakhstanis) went down better than The Punkels (from Hamburg, Germany) who covered everything punk-style at a hundred miles an hour. We had some very angry letters about them.' Such is the desperate lot of those given the apparently impossible job of making their Beatles sound original. 'Some are look-alikes, some are sound-alikes, some are none', said Mr Heckle. 'They're all seeking a new take but there aren't too many novelties left.' The bands' names reflect this painful quest for something a little different. Known variations of the original have included The Beagles, the Beetles (both from Japan), The Buttles (Walsall), The Beats (Argentina), as well the Fab Four, the Fab Faux (both USA) and the Fab Two, an Irish band lacking in numbers. (Herbert 2000)

Georgina Gregory makes a serious contribution to the understanding of such a diverse group of tribute bands in her recent study of 'ghost' acts. Gregory identifies that tribute bands are uber-fans and that their existence is due to the trauma felt by the Beatles' split in 1970. The fan activity from the 1970s Beatle conventions to tribute acts has been a desire to fill the gap in fans' lives when the object of their obsession no longer existed as functioning unit producing new music and film. This production was now left up to the consumers, and certainly the most theatrical and dramatic act of fandom plugging the gap in this loss was Beatle tribute acts. In *Send in the Clones* Gregory writes,

> Reasons for the appearance of three of the earliest tribute bands, The Bootleg Beatles, Rain and The Beatnix, can be attributed to an emotional vacuum created by the original band's break up in 1970. ... The Beatles demise should not be underestimated – fans reeling from the shock of the split – continued to hanker for a reunion, but despite rumours their wishes were to fulfilled and no outlet was available for the pent-up emotions. ... The process of grieving is not restricted to death ... their desire to be united with the lost loved one may lead them to experience and sometimes welcome hallucinations of the deceased. It is easy to see how, in the process of coming to terms with the loss of the Beatles, their tributes fulfilled an important role in representing a tangible link with lost loved ones, allowing the grief feelings to be discharged. (Gregory 2012: 41)

Every night that a tribute act plays is at once nostalgic, but it is also a performance that produces a new interpretation, whether that is a subtle chord change, a quip from one of the performers, a heckle from an audience member or note that is slightly off-key. What we have every time a Beatles tribute act performs is a simultaneous act of fan devotion which yearns to produce an exact copy of the Beatles art, but what we are offered is a different theatrical context for the song and the song itself morphs into something new. A tribute act is an ultimate act of fandom, because of its fidelity to the original and the fact that this act of devotion twists the original into a new shape. It's not simply an exercise in dreamy nostalgia that harks back to the halcyon golden summer of the 1960s: it is a new event and an original text. For instance, The Bootleg Beatles have fun with the canon and the prescribed chronology of Beatles history. A fan famously shouted at the Bootleg John Lennon who was dressed as a mop top 1965 Beatle-suited Lennon. 'Mr. Lennon,' she shouted, 'play Imagine'. 'I haven't written it yet love,' Lennon responded. Here the tribute act is concurrently gently subversive and at the same time faithful to the spirit of the original work: this is the ultimate superfan, a tribute act which changes constantly.

In a sense being in a tribute act is a mixture of contradictory psychological impulses. There is a desire to return to past (necrophilia and *mal d'archive*) but playing in a tribute act goes far beyond a retrospective impersonation or simulation of the original act. From interviewing the Bootleg Beatles it becomes obvious that tribute bands inhabit a liminal 'third-space' between, to use Matt Hills's phrase, 'self and other' (see Appendix 3). Hills contends that

> replication, then, is not the end of the story: it is a moment (or stage) in the impersonator's dynamic career trajectory. Reproducing a 'wholeness' of the other, the successful impersonator finally returns to his or her own body and their own expressive idiom: ideally, the other is used as an object to assist in the unfolding of self and subjectivity. This object-use can be viewed neither as a pure replication of the cult icon, nor as a matter of 'passive' impersonation on the part of the cult fan. The cult fan's sense of self is not subordinated to the other, *being realized through this process of attachment*. (Hills 2002: 166)

When tribute bands such as The Bootleg Beatles play live every performance is an extension of self: a replicated performance is new for two reasons. Firstly, the act of dressing and imagining being someone else challenges primordial fixed identity (Bhabha 1994) as the psychological human essence is as mutable as it is a sign that it can be transcended by inhabiting another identity (self is predicated on semiotic codes) and can be changed 'by blurring the lines between self and other, fan impersonation challenges cultural norms of the fixed and bounded self' (Hills 2002: 171). Secondly, each performance is a bricolage of the new and the old, this can be micro details like the Bootleg John Lennon name checking Oasis throughout the set or it can be a creative mashing of two difference tribute acts creating a dynamic and reimagining of the old, for instance, Beatallica, who are a tribute band who fuse the Beatles and Metallica together:

> Beatallica's complex synthesis of heavy metal and pop challenges authorship just as much as it confronts genre boundaries. Beatallica are not really a tribute band, they prefer to describe their work as a live 'mash-up', an approach which involves combining fragments of the music and lyrics those of Metallica, to which they then add their own lyrics, and just to complicate things further, they make changes to the original tempo, key and time signatures. (Gregory 2012: 74)

Although 'grief', 'sentiment', 'nostalgia', 'cultural trauma' and 'psychological trauma' play a part in fandom's desire to keep the past alive, as we have seen a tribute act is much more complicated than that: it is a method performance where the self is reconfigured into a different persona for every performance. Tribute acts are not ventriloquists and they are not reducible to the status of mimetic karaoke; they change the performance every night because of the live context (the audience and the venues) and the human element of performance, as Gregory argues,

> rather than judging a tribute as failed execution of a text, it is more constructive to appreciate the individuality of single performances, the responses of the audience and the diversity of approaches within the process. The human component and real-time setting ensure that each act and each event is unique, and in this sense, the performance contains an element of the aura which Benjamin ascribed to original artwork untainted by mass production. (Gregory 2012: 128)

My experience of Beatles tribute bands at Beatleweek in Liverpool bears out this thesis of performative uniqueness. The tribute act line-up in August 2017 comprised bands whose performances were different in their performative context and who also mashed Beatle songs into their own eccentric bricolage. In 2017, eight Brazilian tribute bands played at Beatleweek: Nelson and his Beatles (Nelson e Os Besouros) play Beatles songs with a close fidelity but each night their interpretation has a Latin hue; Beat and Shout are a trio who play Beatles songs at a rapid high tempo pace; The BlueBeetles are very faithful to the Beatles sound, but every performance is idiosyncratic with Latin accents and stylings in the music and lyrics; The Colangles Rock Band play a hard rock version of the Beatles' work. The brochure for Beatleweek describes their oeuvre as 'Calangles Mash-ups', seamlessly fusing Beatles classics with other well-known pop and rock songs, riffs and motifs. The idea is to take you to a different 'parallel' during the shows, where you can be listening to the Beatles, while simultaneously listening to arrangements by other well-known musicians and bands!' Clube Big Beatles make every performance different and at Beatleweek they augmented their sound with Andreas Kisser from Sepultura (a famous heavy metal band); Gui Lopes isn't technically a Beatles tribute act, but his inclusion in Beatleweek and the fact that his own songs are very reminiscent of John Lennon's confession-style song writing means that he deserve a mention. Sonido Club are from Florianpolis in Brazil and interpret Beatles songs with the cajon and the pandeiro and experience Beatles songs in a fresh manner. Vini, Lindsay and Isaac are a trio who play Beatles songs with original interpretations of Beatle songs.

The common nationality of tribute band at Beatleweek is English with nine bands, but Brazilian is a close second with eight. The English tribute acts at Beatleweek are The Bootleg Beatles, who will be dealt with at length in this chapter. The other English acts are Tony Coburn, moon-faced, doe-eyed McCartney look-alike who fronts Tony Coburn's Pure McCartney Show; the brilliant Hamburg Beat, who wear black leather jackets and trousers, sunglasses and replicate the sound of the Beatles in Hamburg by pumping out frenetic versions of rock and roll classics by Carl Perkins, Chuck Berry and Little Richard. The Icon, a young Beatles tribute act, came out of musical theatre such as Oliver, Hairspray and Miss Saigon and Our House and play simulations of Beatles classics. The Overtures are an expert Beatles cover band that has performed for Paul McCartney. The Psychedelic Love Orchestra specialize in performing albums in their entirety such as The Beach Boys' *Pet Sounds* and *Sgt. Pepper's Lonely Hearts Club Band*. The Rockits are a nostalgia tribute band that plays crowd-pleasing Retromania such as their show 'Simply 60s'.

Japan had four tribute acts: the Belittles, who were led by Ocean (Paul), who 'Thanks God. Thanks Buddha.' The Clover, an all-female band from Tokyo, who specializes in lesser-known Beatles tracks. The Quarrybeat, whose leader is Pockey Shimiz (John and band leader), and the band have the strapline, 'Welcome to our show. Have a look and enjoy our Paul's smiley face and George's stoned face!' And the Reunions, whose Naoki provides a very 1960s psychedelic description of their act: 'Yes, this could be the final statement of my musical life. I'd love to dye you all a Beatles colour'; and Kaz is correct when she says that their music is 'soulful vocals and a heavy groove' (Beatleweek 2017: 72).

Sweden was represented by Acoustic Beatles, whose USP was 'no electric instruments' even playing complex studio Beatles songs from *Sgt. Pepper* and *Revolver*; Jan Leonard Borgh from the Repeatles, who is 'a vagabond of the western world and played all over Europe and Americas' (Beatleweek 2017: 2); The Bertils, who brought two hundred fans with them; weirdly, Beatleweek extended the remit to include a Rolling Stones tribute act, Rocks Off; and The Stenungekoren, which is translated as Young Rock Choir, performing *Magical Mystery Tour*.

Four Beatles tribute acts from Spain were performing at Beatleweek in 2017. 3Q3 who completely rethought Beatles songs turning them into improvised jazz (with free jazz elements); The Flaming Shakers, who play the early rock and roll songs of the Beatles and who have played with Pete Best; and the Funkles, whom I mentioned in Chapter 2, use funk and soul to completely reimagine the Beatles' texts; and Mother Nature's Meanies, a regular band at the Beatle Day in Gothenburg, Sweden.

Cirrone are one of the four Italian bands at Beatleweek. They describe themselves as 'The Beatles Mash-up' and this bricolage is their distinctive feature, keeping Beatles' music fresh by 'leaving the evergreen melodies of the Beatles just like the originals' (Beatleweek 2017: 33), but Cirrone have melted the songs with many iconic riffs, solos and song bits of other famous artists such as Bowie, Queen, Hendrix, AC/DC, Kinks and Led Zeppelin; when I watched them in the Adelphi Hotel on a Saturday night this 'mashing' did not seem nostalgic: the collision of classic rock texts transformed the old into the new. Rolando Giambelli is a solo artist who started the Beatle Association of Italy and specializes in acoustic sets of Beatles songs. He is something of a Beatles' evangelist dedicating his life to promoting the Beatles in Italy. The Rival Poets are a trio who 'create an unique sound with a unusual line-up, acoustic guitar providing the rhythm, mandolin creating textures and the two voices, Angelica Pallone's lead with Daniele Bazzani's harmonies, often singing together'. The Wonders are Italy's youngest Beatles tribute band: 'The band play total live, with no pre-recorded tracks or samples, keeping the original tones and keys of the originals. With their period outfits and vintage style instruments, the band encapsulates the spirit of 1960s' (Beatleweek 2017: 45).

The United States had Beat-lele: a Hawaiian Beatles tribute act from Oahu in Hawaii: 'Previously a Beatles tribute band called Day in the Life, in 2015 they decided to reinvent themselves as Ukulele Beatles tribute' (Beatleweek 2017: 17). The Bolin/Posner Family are 'a married couple from Maplewood, New Jersey, just outside New York City' (Beatleweek 2017: 24). The video of their three-year-old son, Walter, playing 'Name That Tune Beatle Edition on a drive home, flipping through the "1" CD while Walter rattled off the titles, one after the other. Eli was in the backseat filming it all, and a video posted for friends on Facebook quickly went viral among Beatles fans'. The Tearaways pop cultural weave is Beatles songs combined with the 'California Surf Sound'. Celebrity fans include Tom Hanks and Piers Morgan.

Argentina's Helter Skelter won 'the annual Beatle band competition at The Cavern, Buenos Aires in Argentina: the prize was an invitation to play at International Beatleweek in 2017'. Nube 9 was an opening act for Ringo's concerts in Argentina in 2011. The Star Beetles are 'the official band for the first Beatle Museum of Brazil, named "Magico a Misterioso", which is located in Canela (state of Rio Grande do Sul)' (Beatleweek 2017: 47).

The Breets from Morelia, Michoacan, Mexico, blend a Latin salsa sound with Beatles' music. Las 4 Melenas, whose name translates as the Four Mop Tops, are notable for being very young (they were formed in 2011) and for coming from 'a town on the outskirts of the main Mexican volcanoes Popocatepeti and Iztaccihuatl', demonstrating that the Beatles cultural influence is ubiquitous and is constantly morphing into new hybrid forms. Onion is from Mexico City and their aesthetic is about 'establishing a generational bridge between the essence of the Beatles' music and contemporary rock bands influenced by their legacy' (Beatleweek 2017: 27).

Hempel, The Roaring Forties, Beapple and Two of Us play Beatles songs in a distinct way adding new instruments and whose stagecraft ranges from a solo performer, a band of forty somethings who fetishize 1960s instruments and reinterpret the songs in an idiosyncratic manner instead of copying the original songs note for note, and Two of Us who play song in duet focusing on the Lennon/McCartney dynamic in the Beatles. Stefanie Hempel is the founder of the Beatles Tour in Hamburg. She has recorded her own Beatles tribute album, *Why Don't We Do It in the Road*, on ukulele and guitar. The Roaring Fourties were founded in Cologne in 1993, grey-haired middle-aged men in black Beatles suits and white shirts and who use vintage instruments such as Rickenbackers and Hofners. Holland's Beapple are a Dutch band who 'put a different spin' (Beatleweek 2017: 16) on Beatles' music. Two of Us are a two-man band who reinterpret Beatles material with one guitar, two vocals, a sax or flute (instruments not often used on Beatles songs) and a tambourine.

The Jarnos 'are an instrumental tribute who combines the music of the Beatles with the surf sounds created in California in the early 60s. The Jarnos could be best described as the Beatles mixed with The Ventures and The Shadows'. They are a 1960s mélange that revitalize nostalgic sounds and make them new. Beatles Artifact are a French tribute band who, like The Jarnos, began life as an instrumental Beatles covers band, but gained a singer and moved from a 'clone band' to 'recreating' Beatles texts (Beatleweek 2017: 18). The Bits are a Hungarian tribute band who, sponsored by Hofner, are 'die hard Beatle fans, and deliver an authentic sound' (Beatleweek 2017: 22). McDonald's Farm are a Scottish tribute act that have been performing at Beatleweek for thirty-one years, and who breathe life into the Beatles canon by their inventive collaborations such as performing a whole Rutles album with Neil Innes at the Blue Coat in Liverpool in 1989.

Jiri Nikkinen Band billed as The Beatles Tribute Band played the whole Magical Mystery Tour album on the main stage of the Adelphi Hotel. Russia's Back from the USSR are fronted by Alyona Yarushin, who is an international award-winning singer. Father McKenzie are a rock band from Rostov-on-Don, Russia. Their specialty is performing the entire *Sgt Pepper* album. Switzerland's Les Sauterelles were formed in 1962 and have been reworking 'unplayable' Beatles material. Marco Zappa has been performing since 1967 and describes his mashing of Beatle texts as a 'transformation and pilgrimage' (Beatleweek 2017: 59).

Canadian Hal Bruce has performed seventeen times at Liverpool's Beatleweek: 'He set a world record by performing all 214 Beatles songs in a non-stop medley, all in order of release, and all in the original keys. He accomplished this feat seven different times.' Costa Rica's Dtour were also formed with the intention of 'performing the entire discography … as Beatlemania Costa Rica' (Beatleweek 2017: 28). The Boom Beatles Revival Band are from the Czech town of Usti nad Labem. They perform with a full orchestra which is in keeping with their raison d'être of never trying 'to be The Beatles … they just love to play their music' (Beatleweek 2017: 25). Watching all these tribute bands in Liverpool it is evident that they are all self-consciously attempting to reinterpret the music and to provide new stagecraft to put the songs across. The performances and the songs, as the band testify in the Beatleweek programme, are progressive nostalgia as they take the past and change it into a contemporary sound and also each performance is different every evening depending on the musicians and the audience: each show instead of paralyzing the crowd with romantic and conservative longing for the 1960s invites the audience to reimagine the Beatles in a transformative cultural space, each performance and each crowd's reception of the show is different every night, and that is transformative nostalgia.

There were sixty Beatles tribute acts in Liverpool's Beatleweek in 2017; nine were English, eight were Brazilian; five were Swedish; Italy, Japan, Spain had four. The United States, Argentina and Mexico had three; Germany, Holland, Finland, Russia and Switzerland had two bands; Canada, Costa Rica, Czech Republic, France, Hungary and Scotland had one; and every tribute act at Beatleweek is a fresh spontaneous performance and not just a case of 'playing the part well'. Jimmy Coburn, who plays with the Cavern Club Beatles, described playing at a convention as 'nostalgia that looks back to look forward' and that the Beatles' artistic legacy was so important that playing at the Cavern was like curating a 'museum' (Coburn 2018). Coburn has a point; on Trip Advisor, the Cavern was voted number 8 in a Top 10 UK Landmarks 2010, above Buckingham Palace and St Paul's Cathedral. After watching the Dutch band the Analogues playing *The White Album* in its entirety on 24 August 2018 at the Liverpool Philharmonic Hall, I can say that the Analogues did just that: they looked back to deliver a note-perfect simulation of *The White Album*, but added a creative new sound as well. The Analogues embellished their performance with visuals accompanying each song. Sonja and Robert Muda van Hamel (Spacebar) helped the Analogues successfully stage the unstageable: the sound collage 'Revolution No 9' on a huge screen behind the band, every song on *the White Album* had a film to add to the music. The effect was stunning and brought 1,700 convention fans to their feet. There was a consensus among the crowd that the Analogues were not only the best Beatles tribute act they'd ever seen, but that it was the best gig they'd ever seen. Frank Martens (53) from Hamburg, described it 'as the best concert he'd ever seen'. Between 1986 and 2017, a total of 667 Beatles tribute acts have played at Liverpool's Beatleweek and most bands are inventive and original with their song choice and song interpretation, and of course, each performance is different and the audiences' reactions vary from show to show.

Gregory feels that there is less distance between fans of tribute bands and fans of 'original' acts:

> One of the most striking and enjoyable aspects of the tribute scene are its fan-friendly fan-led ethos. The traditional division between performers and audience is less clear cut, since both could be defined as fans – a sizeable proportion of the musicians are uber fans whose love of the music compelled them to perform in the first place. In enacting the role of their chosen icon, performers are able to extend the parameters of their fandom to a level many of us aspire to but few will ever reach. However, mindful of the egalitarian nature of the tribute event, they are normally careful not to assume a position of superiority. (Gregory 2012: 138)

These bands are assuaging nostalgia grief of first-generation fans by representing a desire to return to fond, early memories before the trauma of the Beatles break-up. This is another reason for fans to escape into the past. This impulse is a *mal archive* (Reynolds 2011: 28): a desire to return to a childhood Eden before the fall, a time when Beatles' music and image flickered across nascent minds. The Beatles themselves were not immune to this sickness and a Paul McCartney concert in 2014 is an unusual spectacle as he is prone to the allure of fandom as his fans. In fact, Paul McCartney is the ultimate Beatles tribute act because his sets almost entirely comprise Beatles cover versions: his shows are a Beatles retrospective complete with video montages of the band in their heyday, and McCartney dressed in Cuban-heeled Beatles boots and a mop top hair style.

Beatles tribute acts have reimagined the Beatles cultural phenomenon; these tribute acts are fans who have created something new, they have looked back to imagine a new future, as Mark Porcaro explains:

> Because the Beatles stopped touring the summer of 1966, none of their albums from *Revolver* forward was performed in live in concert. Thus the tribute bands are forced to recreate the wardrobes of the famous album covers, *Sgt. Pepper's*

Lonely Hearts Club Band and *Abbey Road*, since these are the strongest visual clues they can give an audience as to which time period they are creating. However, by wearing these costumes they have created a reality which never existed, a reality that has gone beyond the original and become an thing of its own – a hyperreality of Beatle performance. (Porcaro 2008)

Ian Inglis cogently prescribes this future of tribute band scholarship and puts the audience on an equal footing as the Prefab Fours:

The proper investigation of Beatles tribute bands therefore has to be situated within a number of interrelated contexts – musical, commercial, cultural, historical and personal. Either through pastiche or parody, the fabrication of a (more or less) credible production requires inputs from performers and audiences alike. Far from being a passive spectator at an event, the audience member is an active participant in the creation and celebration of the event. (Inglis 2006: 132)

At tribute concerts, band and audiences are playing their respective parts so well. A performance by a tribute band is a reinterpretation of the Beatles' canon, and the audiences' reactions are different at each show. The tribute bands and their audiences are engaged in a 'creative reinterpretation that each individual performance evokes. From the back of the auditorium or pub bar, the fan remains aware of the tensions between the past and present, even as he or she temporarily forgets the layers of reconstruction' (Homan 2006: 5).

8

'Ticket to Ride': English cultural tourism and Beatles fans

The final chapter will discuss Beatles-related tourism, museums, city walks and urban renewal with reference to Liverpool and London's tourist industry. Stephanie and Mark Fremaux contend that, 'With the increasing ease and affordability of travelling in the mid-twentieth-century, tourism focused on catering to individual needs. Postmodernity ushered in a focus on the individual and through the rise of popular culture, consumerism, and the ease of reproduction, museums were no longer places for high culture where the relics of an imperial past were on display' (Wearing, Stevenson and Young 2010: 20; cited in S. Fremaux and M. Fremaux), to put it simply, fans now have access to a highly personalized culture remote from 'imperial' museum culture and Freud's 'death-drive' (Thanatos): what Derrida refers to as a ghoulish *mal d'archive*. Simon Reynolds calls this unwholesome process a blending of 'museum and mausoleum' (Reynolds 2012: 12), but the 'living culture' of cultural tourism discussed in this chapter is concerned with a new empirical and immersive experience: new social spheres for fan interaction. For instance, Richard Porter's London Beatles Walks are an opportunity for fan interaction and fresh 'meaning-making' (S. Fremaux and M. Fremaux 2013: 10). Speaking to Richard Porter and the fans that go on his walks, we find that fans are a heterogeneous mess of divisive and contradictory impulses and that cultural tourism adds something new to enjoying and understanding music in a fresh context: 'Popular music is not a national industry. It comes from cities, but negotiates with myths and narratives of the urban and pastoral past. Through popular music, new groups and communities negotiate the meaning of city to find an identity' (Brabazon 2012: 54).

Nostalgic memories of the past, which cultural tourism is predicated on, are wedded to digital memory and the result is a physical walk that stimulates a cognitive experience of progressive and forward-looking thoughts that are then spread communally by the internet; my findings from the questionnaire I used in London and Liverpool reach a similar conclusion, with the participants suggesting that Beatles tourism made them feel 'optimistic'. Worcman and Garde-Hansen call this *Social Memory Technology* (2016); and express memory as a creative reworking of past memories:

> It is from the past that we take the 'meaning' that we give to our present. This same logic is reproduced in the sphere of the collective. Yet, even though we have the 'sensation' that the past we remember is exactly the same as what actually happened, we cannot fail to highlight that our memories are dynamic and the narratives we construct come from our present moment as a story we tell ourselves and others. They are creative choices, and, as the historian Peter Burke confirms, memory is much more about what we forget than what we remember: 'the process of "re-remembering" is influenced by changing situations in which are recalled (2005: 115). What is recorded in our memory is that which … is important at that time and will change from moment to moment. Moreover, we cannot assume that producing a history of a group's mental process will inextricably produce a 'collective' to focus on collective mentalities is to forget that individuals do not think exactly alike' (Burke 2005: 97). This is a constant and dynamic process of recording and constructing narratives on behalf of the self or the group's members, and sharing those selves amongst the group and beyond. (Worcman and Garde-Hansen 2016: 54)

Consequently the experience on a Beatles walk is a transformative one: changing a *mal d'archive* into a forward-looking, progressive living culture that is not anchored to the here and now of the walking tour or the museum. For example, the fans on Richard Porter's London Beatles Walks are recording the experience on their phones. So in a manner to Lincoln Geraghty's analysis of the collectibles such as the print copies of *Beatles Monthly* being loosed into cyberspace by technology, tourism has transformed

> our understanding of the present, community and territory. The new possibilities of connection and sharing our life stories have somehow been transforming our relationship with memory. Any moment, even if it is of no importance, is considered to be worthy of recording and … can become part of 'our past', at the same time as it becomes necessary to create a 'present' through a medium that is increasing social (video, photo, text, social network). (2016: 54)

Technology 'represents an enormous possibility for the dissemination of personal narratives' (Worcman and Garde-Hansen 2016: 64); English cultural tourism is a geographical space where Beatles fans can construct and celebrate their private Beatles heritage based on memories prompted by walks such as Richard Porter's, and spread them exponentially in an accelerated present.

London Beatles walks

Richard Porter started London Beatles Walks and is a superfan to the same degree as Beatles tribute bands and superfan journalists Hunter Davies, Philip Norman and Ian MacDonald. Porter's website states that, 'If you picture yourself on a boat on a river with tangerine trees and marmalade skies, Richard Porter can't help you. But if you are in London and feeling nostalgic for the Beatles era then Porter, president of the London Beatles Fan Club, is the man to see' (London Beatles Walks 2017). Indeed his knowledge of Beatles minutiae is impressive, and anyone who has been on one of his Beatles walks will be stupefied by his level of psychogeography. There are five tours a week which follows cultural sites that have played a part (no matter how insignificant) in Beatles history. The *In My Life Tour* follows the opening scenes of *A Hard Day's Night*, the restaurant scene in *Help!*, the registry office where two of the Beatles were married, the apartment immortalized by Ringo, John and Yoko where the infamous Two Virgins picture was taken, the house where Paul lived with Jane Asher, the house where John and Paul wrote 'I Want to Hold Your Hand' and finishing in the legendary Abbey Road studios and crosswalk. The itinerary itself can be dismissed as archive fever or nostalgia: a necrophiliac obsession with the past, however, it is the fans' interaction with these sites that creates new meanings: an unfamiliar transgressive psychogeography.

On 6 July 2017 I met Richard Porter at the Tottenham Court Road tube station (exit one). If anyone embodies Beatles fandom, it is Richard. He introduced the walk by telling the crowd of twenty-five people that it was the sixtieth anniversary of John meeting Paul at Woolton Fete, Liverpool. The crowd was a homogenized group of Beatles fans. I use the word 'homogenized' because, although the age range was from 18 to 66, they were a typical demographic representing Atlantic history and Anglo-American individualism with a family from Malaysia being the one exception. I spoke to Betty and Faith from Nova Scotia, both in their 60s, but when I asked them if Beatles walks were 'an unhealthy obsession with the past', they felt that these walks 'make people feel optimistic'. They agreed that nostalgia was the main motivation behind the whole industry but it was 'an optimistic nostalgia', that is, a forward-looking nostalgia. This theory was borne out by 18- and 19-year-olds on the tour. The fans were relating to the Beatles in the present tense. The fans from Atlanta, Canada, Iowa, Israel, Perth, San Francisco, Sydney embodied the past and future combined in a living culture, neophilia and necrophilia, which creates an amorphous fan identity. Many of the fans on the walk had visited Shakespeare's Globe and Buckingham Palace on their visit to London, so the Beatles Walk and Abbey Road specially are established, conservative cultural tourism; however, the Beatles fans are a refractory and undisciplined coterie that the Beatles cultural phenomenon is constantly morphing into indeterminate shapes that use the past to move forward and who don't revere the buildings as holy shrines. The tours are not solely an exercise in nostalgia as the fans' attitudes are blended with how we understand popular culture and the Beatles now. In 2017 we have a more positive engagement with popular culture: a celebratory cultural community with an 'optimistic' and plural cultural identity. In discussions with thousands of fans I feel their identity is characterized by Walter Benjamin's *Angel of History*, 'a storm is blowing in from Paradise; it has got caught in his wings with such a violence that the angel can no longer close them; The storm irresistibly propels him into the future to which his back is turned' (Benjamin 1968: 257–8).

Porter is a superfan, he does five Beatles walks a week, on Tuesdays and Saturdays his walk covers cultural sites in north London. I met Porter at the entrance to

Marylebone Station on 25 July 2017; and from the start the tour had a strange spectral quality as many of the sites were very little changed from the 1960s. We (a 64-year-old Beatles fan, Val from Essex, a family from Philadelphia who ranged from a 10-year-old Beatles fan to 50-something parents, a Dutch non-Beatle fan, Anya, who was only interested in the locale) were directed to the road alongside the station, Boston Place. This was where the opening of *A Hard Day's Night* was filmed in 1964. The very young fans were fascinated by looking at this sepia road for the first time in colour. I asked the fans what they felt looking at this movie location and Val called it a 'nostalgic feeling' and Anya felt that the 'English are very sentimental'. The 10-year-old was saucer-eyed with delight, and his psychological imagining of this street was a fresh, new and dynamic emotional experience. From here the minutiae of Beatle lore was visited: the location of the Indian restaurant in *Help!*; Richard Asher's huge townhouse at 57 Wimpole Street, where Paul lived with his girlfriend Jane for three years at the height of Beatlemania, and where he wrote 'Yesterday'; the former Apple shop at 94 Baker Street, Ringo's apartment at 34 Montagu Square, where John Lennon was busted for marijuana possession in 1968; and Marylebone Registry Office, where Paul married Linda Eastman on 7 March 1969.

Richard Porter showed still photographs of the Beatles in front of the buildings on this tour, and this mix for past and present made for a psychological experience which lamented the passing of the 1960s, but it was an odd juxtaposition of past and future; it stimulated a feeling of future pasts in me, the past filling the present with spectres of meaning, a hauntology, which was firmly rooted in the here and now, and this present experience is a new feeling with the ghosts of the past mingling with the imagining of the present. Here architectural history is 'turning nostalgia into a creative tool' (Guesdon and Le Guern 2014: 79):

> the past fording us to re-imagine new possibilities and perspectives of meaning: the progression of time, its recollection and omission raise awareness of the tension existing between 'vanishing' and 'return' as a definition of nostalgia. It also opens the possibility of dramatizing the presence – the insistence – in ourselves of an emotional past being replenished with new projections. (2014: 79)

The attitude of the tour group was a mixture of iconoclasm, subversion, silliness and playfulness. A creative psychological state that was translating the rock shrines on the tour into a living experience: 'Rituals, feasts, and friends are all essential for play to continue. Silly rituals or sensible rituals, magic rituals, always arbitrary but all abolishing sense and parodying the real' (Baudrillard 2014: 227).

Simon Reynolds has suggested that the archive is 'deeply entangled with ideas of origin and order, authenticity and order'. 'Arch' is the same arch that is in words like 'archaic', 'archetype' and 'archaeology', but it is the 'arch' that is in words like 'monarchy' (Reynolds 2011: 26–7). The Beatles walks fans tick off Buckingham Palace and Abbey Road Studios on their cultural itinerary, but Beatles cultural tourism has a more uneven, bumpy and high-spirited character than tours of regal and imperious edifices. Abbey Road is a busy thoroughfare where pedestrians are castigated by angry motorists as they cross the famous zebra crossing, and the walls outside Abbey Road Studios are covered in guerrilla graffiti which changes from second to second. Reynold feels that 'we can't past the past' with 'endless Beatles/Stones/Dylan covers on magazines like Mojo and Uncut' (Reynolds 2011: 411). It seems that the way to transcend the past is 'a frictionless, near instantaneous transit within networks' (Reynolds 2011: 412). In fact this de-anchoring of the archive and revered cultural sites happens on these walking tours: phones and iPad capturing each cultural site and transforming Abbey Road, MPL Communications, Carnaby Street and Savile Row into simulacra that is disseminated instantly from fan to fan enacting emotion architecture that furnishes fans' minds with a strange amalgam of personalized Beatles history remote from canons and traditional heritage culture; this appropriation is true of other cultural sites such as Buckingham Palace and the Globe, English heritage such as Shakespeare and the cult of Princess Diana is also appropriated by monomaniacal, vibrant and extreme fans 'inspired by media output into but not restricted to it. Its concerns escape the matrix of corporate production by raising more humanist issues: seeking pleasure, exploring creativity and making social connections' (Duffett 2013: 285).

This technological appropriation of cultural sites shifts Beatles cultural sites into the sphere of the virtual, into the 'community of imagination', a community which constantly reimagines the fan experience and translates it into a powerful emotional and transgressive experience that is immediately commented upon, edited and its meaning fractured by many diverse fans: 'Reassuringly, by going online this intense but somehow "almost" non-verbalistic experience can be picked, restaged, and reperformed through self-reflexive and humorous analogies' (Hills 2002: 180). This 'technique of reproduction detaches the reproduced object from the domain of tradition' (Benjamin 1998).

The virtual has very strong ties to psychogeography on these Beatles walks. While not exactly flâneurs in the Benjamin sense, because these walking tours are structured and organized by the tour guide, there is definitely a latitude of fan experience. Non-paying passers-by join the official tour to heckle and disrupt and we have seen how the psychogeography of the tour is transformed into a virtual imagining by the fans. Although the Beatles fans are not explicitly disorientating capitalism, nor have they a political intention as, say, the situationist Guy Debord, my experience of many walks in London and Liverpool is close to Debord's concept of dérive:

> One of psychogeography's principle means was the dérive. Long a favorite practice of the dadaists, who organized a variety of expeditions, and the surrealists, for whom the geographical form of automatism was an instructive pleasure, the dérive, or drift, was defined by the situationists as the 'technique of locomotion without a goal', in which 'one or more persons during a certain period drop their usual motives for movement and action, their relations, their work and leisure activities, and let themselves be drawn by the attractions of the terrain and the encounters they find there'. The dérive acted as something of a model for the 'playful creation' of all human relationships. (Plant 2016)

In a very real sense this is exactly what happens on Beatles walks. In Liverpool I took a tour with Joey on the eponymous Ask for Joey Taxi Tour: The Fab Four Taxi Tour, ranked number 1 of 67 tours in Liverpool according to its website. Outside Ringo Starr's first home at 9 Madryn Street, Dingle, Liverpool, Joey told me that 'Paul McCartney was his favourite Beatle' and that Ringo Starr was 'the luckiest man in the world'. There was a carnivalesque lack of idolatry on this tour that was funny and refreshing; and the story of a topiary Ringo Starr being decapitated after he dissed Liverpool on the Jonathan Ross Show was told with relish.

Joey's Taxi Tour is symptomatic of the huge boom in Beatles cultural tourism in Liverpool; his tour is just one of many cultural attractions that demonstrates the cultural and economic benefits of UK Beatles tourism. The first report on contemporary Beatles tourism in Liverpool found the following:

> The groups legacy is worth £81.9 million each year to Liverpool's economy – a figure likely to continue rising – and is supporting more than 2,300 jobs, according to the first report into the burgeoning Beatles tourist industry ... The report commissioned by Liverpool City Council represents the first-ever study of the contemporary value of the Beatles and links earlier academic work with economic data and interviews with key people in the city. It shows that the Beatles related economy is growing by up to 15% per year and that there remains 'significant' growth potential for the future, including the planned relocation of the British Music Experience to Liverpool, and the potential redevelopment of Strawberry Field, where John Lennon played as a child. (*The Independent* 2016)

Speaking to Stephanie Hernandez, a 20-year-old Beatles fan from Houston, Texas, who lives in the UK and works at the Beatles Story (Beatles Museum in Liverpool), was very revealing about the heterogeneity of Beatles fans who are employed in and who constitute the fans who participate in Beatles cultural tourism. She is a Mexican-American who divides her time between London and Liverpool. Her personal fandom narrative illustrates three very important points about fandom. Firstly, her 'unnostalgizing' or progressive fandom, by which I mean in her context she first became a fan in 1998 when she was 9 years old, her choir was singing 'I Want to Hold Your Hand', and her teacher give her a picture of the Beatles and she immediately developed a 'crush' on John Lennon; however, although this anecdote is illuminating regarding the Beatles' appeal of image and music, it is more important for the fact that the Beatles' music and image is not retrogressive nostalgia: here is an example of a fan who encounters the Beatles thirty-five years after Beatlemania and to this fan the band are relevant to her childhood and her reaction is unnostalgizing or progressive as the Beatles are unanchored from their 1960s context and enjoyed in a contemporary cultural setting. Secondly, her personal narrative is important as her job at the Beatle Story Museum gives her access and unique insight into an incredibly diverse demographic of fans; while working in the shop, and as a Spanish speaker, she talked to fans who spoke very little English; she found out that 'one of the most common nationalities of fans was Argentinian'. The age group at the museum she characterized as ranging from '10 to 80' (Hernandez 2017), and the psychological motivation for these fans visiting Abbey Road, the Beatles' homes in Liverpool and very other conceivable cultural site that had any connection to the Beatles was 'taking things from the past and making them present to them now'. One of the ways they do this is by collecting from the shop, Stephanie says that they buy 'one of everything, key rings, dolls, bottle openers, they make a point of buying a record': not only do fans have a contemporaneous experience of walking around old Beatles haunts, but they furnish their lives with merchandise that seems to bring them a sense of security and comfort; Stephanie adheres to this theory describing her room in London as a 'shrine' to the Beatles. Thirdly, her age links to the previous two points; she is young and the Beatles phenomenon to her is present and progressive so working in Beatles cultural tourism is engaging with fans in the here and now and looking forward.

Her fan narrative is a fascinating case study as her references to the Beatles mostly reference the years 2016, 2017 and 2018. When she arrived from the United States she took a taxi straight to Abbey Road (before seeing Shakespeare's Globe and Buckingham Palace) and from there went to the main cultural Beatles sites in Liverpool (the National Trust Houses and the Beatles Story Museum); and she adds 'that when visiting these places it's not 1962, and you can't possibly know how it was then, so you make it up in your head'. In a sense, this is active cultural tourism in the moment.

Her characterization of young fans is also enlightening regarding the fan demographic: she has met very few fans in the 20-year-old age group, but numerous fans 'about ten years older or five years younger'. Her interaction with baby boomer fans is also very revealing about fandom, a Polish fan in his sixties told her that 'you don't know this music', 'you are not old enough' (Hernandez 2017), and was incredulous to find out that a 20-year-old was such a fan.

To Stephanie, the main cultural locus in Liverpool is still The Cavern Club; she recalls seeing the Cavern Club Beatles playing at Beatleweek in 2017, and a drunk female fan standing on a table and shouting that she wanted to have sex with John Lennon; revealingly she wanted sex with Lennon and not the Cavern Club Beatles' lead singer Jimmy Coburn. The fan was so immersed in the moment that the performance of Lennon brought the simulacrum Lennon powerfully into her life in the performative moment.

We discussed that at the root of cultural tourism for baby boomer fans is the trauma of the death of the band, and she added that there will be more Beatles musicals, Beatles tribute bands and increased Beatles tourism 'when Paul and Ringo pass'. Her stories of Beatleweek unnostalgizes the Beatles cultural tourism; she relates a story where a coach full of 10-year-old Italian children arrive at the museum looking bored and travel weary but after the visit they had morphed into energized fans who were begging their parents to buy them every kind of conceivable Beatles merchandise in the shop. Her job at the Beatles Story Museum and her fandom epitomize progressive nostalgia or unnostalgizing of the Beatles cultural phenomenon as young fans interact with cultural space and memorabilia to create new meanings that take the old and reboot for the present. Stephanie Hernandez is an example of a fan who reinterprets fandom through psychogeography and collecting; her job in the Beatles industry is an example of twenty-first-century Beatles fandom; her collections of 1960s vinyl, 'sixties candy store jewellery, and sixties badges' is a psychological romanticizing of 1960s but is a progressive nostalgia of a 20-year-old fan who couches her fandom in the present and future tense when she tells me that 'the human race is a Beatles fan' (Hernandez 2017).

Beatles tours attract an international audience and the tourist numbers in Liverpool are very impressive. In 2016 the UK creative industries published three reports on the state of UK music tourism:

> In the summer of 2016, the music industry trade body UK Music published its latest in-depth Measuring Music study that showed the sector's contribution to the UK economy was worth £4.1bn in Gross Value Added (GVA) during 2015. The music industry also generated £2.2bn in exports and accounted for 119,000 full-time jobs. The latest research from another of UK Music's annual reports, Wish You Were Here 2016, found there were 10.4 million music tourists who attended a festival or gig in 2015 (up 13 per cent year on year), generating £3.7 billion spending in the process. The music industry has also identified huge opportunities for the development of music heritage tourism, which could provide further economic and cultural value. UK Music's Imagine report looked in more detail at the role of music heritage in driving tourism, and the potential heritage resources that could be marketed to music fans. It argues that if visitors to The Beatles Story and The Beatles Magical Mystery Tour were to increase in line with the government's targeted growth in international visitors to the UK, these attractions would have over 350,000 annual visitors. (http://www.thecreativeindustries.co.uk/industries/music/music-case-studies/music-case-music-heritage-tourism)

These statistics demonstrate the extent to which music heritage is enshrined in UK culture, and that these heritage institutions are ubiquitous in UK culture providing spaces for a wide demographic to interact with in unique ways according to their age, class and gender.

Beatles walks are a locus where the physical, the local, the international, the psychological and the virtual meet to create fan space that is evolving and changing. The experience is heterogeneous depending on the tour group, the guide and caprices of the public on any given day. In her book *A Field Guide to Getting Lost*, Rebecca Solnit has a poetic, lyrical and new age evocation of the emotion of cityscapes. In a profound sense her writing has an important contribution to make to the understanding of fandom as 'a special bundle of processes that interact in contingent ways' (Duffett 2013: 288). She writes about the emotional nexus between people and places:

> The places in which any significant event occurred become embedded with some of that emotion, and so to recover the memory of the place is to recover the emotion, and sometimes to revisit the place uncovers the emotion. Every love has its landscape. Thus place, which is always spoken of as though it only counts when you are present, possesses you in its absence, takes on another life as

a sense of space, a summoning in the imagination with all the atmospheric effect and association of a powerful emotion. The places inside matter as much as the ones outside. It is as though the places stay with you and that you long for them when they become deities – a lot of religions have local deities, presiding spirits, geniuses of the place. You could imagine that in those songs of Kentucky or the Red River is a spirit to which the singer prays, that they mourn the dreamtime before banishment, when the singer lived among the gods who were not phantoms but geography, matter, earth itself. (Solnit 2006: 18)

Beatles fans' experience of English cultural tourism is a psychological space where future fan cultures collide with past cultures in the circuitous Mayfair, Soho and West End streets. The experience is similar to Cecil Sharpe's definition of folk music as a present future, the folk song 'comes to us … like a building newly restored, with its walls scraped and cleaned and stripped of their moss and fern' (Young 2010: 67). A walking tour reimagines old experiences and makes them new, it is a hauntology if you like, a flashback, 'an intrusive, anachronic image that throws of the linear temporality of the story' (Luckhurst 2008: 10); the fan is Janus faced: looking back to look forward. The strollers on the tour and the superfan guide are transgressing linear history and contributing to a mental space that is difficult to quantify no matter how many interviews I conducted. The fans and the guides have an agency that makeshifts mental furniture into concepts that are very complex, 'a relationship between cities and music that is not linear or causal' (Brabazon 2012: 57). An experience that is 'in the dusty, cluttered corridors of the arcades, where street and interior are one, historical time is broken up into kaleidoscopic distractions and momentary come-ons, myriad displays of ephemera, thresholds for the passage of what Gerard de Nerval calls "the ghosts of material things"' (Benjamin 1999: 7).

A non-causal psychological and impressionistic feeling is that it is difficult to articulate and characterize my experience and many fans' experiences of walking tours. The hauntology of material things, buildings on walking tours, demonstrates 'the monumental distinctiveness of cult fans' relationship to space and place' (Hills 2002: 154). If I substitute Abbey Road Studio, Savile Row, Trident Recording Studios and so on for Elvis's Graceland in the following passage, we see that Matt Hills writes out the importance of physical space to fans: 'Through Graceland the significance of Elvis – something which would otherwise tend to be free floating and accidental to processes of signification – can be contained or "anchored" in a visible, physical and public fashion. This process of anchorage is important since it provides a form of permanence to what would otherwise be a potentially fleeting pre-verbal experience' (Hills 2002: 154).

Hills stresses the extent to which space and place are important in 'conceptualising cult fans' practices as extensions of fan-text affective relationships, affect has been considered not as an abstract and context-free quality, but rather as an component within (seeking legitimation) the social and individual contexts of fan "pilgrimage" or tourism' (Hills 2002: 156). Hills's work is fascinating as it shows that fandom cannot be 'reduced to metaphors based around "reading", "meaning" or interpretation' (Hills

2002: 156). In other words, fandom is a very diffuse and amorphous psychological interaction with space; and it is because of this indeterminate psychological sense that English Beatles tourism is important for anchoring, however momentarily, a deep connection between people and buildings.

London Beatles Walks is created by a superfan (Richard Porter) for superfans and the lasting impression that this author took from interviewing fans and taking many of Porter's tours was that if he could, Porter would merge with the unpigmented walls of Abbey Road Studio, impaling himself as a living sculpture publicizing the Beatles to the thousands or so fans that cross the famous zebra crossing every day. The fans on these walks look back but transform the past into their present and future lives: on these tours, fans are buoyant and hopeful. As Tammy from San Francisco told me, the tours made her 'feel good' and 'happy' and here the emphasis is on the present tense. The fans on these walks epitomize 'grassroots convergence' (Jenkins 2008: 326) where strollers interact with buildings and streets imbuing these monuments with their emotions and feelings. Each walker/fan experiences a progressive sentimentality, a 'nostalgia [that] could be described as being a liminal, ambiguous phenomenon that migrates into deep emotional and psychological structures as well as into larger cultural, social, economic and political ones' (Niemeyer 2014: 6).

When I interviewed Richard Porter, the conversation ranged from the origin of his own Beatles fandom, how he started the Beatles walking tours, of the age group and nationalities that went on his London Beatles Walk tours. Porter began by telling me about his uber fandom, and he turned out to be a second-generation Beatles fan, 'I was thirteen years old and on new year's day 1976 Capital Radio in London did a rundown of the top one hundred most requested songs of all time by their listeners and over twenty were by the Beatles and the next day I bought the *Red Album 1962–1966*' (Porter 2018). Porter talks about his introduction to Beatles' music with a mixture of nostalgia and of progressiveness. His memories are a psychological melange of the past and the present which is living culture. A progressive nostalgia that is of the moment; and he agrees that this is the feeling that participants on his walks have, that of a forward-looking and lived culture, and very often he says that it is teenagers who bring their parents on walks.

Porter says that he didn't know many Beatles fans until John Lennon was murdered and that after Lennon's murder he began to reach out to Beatles fans as a pen pal and then through reading and sharing his interest in *Beatles Monthly*. It shows the vast scope of the Beatles phenomenon that second-generation Beatles fans came to the band through the republication of *Beatles Monthly* and the release of the greatest hits *Red Album*: both cultural texts, the fanzine and the album, are an example of old product being rebooted and repackaged into a new piece of art: 1960s *Beatles Monthly* was given a new cover, new introductions and photographs of the Beatles in 1976, and the greatest hits *Red Album* was lovingly packaged and tastefully arranged into a new product covering the Beatles careers from 1962 to 1976; and the music was not just singles, it included album tracks that thoughtfully followed the band from lovable mop top pop stars to psychedelic artists, in fact both artefacts are examples of transformative or progressive nostalgia. The product is streamlined into new and slick pop art that mines the old to create a fresher and updated text of images and songs respectively.

The beginning of Porter's walks and his fandom are a fascinating case study in how the Beatles art is living culture. The road to Damascus moment for Porter was regularly visiting AIR Studios on Oxford Street 'quite regularly' between 1980 and 1984, where he would often bump into McCartney. From the early 1980s he was a dedicated and, as my participant observation in chapter 7 demonstrates, a fairly typical fan. Porter began going to the Beatles convention in Liverpool, the first convention in 1981, and to illustrate how Liverpool's attitude to the Beatles has changed, in 1981 the city was undergoing high unemployment and socio-economic problems that culminated in the Toxteth riots; Porter's parents were very apprehensive about his visiting the city in this harsh political climate. Porter also told me that these nascent beginnings of Beatleweek had no money and Cavern Mecca as he was called was 'completely broke'; and the money raised by Cavern Mecca to create a Beatles statue was unceremoniously rejected by Liverpool Council who had ignominiously threatened to 'throw a statue of the Beatles in the river Mersey' (Porter 2018). Nevertheless, post Lennon's death the statue went ahead and Porter told me that at its unveiling in 1981, 'he stood with Victor Spinetti, and a thousand Beatles fans and sang "Give Peace a Chance"' (Porter 2018).

Richard Porter's fandom continued in the 1980s through fanzine culture. He contributed articles and photographs to a fanzine called *Revolver*, he started his own fanzine called London Beatle fan club which developed into another fanzine, *Off the Beaten Track*. The year 1989 was his first walking tour or, rather, he went on another walking tour with three friends from the *Off the Beatle Track* fanzine, and Porter was asked to do the tours after knowing considerably more about the Beatles than the tour guide. After giving up a job in a bank he was approached by London Beatle Walks in 1992 and he has been doing the tours ever since.

The nationalities on tour are very diverse and Porter says that North Americans are the most common nationality on the tours because iTunes is in English, but the Beatles are still huge in South America; and although the Beatles are massive in non-English speaking countries, the tours are represented by English speakers. Nationality is of secondary importance on these tours, apart from demonstrating the ubiquity and range of Beatles fandom. Porter feels that walks are blue-plaqued heritage culture but a forward-looking progressive nostalgia because Beatles fandom is 'almost a creed of peace and love; it's the way people see the world, the anti-war attitudes, vegetarianism, you get people who like the music but they have these other views' (Porter 2018). In a sense Porter is ascribing Beatles fandom as an ongoing, living political stance that has a very lofty and quixotic worldview. It's as if the countercultural values of the 1960s are a torch that is passed to fans: fans are a certain type of idealistically political person. Beatles fandom is not bounded in blue plaques to be looked at but is alive in the psychogeography of fans. In fact Porter supports this argument of the Beatles as progressive art as the Beatles are huge on iTunes and Spotify, which is very popular with young fans on the walking tours. When talking to Porter, and to numerous fans on the walking tours, they often refer to the walks as making them feel optimistic, and the most downloaded track on iTunes, as on 26 June 2018 as I'm speaking to

Porter, is 'Here Comes the Sun', a song suffused with the golden light of 1960s idealism and written in the present tense. Most significantly it is downloaded by new fans who have never listened to the Beatles but love the optimistic sentimentality of the song. Porter says the 'song sounds so fresh', and it is revealing that this is an example of transformative nostalgia, a melodious song of 'progressive sentimentality' that looks forward: it is not called 'There Goes the Sun' or 'There Goes the Sun in the 1960s'. 'Come Together' is always very high as well (Porter 2018), and a song about communal togetherness is appropriate to a discussion of Beatles walks.

Progressive sentimentality

Mike Brocken, who started the first ever Beatles MA at Liverpool Hope University, argues that cultural tourism is indeed a 'progressive sentimentality'; it is a forward-looking cultural phenomenon

> of greatest significance to the lovers of Beatles music visiting the city of their birth are the spaces and places of the imagination whereby a tourist or fan might invoke an imagined space, which is then confronted by the reality of tangible habitation from a matrix, a 'third space' can be brought into focus. Perhaps through such a spatial model, individual fans – and specifically tourist as fans – might be better understood, and regarded far less as holders of fantasist, pathological tags. (Brocken 2016: 3)

Brocken here is iterating the Benjamin idea of 'that anamnesiac intoxication in which the flâneur goes about the city not only feeds on the sensory data taking shape before his eyes but often possesses itself of abstract knowledge – indeed of dead facts – as something experienced and lived through' (Benjamin 1999: 417). An 'abstract knowledge' is a third space of a mess of kaleidoscopic imaginative impulses that are constantly reimagined ad reinterpreted as the fan interacts with Beatles tourist sites or as Broken puts it: 'the Beatles have offered Liverpool a horizon, an empty locus, a point from which Liverpool can engage in a new exciting groundlessness' (Brocken 2016: 8). Beatles cultural tourism in London and Liverpool is much more nuanced and complex than nostalgia and it cannot be reduced to a reductive ideological narrative of reactionary bourgeois fandom; Beatles cultural tourism is creative and emancipatory:

> Overall, the argument put forward is that there has existed an entire body of constraints, a set of conventions, even within popular music fandom itself, that have paraphrased Beatles images, and imaginings, authenticates and authorities into orthodoxies and traditionalisms of representation. One might argue that, during a large part of the-mid-to-late twentieth century, such limitations (disguised as ideologies) guided many Liverpudlians towards an agreed set of rules concerning 'the popular', Liverpool and the Beatles. The organic successes of Beatles heritage tourism have been at times part of a battle against such ideologies and binarisms: a

triumph over the limitation of space by ideology. This now creatively managed landscape was for years a space where decades of fighting over oppositions of anti-populist, foundational logistics took place – and yet the scars are healing remarkably quickly. It is becoming clear through the emergence of Beatles-as-heritage, and popular as discourse, that the contrapositions previously adopted between foundation and horizon have been challenged, and emancipatory have emerged victorious. (Broken 2016: 7)

Raymond Williams's definition of culture is relevant to Beatles cultural tourism:

Williams viewed culture as being about the whole way of life of a distinct people or social group with distinct signifying systems involving all forms of social activity, and artistic or intellectual activities. His comprehensive definitions cover both the development of individual and group culture conveying the importance of heritage and tradition, as well as contemporary culture and lifestyles. Culture is just not about the arts and the aesthetic judgements of a select minority who have been educated to appreciate certain cultural activities; it is also about the lives and interests of ordinary people. (Smith 2016: 2)

Peter Atkinson uses Urry and Larson's concept of the 'tourist gaze' to explain the changing nature and complexity of tourist psychogeography:

Urry and Larsen note the changing nature of the tourist gaze in the era of globalisation and paraphrase Bauman who defines such conditions as a move 'from a solid, fixed modernity' to a 'liquid modernity'. In the latter, the 'time-space compression' evident since the late 1990s involves not only 'rapid flows of travellers and tourists' but, also, 'complex intersections' between increased 'corporeal travel' and 'virtual and imaginative' travel enabled by digital communications technology. (Urry and Larsen 2011: 23)

Beatles cultural tourism is a psychological indeterminate space where fixity and Adorno and Horkheimer's ideas of standardization are eschewed by a heterogeneous fan demographic who translates concrete Beatles shrines into unpredictable and unspecified imaginative spectres of the real.

Over the Easter weekend of 13 March 2018, I stayed at the Hard Day's Night Hotel in Liverpool, which was my hub for a weekend of Beatles cultural tourism; the hotel was the idea of Bill Heckle and Dave Jones of The Cavern Club and Cavern City Tours, and it is for many of the fans I spoke to the base camp for their trek through Beatles Liverpool. The night manager of the hotel, Tim Brown, took me to the John Lennon Suite: an all-white room with the 'Imagine' piano in one corner flanked by two huge portraits of Lennon: a number one haircut Lennon from his *Top of the Pops* appearance in 1970 to promote the single 'Instant Karma', and Lennon at the opening of Apple Boutique in 1968: granny glasses, fur coat and curtain fringe. Another Lennon portrait by the artist Shannon was on the mantelpiece of the room: a John Lennon painting based on the famous Mad Day Out photo session from 28 July 1968 by Don McCullin, here Lennon is wearing his NHS spectacles, has a curtained fringe and has a parrot on his left shoulder. As I was taking photographs of the room, and feeling that this cultural space was part mausoleum and part living culture as the space was enlivened by a constant stream of tourists from all over the world, Brown used the word 'fandom' when talking about guests and told me that Justin Bieber stayed in the room, and that another recent hotel guest was Jennifer Hudson. Tim was wearing a purple tie with the hotel's logo: a chord shape of the opening G7 sus4 chord from a *Hard Day's Night*, and a plectrum badge celebrating the hotel's tenth anniversary. He showed a view of Liverpool from the room's balcony and as we looked at nocturnal Liverpool he told me that he had spoken to two Japanese families who could only afford one international holiday in their lifetime, and they chose Liverpool and the Beatles trail. We arranged a plan for me to work behind reception for a day as proper empirical research and participant observation, and that was the only way I could obtain a tie.

Tim Brown's anecdotes were typical of the myriad stories I heard from workers in Beatles cultural tourism. The cultural spaces and the tone of speakers can seem gloomy and melancholy as the culture they are celebrating is mired in the past, but this is dissipated by the enthusiasm of 'fans' and most of their stories are focused on the present: Adrian Dando, who works in the Beatles shop next door to the Hard Day's Night Hotel, effervescently tells me that an American Beatles fan had paid £7,000 for an Astrid Kirchherr photograph of the Beatles in Hamburg, and that Russian fans bought 'ten T-shirts at a time'. Joe Flannery, Beatles promoter and author of *Standing in the Wings: The Beatles, Brian Epstein and Me* (2013), told me that the Beatles Story museum had 40 million visitors a year, as he was telling me this on the Easter weekend 31 March 2018, school trips full of 10-years-olds filed past. The Beatles cultural workers I met spoke in the present and future tense about the Beatles phenomenon: Sam Laverty, a graduate of the Beatles MA from Liverpool Hope and who works in the British Music Experience museum at the Cunard Building in Liverpool (recently moved from the 02 in London), spoke about the progressiveness of fandom: as a lived culture and industry to work in, study and enjoy.

In fact the paradoxical nature of the tourist industry is constantly apparent: there is a strange backwards melancholy interlaced with a forward-looking appropriation of the old: this collision of old and new is very apparent in the National Trust Tour of John Lennon's and Paul McCartney's childhood homes. The National Trust bus picked me up in Speke Hall, and juxtaposition of a young Lennon and McCartney on the side of the bus with the National Trust oak leaf logo symbolizes either the Beatles being ossified in English heritage culture or conversely the Beatles invigorating English heritage culture. This slightly unsettling clash of the old and the new was the leitmotif of my tour of John and Paul's houses. I tested my thesis, that the Beatles phenomenon looks back and remixes the old to look forward, on the bus driver Joe Roberts. He agreed saying that often on the tours 'kids were often the fans and not the parents'. He told me of many instances of the 5-year-old kids being taken on the National Trust tour by their parents. He told me that the tour attracted many celebrity fans such as ELO's Jeff Lynne, who played the piano in the front room of Paul's house at 20 Forthlin Road.

When I arrived at Paul's childhood home, another tour guide Sylvia Hall took us through the interior and the front and back gardens. The McCartney home was redecorated in its original 1950s wall paper, reupholstered chairs and black-and-white Michael McCartney photographs taken of Paul and his father Michael in the 1950s and early 1960s. There were childhood snaps of Paul and his mother Mary taken by Paul's father. The curation did its best to evoke McCartney's childhood; box bedroom had a single bed against a wall and a small reading desk with his favourite reading: Dylan Thomas's *Under Milk Wood*; John Osbourne's *Look Back in Anger*; and the British Book of Birds. The fidelity to the 1950s and 1960s — McCartney lived there from 1956 to 1963 — was such that the noise and bustle of Liverpool in 2018 seemed very remote in this sepia interior.

John Lennon's home, 'Mendips', 251 Menlove Avenue, a mile's walk from Paul's house over the golf course, was a melancholy time capsule that captured the nascent culture life of a boyhood Beatle. The house was cold as it was in the 1950s: too many expansive windows, and like McCartney's, Lennon's cultural life was on display. Lennon's bedroom had Richmal Crompton's *Just William* book as bedside reading, a cheap acoustic guitar and poster of Lennon's pin-up, Brigitte Bardot.

The guide to Mendips was Colin Hall, husband of Sylvia, a Woolton native, and contemporary of Lennon's. He told me that Bob Dylan was fascinated with Lennon's *Just William* book he'd never heard of Richmal Compton. He told me about celebrity Beatles fan visitors including Paul Brady, Jeff Lynne, Debbie Harry, James Taylor and Bonnie Raitt. Lennon's house was fascinating because it did seem to drop visitors into the 1950s, such was the verisimilitude of the restoration project. Both Lennon's and McCartney's houses were like visiting a well-curated cave of dusty melancholy; the interiors of both time capsules were heartbreakingly nostalgic and were *mal d'archives* of Derridian sickness, but this melancholy enclave of sadness was transformed by the act of leaving the museum: the emotional impact meant that this visitor will transform an antique culture into a psychological state that transcends the museum context. My feeling was of the past resonating into the present and by influencing this fan at a visceral and psychological level prompting a mix of imaginative reactions: it was the effect of cultural space shaping ideas and imagination: a Beatles psychogeography that stimulated future ideas and fan creativity. However, photography is not allowed inside the respective houses for copyright reasons, but you can buy postcards of the interiors. Emotional memories of this tour are, however, ring-fenced from this commodification of Beatles childhoods for sale, and my psychogeography recollections are not memories of postcards, but of the deaths and spectral psychological hauntings of John Lennon, James McCartney and Aunt Mimi, and a liberal humanist universal regret of all our lost childhoods; however, even this nostalgia is progressive as the characters from the old familiar Beatles narrative morph into new thoughts on how curatorship of the past can be forward facing; and one of the ways it remains such is the National Trust's imaginative and creative evocation of the past. The National Trust is not necrophiliac, instead it reshapes the past into a neophiliac thirst for an updated and renovated past even when many of the subjects of the curations here are dead.

Death too formed the basis for Beatles cultural tourism in Liverpool; Paul Du Noyer writes in *Liverpool: Wondrous Place* (2007) that John Lennon's death was the birth of the Beatles cultural tourist industry, 'John Lennon's assassination on 8 December 1980, awoke the slumbering Liverpool people to a legacy they'd ignored because they took it for granted. As Stratford-upon-Avon was to Shakespeare, so Liverpool could be to the Beatles. And now, with Lennon dead, the Beatles were so much old news as an instant heritage industry' (Du Noyer 2007: 16). Mark Lewisohn supports Du Noyer's contention, telling me that 'it changed (Liverpool's attitude to the Beatles) when John died, this was the great accelerant in interest in the Beatles' (Lewisohn 2018). Du Noyer writes that the city fathers had despised the Beatles before Lennon's death (Du Noyer 2007: 16); they were seen outré, rebellious and drug-taking hippies was not the image the city fathers wanted to promulgate pre-Lennon's murder. Liverpool Council pre-Lennon's assassination saw the Beatles as the City Fathers in Joe Orton's play *Up against It*, where McCartney (Ian McTurk) and Lennon (Christopher Low) are banished from Liverpool for sexual promiscuity and vandalism to a Liverpool war memorial, 'It's my painful duty to have to inform you, McTurk, that my niece, upon careful scrutiny, appears to be as much in need of repair as the Memorial to the Fallen. For your outrage upon the living and your friend's outrage upon the dead the city Fathers have decided to expel you both from this city' (Orton 1998: 4). Du Noyer demonstrates that this fictional depiction of the Liverpool Council was very accurate to their real attitude towards the Beatles and he identifies how the council made a complete *volte-face* after Lennon's death. Not that Du Noyer feels that Heritage Culture is retrospective; Du Noyer's fictional imaginings of John Lennon visiting Liverpool in the 1990s is inventive and forward looking: progressive nostalgia if you like. Du Noyer, another male journalist-Beatles superfan, captures the progressiveness in seemingly retrospective melancholy nostalgia by juxtaposing Lennon's ghost walking through the new cultural reimagined Liverpool. Du Noyer's creativity is an example of how heritage can be made progressive and new; his Beatles' fixated psyche collides with geographical space:

> How would it look to Lennon now? Suppose to be romantic he returned from the Other Side by ferryboat. The Pier Head would surprise him, for the Liver Building is no longer black and with velvety soot but hard and bright after sandblasting. The Albert Dock is equally clean: thanks to the steady Covent Gardening of the waterfront, it's more like Disneyland than the clanking, cursing, frowning hellhole that generations of labouring men knew. (Du Noyer 2007: 16)

Du Noyer's ghost Lennon continues his Liverpool haunting and Du Noyer's conceit raises his Liverpool cultural history to the status of creative non-fiction by combing fiction (ghost Lennon) and documentary fact to put the renovation of Liverpool into sharp relief: the old (Lennon) collides with the new giving fresh insights on cultural tourist Liverpool:

> Had he flown into Liverpool Airport, of course, he would have found it now named after him. Wandering up to his old home on Menlove Avenue he'd see

a National Trust plaque on the front. Across the golf course, Paul's little house is a NT museum too. ... but if he took a notion for old times' sake to go back to Mathew Street, then he'd discover the strangest alterations of all. If by coincidence there happened to be a Beatle convention in town, he'd be startled by the sight of lookalike quartets – they might be Hungarians, Brazilians, whatever – strolling to their next engagement in fab attire. Sitting in tourist pubs there would be visitors held spellbound by old associates from Beatle days: faces grown wrinklier with the passing of time, but their anecdotes worn smooth as pebbles in a stream. (2007: 16)

Here Du Noyer is bathing the Beatles tourist shrine in the light of the writer's imagination: he is shifting the geographical space of Beatles cultural tourism into a psychological fiction which takes the threadbare cloth of Beatles nostalgia and restyles them as rococo vestments. Du Noyer sees Beatles tourism as emancipatory for people's imaginations and also gently subversive when statues of hippies replace war heroes: 'There are Beatles statues going up all over. One day they'll outnumber the Victorian war heroes' (Du Noyer 2007: 17).

Debbie Greenberg, the owner of the Cavern between 1966 and 1970 and who saw the Beatles 'over two hundred times at the Cavern' (Greenberg 2018), tells me that Liverpool's attitude to the band was deeply ambivalent in the 1970s and concurs with Du Noyer's thesis, and Orton's satire, when she says, 'if the purchasers we sold the Cavern to weren't prepared to save the Cavern; the councillors could have stepped in' (Greenberg 2018). She maintains that 'while sale negotiations were underway, British Railways sent a letter to the new owners saying they were willing to resite the Cavern further down Mathew Street, but his didn't happen and the Cavern was filled in' (Greenberg 2018). Greenberg's book *The Cavern Club* (2016), on her time involved with the Cavern, sets the record straight on a shameful historical episode of cultural vandalism.

Du Noyer is an astute observer of the Beatles cultural industry in Liverpool; he contends that the deification of Lennon was the point where the city elders began to see the commercial potential in the band, a complete *volte-face* on the council's part. Post Lennon's death the Beatles were idealized for commercial advantage, he finds this uncomfortable while visiting the Hard Day's Night Hotel. 'If anything jarred, it was the big, hairy John Lennon (Plastic Ono Band period) peering from my bedroom wall like a secular saint, tiny white doves of peace inside his irises. Sanctimony and Scouseness always warred in Lennon's soul, and here the former wins' (*The Guardian*, 2008). For the most though Du Noyer argues that Liverpool has curated its history in a tasteful, forward-looking, living culture that avoids Disneyfication:

Had the Beatles come from anywhere else (America springs to mind), one could envisage Disney-styled extravaganzas, with Pepperland fantasy parks, mile-high Helter Skelters, real Yellow Submarines ... Liverpool limits itself to an amphibious vehicle from the Second World War – the Yellow Duckmarine, no less. (*The Guardian*, 2008)

Another important aspect of Beatles walks and Beatles museums is their links to national identity. Heritage culture and Englishness are wedded to the British Empire and globalization. A combination of heritage culture and Englishness goes some way to explaining their global appeal. English culture radiated all over the British Empire, and the disparate cultures on the Beatles walks and visiting the Beatles museum embody globalization/empire returning to the colonial centre (London and to a lesser extent Liverpool). The culture returns as a radical mix of nationalities on the streets of London and Liverpool:

> The Beatles' 'Englishness' may also, to my mind, be a factor in their phenomenal success outside Britain. As with many other English successes beyond the boundaries of the island throughout the 1960s in musical and other genres (the 'British invasion' of the USA in 1964, James Bond films, Swinging London fashion), the Beatles' Englishness was a relic of Imperial British pride founded largely (even before its disintegration following the Second World War) on popular English cultural values. But in contrast to the musical 'invasion' of 1964 which was characterized by English groups influenced by American rock 'n' roll, blues and American consumer culture, the real British musical 'invasion' started after 1965, when many English groups, led by the Beatles, represented the English way of life in their songs to American and European audiences. (Heilbronner 2015)

The spread of English culture through the British Empire represents the grand narratives of history colliding with the mini-narratives of fans' lives and so creating heterogeneous fans whose perception of Beatles history is a mosaic of interconnecting and disparate cultural strands where 'cultural identities are constantly hybridised as they move across the globe in space and time' (Benshoff 2016: 255). My experience of meeting fans on Beatle walks is encountering subjects of many contradictions and paradoxical perceptions of the Beatles, which are dependent on a complex interplay of age, class, gender and nationality.

Similarly Karen Worcman and Joanne Garde-Hansen contend that

> ordinary people have to tell their story, to share their memories and to be part of the many heritages their life story enfolds. Museums may wish to curate and preserve these memories, but more and more people from different social and cultural groups are taking ownership of their own memory work and making their memories open to the world. (Worcman and Hansen 2016: 2)

Cultural tourism offers fans emancipatory spaces to customize their fandom based on experiences of physical space that are then translated anew into digital individually bespoke experiences:

> Orhan Pamuk, in *The Innocence of Objects* (2012), curates and displays the memory-objects represented in his novel *The Museum of Innocence* (2008). The ticket printed on the final pages of the novel grants you access to the exhibition,

which is now located in the Çukurcuma neighbourhood of Istanbul, Turkey. The convergence of novel, museum and online space provides a mediated repertoire of engagement with a theory and practice of memory. This is based on the smallest of objects and the most intimate of personal memories. The Nobel Prize-winning novelist offers a manifesto on the past, present and future of museums. They must seek to 'explore and uncover the universe and humanity of the new and modern man [sic] emerging from increasingly wealthy non-Western nations' (Pamuk 2012: 54). As Pamuk suggests, the time is right now for a different kind of museum to emerge, not monumental 'national symbols' presenting history to global tourism but the stories and memories of individuals; whose everydayness is 'richer, more humane, and much more joyful.' And so, the 'aim of present and future museums must not be to represent the state, but to re-create the world of single human beings. … The future of museums is inside our own homes' (Pamuk 2012: 56–7). (Worcman and Hansen 2016: 2)

It is fascinating that Beatles fans are now fans of tourist destinations, and as Linden and Linden citing Urry and Larson (2011: 206) argue, 'The "gaze" despite being largely "performed" through architectural theming and representations, is "never predetermined and fully predictable". Booth suggests that fandom is 'situated between commercial concerns and resistant hegemonies', and using Paramount Pictures as an example, he argues,

> By retaining ideological and textual boundaries and textual concomitance, contemporary fan work negotiates the boundaries between producer, and audience while still maintaining a reverence for those boundaries. For example, the fan-created web series Star Trek: New Voyages extends the narrative of the original Star Trek series. But by resisting the original series, *New Voyages* also enlarges it. New Voyages' transgression is even condoned, as Derek Johnson points out: 'Despite Paramount's draconian history of enforcing its intellectual property rights, it seemed content to permit fans interim stewardship of the franchise.' Fannish work, in subverting this system, supports it. (Booth 2015: 15)

In a sense, Beatles fandom, whether that is walking tours or slash fiction, resists fixity and floats between passivity and transgression in a fluid and radical 'third space'. The tourist gaze is not 'fully predictable' although it is couched in the machinery of the industrial superstructure. The Polish academic Jerzy Jarniewicz has written about the extent to which the Beatles were part of the hegemonic structures of the music industry and state institutions in 1960s; and yet their 'subversive potential' came not 'from their radical political sensibility and the ability to define critically the areas of madness of the turbulent period, but from their general disposition to treat everything that becomes sacred and unquestionable with reserve, to turn pathos into absurdity, to undermine the dead certainties of the tribe, and to eventually to speak in different conflicting voices' (Jarniewicz and Kwiatkowska 2010: 77). These inherent contradictions or 'conflicting voices' are a constituent part of Beatles fandom: walking tours, tribute bands and the aspects of fandom traced in this book are spaces of joy and playful paradox.

Ken Womack differentiates between millennial Beatles fans and first-generation Beatles fans when I spoke to him about cultural tourism; Ken contends that millennial fans want to interact with geographical space; they want to inhabit the space: go into it. He gives the examples of a 20-something fan who visited St Peter's Church Hall where John Lennon met Paul McCartney on 6 July 1957, and the first-generation fans basked in fuzzy and warm nostalgia while this millennial fan had to video herself acting and playing in the cultural space. Here we have a clear distinction between nostalgia and progressive nostalgia: millennials want to walk all over the respected canon and make it serviceable to their lives in the here and now: older fans are reminded of the past and what their lives were like during *The Ed Sullivan Show* on 9 February 1964, for instance. Fans have a very different experience of Beatles cultural heritage depending on their age. Womack contends that Beatles cultural tourism and Beatles conventions such as Liverpool's Beatleweek and Chicago's The Fest for Beatles Fans are too nostalgic and need to change to attract millennial Beatles fans:

> Nostalgia is a central plank in these kinds of events ... what I would like to see is a shifting away from nostalgia because most of the people. In fact everyone who is living the Beatles now is not a first generation fan, they discovered the Beatles fully formed; they can buy everything fully formed or they can download it in minutes; they probably won't discover them chronologically, so nostalgia will be increasingly less interesting. What will be interesting is that people will be able to put themselves in the time not for nostalgia purposes, but for entertainment purposes. Take The Fest For Beatles Fans, for instance, I have long felt that that convention would be really well served by becoming a Comic Con where you continue to have panels, obviously a bevy of great musical acts, when you can get them, but you increasing move towards the interactive. Kids today want to be involved. They don't want to sit on the side-lines. They want to have discussions; they want to have activities. I totally get that. I do too. (Womack 2018)

Museums, conventions and walks need to be participatory. For example, 'the Museum of Modern Art's (MoMa) ... in which German band Kraftwerk produced a retrospective ... bolstered by a digitally embedded museum strategy (of Facebook, Twitter and social media tool use), ... and production of "spreadable media" for the blogasphere. Moma recognised that heritage had to refresh our ideas about what is valuable to reflect upon and remember' (Worcman and Garde-Hansen 2016: 42). By experiencing the Beatles Story Museum in Liverpool or taking one of Richard Porter's walks to Abbey Road, Beatles fandom is melding physical space and cyber space to create a new interactive forum for fans. Booth calls this demediation 'Playing Fans' where 'where technology exists seamlessly with audience production' and 'generating affective play, and reorganising the spatial and temporal location of fandom' (Booth 2015: 217).

Museums can be sites of 'progressive nostalgia' where 'objects become animated by way of patrons' memories and the affect generated' (Baker 2016: 79). In this manner, popular music museums, Beatles walks and the National Trust, 'People bring their own memories and project their own emotions onto the content and come away with something far richer than anything that's inherent to the empirical quality of the object. So we are keepers of memories but we are also triggers of memories that people bring along and I think it's very different from an exhibition about ceramics' (Baker 2016: 79).

Conclusion
Paul is dead: A fan's story

Beatles fans have reinterpreted and appropriated the Beatles cultural phenomenon to their own ends. Fandom has produced a wealth of archival material which is shifting constantly and reconfiguring Beatles art at a speed it is difficult to keep pace with. The Beatles' history is frozen in aspic to many cultural commentators and journalists, who consigned the Beatles to a series of clichés synonymous with the 1960s. Fans keep the Beatles art alive because they have adopted the songs and iconography from 1960s and have changed these media clichés into texts which have relevance to their own lives. What fans see and hear on television or listen to on records or watch on film is sucked into their heads, and once there it becomes translated into a private, personal and unique experience for the individual. In other words, art is changed into a fresh idea by the receiver of information: popular culture is as much about the fan as the artist who creates the product. My survey of fandom captures the dynamism and creativity of Beatles fans that customize their own Beatles videos. They illustrate a famous Beatles song with a subjective selection of imagery which has relevance to them: fans re-theme the Beatles' work.

Beatles fandom has resulted in new hybrid forms produced by the consumer: mashed fan vids, slash fiction, *Beatles Monthly* letters and tribute acts. Fans have posted outtakes and unreleased performances of songs on YouTube. It is, for example, the first time that the song 'India' has been available to a mass of people. The same goes for experimental music such as 'Carnival of Light'. There are out-takes from the Maharishi's ashram in Rishikesh. In 1968 in Rishikesh, the Beatles recorded songs such as 'Brian Epstein's Blues', 'Child of Nature' and 'Spiritual Regeneration', which had never been heard beyond a niche of hardcore Beatles fans. On YouTube, their songs have been augmented by the fans' own creativity: they had posted video images to accompany these songs. As we have seen, fans use the raw material of Beatles' music, film and iconography to make their pop videos: it is the fans' art, they are cultural pop cultural magpies, and although the results vary in quality they never cease to be original and interesting.

Beatles tribute bands, for instance, have inhabited the Beatles' skins to such an extent that the familiar Beatles songs are remixed and reworked into new performative texts for the fans. The same process has been applied to unseen material such as the famous The Mad Day Out session on 28 July 1968 and to rarely seen images of the Beatles backstage at their 1966 concerts at the Budokan in Japan. The result of this minutia of Beatles imagery is a changed perception of their lives and work, diverging from the music and image that previously comprised the Beatles canon for two reasons. Firstly, we have access to fan vids that use the Beatles' image and music to create a new work of art, for instance, an innovative collage of Beatles photographs and videos created by the fans: they have bastardized the Beatles' product. Secondly, there is unseen Beatles material on YouTube that fans have unearthed for the first time.

The creative consumerism of YouTube has resulted in the Beatles' work being reinvigorated by the fans' input. The numerous reworking of their songs is seemingly endless. The consequence of this is a celebration of the transitory. Their canon is removed from its old signature in space and time. Their work has been cut loose from its 1960s event and context. Fans and musicians have radically altered the Beatles canon.

Many contemporary musicians such as Jay Z and Danger Mouse have posted their own reworking of classic Beatles songs. They have famously mashed the Beatles' canon, adding a hip-hop and dance dimension to their music. They and many other contemporary artists use innovative techniques to produce 'new' material and in fact so much of it is so convincing that it is often difficult to distinguish the imitators and the satirists from the Beatles themselves. Fandom and particularly YouTube translates their work in a variety of texts which tell us about 2014. As Benjamin puts it, 'The mass is a matrix from which all traditional behaviours toward work of art issues today in a new form' (Benjamin 2011: 212).

What we are left with is a dual interpretation of old and classic works of art. The traditional canon of the Beatles' songs opens a vista on the 1960s while a reinterpretation of their work by a contemporary audience conveys society as it is today and also creates a new consumer-led form of art. The cultural ramifications of this are immense, the empowerment of the audience and their ability to control Beatles product for a new audience and to keep alive the optimism and power of those beautiful songs. The songs are now our property: they are the product of the consumer.

YouTubers now 'brush aside a number of outmoded concepts, such as creativity and genius, eternal value and mystery-concepts whose uncontrolled application would lead to a processing of data in the Fascist sense' (Benjamin 2011 : 232). New technology is a limitless vista of imaginative possibility. For instance, the multifarious rare outtakes, rare press conferences, lost studio tapes, Beatles parodies (The Rutles, Peter Serafinowicz; a slew of spoofs by unknown fans such as The Teables and the Rutbeats and even a Sesame Street parody) along with posting of the home videos of John, Paul, George and Ringo demonstrate how technological innovation has translated the Beatles' work anew and how this material is a necessary resource for Beatles scholars and a riposte to Beatles mythology. YouTube refutes Beatles mythology because it offers fans an interactive smattering of new and dynamic Beatles-related material.

The user-generated content on YouTube has permanently dented the monolith of the Beatles cultural industry. It has promulgated an interactive forum that deconstructs and translates the Beatles' image and music anew. Simultaneously it puts an alternative cyber canon into effect. A canon that does not exist physically the way the previous cultural artefacts of the 1960s and 1970s did; but it is an alternative canon nonetheless. Jean Burgess and Joshua Green discussed the archival possibilities of YouTube in 2009.

> In fact, if YouTube remains in existence for long enough, the result will be not only a repository of vintage video content, but something more significant: a record of contemporary global popular culture (including vernacular and everyday culture) in video from, produced and evaluated according to the logics of cultural value that emerge from the collective choices of the distributed YouTube user community. YouTube is thus evolving into a massive heterogeneous, but for the most part accidental and disordered, public archive. (Burgess and Green 2009: 88)

Although there is a creation of an alternative archive it differs in many significant ways to the traditional Beatles canon. The user participates in the meanings of the text and when the canon is reviewed, changed and updated, it doesn't have to go through the official of the music business. In the case of the Beatles that is the Apple organization. In a real sense, we have a constantly shifting archive, the pace of which is dictated by the audience interaction and not established record companies. The way the Beatles' work is disseminated has been completely reconfigured by YouTube. Their work is now more random, more fragmentary and creatively evolving into a public sphere that is dictated by the audience. YouTube has radically changed how we spread and receive information.

YouTube and Beatles Fandom are predicated on individualism and entrepreneurism like the 1960s counterculture which produced the Beatles and their work. Subcultures in the 1960s and the noughties were the result of 'doing your own thing. ... they were uninhibited examples of private enterprise' (Marwick 1998: 17). From fanzines in the 1960s, through fan conventions in the 1970s, journalist superfans such as Davies, Norman and MacDonald, Dangerous fanaticism, YouTube, Fan Fiction and tribute bands the Beatles story is about Fans and, the extent to which, individual fans have manipulated and appropriated the Beatles phenomenon and music to their own ends.

Fandom is a narrative thread which runs parallel with the Beatles phenomenon. It is the Beatles story told (and owned) by their fans: its unofficial history which challenges the official history of the Beatles and Apple. Beatles fan activity is story of the Beatles told by the fans and which chips away at the Beatles cultural monolith: the deconstructed fragments of which reveal a story that would bemuse even the surviving Beatles. Fandom has developed into a life of its own as a way for fans to deal with the loss of the Beatles cultural phenomenal. The spread of Beatles fandom has been so vast that any attempted survey of its development is redundant as soon as fingers hit the keyboard. Jenkins's pioneering work on fandom commented on this seemingly endless production of alternative archive: 'Fan culture is a complex, multidimensional phenomenon inviting many forms of participation and levels of engagement. Such an approach also traces a logical progression from the immediate reception of a broadcast toward the construction of alternative texts and alternative social identities' (Jenkins 1992: 2).

Fandom is a narrative of the Beatles story from the 1960s to the present through the eyes of the fans. By participating in and studying this parallel history, our knowledge of Beatles fans continues to expand and diversify into new areas. In the song 'Within You Without You', George Harrison sang that 'with our love we could change the world' (*Sgt. Pepper* 1967). Even Harrison could not have anticipated to what extent the Beatles' music and iconography could have been reinterpreted by the fans and changed the world.

The beginning of Beatles fandom is captured in the final concert scene of *A Hard Day's Night*. The closing scene is similar to the *Hey Jude* film in that its spontaneity is in fact a rehearsed and highly constructed text. The film's director, Richard Lester, shot the scene in an attempt to capture Beatlemania. Many of the shots in this scene are taken from behind Ringo's drum kit and the camera repeatedly focuses on the fans. The majority of the shots in this closing sequence are directed at the audience. The camera placement was a deliberate act to acknowledge the importance of the fans. In fact the original title of the film on the Beatles was going to be 'Beatlemania', such was the debt the Beatles organization felt to the fans. Onstage, the Beatles are saucer-eyed in awe of what the fans are going to do next: scream, sing along or invade the stage: These scenes chronicle the birth of Beatles fandom and are a visual testament to the fact the Beatles have no control of how the fans are going to react. From fanzines to 'mashed' fanvids, the fans continue to innovate and shift the Beatles canon into fresh and exciting cultural spaces.

One of these cultural spaces that illustrate the ubiquity of the Beatles phenomenon is children's cartoons. The Beatles culture industry was always predicated on youth: many of the screaming girl fans were children in the 7- to 8-year-old age group and the Beatles cartoon in 1965 was obviously to target a young demographic. Modern Beatlemania continues with a Netflix series called Beatbugs which set out to capture the imaginations of children worldwide. The creator, writer and director of Beatbugs, Josh Wakley's mission statement is evangelical about the Beatles: 'It's the greatest music catalogue of all time, and I knew they had messages of hope, love, community and peace,' Wakely says, 'I thought "All You Need is Love" is a great message to bring to children' (Wakely 2017). Wakely is a huge Beatles fan and his zeal is typical of fans who are so consumed with the Beatles they feel they have to adapt the Beatles songs and imagine new contexts. It is impossible to think of a comparable twentieth-century phenomenon that has spread its tentacles into so many disparate areas, Star Wars perhaps, but even there the Beatles are at an advantage, each of their two hundred plus songs is text that can be reimagined and reinterpreted into almost any genre from slash fiction to anthropomorphic beetles:

> Beat Bugs will feature original characters living in an overgrown backyard, learning lessons and going on adventures, with a Beatles song tied to the theme of each episode. Children can experience the episodes in short bursts of 26 11-minute episodes or view 13 half-hour episodes, depending on their preference. ... Wakely explains. 'Every episode has been crafted and poured over so that it lasts more than 20 years – the same way the Beatles music is ever-present in pop culture. We've

taken those songs, made them really child-friendly with awesome animation and the musical storytelling of the Beatles. It is a beautiful combination and a series I believe in'. (Wakely 2017)

Wakely's case study illuminates an important aspect of Beatles fandom: fans are so inspired by the Beatles that they are impelled to become fans who create, 'Wakely hopes the show will inspire a new generation of Beatles fans. "There's a reason for the mania that surrounds the Beatles," he says. "Children love being around joyful music and bright melodies. Bringing that to a new generation with Beat Bugs has been my life goal' (Wakely 2017). Another aspect of the Beatles appeal to children is that this Wakely/fan/creator case study demonstrates that Beatles fandom grows because it is disseminated globally through the cultural industries. As we shall see, my first experience of Beatles fandom was due to the technological ubiquity of their fame: one of the reasons that Beatles fans are so widely spread and so diverse is that they were the first cultural phenomenon to benefit from the 'white heat' of technological progress which was responsible for disseminating the band everywhere and giving fans the opportunity to appropriate them into porn characters or Beat Bugs.

One of the erroneous and most persistent rumours about the Beatles is the 'Paul is dead' rumour that broke all over the world in October 1969. The internet teems with links to this insane conspiracy theory. Adherents to this lie are not deterred by the simple truth that McCartney is alive. There are thousands of online links that continue to promulgate this theory. Believers in this theory argue that McCartney died in a road accident in 1969 and was replaced by a clone called William Campbell. *The Guardian's* Elena Cresci takes up the story:

> Possibly the best known example is the claim that Paul McCartney was replaced with a lookalike after he was killed in a car accident. The urban legend took root in 1969, following the release of the Beatles' Abbey Road. Fans hunted for clues – they were convinced John Lennon was saying 'I buried Paul' in Strawberry Fields Forever, for example (Lennon said he was actually saying 'cranberry sauce'). Unlike some more recent conspiracy theories, the person at the centre actually rebutted the claim. In an interview with Life magazine in November 1969, McCartney said: 'Perhaps the rumour started because I haven't been much in the press lately.' (*The Guardian*, 2017)

Fans who disseminate this rumour call the imposter Faul and the rumour continues to grow exponentially each year. For example, a Google search for Paul is dead on 8 November 2017 threw up these specious stories with titles such as Mysterious Death of Paul McCartney; The Proofs that Faul is Paul; Bass Techniques and Stage Presence Paul to Faul Musicians Know the Truth; Who Buried Paul McCartney; and Paul McCartney's Death in 1966 Goes Much Deeper Than a MI5 Replacement Operation. The Faul conspiracy can be rejected simply. David Aaronovitch, writing about conspiracy theories, perhaps gives the best rebuttal of such weird fan appropriation. He writes,

> I was influenced by the precept know as Occam's razor ling before I knew what this famous implement was. In Latin this precept reads, *'Pluralitas non est ponenda sine neccesitate'*, translated as 'Plurality should not be posited without necessity'. This can be restated as, 'Other things being equal, one hypothesis is more plausible than another if it involves fewer numbers of new assumptions'. Or, far more vulgarly, 'Keep it simple'. And the razor is given to William of Ockham, a fourteenth-century Franciscan monk and theologian not because he invented it, but because it was his favourite tool in a dispute. ... The eighteen-century radical and sceptic Tom Paine applied exactly this thinking to religious doctrine in his book The Age of Reason. 'If we are to suppose', wrote Paine, 'a miracle to be something so entirely out of the course of what we call nature, that she must go out of that course to accomplish it, and we see an account given such miracle by the person who said saw it, it raises a question in the mind very easily decided, which is, is it more probable that nature should go out of her course, or that a man should tell a lie. (Aaronovitch 2010: 6)

Now the Faul/Paul rumour is an example of what Aaronovitch is writing about: all evidence points to McCartney being alive and that 'fans' are simply inventing crazy stories and spreading dangerous rumours. Occam's razor cuts straight to the truth: the simplest explanation is the best. The truth is that Beatles fans made up a whimsical and pernicious story rather than the Beatles and their management managing to fool the world by replacing McCartney with a clone.

The stigma of fandom

One of the reasons for writing this book is to reject the stigma that fandom continues to carry in the press and academia concerning fan studies. This snobbishness is nothing new; in 1964 the future *New Statesman* editor, Paul Johnson, repeated Adorno and Horkenheimer's mass audience theory of fans who were duped by the 'standardization' and 'rubbish' culture such as mainstream music and film. Adorno wrote, 'Capitalist production hems them in so tightly, in body and soul, that they unresistingly succumb to whatever is proffered to them ... Mickey Rooney rather than the tragic Garbo, Donald Duck rather than Betty Boop' (Adorno and Horkheimer 1944: 134). Paul Johnson eschews mass art in a similar manner:

> Before I am denounced as a reactionary fuddy duddy, let us pause an instant and see exactly what we mean by this youth. Both TV channels now run weekly programmes in which popular records are played to teenagers and judged. While the music is performed, the cameras linger savagely over the faces of the audience. What a bottomless chasm of vacuity they reveal! The huge faces bloated with cheap confectionary and smeared with chain store make-up, the open, sagging mouths and glazed eyes, the broken stiletto heels: here is a generation slaved by a commercial machine. (P. Johnson 1964)

There is no musicology in this analysis and Johnson's writing is pop sociology. What he is revealing is a condescension which belies a class divide. To Johnson, pop music fans are to be despised: 'Those who flock round the Beatles, who scream themselves into hysteria, are the least fortunate of their generation, the dull, the idle, the failures: their existence in such high numbers, far from being a cause for ministerial congratulation, is a fearful indictment of our educational system, which in ten years of schooling can scarcely raise them to literacy' (P. Johnson 1964).

Johnson's attitude is still prevalent today:

Teenage girl fans are still patronized by the press today. As Grant says, 'Teenage girls are perceived as a mindless horde: one huge, undifferentiated emerging hormone'. In an influential 1992 essay, Fandom as Pathology, US academic Joli Jensen observed: 'Fandom is seen as a psychological symptom of a presumed social dysfunction.... Once fans are characterised as a deviant, they can be treated as disreputable, even dangerous "others".'

'Lots of different fans are seen as strange', says Dr Ruth Deller, principal lecturer in media and communications at Sheffield Hallam University, who writes extensively about fan behaviour. 'Some of that has to do with class: different pursuits are seen as more culturally valuable than others. Some of it has to do with gender. There's a whole range of cultural prejudices. One thing our society seems to value is moderation. Fandom represents excess and is therefore seen as negative.' (*The Observer*, 2013)

Any objective and unbiased analysis will see that the simplest argument is the best. This is best defined as Occam's razor, if there are two possible explanations, the simplest explanation is the most likely, and here these opinions are predicated on class. The aesthetics and musicality of any early Beatles song can be ranked alongside any primitive or minimalist art. For instance, Kylie Minogue's dance track 'Can't Get You Out of My Head' is almost identical to many of Steve Reich's repetitive minimalist experiments, but it is Reich who has the cultural capital and the critical kudos. Contrary to Johnson's assertions, Beatles fans were not an indoctrinated mass: Although stereotyped as brainwashed consumers, the fans were far from passive. 'They loved the music, of course, but they'd heard these songs a thousand times. When they screamed they were also celebrating themselves, their freedom, their youth, their power. Screaming didn't drown out the performance: it was a performance' (*The Observer*, 2013). A *leitmotif* of *The Beatles and Fandom* is this discussion of audience theory and the emancipatory of psychological and performative aspects of Beatles fandom.

The historian David Fowler agrees with the standardized rubbish arguments of Adorno/Johnson concerning mass pop culture, although in *Youth Culture and Pop Culture: From Beatlemania to the Spice Girls*, he writes cogently about the Beatles apolitical hippie ethos and how they ignored strikes of 1966 and 1967 in Liverpool by national dock workers and the motor car industry. He has this to say about fans regarding Beatles relationship to their fans:

For the Beatles to have reflected Youth Culture they would, presumably, needed to be in contact with young people. But they stopped touring in 1966, and what seems most striking now is how detached they were from youth culture in the late 1960s. One of the more telling comments on Beatlemania, their main contribution to youth culture, was made by John Lennon. He was by this time living in a stately home, Tittenhurst Park in Twickenham, Surrey, and one day he noticed a group of Beatles fans outside his house. He told a reporter:

'They treat my house like a bloody holiday camp, sitting in the grounds with flasks of tea and sandwiches thinking they have come to Beatle National Park.' (Fowler 2008: 174)

To Fowler, older teenagers who were mods and the student left were the 'authentic' youth culture of the 1960s; and not 'girls of 10 to 14 who lost interest in pop culture at around 20' (Fowler 2008: 174). Fowler is a type of anti-aca-fan and his dismissal of the Beatles as not representing youth culture is the polar opposite to super-journalist-fan Ian MacDonald, who argues that the Beatles are the apotheosis of 1960s youth culture: their interest in revolutionary politics (the Revolution songs on *The White Album*), transcendental meditation, mysticism, yoga and LSD, according to MacDonald, accurately mirror 1960s youth culture. So in a manner similar to the biased journalism about the Beatles we read in Davies, Norman and MacDonald, Fowler is using the Beatles as a *tubula rasa* on which to imprint his subjective truth. The differences here are that Fowler is not a fan, but an anti-fan. His rebuttal of the Beatles is important as it shows that Adorno's propaganda mass audience argument remains very persuasive and that Fowler's dismissal of young girl fans missing their incipient feminism and radical inversion of the Beatles phenomenon by making the Fabs the object of their feminine gaze. Fowler's thesis seems erroneous when we consider the political and cultural impact of sublimated sexual euphemism of *Beatles Monthly*; consider his words in the context of Chapter 1 of this book: 'a Cambridge University historian today argues that the Beatles were not heroes of the counter-culture but capitalists who cynically exploited youth culture for commercial gain.' David Fowler claims, 'They did about as much to represent the interests of the nation's young people as the Spice Girls did in the 1990s' (*The Guardian*, 2008). His words epitomize two features of my study of fandom: first, a petty intellectual snobbery towards young fans of pop music and, second, how academics, fans, journalists, fiction writers and YouTubers appropriate the Beatles to their own class, gender and background; Fowler appropriates the Beatles into his own *Weltanschauung*, which is bad because he dismisses young fans, but good because he shows the extent to which we can reappropriate art/culture into the web and weft of our lives: 'The Beatles did not generate a youth culture at all; merely a youth audience of passive teenage (mainly female) fans who became superfluous when the group stopped touring Britain in 1965' (*The Guardian*, 2008).

Fandom is a riposte to Adorno's, Fowler's and Johnson's fear that popular art is not only 'rubbish' but also dangerous propaganda. Emile Durkheim managed to juggle these two positions when writing about religious festivals of indigenous Australian people, 'every festival has certain characteristics of a religious ceremony ... In every case, its effect is to bring individuals together, to put the masses into motion and thus induce a state of effervescence – sometimes even delirium' (Durkheim 1995: 386). Here Durkheim shows that you can be in and of a group but at the same time exist *sui generis*: essentially this piece written originally in 1912 describes fandom, a state where groups come together to be 'pulled outside himself, pulled away from his ordinary occupations. ... cries, songs, music, violent movements, dances' (Durkheim 1995: 386), but retain their individuality: the mass audience theory of Johnson and Adorno is eschewed by pointing out that you can be of the crowd during a ritual (a Beatles concert) and apart from it: a fan's identity being predicated on differences in class, age and gender (even though the Beatles fans were teenage girls; homogenizing this group is deeply problematic).

The Beatles and Fandom: Sex, Death and Progressive Nostalgia demonstrates the extent to which the Beatles and their fans are now considered worthy of serious academic study; and how art is appropriated into new contexts by fans. In the book's introduction I examined the resistance to taking the Beatles and their fans seriously (fortunately most of this elitism has faded): a rebuttal I characterized as a classist rejection of pop culture and its fans:

> Willis declared that 'This is not culture. This is a cult – a cheap, plastic, candyfloss substitute for culture.' He charged that popular culture was not simply distinct from and inferior to high culture. It was destructive of it, supplanting its rightful place in the nation's hearts and minds. He used the metaphor of a 'tidal wave ... under which we are in danger of becoming submerged' and lamented that firms had switched from making busts of Shakespeare to those of the Fab Four. Thus, the twentieth century was becoming 'the century of Beatles and Bingo' in contrast to the eighteenth century ('the century of Bach and Beethoven') and the nineteenth century ('the century of Brahms'). (Collins 2013)

My analysis of Beatles fandom demonstrated that young fans' hysteria in the years of Beatlemania circa 1963–6 was prescient and that visceral passion correctly perceived the inventiveness of the Beatles art; while the vitality of the Beatles primitive folk art was dismissed by intellectuals, it is ironic that Hoggart rejected Americanism and extolled the virtues of organic folk while failing to realize that the Beatles and their fans were enjoying folk music couched in the machinery of the capitalist music industry. Morris dancers may be fine, but as soon as they are incorporated into the creative industries it gives the intellectuals *carte blanche* to dismiss the culture. The intellectual cultural context of the early 1960s regarded mass culture is produced industrially for a mass society in order to generate profit: this is its ultimate purpose. Mass culture is standardized and mass produced (like a Ford car), is repetitive and indistinct ('formula'); the mass culture audience is passive and subject to manipulation by its producers; mass culture is aimed at the mass society and disseminated by the mass media. To Hoggart, American mass culture leads the 'juke-box boys away from lived authenticity of their working-class backgrounds and into the empty fantasy world of Americanised pleasures' (Hoggart 1957: 219), whereas the distinctions drawn by mass culture critics between mass and high culture are not as clear-cut or as static as mass culture critics claim. F. R. Leavis dismissed cinema as a serious cultural form. Eisenstein's (and other silent) films are now considered art; Alfred Hitchcock is considered an 'auteur'; jazz is now often considered as art whereas the Frankfurt School used to condemn it as mass culture. Audience studies reveal that popular crime fiction and films gave working-class men and women meanings and pleasures unavailable from class-conscious British culture. Dick Hebdige's book on *Subcultures* (1979) sees youth subcultures as a revolt in terms of style Punks, mods, skins, rastas recycle elements of style that are available in new combinations: *bricolage*. These subcultures are a response to post-war immigration and the parent culture: a 'magical' resolution of contradictions, via style. In 1948 German critical theorists published the widely influential book *Dialectic of Enlightenment* containing the essay 'The Culture Industry: Enlightenment as Mass Deception'. They argue that the culture industry distracts the masses from a system that exploits them with superficial amusements. And 'the concepts of order [the culture industry] hammers into human beings are always those of the status quo' (cited in Strinati 2004: 57). Whereas Beatles fans intuited, while screaming at concerts or lusting over *Beatles Monthly*, a transgressive meaning and depth in Beatles music. Beatles fans are 'knowing, active and discriminating in their consumption of popular culture' (Strinati 2004: 57). Adorno/Horkheimer ignore the 'active audience paradigm' (Barker 2005: 67). They also ignore creative consumption. Audiences are active producers of meaning. *Bricoleurs* are audiences who create meaning: subcultures, fan cultures, fanzines and online forums, cosplay, Beatles DIY! Beatles' music erodes distinctions between high and low art; and Beatles fandom interrogated the idea that Beatles art is false consciousness or part of the capitalist superstructure: and even if Beatles product can be considered such, the fans appropriate the Beatles into their own lives: fans subvert dominant hegemonic contexts into their own idiosyncratic fandom.

Cultural capital

Bourdieu's theory of cultural capital is a concept that informs the book, especially in the slash chapter where I favourably compare the aesthetics of slash to Kevin Barry's more 'literary' writing. However, the idea of cultural capital is germane to the book as a whole as fandom is often dismissed because it deals with populist art that people enjoy, buy and consume. Bourdieu theories help to explain this pernicious and ubiquitous classism:

> But Bourdieu also points out that cultural capital is a major source of social inequality. Certain forms of cultural capital are valued over others, and can help or hinder one's social mobility just as much as income or wealth. According to Bourdieu, cultural capital comes in three forms – embodied, objectified, and institutionalized. One's accent or dialect is an example of embodied cultural capital, while a luxury car or record collection are examples of cultural capital in its objectified state. In its institutionalized form, cultural capital refers to credentials

and qualifications such as degrees or titles that symbolize cultural competence and authority. (Social Theory Rewired 2016)

It is also worth noting that objections to fan studies are socially constructed, and significantly these objections are what Bourdieu calls Habitus, that is, artistic elitism that is socially conditioned by a childhood hidden curriculum. He contends,

> Habitus also extends to our 'taste' for cultural objects such as art, food, and clothing. In one of his major works, *Distinction*, Bourdieu links French citizens' tastes in art to their social class positions, forcefully arguing that aesthetic sensibilities are shaped by the culturally ingrained habitus. Upper-class individuals, for example, have a taste for fine art because they have been exposed to and trained to appreciate it since a very early age, while working-class individuals have generally not had access to 'high art' and thus haven't cultivated the habitus appropriate to the fine art 'game'. The thing about the habitus, Bourdieu often noted, was that it was so ingrained that people often mistook the feel for the game as natural instead of culturally developed. This often leads to justifying social inequality, because it is (mistakenly) believed that some people are naturally disposed to the finer things in life while others are not. (Social Theory Rewired 2016)

So my thesis argues that objections to slash, tribute bands, fan vids mashing the Beatles canon, conventions and glossy fanzines are classist and, in fact, oblivious to the art of bricolage: fan vids, mash-up and tribute bands are derivative but they take the old and reinvigorate it with the new and unique: Beatles fan art is often palimpsest, that is, Beatles product altered but still bearing visible traces of its earlier form.

Another revealing incident concerning mass audience theory/Adorno's dismissal of 'low' culture occurred at the beginning of the Beatles career in the United States. The American Federation of Musicians and the Immigration and Naturalization Service of the US government in 1964 attempted to ban Beatles concerts in the United States. Beatles fans were naturally outraged by this incident and the story demonstrates the triumph of Beatles fandom over cultural elitism. A struggle that hasn't been completely won, although documentaries such as Howard Goodall's *Sgt Pepper's Musical Revolution* (BBC 2017) validate the fans' far-sightedness concerning the band: Goodall's inclusion of the Beatles in the corpus of Western music is something instinctively understood by fans in 1960s, and Paul McCartney who called 1960s rock music the 'classical music of today' in an interview in 1968 (McCartney Interview 1968). American Beatles fans rejection of the union's position demonstrates the historical struggles that fandom has to make. If you doubt this, try what I've done in preparation for this book; I tell people what Beatles slash fiction is and watch as their reactions move through incredulity, amusement to disdain, this is exactly what Beatles fans were up against in 1964:

> Beatles' fans, on the other hand, developed a point of view on culture similar in many ways to that of Raymond Williams. For Williams, the division between high and lowbrow culture is not an issue of 'levelling down', as it was for Leavis, but

instead the very idea of the 'masses' is seen as a device used by elites to justify their dominance over society. Beatles' fans certainly understood their struggle with the AFM in these terms. Kenin's disparaging remarks that the Beatles were not 'culture 'was viewed by Beatles' fans as the principal terrain of the struggle. The AFM's position can be understood as an expression of what Williams (2005) referred to as the 'effective dominant culture'. The Beatles' fans, on the other hand, were creating what Williams referred to as an 'emergent culture', where new practices, meanings and values develop outside or in conflict with the dominant culture. From a perspective like Williams', rock and roll culture does not represent a 'degradation' of culture, or a levelling down, but an emergent counter-culture. (Roberts 2010)

Here Michael Roberts elucidates the extent to which Beatles fans were ahead of the curve (and they remain so). *Beatles Monthly* was considered fan pap and shallow rubbish in the 1960s; fan conventions were dismissed as fora populated by eccentric anoraks; YouTube fan vids, tribute acts and slash are still dismissed as populist and unregulated flotsam and jetsam of a tabloidized culture by Leavisite leftists and English heritage conservatives. So one of the intentions of this book is to shine a light into the weird and wonderful dark recesses of Beatles fandom and such a literary endeavour is political as it demonstrates the extent to which fans lead mainstream culture by the nose into progressive and *avant-garde* areas; for instance, the feminism of *Beatles Monthly*, the sexuality of screaming fans and emancipatory sexuality of slash fiction. As Georgina Gregory demonstrates, Beatles tribute bands are dismissed as inauthentic simulacra by the music industry. But perhaps one of the most significant victories for fandom are the Beatles walks in London, where Abbey Road competes with Shakespeare's Globe and Buckingham Palace for cultural capital. Again Beatles fans psychogeography is culturally prescient.

'Hey Jude' and fandom

All Beatles scholars and fans will be familiar with the 'Hey Jude' video, a promotion film first broadcast on the David Frost Show on 8 September 1968. This film is a visual illustration of the Beatles and the concept of fandom. The film reminds us that the Beatles' work, and indeed, all art, is a profound negotiation between artists and their followers. The Beatles have been singing 'Hey Jude' for three minutes and nine seconds when there is a frisson of excitement in the audience, Paul McCartney is jostled by fans, who then invade the stage and sing along to the refrain, as familiar now to British people as the national anthem. In reality the stage invasion was rehearsed in Twickenham Film Studios four days earlier, the overflow of communal emotion is, in fact, rehearsed spontaneity. As the song is interrupted, the eye is drawn away from the four familiar faces to the fans. The Beatles are no longer the focus of the viewers' attentions. 'Hey Jude' is a reminder that there is an alternative history of the Beatles phenomenon: a fans' history that runs concurrently with the popular story we all know.

Conclusion 213

The Beatles and Fandom: Sex, Death and Progressive Nostalgia argues that the fans transform the past into a living culture by their own idiosyncratic fandom; however, an important constituent part of progressive nostalgia is 'imagined memory': that is, fans' fantasies that are rooted in real events, but these memories are constantly modified by successive generations who are experiencing a pop cultural event, such as the Beatles in Shea Stadium in 1965, as memories of memories; and these fantasies are commodified by magazines such as *Mojo*, *Uncut* and *Q*, BBC4 documentaries and the Beatles tourist trail. Mark Duffett explains:

> Seeing the Beatles early live shows at the Cavern and seeing the Sex Pistols taunt Bill Grundy on *The Today Show* at the end of 1976 are classic examples of imagined memories. The first thing to notice is that these incidents really happened: they can be located in time and place. For any individual audience members who experienced these, they were supposedly transformative moments. Yet there is also a mass of fans who never had these experiences but wished they did. In that sense they are investing in imagined memories. (Duffett 2010, http://pop-music-research.blogspot.com/2010/07/what-are-imagined-memories-and-how-are.html.)

In a sense, here is that crux of fandom, Beatles fans appropriate the Beatles' image and music into a living culture that is relevant to their lives. There is a capitalist imperative to this and Beatles fandom is a disconnect between the paradoxical thought processes of fans (which is impossible to discern in all their contradictions) and the media hypodermic needle of the superstructure which gives fans access to many memories in the first place (television, YouTube, fan fiction). Again, Duffett contends that,

> Each imagined memory is the thing you wished you had experienced, but never did. It is not exactly a fantasy, because it really happened to someone else. However, it is not *your* memory either, because it happened to someone else. By a process of valorisation in the narrative of history and in the media it is therefore a kind of fantasy which authenticates itself as a (false) memory. The term points to the paucity of phrases like 'cultural memory' in describing popular music's past: for a few people these memories are real enough (although, even for them, the memories have been inflected by the subsequent success story of the performers). Imagined memories are spaces of emotional investment that are necessarily contradictory since they only matter because of what came after them. In a sense, then, they are memory commodity templates: they are both valorised (made to matter by stories) and characterized by their own rarity value. Not everyone has the 'real' memory. This is precisely why they become starting points for further commodities (media documentaries, heritage tourism, anniversaries, re-enactments, etc.). (http://pop-music-research.blogspot.com/2010/07/what-are-imagined-memories-and-how-are.html.)

So in a profound sense, transformative nostalgia is a forward-moving, progressive concept, as each memory is changed by fans, and in many cases it is a memory of a memory. Concepts of memory and nostalgia are an appropriate way to end the book as an episode from my early childhood demonstrates. This story is nostalgic because it was one of the first (in my subjective recollection) that I remember hearing about the Beatles and it is useful as a discussion of memory as my reminiscence has surely been remodified over the years by retelling so that the original incident is more than likely a memory of memory passed from my parents, through my elder brother to me.

My first Beatles memory was from 22 October 1969: the beginning of the Paul rumour. It was the day the rumour broke that Paul McCartney had died. On my fifth birthday, a few weeks earlier, I had been given a blue budgerigar which I called Paul. I loved this bird and spent hours doting on it. My elder brother, Neil, also seemed to like it. He rattled its cage and shouted 'Who's a pretty boy then'. Paul looked at my brother, and fell off his perch dead. I was in floods of tears. 'Paul's dead, Paul's dead,' he shouted to my mother, who was downstairs, listening to the news; 'I know I just heard it on the radio,' she replied. This personal recollection shows the extent to which audiences misinterpret, appropriate and change the meanings of a cultural phenomenon. The rumour of Paul McCartney's death was obviously false, and our reaction was what we call fandom: a personal or communal reappropriation of a performer's music and image. Since the release of the Beatles' first single, 'Love Me Do', an address to the fans to buy Beatles records according to Lennon and McCartney, Beatles fans have been reacting to the Beatles through devotion and obsessive, eccentric and occasionally psychopathic behaviour. In sum, then, a definition of Beatles fandom is an instance when the Beatles are translated anew by fans into constantly changing and unexpected areas. Fandom is an active and participatory act: as 'Hey Jude' instructs, 'Take a sad song and make it better' ('Hey Jude' 1968).

Notes

1 She Loves You: Beatles Monthly

1. On 22 November 1969 a rumour was circulated by fans that Paul McCartney had been killed and replaced by a Scottish musician William Campbell. The most extreme example of fans appropriating Beatles' texts is the 'clues' on the *Abbey Road* album cover. The prosaic cover of four Beatles crossing Abbey Road is given symbolic meaning by fans. The iconic picture is read as a funeral procession. John, in white, is the priest leading the procession, Ringo in a black suit is supposed to represent the undertaker, George in denim is the gravedigger and Paul, who is barefoot, signifies the corpse.

3 'Paperback Writer', journalists as superfans: Hunter Davis, Ian MacDonald and Philip Norman

1. See Matthew Schneider's *The Long and Winding Road from Blake to the Beatles* (London: Palgrave, 2008). Here Schneider links the Beatles to the romantic revolution in 1790s England, where convention was challenged in a manner similar to the Cultural Revolution of the 1960s. See also W. B. Yeats (2001) *The Major Works*, 'The Lake Isle of Innisfree'. Oxford: Oxford World Classics, 19; and W. Wordsworth *Lyrical Ballads*, 'The Tables Turned'. Edinburgh: Longman, 100.
2. Adorno and Horkheimer argue in their essay 'The Cultural Industry as Mass Deception' that 'the cultural commodities produced by the Cultural Industry … while purporting to be democratic, individualistic and diversified, are in actuality authoritarian, conformist and highly standardised' (Barker, *Cultural Studies: Theory and Practice*, 2005).
3. Herbert Marcuse (1898–1979): German–American philosopher and prominent member of the Frankfurt School. His critiques of capitalist society influenced the 1960s student movement. *Freud, Eros and Civilisation* (1955) and *One-Dimensional Man* (1964) were influenced by Marx and Freud. Norman O. Brown (1913–2002), American author of *Life against Death: The Psychoanalytical Meaning of History* (1959). Angela Davis (1944–): born in Alabama, radical feminist, activist and Black Panther. John Lennon and Yoko Ono released 'Angela' in 1972, dedicated to her, and the Rolling Stones' 'Sweet Black Angel' is also about her. Abbot Howard 'Abbie' Hoffman (1936–89): political activist, formed Youth Internationals Party in the 1960s. He was also a friend and confidant of John and Yoko.

5 'Images of broken light': The Beatles on YouTube

1 On 22 November 1969 a rumour was circulated by fans that Paul McCartney had been killed and replaced by a Scottish musician William Campbell. The most extreme example of fans appropriating Beatles' texts are the 'clues' on the *Abbey Road* album cover. The four Beatles crossing Abbey Road is given symbolic meaning by fans. The iconic picture is read as a funeral procession. John, in white, is the priest leading the procession, Ringo in a black suit is supposed to represent the undertaker, George in denim is the gravedigger and Paul, who is barefoot, signifies the corpse.

Appendix 2

1 1 See Bourdieu, Pierre. 1987. *Distinction: A Social Critique of the Judgement of Taste*, Cambridge, MA: Harvard University Press. *Distinction* for his classic analysis of 'cultural capital'.
2 1 *H. of L. Debs.*, vol. 267, col. 583.
3 1 *H. of L. Debs.*, vol. 263, col. 1183; *H. of C. Debs.*, vol. 696, col. 896.
4 1 *H. of L. Debs.*, vol. 258, cols. 494–5; *H. of C. Debs.*, vol. 691, cols. 1468–9.
5 1 *H. of L. Debs.*, vol. 281, col. 973. Drawing upon Matthew Arnold's *Culture and Anarchy* (1869), Richard Hoggart's *The Uses of Literacy* (1957) and Paul Johnson's *New Statesman* article 'The Menace of Beatlism' (1964 Johnson, Paul. 'The Menace of Beatlism'. New Statesman, 28 February 1964.).

References

Aaronovitch, D. (2010), *Voodoo Histories: How Conspiracy Theory Has Shaped Modern History*, London: Vintage.

Abraham, N., and Took, M. (1994), *The Shell and the Kernel*, Chicago, IL: University of Chicago Press.

Acker, K. (1997), 'All Girls Together'. In *The Weekend Guardian*, 3 May, p. 16; cited in Whiteley, S. (2000), *Women and Popular Music: Sexuality, Identity and Subjectivity*, p. 35. Oxford: Routledge.

Adams, R., Ernst, A., and Lucey, K. (2014), 'After Jerry's Death: Achieving Continuity in Deadhead Identity and Community'. In M. Buffett (ed.), *Popular Music Fandom: Identities, Roles and Practices*, New York and London: Routledge, pp. 186–207.

Adorno, T. (2002), 'On the Fetish-Character in Music and Regression of Listening'. In S. Dun combe (ed.), *Cultural Resistance Reader*, London: Verso.

Adorno, T. and Horkheimer, M. (1944), 'The Cultural Industry: Enlightenment as Mass Deception'. In Theordor W. Adorno and Max Horkheimer, *Dialectic of Enlightenment*, Verso, 1997; first publ. Social Studies Association, Inc. New York.

Adorno, T., and Horkheimer, M. (1997; 1st publ. 1944), *Dialectic of Enlightenment*, London: Verso, p. 127.

Adorno, T., and Horkheimer, M. (2005), 'The Culture Industry as Mass Deception'. In C. Barker (ed.), *Cultural Studies: Theory and Practice*, London: Sage.

Allen, W. (1973), *Sleeper*, USA: United Artists.

Anderson, M. (2003), *The Independent*. Available online: www.independent.co.uk/news/obituaries/ian-macdonald (accessed 12 September 2017).

Armstrong, D. (2014), Material Sounds: 'Notes on Pop Music and the Arts: The Beatles and the Deconstruction of Gender Identity'. Available online: http://www.donaldearmstrong.com/2014/01/21/the-beatles-and-the-deconstruction-of-gender-identity/ (accessed 23 October 2017).

Ask for Joey Taxi Tours: A Fab Four Taxi Tour. Available online: https://www.tripadvisor.co.uk/ShowUserReviews-g186337-d1167364-r257941005-The_Beatles_Fab_Four_Taxi_Tour-Liverpool_Merseyside_England.html (accessed 8 July 2017).

Atkinson, P. (2015), 'Abbey Road Studios, the Tourist and Beatles Heritage'. In Ewa Mazierska and Georgina Gregory (eds), *Relocating Popular Music*, London: Palgrave Macmillan.

Badman, K. (2001), *The Beatles Diary Volume 2: After the Break-Up 1970–2001*, London: Omnibus Press.

Barker, S. (2005), *Cultural Studies: Theory and Practice*, London: Sage

Baker, S. (2016), 'The Sound of Music Heritage: Curating Popular Music in Music Museums and Exhibitions'. *International Journal of Heritage Studies*, 22(1), 70–81.

Bal, M. (1996), *Double Exposures: The Subject of Cultural Analysis*, New York: Routledge.

Barker, E. (2015), NME. 'The Beatles: See 12 Rare Photographs Taken by Their Most Trusted Photographer'. Available online: http://www.nme.com/photos/

the-beatles-see-12-rare-photos-taken-by-their-most-trusted-photographer-1423803 (accessed 4 July 2017).
Barry, K. (2015), *Beatlebone*, London: Canongate.
Barry, P. (2009), *Beginning Theory: An Introduction to Literary and Cultural Theory*, Manchester: Manchester University Press.
Barthes, R. (1977), *Music-Image-Text*, London: Fontana
Baudrillard, M. (2014), 'Poetic Transfer of a (Serious) Situation Spectrality'. In K. Niemeyer (ed.), *Media and Nostalgia: Yearning for the Past, Present and Future*, Basingstoke: Palgrave Macmillan, p. 227.
Baym, N. (2017), 'Text and Representation: The Community and the Individual'. In Linden and Linden, *Fans and Fan Cultures: Tourism, Consumerism and Social Media*, Palgrave Macmillan,
Baym, N. (2018), *Playing to the Crowd: Musicians, Audiences, and the Intimate Work of Connection*, New York: New York University Press.
Beatle News.com. Available online: 24 Hours A Day, Eight Days A Week/. https://www.techdigest.tv/2017/05/eight-days-a-week-the-beatles-channel-to-launch-on-siriusxm.html (accessed 1 September 2014).
Beatles Fest. Available online: https://www.thefest.com/and-so-it-began-beatlefest-74-97-81974/ (accessed 5 July 2014).
Beatlefest (19980, YouTube 'Beatlefest 1998 Interviews'. URL: https://www.youtube.com/watch?v=YvlyVf6aIgQ (accessed 5 August 2017).
Beatles Sex. Available online: misscharison.tumblr.com (accessed 28 September 2017).
Beatles Slash. Available online: http//beatlesslash.livejournal.com/profile#/profile/ (accessed 3 September 2014).
Beatlemania: The 'Screamers' and Other Tales of Fandom, *The Observer*, 2013. Available online: https://www.theguardian.com/music/2013/sep/29/beatlemania-screamers-fandom-teenagers-hysteria (accessed 18 October 2017).
Beatleweek Programme (2017), London: Pretty Green.
Benjamin, W. (1968), *Illuminations*, edited by Hannah Arendt. New York: Harcourt, Brace and World. Originally published by Suhrkamp Verag, Frankfurt, 1955.
Benjamin, W. (1998), 'The Work of Art in the Age of Mechanical Reproduction'. In H. Arendt (ed.), *Illuminations*, London: Routledge.
Benjamin, W. (1999), The Arcades Project, translated by Howard Eiland and Kevin McLaughlin, Massachusetts and London: Harvard University Press.
Benjamin, W. (2011), *Illuminations*, London: Vintage.
Bennett, A. (2006), 'Even Better Than the Real Thing? Understanding the Tribute Band Phenomenon'. In Shane Homan (ed.), *Access All Eras: Tribute Bands and Global Pop Culture*, London: Open University Press.
Benshoff, H. (2016), *Film and Television Analysis*, London: Routledge.
Benson, A. (2013), 'Blurring the Lines'. In A. Jamison (ed.), *Why Fanfiction Is Taking Over The World*, Dallas: Smart Pop/Benbella, p. 388.
Berman, G. (2008), *'We're Going to See the Beatles': An Oral History of Beatlemania as Told by the Fans Who Were There*, Santa Monica, CA: Santa Monica Press.
Bhabha, Homi K. (1994), *The Location of Culture*, London: Routledge.
Booker, C. (1992; 1st publ. 1969), *The Neophiliacs: The Revolution in English Life in the Fifties and Sixties*, London: Pimlico.
Booth, P. (2015), *Playing Fans: Negotiating Fandom and Media in the Digital Age*, Iowa: University of Iowa Press.

Booth, P. (2016; 1st publ. 2014), *Digital Fandom 2.0: New Media Studies*, New York: Peter Lang.
Brabazon, T. (2012), *Popular Music: Topics, Trends and Trajectories*, London: Sage.
Bradby, B. (2005), ' "She Told Me What to Say". The Beatles and Girl-Group Discourse'. In Gary Burns and Thomas M. Kitts (eds), *Popular Music and Society*, Routledge, pp. 359–92.
Brocken, M. (2012), *The Beatles Biography: A New Guide to the Literature*, The Beatle Works Limited, Manitou Springs, Colorado.
Brocken, M. (2016), *The Twenty-First-Century legacy of The Beatles: Liverpool and Popular Music Heritage Tourism*, Abingdon, Oxford: Routledge.
Brooke, K. (2013), 'Almost as Big as the Hollies … An Interview with Ian R. MacLeod'. Available online: https://keithbrooke.wordpress.com/2013/04/26/ianrmacleod/ (accessed 22 August 2017).
Brooks, L., Donnelly, M., and Mills, R. (2017), *Mad Dogs and Englishness: Popular Music and English Identities*, London: Bloomsbury.
Brown, M. (2008), 'Historian Says Beatles Were Just Capitalists, and Not Youth Heroes'. Available online: https://www.theguardian.com/music/2008/oct/09/youngpeople. history (accessed 7 December 2017).
Buckley, D. (2012). *Kraftwerk: Publikation*, London: Omnibus.
Burgess, J., and Green, J. (2009), *YouTube: Digital Media and Society Series*, Cambridge: Polity.
Busse, K., and Hellekson, K. 'Introduction: Work in Progress'. In Karen Hellekson and Kristina Busse (eds), *New Essays: Fan Fiction and Fan Communities in the Age of the Internet*, p. 111, Jefferson, NC: McFarland.
Butler, J. (2004). *Undoing Gender*, London: Routledge.
Carter, C. (2002), 'George Harrison's Attacker Released from Hospital', *The Guardian*. Available online: https://www.theguardian.com/society/2002/jul/05/hospitals. mentalhealth (accessed 5 August 2017).
Carville, C. (2011), *The Ends of Ireland: Criticism, History, Subjectivity*, Manchester and New York: Manchester University Press.
Cavendish, L. (2017), *The Story of the Beatles' Hairdresser Who Defined an Era*, London: Alm Books.
Cline, S., and Gillies, M. (2012), *The Avron Book of Literary Non-Fiction: Writing about Travel, Nature, Food, Feminism, History, Science, Death, Friendship and Sexuality*, London: Bloomsbury.
Coleman, R. (1995), *Lennon: The Definitive Biography*, London: Pan; first publ. McGraw-Hill, 1985.
Collins, M. (2013), ' "The Age of the Beatles": Parliament and Popular Music in the 1960s'. *Contemporary*, 27(1): 85–107. Available online: http://www.tandfonline.com/doi/full/10.1080/13619462.2012.722346?scroll=top&needAccess=true (accessed 8 December 2017).
Collins, M. (2017), A Lecture: 'The Beatles and Historical Interpretation'. Available online: https://www.edgehill.ac.uk/histlearn/resources/beatleshistorical-thinking/ (accessed 29 November 2017).
Colli, B. (2003), 'Clouds and Clocks'. Available online: www.cloudsandclocks.net/interviews/IMacDonaldinterview.html. (accessed 1 July 2017).
Conrad, P. (2001), 'Denunciation, Deviation and Repetition: Foucault's Fascination with Sex and Death Had Seditious Motives, But Does Power Deserve Its Billing

as Part of His "Essential Works"?' in *The Guardian*. Available online: https://www.theguardian.com/books/2001/apr/15/artsandhumanities.highereducation (accessed 28 November 2017).

Cresi, E. (2017), 'Why Fans Think Avril Lavigne Died and Was Replaced by a Clone Called Melissa'. *The Guardian*. Available online: https://www.theguardian.com/lifeandstyle/shortcuts/2017/may/15/avril-lavigne-melissa-cloning-conspiracy-theories (accessed 8 November 2017).

Crets, S. (2016), 'Modern Beatlemania'. Available online: http://web.b.ebscohost.com/ehost/pdfviewer/pdfviewer?vid=1&sid=b44a19fa-25a2-4ed2-afb3-6c9360fb59f7%40sessionmgr103 (accessed 15 November 2017).

Cura, K. (2009) 'She Loves You: The Beatles and Female Fanaticism', *Nota Bene: Canadian Undergraduate Journal of Musicology*, 2(1), Article 8. Available online: Available at: http://ir.lib.uwo.ca/notabene/vol2/iss1/8 (accessed 23 October 2017).

Daily Telegraph. 'Mark David Chapman Explains Motivation behind John Lennon Murder'. Available online: http://www.telegraph.co.uk/culture/music/the-beatles/8008098/Mark-David-Chapman-explains-motivation-behind-John-Lennon-murder.html (accessed 30 June 2017).

Daily Telegraph. 'Doctors Let off Hook in Report over Ex Beatles Attacker'. Available online: https://www.telegraph.co.uk/news/uknews/1360341/Doctors-let-off-hook-in-report-over-ex-Beatles-attacker.html (accessed 27 May 2018).

Davies, H. (2009; 1st publ. 1968), *The Beatles*, London: Ebury Press.

Dean, J. (2005), *Beatles Monthly* (1963–1969) and (1976 to 1982), Issues No 1 to No 77, London: Beat Publication.

Dean, J. (1995), *The Best of the Beatles Book*, London: Beat Publication, pp. 78–9.

Debord, G. (1994), *Society of the Spectacle*, London: Rebel Press, p. 12.

Deleuze, G., and Guattari, F. (1987), *A Thousand Plateaus: Capitalism and Schizophrenia*, Minneapolis: University of Minnesota Press.

Derrida, J. (1993), *Spectres of Marx*, London: Routledge.

Dickinson, E. (2010; 1st publ. 1955), *The Complete Poems of Emily Dickinson*, USA: Pacific Publishing Studios

Didion, J. (2012), *The Year of Magical Thinking*, London: Fourth Estate.

Docx, E. (2015), 'Beatlebone by Kevin Barry Review: A Darkly, Wry Trip to Beatle Island'. Available online: https://www.theguardian.com/books/2015/oct/30/beatlebone-kevin-barry-review-beatle-island (accessed 17 August 2017).

Driscoll, C. (2006), 'One True Pairing: The Romance of Pornography and the Pornography of Romance'. In Karen Hellekson and Kristina Busse (eds), *New Essays: Fan fiction and Fan Communities in the Age of the Internet*, NC: McFarland, p. 79.

Duffett, M. (2010), http://pop-music-research. blogspot.com/2010/07/what-are-imagined-memories-and-how-are.html.

Duffett, M. 'What Are Imagined Memories?' Available online: http://pop-music-research.blogspot.com/2010/07/what-are-imagined-memories-and-how-are.html (accessed 15 August 2017).

Duffett, M. (2013), *Understanding Fandom: An Introduction to the Study of Media Fan Culture*, London: Bloomsbury, p. 108.

Duffett, M. (2017), An Interview with Fred Vermorel. Available online: http://pop-music-research.blogspot.co.uk/2017/10/as-potentially-explosive-as-contents-of.html (accessed 23 November 2017).
Duffett, M. (2018), 'And the Power of Elvis', Keynote, Always on Their Mind: Elvis Presley and Consumer Culture, University of Kent, Canterbury, 3 June 2018.
Duffy, Michael S. (2014), 'Book Review: Cult Collectors: Nostalgia, Fandom and Collecting Popular Culture, by Lincoln Geraghty'. Available online: https://journal.transformativeworks.org/index.php/twc/article/view/584/444 (accessed 6 October 2018).
Du Noyer, P. (2007), *Liverpool: Wondrous Place. From the Cavern to the Capital of Culture*, London: Virgin Books.
Du Noyer, P. (2008), 'I Should Be Sleeping Like a Log, Review of the Hard Day's Night Hotel, Liverpool', *The Guardian*. Available online: https://www.theguardian.com/travel/2008/feb/10/liverpool.hotels (accessed 7 December 2017).
Durkheim, E. (1995; 1st publ. 1992), *The Elementary Forms of Religious Life*, New York: Free Press.
Dyer, R. (1981), 'Don't Look Now: Richard Dyer Examines the Instabilities of the Male Pin-Up'. Available online: https://www.scribd.com/document/86715521/DyerMale-PinUp (accessed 10 July 2017).
Echoi, J. (2014), 'Word Press: Feminism, Music, Sexuality, What's Sex Got to do with the Beatles?' Available online: https://wgs160.wordpress.com/2014/09/12/whats-sex-got-to-do-with-the-beatles/ (accessed 23 October 2017).
Ehrenreich, B., Hess, E., and Jacobs, G. (1992) 'Beatlemania: Girls Just Want to Have Fun'. In L. Lewis (ed.), *The Adoring Audience*, London: Routledge, p. 85.
Ellis, R. (2002), *The Singing Dead*, Skipton: Magna Large Print Books.
Evasion (2017), quiet-profanity, slashtumblr.com.
Everett, W. (1999), *The Beatles as Musicians: Revolver through the Anthology*, Oxford: Oxford University Press.
Facebook (2017). 'The Fest for Beatles Fans', Chicago, 13 August 2017. Available online: https://www.facebook.com/events/450523975300543/ (accessed 26 October 2017).
Fathhallah, J. M. (2017), *Fanfiction and the Author: How Fanfic Changes Popular Cultural Texts*, Amsterdam: Amsterdam University Press.
Feldman-Barrett, C. (2014), 'From Beatles Fans to Beat Groups: A Histography of the 1960s All-Girl Rock Band'. *Feminist Media Studies*, 14(6). Available online: http://www.tandfonline.com/doi/full/10.1080/14680777.2013.866972?scroll=top&needAccess=true (accessed 13 November 2017).
Fisher, M. (2014), *Ghosts of My Life: Writings on Depression, Hauntology and Lost Futures*, Winchester: Zero Books.
Foucault, M. (1980), *The History of Sexuality: Volume 1: An Introduction*, New York: Vintage Books.
Fowler, D. (2008), 'Youth Culture and Pop Culture: From the Beatles to the Spice Girls'. In *Youth Culture in Modern Britain, c. 1920–c.1970*, London: Palgrave Macmillan, pp 166–96.
Fremaux, S., and Fremaux, M. (2013) 'Remembering the Beatles' Legacy in Hamburg's Problematic Tourism Strategy'. *Journal of Heritage Tourism*, 4(4): 303–19.

Freud, S. (1920), *Beyond the Pleasure Principle*, in the Standard Edition of the Complete Psychological Works of Sigmund Freud, ed. and trans. James Strachey, London: Vintage, p. 18.

Freud, S. (1939), *Moses and Monotheism*, in the Standard Edition of the Complete Psychological Works of Sigmund Freud, ed and trans. James Strachey, London: Vintage, p. 18.

Freud, S. (2013; 1st publ. 1895), *Obsessions and Phobias*, London: Red Books.

Geraghty, L. (2014), *Cult Collectors: Nostalgia, Fandom and Collecting Popular Culture*, Abingdon: Routledge.

Geraghty, L. (2018), 'Hallowed Place, Toxic Space: "Celebrating" Steve Bartman and Chicago Cubs' Fan Pilgrimage'. *Participations: Journal of Audience and Reception Studies*, 15(1), May 2018: 348–65.

Gladwell, M. (2008), *Outliers: The Story of Success*, New York: Little Brown.

Goodall, H. (2017), *Sgt Pepper's Musical Revolution with Howard Goodall*. Trailer – BBC Two.

Gray, J. (2003), 'New Audiences, New Textualities: Anti-Fans and Non-Fans'. *International Journal of Cultural Studies*, 6(1): 64–81.

Gregory, G. (2012), *Send in the Clones: A Cultural Study of the Tribute Band*, Sheffield: Equinox.

Gross, L. (1966), 'John Lennon: A Shorn Beatle Tries It on His Own', Look, 13 December 1966.

Grossman, L. (2013), 'Foreword'. In A. Jamison (ed.) *Why Fanfiction Is Taking Over the World*, Dallas: Smart Pop/Benbella, p. xiii.

Guesdon, M., and Le Guern, P. (2014), 'Retromania: Crisis of the Progressive Ideal and Pop Music Spectrality'. In K. Niemeyer (ed.), *Media and Nostalgia: Yearning for the Past, Present and Future*, Basingstoke: Palgrave Macmillan.

Haglage, A., and Durham, S. (2012), 'The Beatles: 50 Years since the Music Started'. In Newsweek, New York: Daily Beast.

Harris, J. (2012), 'The Best Books on the Beatles'. Available online: https://www.theguardian.com/books/2012/sep/26/beatles-best-books (accessed 28 March 2018).

Harris, J. (2013), 'I Am a Beatles Obsessive. But Let's Cut the Fabs-Worship'. *The Guardian*. Available online: https://www.theguardian.com/commentisfree/2011/jan/03/beatles-cut-the-fabs-worship (accessed 29 November 2017).

Harris, J. (2013). 'The Beatles – All These Years: Volume One: Tune in by Mark Lewisohn: Review'. Available online: https://www.theguardian.com/books/2013/oct/02/beatles-tune-in-mark-lewisohn-review (accessed 9 August 2017).

Harris, J. (2016), 'Paul McCartney by Philip Norman Review – The Beatle Finally Gets His Due'. Available online: https://www.theguardian.com/books/2016/may/28/paul-mccartney-the-biography-by-philip-norman-review (accessed 9 August 2017).

Harrison, G. (1987), 'Interview at 57 Street'. Available online: https://www.youtube.com/watch?v=G1wkRVUlCzM (accessed 9 August 2017).

Hartley, J. (2009), 'Uses of YouTube'. In J. Burgess and J. Green (eds), YouTube, Cambridge: Polity, pp. 132–3.

Hebdige, D. (1979), *Subcultures: The Meaning of Style*, London: Routledge.

Heilbronner, O. (2015), 'The Peculiarities of the Beatles: A Cultural Historical Interpretation in Social and Cultural History: The Journal of Social History Society'. Available online: http://www.tandfonline.com/doi/abs/10.2752/147800408X267274 (accessed 14 November 2017).

Herbert, I. (2000). 'Love Me Too: The Fab Faux Industry Support Over 200 Beatles Tribute Bands (And That's Just in Liverpool)' *The Independent*. Available online: https://www.independent.co.uk/arts-entertainment/music/news/love-me-too-the-fab-faux-industry-supports-200-beatles-tribute-bands-and-thats-just-in-liverpool-626057.html (accessed 6 October 2018).

Hills, M. (2002), *Fan Cultures*, London: Routledge.

Hoggart, R. (1957), *The Uses of Literacy: Aspects of Working Class Life*, London: Penguin.

Homan, S. (2006), *Access All Areas: Tribute Bands and Global Pop Culture*, London: The Open University.

Hopkins, N., and Kelso, P. (1999). 'How George Harrison Became a Target', *The Guardian*. Available online: https://www.theguardian.com/uk/1999/dec/31/paulkelso.nickhopkins (accessed 5 August 2017).

Hopper, K. (2011; 1st publ. 1995), Flann *O'Brien: A Portrait of the Artist as a Young Post-Modernist*, Ireland: Cork University Press.

Huberman, J. (2013), 'Forever a Fan: Reflections of the Branding of Death and the Production of Value'. In Karen Alexander (ed.), *Anthropological Theory*, USA: Sage.

Inglis, I. (2006), 'Fabricating the Fab Fourf'. In Shane Homan (ed.), *Access All Eras: Tribute Bands and Global Pp Culture*, Maidenhead: Open University Press, pp 121–35.

In the Loop Magazine. The Fest For Beatles Fans 2016. Available online: https://www.youtube.com/watch?v=i9qOu42I0KA (accessed 7 November 2017).

Jaminison, A. (2013), *fic: Why Fan Fiction Is Taking Over The World*, Smart Pop/Benbella: Dallas.

Jarniewicz, J., and Kwiatkowska, A. (2010), *Fifty Years with the Beatles: The Impact of the Beatles on Contemporary Culture*, Lodz, Poland: University of Lodz Press.

Jenkins, H. (1992), *Textual Poachers*, London: Routledge.

Jenkins, H. (2006), *Convergence Culture: Where Old and New Media Collide*, New York University Press.

Jenkins, H. (2007), 'Afterward: The Future of Fandom'. In J. Gray, L. Harrington and C. Sandvoss (eds), *Fandom: Identities and Communities in a Mediated World*, New York: New York University Press.

Jenkins, H. (2008), *Convergence Culture: Where Old and New Media Collide*, New York: New York University Press.

Jenkins, H., Ito, M., and boyd, d. (2016), *Participatory Culture in a Networked Era*, Cambridge: Polity.

Johnson, P. (1964), 'From the Archive: The Menace of Beatlism'. Available online: https://www.newstatesman.com/culture/2014/08/archive-menace-beatlism (accessed 18 October 2017).

Johnson, T. H. (2010), *The Poems of Emily Dickinson*, Harvard: Harvard University Press.

Jones, G. (2002), 'The Sex Lives of Cult Television Characters'. In *Screen* 43(1), Spring 2002: 79–90.

Jones, J. (1992), *Let Me Take Down, Inside the Mind of Mark David Chapman*, New York: Villard.

Johnson, K. (2015), 'David Bowie Is'. In E. Devereux, A. Dillane and M. J. Power (eds), *David Bowie Critical Perspectives*, New York: Routledge, pp. 1–19.

King, M. (2015), 'The Beatles, Help! and the Creation of the British Modern Man', in The Conversation. Academic Rigour/Journalistic Flair. Available online: http://theconversation.com/the-beatles-help-and-the-creation-of-the-modern-british-man-44436 (accessed 22 June 2018).

Kirby, D. (2016), 'Beatles Legacy Brings More Than £89M to Liverpool's Economy Each Year', *The Independent*. Available online: http://www.independent.co.uk/news/uk/home-news/beatles-legacy-brings-more-than-89m-to-liverpools-economy-each-year-a6859271.html (accessed 4 April 2018).

Kirkup, M. (2015), 'Some Kind of Innocence': The *Beatles Monthly* and the Fan Community'. *Popular Music History* 9(1): 64.

Kosnik, de A. (2016), *Rogue Archives: Digital Cultural Memory and Music Fandom*, Cambridge, MA: MIT Press.

Kovach, B., and Rosentiel, T. (2003), *The Elements of Journalism*, London: The Guardian and Atlantic Books.

Kramer, B. J. (2016), *Do You Want to Know a Secret? The Autobiography of Billy J. Kramer*, Sheffield: Equinox.

Krerowicz, A. (2014), *The Beatles and the Avant Garde*, USA: Create Space Independent.

Kurlansky, M. (2005), *1968: The Year That Rocked the World*, London: Vintage.

Larkin, P. (2012), 'Annus Mirabilis', *Philip Larkin: The Complete Poems*, London: Faber and Faber.

Larry King Live, 17 December 1992. Available online: https://www.youtube.com/watch?v=QUMJdkL0EnM (accessed 11 October 2017).

Leigh, S. (2016), *The Cavern Club: The Rise of the Beatles and Mersey Beat*, Carmarthen: McNidden and Grace.

Leland, J. (2000), 'Bloody Attack on a Beatle'. By: Leland, John, Newsweek, 1 October 2000, 135(2).

Lennon (1974), In the Loop Magazine, 2015. http://beintheloopchicago.com/fest-beatle-fans-come-together-rosemont/ (accessed 30 October 2018).

Leonard, C. (2014), *The Fans' Eye–View: Beatleness: How the Beatles and Their Fans Remade the World*, New York: Arcade.

Leonard, J. (1984), 'Paul McCartney Raw Interview Footage with Roy Leonard' https://www.youtube.com/watch?v=QSebxaVz-I8 (accessed 22 July 2018).

Lewis, L. (1992), *The Adoring Audience*, London: Routledge.

Lewis, S. (1998), 'Beatlefest 1998, Chicago Interviews, Continental Cable Television'. Available online: https://www.youtube.com/watch?v=Yv1yVf6aIgQ (accessed 6 November 2017).

Lindberg, U., Gudmundson, G., Michelsen, M., and Weisethaunet, H. (2005), *Rock Criticism From the Beginning: Amusers, Bruisers and Cool-Headed Cruisers*, New York: Peter Lang.

Linden, H., and Linden, S. (2017), *Fans and Fan Cultures: Tourism, Consumerism and Social Media*, London: Palgrave Macmillan.

London Beatle Walks http://www.beatlesinlondon.com/ (accessed 5 July 2017).

Luckhurst, R. (2008), *The Trauma Question*, New York: Routledge.

Lynskey, D. (2013), 'Beatlemania, the Screamers and Other Tales of Fandom', *The Observer*. Available online: https://www.theguardian.com/music/2013/sep/29/beatlemania-screamers-fandom-teenagers-hysteria (accessed 24 October 2017).

MacDonald, I. (2006; 1st publ. 1990), *The New Shostakovich*, Pimlico, 2006, p. 47.

MacDonald, I. (2003), *The People's Music*, London: Vintage.

MacDonald, I. (2008), *Revolution in the Head: The Beatles' Records and 1960s*, London: Vintage.

MacLeod, I. (2013), *Snodgrass and Other Illusions*, London: Open Road.

Malinowski, B. (1922), *Argonauts of the Western Pacific*, London: Routledge.

McLuhan, M. (1968). 'Marshall McLuhan in Conversation with Norman Mailer'. Available online: http://www.marshallmcluhanspeaks.com/media/mcluhan_pdf_4_gOLK6yS.pdf (accessed 5 May 2018).
Makela, J. (2004), *John Lennon Remembered: Cultural History of a Rock Star*, New York: Peter Lang, p. 250, and cited in Fowler, D. *Youth Culture in Modern Britain, c. 1920–c.1970*, Basingstoke: Palgrave MacMillan, p. 168.
Marcus, G. (1991), *Dead Elvis*, Cambridge, MA: Harvard University Press.
Marcuse, H. (1992; 1st publ. 1955), *Freud, Eros and Civilisation*, Boston: Beacon Press.
Marcuse, H. (2002; 1st publ. 1964), *One-Dimensional Man*, London: Routledge.
Marshall, I. (2006), 'I am He as You He as You Are Me and We Are All Together', Bakhtin and the Beatles'. In K. Womack and T. F. Davies (eds), *Reading the Beatles: Cultural Studies, Literary Criticism and the Fab Four*, Albany: State University of New York Press.
Marwick, A. (1998), *1960s*, Oxford: Oxford University Press.
Masummi, B. (2016), 'The Pleasures of Philosophy', VI, in Deleuze, G. and Guattari, F. *A Thousand Plateaus*, VI, London: Bloomsbury.
McCartney, P. (2009), 'YouTube Fan Vid'. Available online: https://www.youtube.com/watch?v=8aWFIHcYwlo (accessed 5 November 2017).
McGrath, J. (2010), 'Cutting Up a Glass Onion: Reading the Beatles' History and Legacy'. In Jerzy Jarniewicz and Alina Kwiatkowska (eds), *Fifty Years with the Beatles: The Impact of the Beatles on Contemporary Culture*, Poland: University of Lodz Press.
McLuhan, M. (1967), *The Medium Is the Massage: An Inventory of Effects*, USA: Penguin.
McNair, B. (2003), *News and Journalism in the UK*, London: Routledge.
Mellers, W. (1974), *Twilight of the Gods: The Music of the Beatles*, Viking Press.
Miles, B. (1997), *Paul McCartney: Many Years from Now*, London: Secker and Warburg.
Millard, A. (2012), *Beatlemania: Technology, Business, and Teen Culture in Cold War America*, Baltimore: John Hopkins University Press.
Moore, F. (2014), 'The Beatles: In and Out of Literature'. Available online: http://airshipdaily.com/blog/06182014-the-beatles-literature (accessed 2 December 2017).
Moore, R. (2010), *Sells Like Teen Spirit: Music, Youth Culture and Social Crisis*, New York: New York University Press.
Music Case: Music Heritage Tourism (2016). Available online: http://www.thecreativeindustries.co.uk/industries/music/music-case-studies/music-case-music-heritage-tourism (accessed 16 October 2017).
Myall, S. (2016), 'The Beatles Had Pre-Paid Prostitutes Waiting in Hotels as They Toured US, Reveals New Book. Available online: https://www.mirror.co.uk/3am/celebrity-news/beatles-pre-paid-prostitutes-waiting-7830459 (accessed 7 October 2018).
Neale, S. (1983), 'Masculinity as Spectacle: Reflections on Men and Mainstream Cinema'. *Screen* 24(6): 2–17.
Niemeyer, K. (ed.) (2014), *Media and Nostalgia: Yearning for the Past, Present and Future*, Basingstoke: Palgrave.
Norman, P. (2005; 1st publ. 1981), *The Beatles in their Generation: Shout!*, London: Fireside.
O'Neill, S. (2014), *Shakespeare and YouTube: New Media Forms and the Bard*, London: Bloomsbury.
Orton, J. (1998), *Up against It: A Screenplay for the Beatles and Head to Toe: A Novel*, New York: De Capo Press.

O'Sullivan, S. (2017), 'I Saw the Beatles Live, But No, I Didn't Scream. It's Time to Take Fmale Fans Seriously'. Available online: https://www.washingtonpost.com/entertainment/books/i-saw-the-beatles-live-but-no-i-didnt-scream-its-time-to-take-female-fans-seriously (accessed 26 May 2017).

Plant, S. (1992), *The Most Radical Gesture: The Situationist International in the Postmodern Age*, London and New York: Verso.

Plant, S. 'Psychogeography and the Dérive'. Available online: https://www.geog.leeds.ac.uk/people/a.evans/psychogeog.html (accessed 8 July 2017).

Porcaro, M. (2008), Reviewed Work: *Hyperreality in Cyberspace: Web Sites of Three American Beatles Tribute Bands*. Review by: Mark D. Porcaro *American Music*, 26(1) (Spring, 2008): 133–6. Published by: University of Illinois Press Stable URL. Available online: http://www.jstor.org/stable/40071697 (accessed 19 September 2017).

Quinn, A. (2006), 'Hunter Davies, The Beatles, Football and Me'. Available online: https://www.theguardian.com/books/2006/sep/10/biography.features1 (accessed 7 December 2017).

Ramsey, T. (2013), 'Playhouse Presents: Sky Arts 1, Review'. Available online: http://www.telegraph.co.uk/culture/tvandradio/10019144/Playhouse-Presents-Snodgrass-Sky-Arts-1-review.html (accessed 22 August 2017).

Raskin, E (2008), *Unspeakable Secrets and the Psychoanalysis of Culture*, Albany: University of New York Press.

Rebeat (2017), Blog: http://www.rebeatmag.com/ (accessed 10 November 2017).

Rehak, B. 2014. 'Materiality and Object-Oriented Fandom' [editorial]. In 'Material Fan Culture', Bob Rehak (ed.), special issue, *Transformative Works and Cultures*, no. 16.

Reich, W. (1991; 1st publ. 1946), *The Mass Psychology of Fascism*, London: Souvenir Press.

Reinhard, C. D. (2018), *Fractured Fandoms: Contentious Communication in Fan Communities*, London: Rowman and Littlefield.

Reynolds, S. (2012), *Retromania: Pop Culture's Addiction to Its Own Past*, London: Faber and Faber.

Roberts, M. (2010), 'A Working-Class Hero Is Something to Be: The American Musicians' Union's Attempt to Ban the Beatles in 1964'. *Popular Music*, 29(1). Copyright © Cambridge University Press 2010, pp. 1–16.

Rolling Stone (2002), George Harrison Special, 17 January 2002, Issue 887, p .19.

Roszak, T. (1970), *The Making of the Counter Culture: Reflections on the Technocratic Society and Its Youthful Opposition*, New York: Anchor Books.

Rothman, L (2015), 'How the World Reacted to John Lennon's Death 35 Years Ago'. *Time Magazine*. Available online: http://time.com/4131751/john-lennon-1980-anniversary/ (accessed 30 October 2017).

Said, E. (1978), *Orientalism*, London and Henley: Routledge and Kegan Paul.

Salinger, J. D. (1951), *The Catcher in the Rye*, Boston: Little, Brown.

Sandbrook, D. (2006), *White Heat: A History of Britain in the Swinging Sixties*, London: Little Brown.

Sandvoss, C. (2005), *Fans: The Mirror of Consumption*, Cambridge: Polity.

Schmidt, S. (2014), 'The Story of How Mark Lapidos Met John Lennon'. Available online: https://www.youtube.com/watch?v=YaTgzSTOYBc (accessed 6 November 2017).

Schneider, M. (2008), *The Long and Winding Road: From Blake to the Beatles*, London: Palgrave.

Scodari, C. (2007), 'Yoko in Cyberspace with Beatles Fans: Gender and the Re-creation of Popular Mythology'. In J. Gray, L. Harrington and C. Sandvoss (eds), *Fandom: Identities and Communities in a Mediated World*, New York: New York University Press.

Sheffield, R. (2017), VH1's Beatles Fantasy (and Ours). By: Sheffield, Rob, Rolling Stone, 0035791X, 3 February 2000, issue 835. Available online: http://web.b.ebscohost.com/ehost/detail/detail?vid=1&sid=f095dbb8-0edb-4d54-a242-7cfa66e389a4%40pdc-v-sessmgr01&bdata=JnNpdGU9ZWhvc3QtbGl2ZQ%3d%3d#AN=2854215&db=aph (accessed 13 November 2017).

Sherlocked221. *Who Knows How Long I've Loved You*. Available online: http://missmcharrison.tumblr.com/slash. (accessed 1 August 2017).

Shipper, M. (1979), *Paperback Writer: The Life and Times of the Beatles: The Spurious Chronicle of Their Rise to Stardom, Their Triumphs & Disasters, Plus the Amazing Story of Their Ultimate Reunion*, New York: Fred Jordan Books, Sunridge Press.

Smith, M. K. (2016), *Issues in Cultural Tourism (Third Edition)*, Oxford: Routledge.

Social Theory Rewired (2016), 'Habitus, Pierre Bourdieu'. Available online: http://routledgesoc.com/category/profile-tags/habitus (accessed 23 November 2017).

Solnit, R. (2006), *A Field Guide to Getting Lost*, Edinburgh: Canongate.

Spizer, B. (2017), *The Beatles and Sgt Pepper: A Fans' Perspective*, USA: 498 Prodcutions L.L.C.

Stanley, B (2004), 'Chick with Licks', *The Times*, 25 June, p. 16.

Stark, S. (2006), *Meet the Beatles: A Cultural History of the Band That Shook Youth, Gender and the World*, New York: HarperCollins.

Strinati, D. (2004), *An Introduction to Theories of Popular Culture* (second edition), London: Routledge.

Time Magazine (2015), 'How the World Reacted to John Lennon's Death 35 Years Ago'. https://time.com/4131751/john-lennon-1980-anniversary/.

Tyrangiel, J. (2016), Book Review, *Paul McCartney: The Life by Philip Norman*, *The New York Times* (2016). Available online: https://www.nytimes.com/2016/06/05/books/review/paul-mccartney-the-life-by-philip-norman.html (accessed 7 October 2018).

Ultimate Classic Rock (2014), 'George Harrison Attacked'. Available online: http://ultimateclassicrock.com/george-harrison-attacked/ (accessed 19 October 2017).

Urry, J. and Larsen, J. (2011), *The Tourist Gaze 3.0*, 3rd edn, London: Sage.

Vermorel, F. (2011; 1st publ. 1985), *Starlust: The Secret Fantasies of Fans*, London: Faber and Faber.

Vonnegut, K. (1998), *Timequake*, London: Vintage.

Wakely (2017), http://www.retail-merchandiser.com/blog/2948-merchandise-monday-beat-bugs (accessed 2 December 2017).

Walker, J. (2014), *Sex and the Beatles: 400 Entries*, Canada: Something Now.

Wearing, S., Stevenson, D, Young, T. (2010), *Tourist Cultures: Identity, Place and the Traveller*, London: Sage.

Wenner, J. (2000; 1st publ. 1971), *Lennon Remembers*, London: Verso.

White, E. (2017), 'Rebeat. 10 Reasons Why the Second – and Third – Gen Beatles Fan Experience is Unlike Any Other'. Available online: http://www.rebeatmag.com/10-reasons-second-third-gen-beatles-fan-experience-unlike/ (accessed 15 December 2017).

Whiteley, S. (2000), *Women and Popular Music: Sexuality, Identity and Subjectivity*, Oxford: Routledge.

Wikstrom, P. (2009), *The Music Industry*, Cambridge: Polity, p. 159.

Williams, R. (2003), *The Guardian*. Available online: www.guardian.co.uk/news/2003/sep/08/-obituaries.artobituaries (accessed 7 December 2017).

Williams, R. (2010), 'The Legacy of John Lennon', *The Observer*. Available online: https://www.theguardian.com/music/2010/sep/26/john-lennon-at-70-beatles (accessed 30 October 2017).

Woledge, F. (2006), 'Intimatopia: Genre Intersections between Slash and the Mainstream'. In Karen Hellekson and Kristina Busse (eds), *New Essays: Fan Fiction and Fan Communities in the Age of the Internet*, Jefferson, NC: McFarland.

Wolfe, Tom (1973). *The New Journalism*, Tom Wolfe and E. W. Johnson (eds), Picador, 1975; first published 1973.

Wolfe, T. (1989), *The Electric Kool-Aid Acid Test*, London: Black Swan.

Wolfe, T. (1996), Tom Wolfe, the New Journalism. With an anthology edited by Tom Wolfe and E. W. Johnson, Basingstoke and Oxford: Picador.

Womack, K. (2017), *Maximum Volume, the Life of Beatles Producer George Martin: The Early Years, 1926–1966*, Chicago, IL: Chicago Review Press.

Womack, K. (2018), *Sound Pictures, the Life of Beatles Producer George Martin: The Later Years, 1966–2016*, Chicago, IL: Chicago Review Press.

Womack, K., and Davies, T. (2006), *Reading the Beatles: Cultural Studies, Literary Criticism, and the Fab Four*, Albany: State University of New York Press.

Worcman, K., and Garde-Hansen, J. (2016), *Social Memory Technology: Theory, Practice, Action*, New York: Routledge.

Yeats, W. B. (2008), *The Major Works*, Oxford: Oxford University Press

Young, R. (2010), *Electric Eden: Unearthing Britain's Visionary Music*, London: Faber and Faber.

Discography

Bach, J. S. (2008), *Brandenburg Concertos*, Avie [Album]
Baker, Anita (1986), *Rapture* [Album]
Billy J. Kramer and the Dakotas (1963), 'Bad to Me', Parlophone [Single]
Luciano Berio, Sequenza V. (1967), *Wergo* [Album]
The Beatles (1962), 'Love Me Do', Parlophone [Single]
The Beatles (1965), 'Ticket to Ride', Parlophone [Single]
The Beatles (1965), 'Yesterday', *Help!*, Parlophone [Album]
The Beatles (1965), 'You've Got to Hide Your Love Away', *Help!* [Album]
The Beatles (1966), 'For No One', *Revolver*, Parlophone [Album]
The Beatles (1966), 'Eleanor Rigby', Parlophone [Single]
The Beatles (1967), 'Lucy in the Sky with Diamonds', *Sergeant Pepper's Lonely Hearts Club Band*, Apple [Album]
The Beatles (1967), 'Within You Without You', *Sergeant Pepper's Lonely Hearts Club Band*, Apple [Album]
The Beatles (1967), 'I Am the Walrus', *Magical Mystery Tour*, Apple [Album]
The Beatles (1968), 'Hey Jude', Apple [Single]
The Beatles (1968), 'Julia', *The White Album* [Album]
The Beatles (1968), 'Revolution No 9', *The White Album* [Album]
The Beatles (1968), 'Across the Universe,' Apple [Single]
The Beatles (1995), 'Free as a Bird', Apple [Single]
The Beatles (1995), 'Real Love', Apple [Single]
Jay Z (2003), *The Black Album*, Rock-a-Fella-Records [Album]
John Cage (1966), 'Variations VI', *Brilliant Classics* [Album]
Danger Mouse and The Beatles (2003), *The Grey Album*, self-released [Album]
Donovan (1965), 'Catch the Wind', Pye Records [Single]
Bob Dylan (1966), 'Visions of Joanna', *Blonde on Blonde*, Columbia [Album]
The Eagles (1977), 'Hotel California', Asylum [Single]
Archie Fisher (1968), 'Reynardine', *Archie Fisher*, Xtra [Album]
John Foxx (2006), *Tiny Colour Movies*, Metamatic Records [Album]
Davey Graham (1963), 'Anjii', Topic [Single]
George Harrison (1968), *Wonderwall Music*, Apple [Album]
Iggy Pop and the Stooges (1973), *Raw Power*, Columbia [Album]
Bert Jansch (1965), 'Needle of Death', *Bert Jansch*, Transatlantic [Album]
John Lennon (1970), *John Lennon/Plastic Ono Band*, Apple [Album]
The Marvelettes (1961), 'Please Mr Postman', Tamla [Single]
Pat Metheny (2011), 'And I Love Her', *What's It All About*, Nonesuch [Album]

Paul McCartney (2009), 'I Want to Come Home', MPL Communications [Download Single]
Prince (1985), 'Around the World in a Day', *Paisley Park*, Warner Brothers [Album]
The Sex Pistols (1976), 'Anarchy in the UK', EMI [Single]
Rihanna, Kanya West, Paul McCartney (2015), 'FourFiveSeconds', Roc Nation Westbury Road [Single]
Karlheinz Stockhausen (1967), *Hymnen*, Deutsche Gramophon [Album]
The Rolling Stones (1972), 'Sweet Black Angel', *Exile On Main Street*, Rolling Stones Records [Album]
The Vipers (1957), 'Maggie May', Parlophone [Single]
Wings (1972), 'Mary Had a Little Lamb', Apple [Single]
Wings (1977), 'Mull of Kintyre', Capitol [Single]

Personal Interviews

I spoke to the following for this book – thanks to all!

Jeffrey Alan Ross was a former member of the legendary Apple Records band Badfinger and is musical director for Grammy Award-winning producer Peter Asher.

Peter Asher CBE is a British singer, manager and record producer, who as one half of Peter and Gordon, a British pop duo, composed of Peter Asher and Gordon Waller, achieved international fame in 1964 with their first single, the million-selling transatlantic number 1 smash *A World without Love*. The duo had several subsequent hits in the British Invasion era.

Gary Astridge, as Ringo's drum curator, restores and documents Ringo's drums and installs Ringo's Beatle drum kits for display at prestigious venues such as the Grammy Museum in Los Angeles and the Rock & Roll Hall of Fame Museum in Cleveland, Ohio.

Kevin Barry is the author of *Beatlebone* (2015), a novel that blends autobiography, fiction and Beatles fandom to tell the story of John Lennon visiting an Irish island he bought in 1968.

David Bedford is the author of *Liddypool* (2009) and *The Fab One Hundred and Four* (2016). He has also published his latest book, with Garry Popper, *Finding the Fourth Beatle* (2018). He collaborated with the Beatles' official biographer Hunter Davies on *The Beatles Book*, and he was associate producer and historian on the documentary *Looking for Lennon* (2018).

Roag Best has worked in the music industry as a musician, songwriter, promoter and manager. Roag is the brother of former Beatles drummer Pete Best. He opened the Beatles museum Magical History Tour in 2018.

Cheryl Breo is the author of *Happiness Is a Warm Gun: A Vietnam Story*, an autobiography of being married to a Vietnam veteran.

Tim Brown works as the night manager at A Hard Day's Night Hotel in Liverpool.

Leslie Cavendish was the Beatles' hairdresser in the 1960s. He was on the bus in the Magical Mystery Tour film. Leslie's new book, *The Cutting Edge* (2017), chronicles his time with the Beatles as well as his apprenticeship with Vidal Sassoon in 1962.

Jeremy Clyde is an English actor and musician who is part of Chad and Jeremy, an English folk singing duo who had seven Top 40 US hits between 1964 and 1966, including *A Summer's Song* which hit number 7 in 1964.

Jimmy Coburn plays the part of John Lennon in resident Cavern Club Beatles band, The Cavern Club Beatles. Along with his brother Tony, Jimmy has had the acclaim of Geoff Emerick, who described him as the best sounding John Lennon vocal he had ever heard!

Adrian Dando works at A Hard Day's Night Hotel in Liverpool.

Maria Darwin is a Liverpool-based nursery nurse, a Beatles tour guide and author of *John Lennon: The Early Years* (2017).

John, Dylan and Cassidy Dawson are a family of American Beatles fans, who have attended The Fest for Beatles Fans in Chicago for the last twenty years.

Jack Douglas worked as an engineer on John Lennon's album *Imagine* (1971) and was producer for Lennon's final album *Double Fantasy* (1980). He has worked with Aerosmith, the Who, Cheap Trick, Supertramp and the New York Dolls.

Mark Duffett is a reader in media and cultural studies at the University of Chester. Publications include *Understanding Fandom* (2013) and *Counting Down Elvis: His 100 Finest Songs* (2018).

Dan Edwards organizes the Beatles Day 1 in St Margaret's, London.

Geoff Emerick was the Beatles sound engineer on their albums *Revolver*, *Sgt Pepper's Lonely Hearts Club Band* and *Abbey Road*.

Joe Flannery was the business associate and partner of Brian Epstein, he became an integral part of the Beatles' management team during their rise to fame in the early 1960s.

Tom Frangione is the resident Beatles expert on The Fab Forum on the Beatles Channel 18 on SiriusXM.

Stephanie Fremaux is a media theorist, lecturer at Birmingham City University and author of *The Beatles on Screen: From Pop Stars to Musicians* (Bloomsbury 2018).

Debra Garver-Dewalt from Erie, Pennsylvania, is a regular fan at the Chicago Beatle Fest.

Tony Giangreco is a 26-year-old drummer who plays Ringo in Meet the Beatles and bass in another Beatles tribute band *The Time Bandits* and is a multi-instrumentalist who specializes in guitar, piano and sitar.

Jorie Gracen has never missed a Beatles Fest, runs themaccareport.com and sings with the tribute band The Pondhawks.

Debbie Greenberg is the author of *The Cavern Club: The Inside Story* (2016).

Tom Gross has been at forty-one Chicago Beatles Fests and plays lead guitar with mid-western band Head East.

Chuck Gunderson has been attending Beatles conventions since the 1970s; and he has written *Some Fun Tonight: The Backstage Story of How the Beatles Rocked America* (2016).

Nikki 'Little Nicola' Hale was the 5-year-old sitting on John Lennon's lap on the Magical Mystery Tour bus.

Colin Hall for the last seven years has been the live-in custodian of Mendips, John Lennon's childhood home in Woolton, Liverpool.

Sylvie Hall lives with her husband Colin, the custodian of Aunt Mimi's old home which is now run by the National Trust and says that John Lennon's childhood home is 'not a museum, it is not a dead space'.

Bill Harry is the creator of *Mersey Beat*, a newspaper of the early 1960s which focused on the Liverpool music scene.

Terri Hemmert has been at the Chicago Beatles Fest since the beginning and is a Chicago DJ on 93.1 WXRT and she hosts the *Breakfast with the Beatles Show* every Sunday.

Stephanie Hernandez is a Beatles fan, St Mary's University student and works at the Beatles Story in Liverpool.

Paolo Hewitt is a music journalist and writer from Woking, Surrey. He is the author of over twenty books covering music, fashion and football, plus *The Looked After Kid*, a memoir about life in care.

Matt Hills is reader in media and cultural studies at Cardiff University and the author of *Fan Cultures*, *The Pleasures of Horror* and *Triumph of a Time Lord: Regenerating Doctor Who in the Twenty-First Century*.

Ian Inglis has published widely on the Beatles including *The Beatles in Hamburg* and *The Words and Music of George Harrison*. He is visiting fellow at the University of Northumbria.

Mike Kirkup is an academic at Teesside University and his research includes Popular Music History & Culture (particularly the Beatles, Bob Dylan, cultural and social contexts of pop music).

Joanna Kozlowska describes herself as a Beatlemaniac, Maccaholic and fan.

Billy J. Kramer is a legendary English pop star who was managed by Beatles manager Brian Epstein. His single *Bad to Me* reached number 1 on the UK charts in 1963.

Aaron Krerowicz is a professional Beatles scholar, musicologist and author of *The Beatles and the Avant Garde*.

Mark Lapidos started The Fest for Beatles Fans in 1974.

Sam Laverty is a Beatles fan, a graduate of the MA in the Beatles at Liverpool Hope University and works at the British Music Experience in Liverpool.

Candy Leonard is a writer and author of *Beatleness: How the Beatles and Their Fans Remade the World*.

Mark Lewisohn is an English author and historian, he is regarded as one of the world's leading Beatles experts and he has set the 'gold standard' for Beatles scholarship with *Turn On* (2013), the first part of three-part biography of the Beatles.

Joey Lyons is tour guide for A Hard Day's Night Taxi Tours, Liverpool.

Frank Martens is a 53-year-old, second-generation German Beatles fan from Hamburg.

John Merjave is an American musician who plays with his band The Weekenders and Beatles tribute act, Liverpool.

Erica, Shannon, Julian and Stella Mohs are a family of Beatles fans from Minnesota.

Mario Novelli is a Paul McCartney lookalike and a member of the Pond Hawks.

Roy Orbison Jr is a musician and son of the legendary Roy Orbison.

Daniel Philips is a regular at the Chicago Beatles Fest for the last twenty years as Big D Unplugged.

Richard Porter is a tour guide at London Beatles Walks and Tours.

Gail Renard is a BAFTA Award-winning writer, performer and producer. Gail is chair of the Writers' Guild of Great Britain and BAFTA. Gail's latest book, *John Lennon: Give Me a Chance*, is based on her eight days spent with John and Yoko at their Bed-In for Peace in Montreal in 1969.

Charles Roberts took the first picture of John Lennon onstage with the Quarrymen and was in the audience for many of the Beatles' shows. Charles is the author of *Just Like Starting Over: John and the Quarry Men, My Teenage Years* (2016).

Joe Roberts is a driver for the National Trust tours of John Lennon and Paul McCartney's childhood homes in London.

Beatrice Schimdt is a 62-year-old German Beatles fan from Berlin.

Susan Shumsky is the author of *Maharishi and Me: Seeking Enlightenment* and worked for the Maharishi for six years.

Roy Silva is a musician, Beatles fan and has attended The Fest for Beatles Fans since 1996.

Jude Southerland Kessler has been at nine Beatles Fests in Chicago, and volume four of her John Lennon series, *Should Have Known Better*, was published in 2018.

Jackie Spencer, a Beatles guide, has been a professionally qualified Blue Badge guide since 1995 and describes her tours 'as the toppermost of the poppermost!'

Bruce Spizer has written seven volumes on the Beatles including *The Beatles and Sgt Pepper: A Fans' Perspective*.

Al Sussman is the author of *Changin' Times* and has worked for The Fest for Beatles Fans since 1974.

Kenneth Womack is dean of the School of Humanities and Social Sciences at Monmouth University in New Jersey and is author of the magisterial two-volume *Maximum Volume: The Life of Beatles Producer George Martin*.

Appendix 1

Beatles Questionnaire

Beatleweek, Liverpool, 23–29 August 2017
Thanks for agreeing to complete this questionnaire.

1. How long have you been a Beatles fan? (Please circle)

   Less than one year   1–5 years   6–10 years   11–20 years   20+ years

2. How many 'Beatles Conventions' have you attended? (Please circle)

   This is my first   1–5   6–10   10+

3. What are the main reasons for attending the 'Beatles Conventions'? (Please tick all that apply)

   a. Nostalgia for the past
   b. Meet other Beatles fans
   c. Keeping the Beatles alive for the future
   d. Share 'Beatles memories'
   e. Meet people who knew the Beatles (e.g. Geoff Emerick)
   f. Other please write below

4. Have you attended or visited any of the following in the past year? (Please tick all that apply)

   a. Beatles Walk London
   b. Beatles Walk Liverpool
   c. Magical Mystery Tour
   d. Beatles Museum
   e. National Trust Tour

5. Have you attended or visited any of the following in the past year? (Please tick all that apply)

   a. Shakespeare's Globe
   b. Buckingham Palace
   c. Abbey Road

6. **Are you a fan of a Beatles tribute band?**

   a. No (Please go to next question)
   b. Yes (Please write name of band below)

7. **Are you a fan of other bands?**

   a. No (Please go to next question)
   b. Yes (Please write up to three bands below)

8. **Do you collect Beatles memorabilia? (Please tick)**

   a. No (go to next question)
   b. Yes (if yes, please tick all types below)

Vinyl	CDs	DVDs
Mugs	Posters	Badges/pins
Dolls	Key rings	Other, please specify below

9. **Please complete the following sentence:**

   'A true Beatles Fan is ....'

10. **Please indicate how much you agree or disagree with the following statements:**

    Strongly agree (SA)
    Agree (A)
    Neither agree nor disagree (N)
    Disagree (D)
    Strongly disagree (SD)

11. STATEMENT	SA	A	N	D	SD
a) Fan videos on YouTube (e.g. mashing Beatles songs) keeps the Beatles' music relevant					
b) 'Being a fan of "Heritage Culture" (including the Beatles) is an unhealthy obsession with the past.'					
c) Copying is a bad thing when it comes to Beatles tribute bands					
d) Beatles Conventions transform Beatles cultural products into a new emotional experience for fans					
e) Sex and death are at the core of Beatles fandom					

12. **Age (please circle)**

    10–15 16–21 22–29 30–39 40–49 50–59 60–69 70–79 80+

13. **Sex (please circle)**

    a. Male
    b. Female
    c. Other

14. **Nationality (please write below)**

15. **Where do you currently live? (Country, region, etc.) (Please write below)**

16. **What is your ethnic group?**

    Choose one option that best describes your ethnic group or background:

    White

    - English/Welsh/Scottish/Northern Irish/British
    - Irish
    - Irish traveller
    - Any other White background, please describe

    Mixed/Multiple ethnic groups

    - White and Black Caribbean
    - White and Black African
    - White and Asian
    - Any other Mixed/Multiple ethnic background, please describe

    Asian/Asian British

    - Indian
    - Pakistani
    - Bangladeshi
    - Chinese
    - Any other Asian background, please describe

    Black/African/Caribbean/Black British

    - African
    - Caribbean
    - Any other Black/African/Caribbean background, please describe

    Other ethnic group

    - Arab
    - Any other ethnic group, please describe below

Thanks for taking the time to complete this questionnaire.

Appendix 2

Mass audience theory

Collins, M. (2013), '"The Age of the Beatles": Parliament and Popular Music in the 1960s', in *Contemporary*, 27(1), pp. 85–107, http://www.tandfonline.com/doi/full/10.1080/13619462.2012.722346?scroll=top&needAccess=true. Accessed 8 December 2017.

The Beatles were inevitably invoked in debates on the relationship between high and low culture at a time when the 'cultural capital' accorded to each was a matter of intense concern.[1] Most politicians agreed with Viscount Samuel in his sharp distinction between the Beatles and 'serious' art.[2] The Bishop of Southwark and Lawrie Pavitt accordingly contrasted them to the Royal Shakespeare Company and the soprano Joan Cross.[3] But while the likes of Lord Auckland and Sir Herbert Butcher were careful not to criticize the Beatles when distinguishing 'their form of culture' from the more august variety, others did not hesitate to do so.[4] The Duke of Atholl referred to the Beatles as mere 'noise', while Lord Willis saw the Beatles as personifying all that was wrong with contemporary culture and society.[5]

Appendix 3

Chris Olley

Chris Olley's son auditioned for the Bootleg Beatles and wrote a blog post about the dilemma of this. The blog is interesting as it demonstrates the merging of 'reputable' musicians and tribute bands.

View at https://chrisolley.wordpress.com/2017/01/09/charlie-auditions-for-the-bootleg-beatles/.

Index

3Q3 66, 174

Abbey Road 31, 42, 44, 90, 114, 121, 164, 169, 178
Abbey Road Studios 1, 181–3
Abram, Michael 2, 4, 14–15, 19, 99–100, 144, 159
Aca-fan 24–5, 38, 44, 59, 96–7, 161, 208
Acoustic Beatles 174
'Across the Universe' 125–6
Adorno, Theodor 30, 35, 39, 87, 90, 123–4, 126, 131, 191, 206-11, 215
A Hard Day's Night 30, 59, 83, 114, 181–2, 192, 204
Alan Ross, Jeffrey 63
Allen, Woody 13
Analogues, The 176–7
'And I Love Her' 62
'Annus Mirabilis' 2
Aoronovitch, David 1, 205–6
Apple 58, 70, 116, 121, 129–31, 133, 145, 159, 166, 203
Apple Corps 20, 116
Apple Pies 170
Apple Records 115
Asher, Jane 32, 181
Asher, Peter 57, 60, 64
Ask for Joey: Fab Four Taxi Tours 184
Aspinall, Neil 28
Astridge, Gary 61, 64

Bach, J. S. 89, 209
Back from the USSR 176
'Bad to Me' 60
Baker, Anita 5
Baker Street 154, 182
Bakhtin, Mikhail 140, 159
 carnivalesque 21, 76, 130, 132, 139, 142, 145, 148, 157–9, 167, 169, 184
Bangs, Lester 5, 75–6

Barry, Kevin 21, 145–7, 158, 160, 163, 165, 210
Barthes, Roland 118, 147, 149
Baudrillard, Jean 7
Beach Boys, The 63, 162, 174
Beapple 175
Beatlefest 53
Beatlemania 1–2, 4, 18, 23, 27, 30–4, 38, 41, 44–50, 66–9, 94, 96, 113, 121–2, 130, 170, 176, 182, 184, 204, 207–9
Beatles for Sale 114
Beat and Shout 173
Beatles Artefact 175
Beatles Monthly 1–5, 8, 14, 16–18, 27–51, 53, 58, 66, 70, 93–4, 97, 109, 142, 144–5, 148, 153–5, 158, 165–6, 180, 188, 201, 208, 210, 212
Beatles Rock Band 21
Beatleweek 2, 6, 15, 17, 22, 56, 65–6, 68, 72, 153, 170, 173–7, 185, 189, 198
Beat-Lele 175
Beats, The 171
Beethoven, Ludwig 209
Beetles, The 171
Benjamin, Walter 118, 181, 190
Best, Pete 56–8, 140, 174
Binet, Alfred 3
Bit, The 176
Bolan, Marc 47
Bombay Beatles 170
Boom Beatles Revival Band 176
Bootleg Beatles, The 3, 170–3
Borgh, Jan Leonard 174
Bourdieu, Pierre 24, 210–11
 cultural capit al 21, 71, 94, 144–5, 164–5, 167, 207, 212
Bowie, David 2, 8, 46, 47, 99, 107
Brahams, Johannes 209
Bricoleurs 130, 210
Brown, Tim 191–2

Bruce, Hal 176
Buttles, The 171

Cage, John 89
Calangles Rock Band, The 173
'Calangles Mash-ups' 173
Cartoons 28, 204
Cavendish, Leslie 59–61, 71
Cavern Club Beatles 176, 185, 231
Cavern Club, The 72, 110, 141, 148, 175–6, 185, 189, 191, 213
Chapman, Mark 1–2, 4–5, 10–12, 14–16, 19–20, 49, 69, 83, 99, 100–11, 142, 144, 159
Cheatles, The 170
Cirrone 174
Clube Big Beatles 173
Clyde, Jeremy 60, 74
Coburn, Jimmy 173, 176, 185
Coburn, Tony 173
Cohn, Nik 5
Coldplay 169
Coldplace, Coldplay tribute act 169
Comic Con 56, 68, 198
Counterculture 19, 30, 36–7, 39, 43, 48, 81–5, 87–88, 95, 114–15, 121, 126, 149, 189, 203, 208, 212
Crompton, Richmal 193
Just William 193

Danger Mouse 91, 119, 128, 202
Davies, Hunter 5, 19, 22, 30, 56, 75–9, 81, 83, 89, 92–3, 97, 180
Dean, James 104
Debord, Guy 132
  dérive 183
  situationist 183
Deleuze, Gilles and Guattari, Felix
  anti-memory 71
Derrida, Jacques 5–6
  concealment 16
  hauntology 15–16, 107, 128, 182, 187
  mal d'archive 5, 9, 12, 14, 21, 95, 140, 172, 179–80, 180, 193
Didion, Joan
  The Year of Magical Thinking 137
Digit Gratis Economy 21
Douglas, Jack 60, 64, 71

DTour 176
Duffett, Mark 3, 8, 12, 18, 20, 22, 42, 70–1, 99–102, 106–7, 109–10, 113, 131, 133–4, 137, 140, 143, 159, 213
Du Noyer, Paul 194–5
Dylan, Bob 16, 69, 83–4, 183, 193

Eagles, The 63, 171
Ed Sullivan Show, The 9, 30, 41, 68, 198
Ellis, Ron 169
Emerick, Geoff 56, 89
Epstein, Brian 3, 27–8, 45, 47, 54, 68, 77, 94, 113, 118–19, 140–1, 148, 157–8, 192, 201
Evans, Mal 28
Everett, Walter 98

Facebook 66–8, 109, 131–2, 175, 198
Fisher, Mark 16, 127
Freud, Sigmund 10, 29, 49, 62, 142
  Beyond the Pleasure Principal 108
  Eros 4–5, 40, 42, 94, 161
  Melancholia and Mourning 14
  Moses and Monotheism 108
  Obsession and Phobias 3
  psychic wound 108
  repetition compulsion 5, 14
  return of the repressed 12
  Thanatos 4–5, 179
Foucault, Michel 4
Funkles, The 66, 174

Game of Thrones 145
gender 18–19, 39–42, 45–7, 71, 137, 140–1, 143, 152, 164–6, 186, 196, 207–9
Geraghty, Lincoln 6–8, 20, 27–8, 110, 113, 134, 180
Giambelli, Rolando 174
Gladwell, Macolm 35
Goldman, Albert 24, 148
Google 116, 130, 205
Graceland 187
Grateful Dead, The 15, 64
Guardian, The 4, 77, 79, 85, 93, 95, 99, 102, 105–6, 145, 147, 158, 161, 195, 205, 208
Gui Lopes 173
Gunderson, Chuck 59

Hall, Colin 193
Hall, Sylvia 193
Hamburg Beat 173
Harris, John 23, 76, 79
Harrison, George 1, 11, 14–16, 19, 54, 57, 64, 68–9, 72, 102, 141, 148, 204
    attack on 99–100, 105–6, 122
    'Here Comes the Sun' 90, 190
    Wonderwall Music 42
'Help!' 16, 40, 181–2
Hempel, Stefanie 175
Heritage culture 22, 24, 94, 183, 189, 194, 196
Hernandez, Stephanie 161, 184–5
'Hey Jude' 83, 171, 204, 214
Hills, Matt 50, 172, 187
Hoggart, Richard 209

India 70, 119
    'India' 201
    Rishikesh 201
Innes, Neil 176
Instagram 67, 133

Jarnos, The 175
Jay Z 62, 91, 119, 124, 202
Jenkins, Henry 44, 121, 130, 133
Jiri Nikkinen Band 176

Kazakhstan Beatles 170
Kennedy, John Fitzgerald 104
Kramer, Billy J, 60, 141, 148
Krerowicz, Aaron 95–6

Lapidos, Mark 19, 50, 53, 54–5, 70–2
Leary, Timothy 55
Lego 8
Lennon, Cynthia 94
Lennon, John 1, 3–4, 10–11, 24, 34, 45, 48, 49, 53–6, 59–60, 62–3, 71, 75–7, 79–80, 82, 87–9, 96, 101–3, 114, 117–19, 137–42, 145–53, 155–8, 161–2, 165, 167, 172–73, 175, 182, 184–5, 192–3, 195, 198, 205, 208, 214
    death 12–15, 19–20, 57, 64–5, 68–9, 72–3, 82–3, 99–100, 104–10, 122, 188–9, 191, 194
    'Mendips' 155, 193

Lennon, Julian 58
Leonard, Candy 6, 9, 40, 69–70, 165
Let It Be 114, 117, 126,
Lewisohn, Mark 24, 51, 72, 76–7, 97, 194
Liverpool 1, 6, 11, 13, 15, 17, 21–2, 38, 61, 62, 65, 68, 72–3, 153, 159, 170, 173, 176, 179, 181, 183–6, 189–96, 198, 207
    Adelphi Hotel 174, 176,
    A Hard Day's Night Hotel 191
    Beatles Story, The 161
Liverpool Echo 105, 107
Liverpool Hope University 190, 192
Liverpool Philharmonic Hall 177
London 1, 21, 24, 29–30, 49, 59, 61, 71–3, 89, 109, 159, 170, 179–81, 183–5, 188–90, 192, 196, 212
    Buckingham Palace 24, 40, 176, 181–3, 185, 212
    Shakespeare's Globe 24, 181, 185, 212
LSD 77, 93, 102, 108, 114, 208

MacDonald, Ian 5, 22, 24, 76, 78, 80–2, 86, 88, 97, 121, 124, 138, 144, 151–2, 180, 208
MacLeod, Ian 155–7
MagiQuest 21, 133
Manson, Charles 83, 159
Martin, Sir George 20, 59, 89, 116
mash-up 14, 128, 152, 154, 173–4, 211
McCartney, Sir Paul 11, 41, 57–8, 60, 64, 79–81, 88, 114, 141, 148, 153, 156, 174, 177, 192, 198, 211–12
    'I Want to Come Home' 129
    MPL Communications 183
    Paul's house, 20
    Forthlin Road 192
    Paul is dead rumour 42, 44, 54, 121, 201, 205, 214
Marquis de Sade 128, 145
Memorabilia 6–9, 19, 50, 54–8, 63, 65, 69, 71, 76, 77, 185
Monroe, Marilyn 104
Murakami, Haruki 163–4

National Trust, the 185, 192–3, 199
necrophilia 14, 172, 181, 193
neophilia 30, 67, 181, 193
Nelson, George 5, 76

New Journalism 80–2
New York Times 80–1, 164
Norman, Philip 3, 5, 19, 22, 30, 75, 79, 81, 83, 89, 92–3, 97, 101, 130, 156, 180
'Norwegian Wood' 164
Nowhere Men, The 170
Nube 9, 175

Oasis 11, 106, 127, 172
Ocean 174
Onion 175
O'Mahony, Sean 28, 34, 51
Ono, Yoko 109
Orbison Jr, Roy 60
Orgies 3, 4, 11, 141
Orton, Joe 194

Please Please Me 114–15
Ponds Hawks, The 63
pornography 40, 142, 146
Porter, Richard 5, 21, 71–2, 109, 179–82, 188–9, 198
Potter, Harry 68
Presley, Elvis 15, 20, 22, 38, 40, 44, 46, 54, 70, 122, 187
psychogeography 5, 181, 183, 185, 189, 191, 193, 212

Quarrybeat 174

Rabelais, Francois 128, 141, 145
Rain 170
Real Person Fiction (RPF) 143–4
remix culture 16, 122, 124, 126, 130, 132–4, 201
Return, The 170
Reynolds, Simon 6, 16, 21, 179, 182
  Retromania 6, 16–17, 27, 67, 127, 153, 174
Retro-Nuevo 5–6
Revolver 9, 89, 94, 169, 184
Roaches, The 170
Roaring Forties, the 175
Rolling Stones, The 48, 84
Rubber Soul 16, 31, 114, 153, 164

Saudade 7
Savile Row 183, 187

Scarabs, The 170
Sgt Pepper's Lonely Hearts Club Band 13, 32, 44, 54, 57, 77, 89, 114, 174, 176–7
Shannon 191
'She Loves You' 17–18, 28, 33, 45, 73, 109, 126, 140
Shipper, Mark 21, 98, 137–8, 158, 163
Shotton, Pete 141, 158
slash fiction 1–3, 5, 14, 17, 21–2, 32, 39–40, 44, 50–1, 93–5, 97–8, 137–48, 150–3, 156–67, 170, 197, 201, 204, 210–12
Sonido Club 174
Spencer, Princess Diana 54–5, 70, 183
Spockanalia 21
Star Beetles, The 175
Starr, Sir Ringo 23, 64, 76, 80, 141, 184
  Ringo's house, 9
  Madryn Street 184
Star Trek 13, 21, 137, 159, 160–1, 197
Stenungkören, The 174
Styles, Harry 127
Swift, Taylor 133

Taylor, Derek 122
Tearaways, The 175
Top of the Pops 191
Trauma 5, 10–17, 20, 42, 45, 53, 55–8, 62, 65, 69, 70, 72, 76, 97, 103–6, 108–10, 150, 152–3, 155, 163, 171, 173, 177, 185
Trident Recording Studios 187
Tumblr 21, 67–8, 130–1, 133
Two of Us 175
Twickenham Film Studios 212

Valentino, Rudolph 49, 54
Vermorel, Fred 2–3, 49
Vidders 40, 130
Vonnegut, Kurt 163–4

Walker, Jeff 3
Weeklings, The 61
White Album, The 177
Wikis 21
With the Beatles 114
Wolfe, Tom 35, 38, 80–1

Womack, Kenneth 59, 89, 98
Wooler, Bob 72, 110, 141, 148

Yellow Submarine 6, 13
Yellow Submarine Corgi toy 6, 8
'Yesterday' 182

Yeats, W. B. 86, 129
YouTube 1–2, 14, 16, 20, 22, 40, 50–1, 63, 72, 81, 91, 93, 113, 115–35, 142, 152, 154, 156–8, 166, 201–3, 208, 212–13

zombies (Beatles turn into zombies) 137–8

www.ingramcontent.com/pod-product-compliance
Lightning Source LLC
Chambersburg PA
CBHW050325020526
44117CB00031B/1794